Astrology
&
Consciousness

Astrology
&
Consciousness

The Wheel Of Light

By

Rio Olesky, M.A.

NEW FALCON PUBLICATIONS
TEMPE, ARIZONA U.S.A.

International Standard Book Number: 1-56184-123-4
Library of Congress Catalog Card Number: 95-74973

First Edition 1995
Second Printing 1997

Cover art by S. Jason Black

The paper used in this publication meets the minimum requirements of the American National Standard for Permanence of
Paper for Printed Library Materials Z39.48-1984

Address all inquiries to:
NEW FALCON PUBLICATIONS
1739 East Broadway Road Suite 1-277
Tempe, Arizona 85282 U.S.A.
(or)
320 East Charleston Blvd. • Suite 204-286
Las Vegas, NV 89104 U.S.A.
website: http://www.newfalcon.com
email: info@newfalcon.com

DEDICATION

To my parents, Bob and Audrey Olesky, whose unconditional love and support provided the foundation for a good life.

To my wife, Arrow, whose love, devotion and playfulness have filled my life with joy. (And whose ruthless editing helped make this book what it is.)

To my guru, Paramahansa Yogananda, whose love and wisdom have provided the light about how to be.

ACKNOWLEDGMENTS

Thanks to my secretary and friend Carol Bianco whose competence and efficiency gave me the time to get this book written, and to Annabel Ayres who suggested the subtitle.

TABLE OF CONTENTS

INTRODUCTION

Astrology is a system of understanding. It provides a methodology that connects the individual to the group, humanity to the planet, the earth to the solar system and the solar system to the universe. It can help you to understand patterns of behavior and understand how to maintain or change them. It is a way of seeing the interplay of various cycles in life. It is a way to learn where you are, how you got there, and what options are available to you. The fundamental tool of astrology is the horoscope. It can be used as a map of your resources and challenges and as a way of connecting your inner self with the world around you.

The horoscope is a mandala. *Mandala* is a Sanskrit term that means to learn how to focus inward. You may ask, "Why learn astrology and can it help me?" Astrology has value in three ways. The first is self-awareness, learning who you are. The second, is self-understanding, learning why you are here. The third is self-acceptance, the most important, learning to love yourself. Through these three ideas you can expand your potential to its maximum, and maintain a healthy body and a clear psyche.

The natal horoscope is a picture of what the solar system looked like on the day, month, year, time and place that you were born. It's the starting point of all the cycles that will influence you throughout your life. The natal horoscope, or chart, is like a map in that it helps you to find things such as tools and strengths on the one hand, tensions and lessons to be learned on the other. Studying astrology and learning about your natal chart can help you to remove blockages or things in life that you have always assumed were just there. The chart always provides ways out. By applying your tools to your challenges, you can learn how to grow through those blockages, how to use your tensions as motivational factors that stimulate change. You also learn to take better advantage of your tools. You can learn to do the work of removing the blockages and growing through the tensions or the work of arriving at self-awareness, self-understanding, and self-acceptance.

Astrology is a language. It provides an alphabet, a vocabulary and rules of syntax and grammar for a major tool of self-help and self-directed behavioral change. It is a language that can further your awareness of, and your connection to, life. Astrology is an impersonal system for understanding a personal state of being. It's imperative that as you discover your nature, you remain open to surprises along the way. New options and possibilities that you never before thought you could do may exist as potentials within the chart and consequently within your capability. Be open to letting go of things that you've been carrying around for many years that may not even be a part of you. They may also be patterns you've already worked through. As you continue the study of your natal chart, you may be surprised to find that things you always assumed were permanent problems may not be so. Metaphysically, they are patterns that you brought into this life to become aware of, resolve, and let go. You chose your natal chart, the circumstances of your birth and your childhood family and experience to remember those key dynamics. Your childhood family was your first teacher. It helped you to grow by indoctrinating you in ways that you needed and came here, this time, to work through.

As you become more aware of who you are, what your tools are, and even what your work is, you can eliminate those factors from your past. You can concentrate on reimprinting and reprogramming who you are based on your free will choices of who you want to be.

To understand and benefit from astrology, you may need to suspend certain aspects of your old belief system such as the need for scientifically observable, verifiable information. At this time we are unable to give a scientific validation of how astrology works. In this way it's very similar to psychology or psychoanalysis which are also not exact provable sciences. Although there is no one scientific method that will enable us at this time to understand how astrology works, statistical studies with computers are being done. Hundreds of thousands of charts and other astrological data are being used to test the traditional interpretations that correlate behavioral patterns to planetary configurations. Ancient texts are being translated into modern language to establish the origin of astrological theory. In the meantime, as an individual, you can study astrology and interpret your own chart or have it read by a professional and you will see the correspondences between the symbolic influences contained there and the actual experiences of your life. It has been theorized that the chart works based on the traumatic imprint theory. This is also known as *synchronicity* which was originally defined by one of the pioneers of psychoanalysis, Carl Gustav Jung. It states, "Whatever is happening at any given moment of time shares the qualities of that moment." At the moment of your birth, it is a combination of planetary influences that symbolize the energy patterns that will characterize your behavior. These patterns are also called archetypes in that they pervade the psyches and lives of all people. The archetypes define your relationship to yourself, your relationship to others, your work, your body and your concept of God.

I believe that astrology does not work in a cause and affect way. It is not because a planet was in a certain sign when you were born that you are a certain way. What makes astrology valid as a system for understanding the internal and behavioral dynamics is that it connects the individual to the cycles of life. Studying the cycles in play when you were born can provide clarity about who you are and directions to pursue to maximize your growth potential.

Your natal chart represents the foundation of your character. In many ways it indicates how you have chosen to limit yourself in this lifetime. It can suggest what your desires are. It can indicate what you need to resolve and work through, or grow and evolve through. Astrology is objective. It enables you to understand yourself and others in a clear way, without judgment. It enables you to see yourself in other people, to understand more completely the oneness of life, and to understand that we have much more in common than we have differences. Astrology should not be used to control, dominate, criticize or judge others. It is just a system of understanding.

The horoscope as a whole represents the union, the Oneness, the universal consciousness, the place we all came from and the place where we are all going. It is a picture indicating how our energy acts and reacts to various environmental stimuli. Your natal chart provides a diagram of the basic relationship to yourself, your parents and early environment. The chart can suggest your needs to create and communicate. It shows your strengths, weaknesses, harmonies and disharmonies, the knots to untie and the tools with which to untie them. The chart indicates certain past life experiences—things you have learned and can do well and things that you have not done well. The natal chart cannot show us at what level of consciousness or from what philosophical perspective you relate to your energies. The chart is a framework within which are virtually limitless ways of putting together varying combinations of expression. It's the free will that picks and chooses. It decides what to do and when and how to do it. Your free will is as alive as you want it to be.

There are many different types of astrology. Most use a zodiac—a wheel of animals. In *tropical astrology*, astrologers base the zodiac on what the solar system looked like approximately 2000 years ago. The alignment of the fixed stars in the various constellations has changed. One of the things we learn through the study of astrology is that everything is constantly in motion, although the motion of the constellations is very slow. Tropical astrology is two thousand years out of date from the point of view of a contemporary astronomer. Still, from the point of an explorer of inner space, there are correlations between the positions of the planets in the signs of a tropical natal horoscope, and the behavior of that person.

Sidereal astrology considers movement and change within the celestial framework. It allows for the fact that the fixed stars change. For tropical astrologers, the Sun moves into Aries every year on the first day of spring in an unchanging cycle. Due to the wobble of the earth on its axis, the cycle changes one degree every seventy years. From the point of view of the sidereal astrologer, the Sun enters Aries earlier than that. Thus on March 21 the Sun is in early Pisces or late Aquarius, a difference of approximately twenty-four degrees. Sidereal astrologers take the wobble of the earth into consideration; tropical astrologers do not. It has been theorized that tropical astrology works more accurately in defining inner space and psychodynamics, whereas sidereal astrology more accurately describes the movements of large numbers of people, groups, and generations.

We can look at the solar system geocentrically as people from ancient civilizations did and assume that the earth is the center of the solar system. We can look at astrology heliocentrically, which sees the Sun as the center of the solar system. Each system provides a different perspective on the energy patterns of the individual, and each merits its own study.

Astrology has many different uses. Astrology can be used for character analysis to help understand the internal dynamics and motivations of a person's psyche. This suggests how an individual will function in relationships and indicates their career and spiritual needs. Orientation toward the home, a need for emotional expression and a tendency toward dependency or freedom can be seen in the natal chart. Astrology also can be valuable for medical diagnosis. Each of the signs of the zodiac corresponds to specific parts of the body. These parts could be a system—such as the nervous or motor systems—individual organs, the extremities, or the head. By studying your natal chart you can understand which parts of your body may break down under stress, and therefore which need more attention or support.

Astrology can be used for divination. An ancient system called *horary* allows one to ask questions about mundane situations. Questions about relationships, lost possessions, legal matters or investments can all be answered by a horary chart. Before people knew the day, month, year, time, and place of birth, the only available method of horoscope calculation was a horary chart. The astrologer would cast a chart for a specific date, time, and place. Within that horoscope lay the astrologer's responses to the client's questions. Horary is widely used today and, if properly interpreted, can provide answers to questions about external situations. The inner space of a person, however, is best explored through a natal chart.

Electional astrology is the use of a chart that indicates the best time to initiate something.

Mundane astrology is political astrology and pertains to the chart of a specific political body, state or country. Inherent within the framework of that chart are the tendencies, characteristics and values of the people residing in that country. As the government of a country changes, as revolutions take place and perhaps even boundaries change, the chart would change. The new chart would reflect the new state of mind of the people, the new governmental framework, and even the cultural integration among the peoples of that country.

Originally astrology and astronomy were one subject with the primary concern being planetary observation. In most ancient times this was useful for agriculture. When was the right time of year to plant? What was the right time of year to harvest? If a tribe didn't get it right, they often didn't get a second chance. Astrology still has agricultural purposes. As we assess the movement of the moon through its various signs and phases we discover the best time to plant or the best time to harvest depending upon whether we are planting and harvesting for root crops, leaves, fruit or flowers. As human consciousness developed astrology/astronomy was used as a time measuring device. Tablets that measure time date from 721 BC.

People from around the world have contributed to the development of astrology. Rudimentary observation of planetary phenomena occurred independently in Mesopotamia, Egypt, China and Central America. The idea of a zodiac also appeared in all these cultures. The Babylonians of Mesopotamia have the greatest reputation among ancient people for the study of astrology and astronomy. The First Dynasty of Babylon dates from about 1830 BC and it is from this period that the study of the subject began. The first known mention of twelve equal signs was in Babylonia in 419 BC, with the oldest surviving individual horoscope dating from 410 BC. The symbols and animals we use to understand astrological concepts have been contributed by ancient tribes from the Middle East, such as the Sumerians, the Chaldeans, and the Assyrians. It wasn't until the zodiac was brought to Greece, however, in about 400 BC that the names of gods and goddesses were given to the astrological archetypes that we use today.

The Old Testament was sanctified by 70 AD. References to astrology abound. For example, Jacob had twelve sons. The Israelites used the personalities of these twelve sons to understand the twelve signs. References to the planets are found in such stories as Joseph in Genesis and Samson and Delilah in Judges. The prophet Ezekiel claimed to have seen "the wheel in the middle of the sky." On that wheel were pictured the bull, the lion, the eagle and the man. These images refer to the totems of the four fixed signs: Taurus, Leo, Scorpio, and Aquarius.

By 200 AD, astrology had become an accepted part of Persian culture. The Persian astrologers contributed the concept of the four elements (fire, earth, air, and water) to our understanding of the system.

Astrology also existed in the Aztec culture of meso-America in the pre-Columbian period prior to the 15th Century AD. The Aztec calendar, essentially a circular medallion with the signs of the zodiac in order around the circumference, is familiar to those interested in either astrology or the history of Central America.

Astrology is also well represented in Eastern Cultures. As far back as 4000 BC the Hindus made celestial observations. They were strongly influenced by an infusion of Greek culture that began with the campaigns of Alexander the Great in 300 BC. Astrology has always been held in high regard in India and astrologers have been afforded very high social standing. Today there are astrology departments in the finest universities in India and astrology professors are treated with great respect.

In China the origin of the zodiac is traceable to 1000 BC, although modern Chinese astrology has its origins in the *I Ching* and the Sung Dynasty in the 10th Century AD. Chinese astrology is based on free will and the control you have over your actions. The Chinese believe that the individual must accept responsibility for his or her actions and decisions. They use the individual horoscope as a nexus that integrates the external environment, the culture, the family and social relationships. Chinese astrologers correlate significant events and major changes in a person's life to specific time periods and planetary movement, much as in contemporary Western use of the system.

Today astrology is used throughout the world. Groups gather, organizations are created and books and periodicals are published to educate people about the beneficial and practical uses of astrology and to advance knowledge and understanding.

This book is organized to help beginning students understand the concepts and keywords that comprise the basic variables of astrology: planets, signs, houses and aspects. These concepts are expressed to show how they function physically, emotionally, psychologically, socially and spiritually. This enables the intermediate student to gain more depth of understanding as well.

Planets are the most important variable. They are defined as energy types. Each planet in our solar system—plus the Sun and the earth's Moon, which are also called planets when discussing astrology—expresses itself with a different duration, intensity and frequency of energy or manifestation. It is the configuration of the planets in the natal chart that indicates a person's individuality. The chart indicates what your potential is for personal growth and what you have reincarnated to work with and work through. Abundance of energy in one place or absence of energy in another can indicate areas in which you are very strong or areas in which you are relatively weak.

The symbols or glyphs that indicate the different planets are all composed of three primary symbols. The first symbol is the circle [○], that indicates the life force, consciousness and will. The second symbol is the semi-circle [ )]which indicates the individual soul, the subconscious and wisdom. The third symbol is the cross (+), which indicates the material plane.

The motion of a planet can be direct or retrograde. When the planet is direct, its motion is clear. It tends to be expressed and manifested in a straightforward manner. If the planet is retrograde, its expression is indirect, personal in expression or counterpoint to direct energy. All planets, with the exception of the Sun and Moon, take their turn going retrograde. The indication that a planet is retrograde is the symbol ℞ written after the planet. Like the Rx used by a pharmacist to indicate a prescription, we can talk about retrograde planets as being a prescription for health. These planets indicate where remedial work is necessary for growth. A retrograde planet tells us to go back and review how we manifest the energy of that planet.

The signs of the zodiac function as filters. Each planet is said to rule at least one sign. The energy of a planet resonates to the pattern of an individual sign. There are twelve signs, each thirty degrees in length. The characteristics of each sign are determined by which qualities they partake of in three subcategories: polarity, elements, and modes. These designations are determined by dividing the 360 degree circle—the wheel of the zodiac. Dividing by two creates a basic duality, and delineates each pair of signs into polar opposites called *yin* and *yang.*

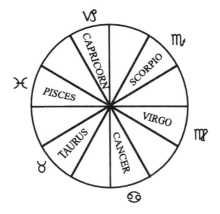

YIN SIGNS

The *yin*, or feminine, signs are Taurus, Cancer, Virgo, Scorpio, Capricorn, and Pisces. These signs manifest their energies in receptive, diffused ways and are internal in focus and orientation.

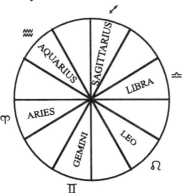

YANG SIGNS

The *yang*, or masculine, signs manifest in a more expressive, active, outgoing and linear way. The *yang* signs are Aries, Gemini, Leo, Libra, Sagittarius, and Aquarius. The designations *feminine* and *masculine* in this context are metaphysical distinctions and do not relate to men and women. Any person can have an abundance of energy in either the *yin* or *yang* signs, regardless of gender.

THE WHEEL OF ELEMENTS

To divide the circle of twelve signs by three leaves a remainder of four, the elements of which are: fire, earth, air, and water. For example, if a circle of 360 degrees is divided by three it leaves a remainder of 120 degrees, which is the degree of separation of each of the signs of one element.

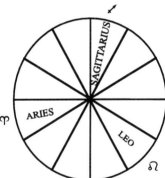

THE FIRE SIGNS

The fire signs are Aries, Leo and Sagittarius. Fire signs tend to be assertive, intuitive, dynamic and illuminating. In positive expression, they can be extremely creative. In a negative form they can be egocentric or self-indulgent. If anyone has an abundance of fire in the natal chart, there may be too much self—one may burn others or be blinded by one's own light. If there is little fire in the chart, there may be difficulty in being assertive, aggressive, creative or confident.

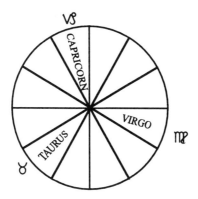

THE EARTH SIGNS

The earth signs—Taurus, Virgo, and Capricorn—are practical.
They are materialistic, hardworking, cautious, grounded and
conservative. If there is an abundance of earth in the natal
horoscope, a person may focus on the body, consumerism, or
possessiveness. Little earth in the chart suggests a neglect of the
practical side of life. This could take the form of abuse of the
body, irresponsiblility, or a sense that the material plane feels
foreign.

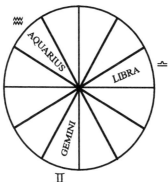

THE AIR SIGNS

The air signs—Gemini, Libra, and Aquarius—are inventive,
gregarious, objective and sociable. People who have an
abundance of air could be socially superficial or too idealistic in
their intellectual pursuits. Little air suggests discomfort in social
situations or an inability to be objective or detached. Sometimes

a lack of air can serve as a motivating force, stimulating a person to become more mentally or socially oriented. It can also lead to overcompensation if one were to become a professional student or develop an overactive social life. When there is a lack of an element, try to compensate by creating balance, not excess.

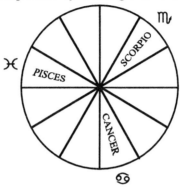

THE WATER SIGNS

Water signs—Cancer, Scorpio, and Pisces—are sensitive, emotional, psychic and compassionate. The only promise and guarantee of water is in the realm of the emotions. Because the water signs are sensitive, they also tend to be secretive. What they are feeling may not be expressed. When this happens, the unexpressed emotions cluster around the solar plexus, the personal power or ego center. If you are not expressing or releasing emotions you are ego-identifying as being stuck in the emotional state you are not expressing. This pattern can lead to emotional dependency or fear of emotional hysteria and can have a negative influence on your relationships. If you are in a relationship and not expressing your feelings to your partner, the relationship will probably end in a state of frustration, ambivalence or crisis. In your next relationship, those emotions will again surface. If this pattern becomes habitual, your experience of relationship will become confused and unfair to all concerned. Blocking the expression of emotions will also block the raising of higher consciousness into mystical, psychic or spiritual realms. It is through communion with our inner self that we connect with God or Spirit.

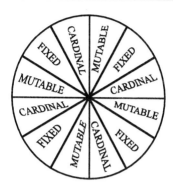

THE WHEEL OF MODES

To divide the circle of twelve by four leaves a remainder of three. This is the number of signs categorized by *mode*: cardinal, fixed, and mutable. Dividing 360 by four leaves a remainder of 90, the degree of separation between signs of the same mode. The modes define the manner of release or expression of energy.

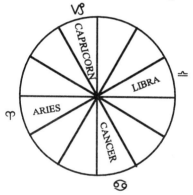

THE CARDINAL SIGNS

The *cardinal* signs—Aries, Cancer, Libra, and Capricorn—are oriented toward action, manifestation and initiation of projects, situations and relationships. They manifest their energy in a direct, active, dynamic manner. They have leadership ability and feel comfortable with trial and error. Too much cardinal energy can get stuck in a pattern of initiation within which nothing is completed or dealt with on a deep level. With little cardinal energy there may be difficulties starting new projects.

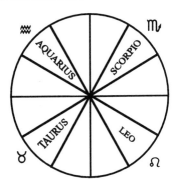

THE FIXED SIGNS

The *fixed* signs—Taurus, Leo, Scorpio, and Aquarius—are oriented toward habitual patterns of behavior, security and preservation. Fixed energy tends to be habit bound and routine oriented. This is fine provided that you are aware that you are manifesting a habit and why. Underlying the habit patterns are value systems, belief systems and assumptions about the nature of life and your place in it. A person with a lot of fixed energy is comfortable with habits because they can provide continuity, security, and stability. If you find that the degree and quality of security are not fulfilling your needs and expectations, however, it is not enough to arbitrarily change the habits and routines. You must penetrate to the values and beliefs themselves. It could be that the values are out of date or that they are not yours. Once you update the value and belief systems and make them appropriate to your needs and experience, you can create new habits that will bring more of the security you find meaningful.

One of the tools of fixed energy is will power. Yet, if the values are not updated periodically, the will power tends to turn around and manifest as "won't power" and you don't grow or change. You trade the comfort of the known for the challenge of the new and create a life of stagnation, not security.

Without fixed energy, continuity and consistency are hard to create. The will power may be weak and the values and beliefs unclear. You can strengthen your will by directing time and energy to something you enjoy. By maintaining your focus you develop your will power and a deeper relationship to the activity.

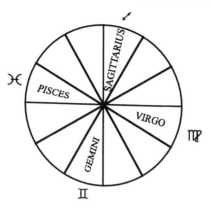

THE MUTABLE SIGNS

The *mutable* signs—Gemini, Virgo, Sagittarius, and Pisces—are adaptable and oriented toward learning, and to serving others. People with a great deal of mutable energy are oriented toward the expansion of consciousness and the development of wisdom. With too much mutable energy you can get lost in theories and ideals. Your energy can become diffuse or confused. If this is a problem, learn to work within systems. This could be something ongoing and external such as an academic program or it could be something you create within yourself, such as a daily spiritual discipline. Systems can provide a framework that can minimize tendencies to be influenced by external forces. Systems exist for a reason. They can provide you with a sense of direction and a place to put the information. This can help prevent you from being sidetracked by some new and seemingly exciting idea, person or venture.

If there is little or no mutable energy you may repeat mistakes because you have not learned from them the first time, especially if you have a lot of cardinal energy. You could tend to be rigid and stubborn, refusing to listen to others' ideas or points of view, especially if you are very fixed. As with elemental emphasis, an imbalance in the modes calls you to develop ways of expressing yourself that are more harmonious.

The dynamics of each sign are defined by the polarity, element and mode with which it is associated. The signs are also represented by a glyph (symbol) and a totem (animal). The background and qualities of the glyph and totem further define the nature of each sign. When we combine these subcategories under the heading of one sign we can perceive their tendencies and underlying motivation, their strengths and inherent weaknesses.

Signs are archetypes. Each provides an image and expression of ways of being that are fundamental and universal in the human psyche. Different cultures value some more than others—even support some and undermine others. This varies from culture to culture and from era to era. But the universality of the psychological patterns is constant. Throughout history, each culture puts its imprint on the archetypes through art and mythology. It is useful, therefore, to explore myths from around the world to gain insight and clarity about the nature of the signs, the twelve primal archetypes.

The third astrological variable is "houses." Houses are defined as areas of life. They indicate where the energy is going to be expressed. Certain houses direct energy outward toward the world, others direct it in more personal ways. For example, the tenth is the house of career and the seventh is the house of one-to-one relationship. The wheel of houses is, in turn, separated into quadrants and hemispheres.

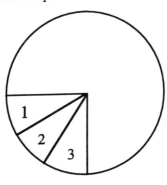

QUADRANT ONE

Quadrant one is composed of houses one, two, and three. It is oriented toward self-awareness, self-definition, and self-development. The cusp, or beginning, of the first house, is also called the ascendant or rising sign. Representing East on the compass, the rising sign indicates what sign was coming up above the horizon at the time of birth. The first house cusp, therefore, is a clear indicator of the personality and body type.

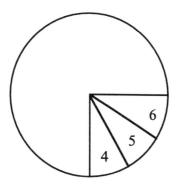

QUADRANT TWO

Quadrant two consists of houses four, five and six. It is the quadrant of home, family and personal creativity. The fourth house cusp indicates your primary relationship to yourself, both in this and prior lifetimes. It can describe your emotional, psychological and spiritual foundation. It represents north on the compass.

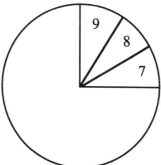

QUADRANT THREE

Quadrant three is composed of houses seven, eight and nine. It is the quadrant of relationship. The seventh house cusp suggests the way in which you receive—and what you need to receive—from others. It is the western point of the compass.

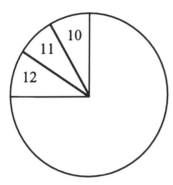

QUADRANT FOUR

Quadrant four, which consists of houses ten, eleven, and twelve, pertains to group interaction and higher consciousness. With a lot of energy here, you tend to perceive life in broad, global terms. The tenth house cusp especially indicates the way you project yourself to others through your job, profession or goals and how you cultivate your public image. It is the southern point of the compass.

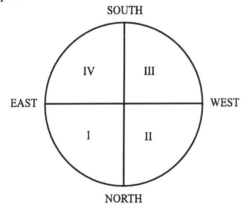

Quadrants one and two form the Northern hemisphere of the horoscope. Planets in this area are oriented toward activities that are personal and internal. Quadrants two and three combine to form the Western hemisphere, in which the orientation to life is objective. Quadrants three and four formulate the Southern hemisphere, in which the areas of focus are external and impersonal. Quadrants four and one comprise the Eastern hemisphere within which the focus is subjective.

To summarize the definitions of the quadrants, quadrant one is internal and subjective, quadrant two is internal and objective, quadrant three is external and objective, and quadrant four is external and subjective. Planets located in the quadrants will tend to express themselves accordingly.

The final variable of the chart is aspects. Aspects are defined as significant angular relationships between any two or more planets. The aspects of a horoscope are what makes it dynamic and exciting. They imply change and stimulation. Angular relationships between plants of sixty and one-hundred-twenty degrees are called sextiles ($\ast$) and trines (Δ) respectively. These aspects generate a positive and harmonious flow of energy. They are indicative of our tools. Angular relationships of ninety or one-hundred eighty degrees are called squares ($\square$) and oppositions ($\mathcal{S}$). They stimulate us to grow and change. Without that development, the squares and oppositions create conflict within us or between ourselves and others. When planets were less than ten degrees apart at your birth, they are conjunct ($\mathcal{d}$) to each other. This creates the potential to focus those energies and accomplish a lot in the house that they are combined in. There is also the possibility, however, that the planets joined within a conjunction don't blend. One planet might be stronger and dominate the other, or they could be energies that are oriented to different levels of consciousness. In this case, the planets are not working together and the conjunction can lead to fragmentation or waste of the energies involved. (For additional and more specific information about aspects, see the introductory sections of the Cancer, Leo and Libra chapters.)

Each of the signs and planets is associated with a part of the body. If you have three or more planets in a particular sign then the part of the body ruled by that sign can become stressed. This can lead to a breakdown when you are under a lot of tension or anxiety. Therefore, it's important that you learn which parts or systems of the body are ruled by that sign so you can feed them. Make sure that they are getting the necessary nutrients so that they can maintain themselves and their functions.

As astrology exists throughout the world, it has also existed throughout time. As we study the texts and the artifacts of various ancient cultures and societies, we find that there has always been this sense of relationship or connection between the self and the heavenly bodies. The further back we go, the more primitive the understanding and usage of the system. As we study history, we see the evolution and development of human consciousness, through the means of technology, politics and philosophy. We find that growth and development of consciousness was also reflected in the development of astrology. The expansion of astrology as a system through which to understand people enables us to gain control over ourselves and to feel empowered.

To study your horoscope within a Western frame of mind, as opposed to the Eastern or Vedic school, is to realize that it's not a fatalistic or predetermined system within which things have to happen and from which there are no ways out. Within the Western system of astrology, the chart shows us all the ways out. Realize that we always have everything we need to work through the various struggles and tensions that exist before us. The interest in the chart, or the commitment to study your chart, is a commitment to liberate yourself, to learn more about who you are and work to free yourself from obstacles in life. In this way you take the responsibility to create the kind of life you want to live, and the kind of person you want to be.

As a serious student of astrology, you might want to read this book in its entirety. As a novice you might make better use of it by focusing on those passages that match influences in your natal chart. For example, if your Sun sign is Gemini you would read about the nature of that sign. If your Gemini Sun is in the tenth house, jump to the Capricorn chapter, and read about the tenth house. If you have two or three other planets in another sign, read the chapter about that sign and the house in which those planets are located. If you have a prominent Pluto, find Pluto in the Scorpio chapter and read that.

The most significant parts of your natal chart are the Sun sign, the Moon sign, and the rising sign. The rising sign is on the cusp of the first house or what would be nine o'clock on the face of a clock. Take some time to look in the Aries chapter under first house, to learn about what a rising sign is. Read also the chapter about the sign that you have rising.

The best way to learn astrology is to look at charts. You may have a hard time understanding what Mars in Cancer in the fifth house is all about until you notice that someone you know well has that combination in their natal chart. Then it moves beyond endless memorization and into the realm of personal experience.

The person you should strive to understand the best is you. Your natal horoscope can enable you to know yourself well. Use this book as a means of delving into yourself more deeply. Use it as a reference book to help you to develop an objective perspective on who you are, how you function, why you function as you do and what might be some other ways of creating your experience.

Learning astrology, like learning about yourself, is the work of a lifetime. Astrology is a tool to help you do the work. Use this book as a way of understanding the tool in a deeper and more inclusive way. As you learn about yourself, your awareness of the world around you grows. Eventually this can include expanding your consciousness to include the whole of life, the Oneness of Being.

ARIES

The first sign of the zodiac is Aries. When the Sun begins its annual journey through Aries it is entering the Northern hemisphere. The Northern hemisphere is comprised of houses one through six and pertains to the personal areas of life. Aries, therefore, is the beginning of the personal world, the inner realm. Aries also initiates the first quadrant, the quadrant of self. As such, it is analogous to the first house. The cusp of the first house is called cardinal point I. The cardinal points are also called the angles of the chart. Each of the angles begins one of the quadrants. The angles represent the beginning of the seasons in annual cycle of the Sun. For example, cardinal point one, the Eastern angle, represents the Spring Equinox, one of the two times each year when the days and nights are of equal length. The Equinox marks the first day of spring and occurs on March 21, the first day of Aries. The Sun is moving North, spreading its light and warmth to the Northern hemisphere, and bringing with it the return of the creative drive and force to that hemisphere. This is a time of year when the vital dynamism of life bursts into manifestation suddenly, seemingly overnight. No hesitation, no deliberation. Nature knows that this is the time to reintroduce the vital life force to this hemisphere. There is a sense of immediacy, even impulsiveness to this process, that is similarly duplicated by Aries. Aries is the personification of the process of renewal in the hemisphere. The legend of Johnny Appleseed is reborn as Johnny Aries-seed, the I'd-love-to-stay-but-gotta-go-lots-to-do sign of the zodiac.

The cusp of the first house, Cardinal Point I, also represents the Eastern point on the horizon. In the course of a day, the planets rotate clockwise, ascending above the horizon in the East. As the Sun comes above the horizon a new day begins. In

31

the course of a year, the Spring Equinox symbolizes the reemergence of the light and life force in the hemisphere; in the course of a day, the Sun has a similar significance, even if only for that twenty-four hour period. As Aries is the sign associated with these points, it clearly represents the dawning of the light. As it also is the sign of East, it begins the first quadrant, the three houses whose task it is to define, develop, and express the self.

Aries also partakes of the Eastern hemisphere that is composed of houses 10-3. As such, it tends to be subjective in focus, preferring to create its own experience rather than perceiving what is already happening and trying to fit into that program. With freshness and enthusiasm, reflecting the dawning of a new day, and the opening of a new growing cycle, Aries pursues its mode of subjective creativity.

Over the next two months, Taurus and Gemini will deepen and expand this creation and expression of self. What Aries must do is get it going. From the physical and mental levels, or even from paying attention and realizing that it's time for action, this is the task and nature of Aries. It represents the need to assert personal energy. Aries says, "I am."

The Sun enters Aries every two years on March 21 and leaves April 21. Every other year the dates are March 20 and April 20. This variance is true for all signs. So although for many people born on March 21 the Sun is in Aries, for some it may be in the last degree of Pisces. In either case, when the Sun, or any planet, is in the last two or three degrees of one sign or the first two or three of another, that planet is said to be on the cusp. As a result, you will manifest that energy through both of the sign-filters at different times in your life. Having planets on a cusp may be more confusing, because it provides more options for expression. But it also allows for more variety and complexity of manifestation.

THE MYTHS

The Arabian astronomer, Abumasar, stated that creation took place when the planets Sun, Moon, Mercury, Venus, Mars, Jupiter, and Saturn were all conjunct in the sign Aries. Although possible that there was such an alignment at one time it is totally speculative and highly unlikely that it was during such an alignment that life began. But this theory is interesting and useful in two respects. First, it suggests that to associate Aries with initiation and beginnings is ancient and universal. Second, it points out the relevance of cycles: that phenomena take place at specific times, and for certain periods. Something preceded that which is just now beginning, and something else will follow.

The Greeks referred to Ares as the god of war. He was one of the twelve original Olympian deities and represents a primal archetype in the human experience. One of the contributions the Greeks made to the development of human consciousness was to emphasize the rational mind "to bring order out of the chaos." In keeping with this cultural and intellectual orientation, Ares was not highly regarded by the Greeks. Ares was aggressive, physical and impulsive. His negative persona was to be violent, hostile and brutal. In the Iliad, Homer depicted Ares in a derisive light, calling him "the curse of men," as if emotionally generated action is reprehensible. Homer did, however, praise Ares for his leadership, courage and bravery. These images of Ares/Mars combine to portray instinctive action generated by an immediate emotional response. Ares was the victory of action over contemplation, of the physical and passionate over the rational and refined. War and sexuality were expressions that defined the energy of Ares.

The Romans changed Ares' name to Mars, ironic in that the planet astrologers define as the ruler of the sign Aries is Mars. The Romans found more value in the passion of this god. They defined him as the protector and defender of the community, and portrayed him as vigorous and virile. His priests danced in full armor. His temple was dedicated to warlike exercises. The Romans thought of Mars as not only acceptable, but desirable. Not only did this god have a revered place in Roman society, but the characteristics he demonstrated were thought worthy of worship and emulation. To the Romans, acts of violence and conquest were given high priority. Mars was also said to be the father of Romulus and Remus, the founders of Rome. Thus the progenitor of their capitol city, the center of their civilization, was the god of war.

Ares' father was Zeus, his mother Hera. The story of their marriage unfolds from a time in history when the ancient matrilineal agrarian tribes of Central and Southern Europe (in which women were priestesses and heads of clans, but men were not seen as subordinant or suppressed) were being overrun and undermined by the invading tribes of hunters and gatherers from the north and south. Zeus was the primal deity, the godhead of the male-dominated invading culture. Hera was the primal deity, the goddess, of the pastoral indigenous culture. Their marriage was supposedly based on the merging of the two societies, blended as equals. Hera was to give up her freedom and sanctified position as prime deity in return for vows of devotion and fidelity from her male partner. This would have symbolized the merging of the two cultures as one, with each maintaining its own integrity and source of power. Soon after the vows were taken, Zeus betrayed them. His infidelities became legend, leaving Hera humiliated, yet no longer free to strike back or leave. Their offspring, Ares, felt the outrage, the anger and the betrayal of his mother. He became the vengeful expression of that anger. It's as if war, the "curse of man," is a result of the subjugation of a civilization that placed sharing, caring and nurturing in high priority to a culture that emphasized might as right.

Greek and Roman mythology offers the story of the golden fleece. A man named Phrixus was sentenced to death as a sacrifice to the gods. Hermes (Greek) or Mercury (Roman) sent a sacred ram who had golden fleece and Phrixus escaped by flying with the ram, hanging on to his fleece. This is a story that emphasizes the drive for freedom and personal independence of Aries. The story of the golden fleece is later expanded through the story of Jason and the Argonauts. Jason was the rightful heir to the throne of Iolcus. When he tried to claim his birthright, he was told to retrieve the golden fleece as the price of the throne. Though the fleece was guarded by a dragon, the daring Jason was successful in his quest and was returned to the throne. This demonstrates the qualities of courage and bravery with which Aries is associated.

The themes of freedom and courage as qualities of the Aries archetype are also expressed by several other myths. The Hebrews called Aries the month of the ram. The Hebrews had been enslaved by the Egyptians for hundreds of years. It was during the month of the ram that the Hebrews, led by Moses, broke the chains of slavery. With little to sustain them in a physical way, they relied on the charismatic leadership of Moses and their own relentless drive to regain their independence. They kept moving until at last they were successful in their quest.

These myths suggest that Aries represents a combination of qualities. The god of war is also the avenging protector. The impulsive expressor of physical or emotional energy is also the brave and courageous leader. The derided forceful brute can also be a progenitor of freedom.

The Aryan Age conforms roughly to the two thousand years before Christ. It was during this time that the Old Testament was written, and provides a sense of what life was like in the Middle East and Southern Europe. This was the age that created the terrifying, vengeful God Yahweh. Anger, judgment and one-dimensional restrictions mark the reign of this deity. The real story, the real hero of the age, however, was the courage and bravery of a small tribe fighting for its freedom. Yahweh also symbolizes the concept of the unified Godhead that emerged during this period. The Middle East had been a multifaceted pantheon of cultures, tribes (some matrilineal, some matriarchal) and deities. They were either comfortable co-existing with each other or ignorant about each other's presence. They were each content to remain in their own area. During the Aryan Age, these pastoral societies were overtaken by a more aggressive people. These groups placed more value and emphasis on the individual than the tribe, on conquest than co-existence and on the primacy of the masculine principle over the continuity of the feminine. This became symbolized by the omnipresence and omnipotence of the single male figure, God the father. Although this promoted individual definition and development, it also created polarizing divisions among the tribes. Ultimately this led to the extreme separation of male and female, the generation of class-oriented, hierarchical societies. Instead of the many tribes, one tribe was being forged by one leader. With that military and economic consolidation and strength came the subjugation of the individual to the will of the leader. Values changed. Property and posses-sions became more desirable than creativity and the arts. With that change began a separation from a sense of connection to the Oneness of Life that we are still trying to reverse today.

This historical development has many parallels in the nature and qualities of Aries. As a *yang* sign it is more comfortable with the individuating principle, and the expression of the masculine, assertive modality. It prefers independence, and can be ruthless and courageous in upholding that principle. However, it is quite capable of perceiving others in a relatively narrow, even parochial way that ultimately limits the freedom of those people. Quite assertive of its own ideas, Aries can nevertheless remain subjectively attached to them, criticizing and judging alternative points of view. Aries can be the leader who forces others to submit to his will.

To bring humanity out of the undifferentiated stew of early hominid tribes, the drive and pioneering spirit was important. The rational process had to be viewed as a valued part of the human experience to develop more perspective about ourselves as a species. As can many enthusiastic true believers, Aries can also become stuck in one-dimensional thinking, and requires the perspective of other archetypes to help the evolutionary process continue.

THE GLYPH: ♈

The glyph associated with Aries is a very simple symbol. It resembles a stick figure rendering of a bird in flight, illustrating the Aries love of freedom. It's a symbol of the effervescent fountain-like flow of life force. The glyph suggests that the energy of Aries is expressive and always moving.

It also resembles the collar leaves of a plant, the first ones that push through the soil. This symbolizes the initiatory force that Aries can demonstrate. It is the sign of Spring, the assurance that the vital energy has returned to the hemisphere and that the growth cycle has been renewed. There is nothing hesitant, shy or inhibited about this energy. It is thrusting, driving and direct. It is as if Nature is telling us through the Arian modality that you have a certain time to begin to plant the seeds of whatever new project you want to begin or parts of yourself you want to develop. To spend time deliberating or discussing is to waste the immediate opportunity at hand. This is the underlying motivation of the Aries nature. Always in the present, dealing with issues at hand in a very clear and forceful manner. Not much for diplomacy or consideration of other people or the subtleties of the situation. There is only the *now*, and now is the time for action.

THE TOTEM:

The animal associated with Aries is the ram. This image continues the association of Aries as thrusting and aggressive. It brings to mind the image of a battering ram. This principle can manifest in Nature as the Dall sheep. This is an independent, dynamic and sexual animal. When its territory is invaded, or during mating season, the ram can become quite belligerent. Whether working to remain free, or attempting to gain dominance in the flock, the Dall ram is always moving.

Putting together the symbols of the glyph and the animal, the fundamental qualities of Aries begin to emerge. It is easy to visualize a strong beast of the mountains, climbing in a bold and pioneering way to the peaks of the range where it can enjoy its own life in its own way. As a *yang* or masculine sign, Aries presents a picture of the dominant male leading its tribe to a place of abundance. His long, thick hair flowing in the wind is a testimony to the pride he has in his direction and leadership.

But there is also a more spiritual implication of this totem. Centuries before the Christian Era, the people revered Aries as the "Lamb of God." It was thought of as the sign of the savior, in that its influence helped cleanse sins. Since this is also the time of year when the Sun ascends in the Northern hemisphere, we can assume that the ancients were actually revering the Sun as the savior and healer. When the Sun returns to the Northern hemisphere, its warmth and radiance encourages people to open their doors and open themselves—to clean the rooms and furniture after the winter's accumulation of dust and debris and to perform similar ablutions on the inner self. After a winter of hibernating with your own thoughts, Aries represents the time to air them out. If the ideas are selfish or negative in any way, you can become more aware of that by listening to them spoken out loud. Then eliminate them from your mind and purify your mind in the process. If they are good ideas that represent your creative nature and are of benefit to both yourself and others that too becomes clear. Spring is the time to act on them.

Both of the primal elements are in the sign Aries. The primal forcefulness, the independence and the courage are the most obvious and well-known manifestations of its influence. It can also display tendencies of honesty and creativity. It dislikes being tied down to anything that is old or extraneous. It prefers change and new beginnings.

MODE AND ELEMENT

Aries is the cardinal fire sign. As the first sign in the zodiac, Aries tends to function in a simple and straightforward manner. It's a young sign and can relate in an overly simplistic, naive way to life. Aries tends to experience life one-dimensionally, even at those times when it is more realistic or appropriate to be aware of the complexities and subtleties of a situation.

As a fire sign, you have a drive to be creative. You can express yourself in a variety of art forms. Mercury in Aries is oriented toward creative writing. With Venus or the Sun in Aries you may tend toward visual art. As an Aries you prefer any form of creative expression that enables you to have hands on contact. You may have difficulty relating to an activity if it is presented solely in an intellectual form. To act on the idea, to see it, touch it, or draw it can make it seen more real, and enable you to understand it more clearly.

The fire of Aries is like that of a lightning bolt—direct, immediate and intense. Sometimes such a burst of electrical energy is single-pointed, like a ray of pure light in the sky. At other times it appears more scattered in random patterns across the sky. Similarly, Aries can act in ways that are very singular and focused, or more dispersed and confused. In the former manifestation, you will usually be more effective in the situation, and more satisfied with your contribution. In the latter scenario you will be more frustrated and ineffectual.

A bolt of lightning against the night time sky can illuminate an entire vista, bringing clarity to that which would otherwise be dark and hidden. Similarly, the fire of Aries can bring the light of truth to a situation clouded by ignorance or deceit. Sometimes this can happen merely by perceiving something in its most basic form, and sharing that perception honestly. This can produce insight and the opportunity for consciousness to develop.

But the fire can be also be used in a detrimental way. The Aries' truth can be expressed rashly, or in a harsh and insensitive way. It can prove to be destructive of whatever lies in its path. In either case, there is no artifice to Aries. Although it can be abrupt, it is always real in expressing its own point of view.

As a cardinal sign, Aries is action-oriented. It enjoys initiating new experiences, projects and relationships. Like the new growth in Spring or the young animal full of its new life, Aries charges forth with energy and exuberance. What it may lack in direction or goal is made up for by its pure energy. It would rather act impulsively, learning its lessons through trial and error, than function in a more deliberate but less enthusiastic manner. Sometimes this type of behavior can be unnecessarily wasteful. It can lead to relationships with people and connections to situations that are superficial or one-dimensional. It can produce immature relationships. If this is continually your pattern, your growth becomes limited or non-existent. If you maintain an attitude of openness, learning from the mistakes, eliminating those actions that prove unfulfilling, this path can be useful. It enables you to understand what is the proper, truthful process for you, and it can teach you how to act decisively in the face of new experience.

Combining the cardinality with the fire, produces the image of a sign that has the best record for initiating projects, a fact that is appropriate for the first sign of the Zodiac. Unfortunately it also has the worst record for following through and finishing what it starts. A lot of Aries energy in the natal chart might indicate a predisposition to chose a house to live in based on the amount of closet and cabinet space. The more the better. This way there would be places to store all the unfinished projects in case someday you wanted to return to work on and complete them.

THE RULING PLANET

The ruling planet of Aries is Mars. Although the contemporary glyph for Mars is the male symbol (♂), the original glyph was a circle with a cross on top (☿). This represents the physical plane emanating from the primal energy of the circle. It indicates that for Mars there is the primacy of individual ego (symbolized by the cross) over Spirit (symbolized by the circle). Will (the circle) is beneath and subordinated to physical plane activity (the cross).

Mars represents the energy that is pioneering and creative. It is the initiating force, driving, and aggressive. If carried to an extreme, it can produce arrogance and out of control action. It has a stimulating influence in whatever area of life it is found in the natal horoscope. It represents the drive to display personal energy. It is energy that is directed outward, moving from within the self and being expressed externally. Expressions such as anger, art or sexual passion are manifestations of Mars.

Even though you may not have planets in the sign Aries we all have Mars in our natal chart. Its sign placement indicates how you express yourself, how you assert your personal energy in physical ways. Its house placement indicates where (what area of life) the energy exists. Mars is the energy that enables you to define, develop and express the "I am." If it is placed in a sign and house in your natal chart in which it feels comfortable, is supported by aspects or angular relationships from other planets, and if you are expressing it in a centered way, its energy will convey courage, vitality and health. If it is placed in a stressful pattern in your chart or you are using its influence in an uncentered way, it can indicate cruelty, selfishness and lust. Mars can be expressed with a me-first, shoot-from-the-hip kind of arrogance for whom winning is the only thing. If Mars is under stress it can also indicate lack of courage, lack of identity or poor health. Competition and conflict act as two guns in the holsters of an out of control Mars. This is the image of the little boy on the playground striving to be seen as okay, as good as all the other guys, and therefore not a target of ridicule or laughter. As you develop yourself in a more conscious, centered and self-loving way you restrain those Martian tendencies by retraining yourself to think of the energy in a broader context.

Mars is the warrior, but this needn't be defined as one who is always looking for a fight. Externally, a true warrior is one who acts with consciousness and courage, and who never does anything without a clear understanding of motivation. A true warrior is one who seeks to pioneer new paths of activity in life in an independent, self-determined way. In a concrete sense, this can manifest as the scientist (Mars in Scorpio), the technician (Mars in Virgo), the inventor (Mars in Aquarius), or the logician (Mars in Libra).

For men these concepts are important. Being male makes it desirable and important for them to maintain such traits as physical strength, athletic skill and sexual vitality. These are all qualities under the rulership of Mars. Individual free will can decide whether this energy manifests in a way that burns others with insensitivity or is to be used in the service of forging new patterns of human relations and activity.

For women the energy of Mars is important to tap into and feel comfortable expressing. You have the option of growing beyond the societally defined dictum that only males can own their leadership ability, athleticism, sexuality or assertiveness. Be yourself, use your Mars in the manner defined by its sign, house placement and the aspects to it. By developing a clear understanding of why, how, when and where you want or need to express this form of masculine energy you become able to use it in fulfilling and appropriate ways. By becoming more comfortable with your Martian/masculine energy you can take a more active role in creating your life. You can function more independently, less reliant on men to initiate activities that are important to you. You can be more assertive in expressing your opinions thereby helping to integrate your values into both your personal life and professional environment. Being more physically active can bring increased recreational pleasure and greater sexual fulfillment. Working with your Mars energy can help you be more conscious of anger and direct in expressing it. This can help eliminate depression and chronic resentment.

The concept of the warrior also has an internal manifestation. In the Buddhist tradition, the way of the warrior is "the courage to know oneself." This involves recognizing and integrating both the difficult and harmonious aspects of your nature. For example, if you have Mars in Taurus, you may have difficulty dealing with anger. You tend to have a very long fuse connected to a very large keg of dynamite. It may take you a long time to register and express your anger but when you do, the explosion could be monumental. As a warrior, you must challenge yourself to become aware of these tendencies. Learning to recognize the emotion of anger as it starts to build is the first step. Learning how to communicate that anger in a way that lets others know how you feel without resorting to rage is the second step. Avoiding the denial/destruction route is part of your challenge in learning about and conquering yourself.

The way of the internal warrior can take many paths throughout the lifetime. Aggression (too much or not enough), sexuality and competitiveness might be a few of the issues to address. Not to negate or repress, but for consciousness—knowing what you are doing and why.

The sign of Mars' placement indicates how you project yourself in life. Mars in the fire signs (Aries, Leo or Sagittarius) suggests a radiant, confident expression of energy. Your ability to define yourself and let others know who you are is clear and can manifest through a strong creative drive. For all your passion and enthusiasm, however, you may be too direct or insensitive in your relationships. Aries and Sagittarius can be direct and immediate in their sexual activity, making up in ardor and passion what they may lack in subtlety and sensitivity. People with Mars in Leo are romantic and playful. Leo is the sign of love, and, with Mars in Leo, sexuality becomes a fine vehicle for sharing it. Anger is also expressed with immediacy and passion. Mars in Aries can be overwhelmed with the feeling of the moment and lash out at others. Mars in Sagittarius can be blunt and unfeeling in its anger. Mars in Leo can be more diplomatic, but can also unleash anger with vehemence and willfulness.

In the earth signs (Taurus, Virgo or Capricorn) your energy is expressed more slowly and oriented to practical activities. Your focus is to get things done, to achieve something that has enduring benefit. A potential drawback, however, is to become too identified with physical manifestations. Even if they are productive and useful, to define yourself primarily by material results is limiting. Taurus and Virgo are especially uncomfortable expressing anger. For Taurus there could be a tremendous explosion after a long period of patience. Virgo can express anger through nit-picking criticism although Mars in Virgo is also helpful in craftsmanship and playing instruments. Capricorn is more authoritarian in its anger, seeking to control others' actions as a way of creating safety for itself. Mars in Taurus is sensual as well as sexual, enjoying a long build-up in times of intimacy. Mars in Capricorn can also be sexually passionate but also can use sex as a tool with which to control a relationship. Mars in Virgo tries to adapt to the partner's needs and be serviceful in sexual activity.

Mars in air signs (Gemini, Libra or Aquarius) puts energy into the mental and social activities of life. Reading and networking provide ways of expressing yourself. You tend to identify with your ideas, your social contacts and your intellectual development. Creative writing or working with crafts can be manifested especially in Gemini. Too much energy expressed this way can lead to hyperactivity or a tendency to think too much and act too little. Anger tends to be expressed verbally, through argument or debate. Librans express anger by playing devil's advocate and can deliberately provoke others by expressing contrary opinions. They can also express anger by instigating a conflict between others. Sexually the air signs prefer activities that are refined. Mars in an air sign enjoys conversation during sexual intimacy. Mars in Aquarius can run the gamut from being highly inspired to detached. This placement enjoys sexual experimentation.

In water signs (Cancer, Scorpio or Pisces) your feelings and sensitivities are heightened. Your intuition and dream life can be strongly developed but you have difficulty with the more external forms of Martian expression. Anger can be expressed quite differently in each sign. In Cancer you can be pouty and petulant in a childlike way or rather biting. Scorpio, known for its stinger, also has a bite although often expressed with greater intensity to the extent that it inflicts more pain. Scorpio also tends to hold on to anger and remain vindictive for long periods of time. Pisces can express anger in a misplaced way. Often Pisces has a hard time recognizing anger and may direct it inward. If they do express it, the anger is often misplaced. They get angry at the wrong time, at the wrong person and for the wrong reason. Sexually, Mars in Cancer can be quite passionate or quite detached. The Moon rules Cancer and the monthly cycle of the Moon will indicate the times of the month when any individual with Mars in Cancer will be interested. During sexual activity, however, Mars in Cancer helps generate a responsive and sensitive manner and can be a very considerate lover. Scorpio is known for its sexual appetite. Assuming a deep emotional connection with the partner, sex can be a vehicle for transformation. Without that bond, however, sex can be boring or draining to Scorpio. Far from the obsessive pattern that is the stereotype, people with Mars in Scorpio can spend long periods of time celibate if true intimacy is lacking in their lives. Mars in Pisces is dreamy and romantic. With Mars in Pisces you enjoy fantasy in your love-making, finding that it opens the way for creativity and self-expression in this area of activity.

When Mars is retrograde, it can indicate the person has a difficult time expressing him- or herself in a clear and straightforward way. The sign within which Mars is retrograde can indicate what part of the Martian influence needs review or what is preventing overt expression. For example, with Mars retrograde in the introspective sign Pisces the tendency may be to direct the anger at self, and feeling inhibited about any overt expression of any kind. With Mars retrograde in Cancer—the sign of the family and the parent-child relationship—one may seek out a person in the present who symbolizes someone from the past and try to recreate situations that have been previously experienced. In Capricorn, who tends to seek approval and recognition from others, Mars retrograde brings a difficult time with peer group relations, and you may seem to get along better with people who are much older or younger than you are. In Leo, a sign of self-exaltation, Mars retrograde provides a fierce desire to win in any situation, whether in an athletic contest or personal relationship. In Aries, the individual may have a difficult time with self-expression or assertiveness, and might tend to over compensate for that by being excessively arrogant, pushy or demanding. The response that these last two Mars retrograde patterns engenders is usually rejection. To the external observer that response may be appropriate and fair. To the Mars retrograde individual this may seem unjust and confusing, just another reason to avoid putting the self out there at all. To be extreme with your Mars retrograde is to create a behavior in which "your best defense is a good offense." You try to avoid being confronted or challenged by creating an intimidating persona that is compensation for feelings of insecurity in that area.

The lesson of Mars retrograde, therefore, is to develop your assertive self in a broader and more balanced way. Be aware of your anger but learn to direct it. Feel comfortable with people of all ages without shirking or fearing your peers. Maintain a healthy competitive drive without feeling compelled to always "win." Sometimes winning takes the form of beating yourself. Conquer those tendencies that separate you from others and cause you to isolate yourself within your protective chamber of ego-armor.

THE FIRST HOUSE AND THE RISING SIGN

The area of life associated with Aries is the first house. The cusp of the first house is a cardinal point. Altogether there are four cardinal points: house cusps one, four, seven and ten. Cardinal points are also called angles. Planets on or around these points are called angular. Angular planets will be manifested in a direct and obvious way. At times it may seem as if people with an abundance of energy around the cardinal points make more mistakes than other people because their errors are more apparent, more out there for all to see. If that is your experience, balance that out by realizing that your successes will also be more evident, for the same reason. At least allow yourself to acknowledge that truth. Better, allow yourself to receive the praise and recognition that is likely to accompany your triumphs. You can also use the feedback from the "failures" as an opportunity to develop a more realistic perspective. Learn from that situation and what may seem like a problem may turn out to be a wonderful learning opportunity. Don't use "selective listening" to give you a distorted picture of yourself.

The cardinal points correspond to the beginning of each season. They are analogous to the solstices and equinoxes. The first house, cardinal point one, relates to the Spring Equinox, the first day of spring. This is that time of year when the Sun is coming north and the days and nights are of equal length. The light is spreading in the Northern hemisphere. Similarly, your rising sign, cardinal point one in your natal chart, can indicate the way in which you spread your light in the world. As such, it is one of the most significant variables in your natal chart.

The sign on the cusp of the first house, as well as any planets therein, defines the expression of your personality. The sign on the cusp of the first house is also called the rising or ascendant sign, because it was the sign coming up in the East at the time of day that you were born. It can indicate the way in which you come across to others. If you visualize yourself as a building, the rising sign is the front door. It is that part of yourself that you willingly open up and show to other people as if to say, "Hi, this is me." That is no more the total you than the front door is the entire building, but it is the first part. It is the persona, the way in which you integrate with the physical plane during an incarnation. The point of persona has a lot to do with your attitude and outlook on life, and with your expression of self through body language, physical appearance and social style. Distinctions can be made by looking at the mode of the sign rising and the mode of the sign in which the ruler of the ascendant resides. Cardinal signs imply being more action-oriented. Cardinal signs on the angles define a person who is a goer and a doer. Fixed signs are more stable and persevering with a demonstrable strength of will. The mutable signs on the angles, or where the ruler is placed are the most adaptable to what is going on around them, and are oriented to service. They usually need external structure, however, to function most effectively.

Aries rising or Mars in the first house enables you to project your persona in a direct and energetic manner. You are an initiator who has the potential to be a leader. You can also be impulsive in your actions and competitive in your relationships. You like being first in whatever you do but sometimes act before speaking or speak before thinking. Physical activity is important to you and you may have a tendency toward aggressive or hostile behavior.

Taurus rising or Venus in the first house puts harmony and aesthetics in high focus. You tend to act in slow, deliberate ways, preferring what is comfortable over what is exciting. Patience is one of your virtues with regard to both your own process and that of others. You can be very affectionate and sensual, but can also be so oriented toward the pleasures of life that you can become overweight or inactive. Security is important to you. If you remain hardworking, that security becomes a foundation of your life. If you don't, you can become extremely materialistic and possessive, seeking to impose your will on others.

Gemini rising or Mercury in the first house promotes a curious nature. You are versatile in your activities and enjoy a variety of people to relate to. Communication skills are a strength and you have good hand-eye coordination and manual dexterity. You could also have a tendency, however, to get confused by having too many projects going at once. You can be glib and charming but may connect with people at a superficial level. Avoid becoming so identified with ideas and the logical process that you lose touch with your feelings or relate in an insensitive way toward others.

Cancer rising or the Moon in the first house indicates a sensitive, receptive and care-giving nature. Your home and relationship to your family are of primary significance. You relate well to children and are a conscientious parent. You can also be playful and childlike yourself. Your sensitivity can also cause you to become overly self-protective, and interpret words or actions as being aimed deliberately at you. This can cause you to withdraw or be moody. Be careful about becoming too dependent on the family or on your identity as a parent.

Leo rising or the Sun in the first house render you an honest person who externalizes feelings and attitudes about yourself. You can be generous to and supportive of others and are a good organizer. You also need support and recognition from others. This can contribute to you being shy with people, if you think you don't deserve or simply will not receive that type of feedback. You can also be demanding of that energy from others in a way that causes them to turn away from you or give you less than they otherwise might have.

Virgo rising impels a strong attitude of service in your projection to others. Being in touch with your body and striving to maintain a balanced program of exercise, diet and rest helps you to function most efficiently. You can feel strongly connected to nature and may feel at home in the woods or your garden. Virgo can also be a perfectionist. You could become critical of your body if you notice a flaw. You can also be critical of other people who don't measure up to your expectations.

Libra rising emphasizes balance in your life. You focus on the harmonious interaction between yourself and others and can be thoughtful and considerate in your relationships. You have the ability to put others at ease in your presence. You also tend to be overly sensitive to displeasing others. This can cause you to placate them and rely on the feedback from other people to give you a sense of identity. Personal appearance, including the style and color of your clothing, is important to you.

Scorpio rising or Pluto in the first house provides an intense, passionate and sensitive persona You need your time alone as a opportunity for deep self-analysis but you also need to lighten up at times and not be obsessive with demands either on self or others. Scorpio and Pluto are the sign and planet of transformation. Pay attention to situations in which others are recoiling from you. They may telling you that they find your energy too demanding or invasive. Also notice when others are taking advantage of your sensitivity and are draining you or hurting your feelings. In either case some part of your persona needs to be transformed. As you let go of old attitudes or forms of persona that are no longer working for you, create new ones to take their place.

Sagittarius rising or Jupiter in the first house help bring about an expansive and enthusiastic attitude and outlook on life. You have a marvelous sense of humor and a generosity of spirit. You love to travel and can be attracted to any activity than enables you to expand your awareness. You can also be athletic, preferring individual sports such as hiking or bicycle or horseback riding to the more competitive team sports. Too much expansion can also lead to excessive idealism and tendencies to expect more from people and situations than they can realistically provide.

Capricorn rising or Saturn in the first house induces a goal-oriented, organized personality. You like structure and organization and tend to create it for both yourself and others. As you work to achieve your goals you can function in an ambitious, competitive yet self-disciplined manner, clearly aware of your limits and boundaries. Without defining your goals, you will tend to feel limited, inhibited or fearful. You can try to counterbalance those tendencies by being controlling of others rather than working to control yourself.

Aquarius rising or Uranus in the first house puts emphasis on freedom and expressing your persona in an often unconventional way. These influences generate an attitude of tolerance, friendliness and acceptance toward others. You can be inspiring to others sometimes even being seen as a role model. You also identify as an individual. These influences can also lead to an attitude of aloofness, remaining detached from others. You could also get carried away with your need for uniqueness and be seen as extreme or eccentric in your social style or manner of dress. Try to define your persona in such a way as to be authentic in expressing who you are, but not to the extent of deliberately generating hostility or rejection from others.

Pisces rising or Neptune in the first house can make it difficult for you to be sure of who you are. You can be plagued by feelings of self-doubt and self-criticism. You can be oriented toward helping and serving others and thus blend in with what is going on. Forced to be more clearly defined can cause you to conform to other people's expectations or to play a role. You are a natural mimic, so your performance can be good. It's also dangerous because you can become convinced that whatever part you are playing is really who you are. A strong connection to a spiritual path can help solve the problem. By identifying with Spirit you feel supported by divine forces of unconditional love. You can develop faith in yourself and your ability to function effectively.

The rising sign, as well as any planets in the first house, can indicate your body type. The parts of the body ruled either by your rising sign or the planets in the first house are also ones that may tend to break down under stress. The influences of the first house need to be considered when looking for clues about health issues.

Trying to assess body type is a complex matter. The sign on the cusp of the first house, the planets in the first house and the ruling planet of the rising sign have to be considered. If, for example, you have Libra rising note the placement of Venus in your chart because Venus is the ruling planet of Libra. If Venus is conjunct Saturn, your body type will reflect that conjunction. Usually, Libra rising (like any air sign rising) grants a thin frame and wiry body. But the conjunction to Saturn may elongate the body, making you taller than most people with Libra rising. Health wise, Libra rules, among other things, the kidneys. With the ruler (Venus) conjunct Saturn, you may have problems in the kidney area due to some type of blockage or restriction (qualities brought by Saturn).

With the ruler of your ascendant conjunct Saturn, you may tend to be more cautious and reserved that would be expected just by noting the sign itself.

Even with no planets conjunct the ruler of your ascendant, the sign in which that ruler is placed can also provide clues about body type and personality. For example, with Capricorn rising it might be assumed that your personality would reflect the qualities of that sign. Among these traits are seriousness, caution and responsibility. The ruling planet of Capricorn is Saturn. If you have Saturn in a playful and changeable sign like Gemini or Aquarius your behavior and persona might be reflective of those qualities as well as those of the more restrictive Capricorn.

Although defining body type by ascendant and first house planets is not an exact science, some general rules are worth noting. With an air sign rising (Gemini, Libra, or Aquarius), the body tends to be willowy or wiry. Fire signs (Aries, Leo, or Sagittarius), often render a larger and stronger frame. Fire signs or Scorpio rising, or Mars in the first house, can indicate red hair. Water signs (Cancer, Scorpio, or Pisces) suggest a stocky frame. Earth signs rising (Taurus, Virgo, or Capricorn) large boned, with thick hands and fingers, and solid frame. With Jupiter, which is the energy of expansion, is rising or the signs ruled by Jupiter (Sagittarius and Pisces) are rising, you may have a tendency to gain weight (the body expanding).

These points may be interesting, but have a generally limiting significance. Not only is the body type a relatively superficial way of defining a person, but there are many exceptions and specific applications which make each case unique. I gave a lecture one time to a group of women. I noticed one young lady in particular sitting in the front row. It seemed evident to me by her facial features that she had Gemini rising. After the talk, she gave me her birth data so I could cast her chart and give her a reading. According to the data, she had Capricorn rising. Confused, I went home and cast the chart. Sure enough, she had Capricorn rising, but Mercury (the ruler of Gemini) was exactly conjunct her ascendant. Sometimes the influence can come from the sign, other times from a planet, and still others, from a planet in aspect to the ascendant or its ruler.

Of greater significance is the way in which the sign on the cusp and the planets in the first house define yourself and express your attitude about yourself in a broader framework than appearance.

Don't confuse the sign Aries, the planet Mars, and the first house. You may or may not have any planets in the sign Aries. But we all have the planet Mars in our natal horoscope. It could have been in Aries at the time of your birth, or any of the other eleven signs. Wherever you have it indicates where (by house) you have the drive to express yourself, and how (by sign) its energy will get expressed. We all have a rising sign because there is always a sign ascending above the horizon at the time of day that we were born. The wheel of signs rotates clockwise, rising in the East and setting in the West. Think of the horoscope as the face of a twenty-four hour clock. If you follow the Sun in its daily journey, it rises at dawn on the ascendant or first house cusp. It culminates, or achieves its most elevated position at mid-day around the mid-heaven or tenth house cusp. At sunset, the Sun descends below the horizon and is at the descendant or seventh house cusp. At midnight it is directly below the earth at its nadir, the fourth house cusp.

If you were born at dawn, the sign that the Sun was in was also rising in your natal chart. If you were born at another hour of the day picture where the Sun was at that time, relative to the twenty-four hour clock of the chart. Since the order of the signs is invariable, because each one always follows the same sign and precedes another, you can see what sign was rising at the time you were born, and understand why. Each sign rises for about two hours each day (twelve signs in the zodiac, twenty-four hours in a day).

The rising sign, (the sign on the cusp of cardinal point one) and the planets or energy in the first house get things going. What they get going is the way in which you define yourself and express that self, socially and physically, and integrate that self into the immediate environment.

ARIES AND THE BODY

Anatomically, Aries rules the head, the cranial area, the facial bones, and the motor centers in the brain. Several planets in Aries can indicate a propensity for headaches and accidents involving the head. There must be some connection between your Aries energy and the body or Aries and health, however, for this pattern to manifest. If you have Aries planets in the first house (body and body type) or the sixth house (health), your head can be prone to pain or injury. If your Aries planets are in hard aspect (square, opposition) to planets Saturn, Uranus, Pluto or Mars, it could suggest illness, accident or suppression of energy. Aries energy in the third house (transportation, short trips) in hard aspect to Uranus, or Mars in the third house in any sign but in hard aspect to Uranus suggests traffic accidents. Planets in Aries or Mars in the ninth could indicate accidents during long journeys. Mars or energy in Aries in hard aspect to Saturn can lead to low energy or chronic health problems.

The experience of Aries is one of energy expressed in a direct way. If you have several planets in Aries, you may tend to be very active and function in impulsive ways. This can increase the

likelihood of accidents and injuries, but also generates vitality
and the energy to engage life directly. If Mars is in Aries, in
supportive aspect (sextile, trine) to the Sun or Jupiter or on one
of the four angles, your energy level is high. Your overall health
will tend to be good and you will exhibit the ability to fend off
illness. Mars sextile or trine to Saturn or Pluto indicates physical
stamina. Mars squared or opposing Neptune generates dissi-
pation of vitality and energy level.

Mars functions physically like the drive wheel in your car: it
supplies the friction that enables action to take place. By sign
placement it suggests how active, competitive or athletic you are.
Mars in a fire sign generates the most energy and drive. The
activity needs to be balanced by periods of rest to alleviate
potential burnout. In air signs Mars provides energy for the mind
and helps in creating social activities. The nervous system can be
over charged, however, creating tension and mental exhaustion.
Fire and air signs can also signify a more rapid recuperation from
illness than if Mars is in earth or water signs. In the earth signs
the energy level is less dynamic. The movement is more deliberate and oriented to generating a long range physical stability.
With Mars in the water signs, the emotions are heightened to the
extent that the energy can be easily depleted.

If Mars is heavily emphasized in the chart (Mars in Aries,
Leo, Scorpio, or Sagittarius) conjunct the Sun, or in hard aspect
to Uranus or Jupiter, it can create almost too much energy.
Competitive and athletic by nature you could also be so driven
by your physical energy that you could, at times, be violent.
These influences can also lead to actions that are so indiscrim-
inate as to render you accident prone (especially in hard aspect to
Uranus).

Mars energy is hot and dry. Illnesses that can correspond to
Mars reflect its nature: infections, fevers, inflammations, burns,
surgery, and pain. Mars can also indicate experiential illness, that
is, problems arising from doing things, from being active. With a
prominent Mars in your natal chart, you need to learn patience,
and how to allow your activities to develop in their own time.
Learn how to integrate the expression of your own energy with
the rate appropriate to your activities.

CONCLUSIONS

Aries is the sign of the *now*. As the first sign of the Zodiac, Aries influence is simple and without artifice. What you see is what you get. They constantly require and seek new challenges and opportunities. Sometimes this here-and-now orientation can make them impatient or one dimensional. They can be narrow-minded and tend to be opinionated. Their impulsiveness can cause them to pre-judge people or situations to the extent that they jump to conclusions about things. Most of the time they will be wrong in their assumptions. They can be right often enough, however, that this pattern gets reinforced. They can be unaware of the subtleties and complexities of a situation, of a relationship or of life itself. At times this can make them insensitive to the needs and feelings of others or uncompromising in demanding that their ideas be acceded to. Aries energy can be artless, but it can also be expressed with spontaneous, unpremeditated purity. Aries can be at once idealistic yet naive.

Each of the twelve signs of the zodiac contributes something of value to the human experience. Each sign represents the manifestation of a human archetype, an experience which people everywhere resonate with because it is part of the collective psyche. Aries is the archetype of the initiator. Its contribution is to get things moving. It is the pioneer, who helps to create new ways of being, or perceiving and relating to life. In your car, the strongest gear in the transmission is first, because it takes the vehicle from one mode of inertia, rest, to another mode, movement. As the sign of the first step in action, Aries needs to understand the Law of Karma. Karma means action. The Law of Karma reminds us that actions have reactions. As we sow, so shall we reap. The results of our actions are predicated upon the actions themselves. If we consider others, if our actions lead to beneficial results for ourselves and others, we receive positive reward, or good karma. If the actions are solely self-serving, if we are the exclusive beneficiary, the karma we reap would be similarly restrictive. Sooner or later we would be excluded from desirable situations.

The motivation behind the action is as important as the action itself. Even if we are the sole beneficiary of something, if our intention was to produce the greatest good for the greatest number, the karma we create is still good. If we do something of benefit to others but intend only to benefit ourselves, the karma is not as positive as it would be had our intentions matched the results. Headstrong, impulsive Aries can benefit from understanding the importance of this law. Looking to the results of action can be more important in the long run than immediate actions themselves.

The Sun in spring rejuvenates the Northern hemisphere and stimulates the growth cycle to begin. So does Aries generate action and new beginnings. Like a cosmic Johnny Aries-seed, it activates the divine spark of life, and moves on. Relative to the development of human civilization, Aries represents the hunter-gatherer. This stage of experience involves being present to the needs of the day and the activity of the *now*. Pay attention, satisfy the need and move on.

Sometimes that head-first, head-long dive into something can be a liability. If others are confused, Aries is clear. Where others are vague, Aries is direct. This can lead to a situation where Aries is the energy that is taking a risk by expressing an opinion, or by asserting leadership where it is needed. As a result, Aries can become a target of those who disagree with that action, or had a bad experience as a result of that decision. It's as if by contributing as a leader, Aries also becomes a target. Similarly, the impulsive drive to act can also lead to decisions made in haste and wrong actions taken.

Aries is an adventurer, the Indiana Jones of the zodiac. Aries is drawn to exciting activities, things that are new to their experience and sometimes risky. Eagerness and confidence, two fundamental Aries traits, can help maximize success in new and intriguing adventures.

Aries is the rugged individual. Like being John Wayne in a movie, people with Aries energy prefer to be their own person and go their own way. Others could perceive them as harsh, uncaring or willful. This pattern can lead to superficial, simplistic, or insensitive relationships. Growth for Aries comes from slowing down. This can manifest as developing patience and taking time to notice the subtleties of a relationship or situation. It can also suggest the need to become involved with their activities for longer periods and at deeper levels of awareness.

Aries can be a particularly difficult experience if several planets are in that sign in a woman's chart. As a rule women are not encouraged to develop Aries-like qualities. They are not supported in the expression of those already developed. Although these societal patterns are changing, and younger women may not have the same experience as older ones did, the traits of independence, directness and leadership have been repressed or at least not noticed or appreciated in women. This forces women with significant energy in Aries to make a decision. You can either choose to be who you are and run the risk of being seen as "different," or betray your nature and conform to societal expectations. Regardless of how long or how frequently you may choose the latter option, the first one is always there. It is waiting for you to make the decision to be yourself, a fundamental characteristic of Aries anyway. Perhaps your parents were overprotective and concerned that a strong aggressive woman would be found unattractive by men, never marry and live a lonely, impoverished life. Maybe your parents believed in the superiority of men or that women are by nature submissive. They would have seen your ruggedness and honesty as an aberration. You don't have to take on their fears or philosophies. Aries is about being yourself, about expressing the "I am" in a clear, assertive manner.

Aries are the warriors of the Zodiac. Not in the sense that they are looking for a fight, but in the sense that they are looking for new challenges and horizons to explore. If someone is working at cross purposes to them, Aries will suggest that the individual fall in line behind them, since Aries are good leaders; or that the person step aside and let the Aries pass, since Aries are very independent people; or that the individual acknowledge that the Aries is right (Aries can be very opinionated and hold passionately to their ideas); or they may suggest that if the person stays there, they will be bowled over by the assertiveness or aggression of the Aries.

In the early 1960's Carl Foreman made a movie called *The Victors*. It takes place in Germany right at the end of World War II. Unlike most of the movies made about W.W.II or the Korean War in the 1950's, this did not glorify war or seek to portray soldiers as heroes. At the end of the movie a drunken Russian soldier comes staggering out of a bar and walks down a narrow, dark alley. It had been raining and the street is covered with puddles. As he ambles along, quietly singing to himself, he comes upon a puddle deeper than others. In fact it is so deep that a board has been placed across it to act as a bridge. Just as he gets to the middle of the "bridge" he is met, quite suddenly and alarmingly, by an American soldier, also drunk and going in the opposite direction. Each soldier yells at the other to move, in his own language, of course, to insure lack of communication. These two warriors are alone in this alley. They fought as allies to defeat a common enemy. Yet neither can compromise or back down. In a scene which chillingly presages the cold war, the movie delivers its message: in war there are no "victors," only victims. People who have become so caught up in their own rightness, that they become limited in what they actually can see. It also points out the futility of the willful, one-dimensional Aries approach to life. For the Aries to grow and evolve, it must somehow emerge out of its narrow minded impulsiveness. Real progress does come to the Aries as they learn to develop their ability to explore deeper levels of themselves and of here-and-now realities.

We are all a blending of many symbols, themes, and energy patterns. For those who embody the principle of Aries, real growth may involve inter-weaving the totality of their influences, and not being satisfied with only starts and assertiveness. It may be important, for example, to develop the qualities of balance and sensitivity in your relationships to yourself and others. Learn to discriminate those times when sewing the seed and moving on is appropriate, and when expressing calmness, patience, and perseverance is desirable. This subtlety of awareness and action may not be easy for the Aries, and may even feel uncomfortable and awkward but it does represent a path of real growth and personal development.

Aries represents the energy of the personal self. It is the journey of the Aries to initiate, to activate and to lead. It is the manifestation of Divine Spark. Aries represents the hero, the courageous one who takes a first step in a new direction. Usually this is a step that few might want to take because there is some danger or risk involved. Going into a burning building to rescue a trapped person is the mark of a hero. Interrupting the comfortable behavioral patterns of an unhealthy relationship is the mark of a hero. Challenging society to explore new definitions of reality is the mark of a hero. Being willing to pursue new understandings and perspectives of yourself is the mark of a hero. Too often people are inclined to wait for heroes to appear who provide incentive and example for change and new beginnings. We live in an age when so much is changing so fast that it's inappropriate to adopt a wait and see attitude and dangerous to want someone else to go first. We live in an age when new heroes are needed. Aries is the spark that enables anyone to be a hero. It inspires us to define ourselves and create our reality in ways that work for us and, hopefully, can provide a living stimulus for others to do the same.

TAURUS

The second sign of the zodiac is Taurus. Taurus represents the need to stabilize the new beginnings of Aries. Taurus' task is to be a nurturing influence for the newly emerging vital life force which Aries represents. As a *yin* sign, Taurus' focus is internal. It is receptive and intuitive. Taurus is also a "succeedant" sign. It continues the experience of the previous angular sign, but at deeper level. Taurus functions more continuously and to a greater degree of completion.

Taurus also continues the activity of the first quadrant. Aries, the rising sign and planets in the first house initiates the journey of self and the expression of "I am." Taurus extends that journey by developing a deeper awareness of the identity. From its feminine perspective, Taurus is less concerned with acting out as a way of personal discovery, and more likely to look within and feel what is real and sustainable about the self. Taurus says, "I have." It wants to capitalize on what has already happened, building on it for the future.

Aries is the sign of early spring, the initial expression of the Life Force. Taurus comes along in mid-spring. The primal rush has been replaced by slower growth, and a deeper appreciation of the beauty of the season that can only happen when phenomena persists.

The sun enters Taurus on April 19 and leaves on May 20.

THE MYTHS

Many of the myths associated with Taurus come from the ancient world, the Neolithic Period, known as the Taurean Age. This took place from approximately 4000-6000 BC. This was a time when the culture of the Mother Goddess was pre-eminent in the world from central Europe to the (then) grasslands of the African Sahara. The tribes of that time and place were agrarian, they lived in intimate connection with the Earth, and they defined the primal female force as their main deity. They celebrated the cycles of nature with emphasis on fertility rites in Spring and death-and-regeneration rites in Fall. Some of the Taurean myths come from the ancient Egyptians. Some of their spiritually-oriented artwork often depicts the bull carrying the Sun between his horns. The Sun symbolizes creativity, consciousness and will. It is our link to the source of life. The carrier of the Sun is powerful in two ways. Most obvious, is the intense strength needed to bear the weight of such an imposing burden. More importantly, if also more subtle, is the honor of being so close to the source of life, and responsible for holding it safely and securely. Taurus, through its totem the bull is oriented toward security and capable of providing stability. As the protector of and provider for the Sun, the bull received veneration from the people, and the bull became associated with spirituality. The bull was also said to be the incarnation of Osiris, god of the Nile, and symbol of eternal life. Osiris was a central deity of spring fertility rites, and was depicted with large and prominent sex organs. Models of him with a triple phallus were borne in religious ceremonies in which sexual union was a symbol for a vigorous and long life. It's interesting to note that it was during the Taurean Age that Egypt was organized as a country, indicating that the roots of its culture emanate from these symbols and ceremonies.

In ancient Crete the association between the bull and the spirit was continued. Young people were selected to play on the backs of bulls in religious ceremonies. Again the bull is used as a symbol of fertility. How ironic that although Taurus is a *yin* or female sign, its primary totem is male. The horns of the bull especially are seen as symbols of the male principle.

The Taurean Age was one in which the image and concept of the Goddess was venerated as the prime deity. This seemingly implies female dominance over men, but such was not the case. This was not a period or social order in which dominance of any kind was perpetrated. Women didn't exert power over men, but they did define the societal patterns. These patterns were based on more feminine traits, such as sharing, nurturing, and love of nature. The society of Crete was matrilineal (although in some ways matriarchal) in that the woman (mother) was given the prominent position in the household. Emphasis was on the tribe and included all family members within that construct. There doesn't seem to be much evidence that either sex was dominant.

Taurus is a spring sign in the Northern hemisphere. The power of nature is very obvious in spring as the male and female principles combine to re-invigorate life on earth and insure continuity of the species. The ancient veneration of the bull as a connection to the source of life has devolved in the modern world to bull fighting, in which death of the bull represents the triumph of humanity over nature. Or the stampede at Pamplona in which people are gored and killed each year as the bulls go marauding through the narrow streets. This may be fun for some and ceremony for others, but it certainly undermines the meaning of our earliest cultural roots. The sense of renewal, of the veneration of nature and honoring of the female and male principles in ceremonial celebration of the life force, seems desecrated by these macho displays and adolescent posturings.

In India, the Hindus venerate cattle as being the most sacred of animals and representative of divinity. Images of bulls decorate homes and temples, The animals themselves roam freely in town squares. Their dung has been used as both fuel and holy ointment and their urine used to purify the human body both internally and externally. It is taboo to eat any part of the bull or cow, or use any part of its anatomy in any way. Their death is used as an occasion for religious ceremony. The kind and placid cow is seen as an object of devotion.

In the United States, we have borrowed some of this ancient symbolism for our own culture. On the back of the dollar bill is a pyramid with an eye at its peak and the green earth below. The pyramid is a clear reference to Egypt, while the eye represents the eye of Osiris, the Egyptian god of the Nile. Osiris was frequently depicted in both mythology and art as being embodied in the bull. This symbolizes spirit (Osiris) that is incarnated in the physical world of nature. This also suggests that within the terrestrial form lie the secret teachings of the spiritual soul. Relative to our currency, this symbol suggests the stability of our financial system. It implies that our wealth comes from the soil and that our spiritual foundation is rooted in the ancient world.

These four myths combine to introduce us to the nature of Taurus. As the supporter of the Sun it embodies immense strength and the desire to preserve the stability and security of the life-giving Sun. Its horns and its symbolic connection to Osiris suggests sexual fertility and emotional sustenance. In its most mundane form, the bull represents the continuity of the cycles of the Earth and its resources that sustain our physical existence, either in the form of food, or translated into the form of money.

THE GLYPH: ♉

The glyph associated with Taurus is the circle with a semicircle above it, as if it were a stylized image of a bull. This is a symbol of fecundity, or fertility. The semicircle represents soul, the subconscious mind. The circle stands for will and consciousness. The ascendance of the semicircle suggests that the internal and intuitive is more important to Taurus. It is as if the wisdom of the subconscious mind is being supported by the will of the consciousness. There is a simple duality for Taurus: depth within, strength without. Both features are combined through the indomitable will of the Taurean. This simple image illustrates a simple principle and function: to maintain and preserve the flow of the Life Force as it manifests in physical form.

THE TOTEM: 🐂

The bull is the animal associated with Taurus. It seems incongruous that the *yin* sign Taurus has a masculine image as its totem. It suggests that in a primal context, the masculine and feminine roles can be interchangeable. That the male can be as nurturing as the female, and the female as strong and persevering as the male. It also suggests that the bull can exhibit traits that are traditionally associated with feminine behavior such as patience and docility.

The bull has evolved as a spiritual icon in India, where the Hindus are devoted to this animal, valuing its tractability and gentleness. Its life is preserved and it has uses such as ritual celebration and healing purification. They bull is valued for its tremendous internal strength which is not necessarily expressed or manifested. Western civilization, however, has created such images as the "bull in the china shop" or the expression "the bull sees red." This is quite a difference in the perception and definition of this animal. This can partly be explained by cultural differences, the West is more active and aggressive than the East. But it is also characteristic of the patient bull who, at times, can become enraged. What makes the bull, this otherwise genial animal, suddenly explode?

Taurus is a young sign, much like Aries. The Arian function is to sow the seeds of the vital life force in Spring, but then it moves on. It doesn't like to stay too long in one place. The cardinality of the Aries suggests action. This tendency to act provides stimulus and energy which is impulsive, driving and assertive. Taurus, however, seeks to act in a more continuous fashion to build the momentum that stabilizes those seeds of new beginnings sown by Aries. It is Taurus' task to remain constant as the plant comes bursting through the ground in the Spring. Taurus stays with that plant and cultivates it, watering and feeding it until eventually it comes to fruition. This is not only what Taurus *does*, it's what Taurus *needs*. To thrive, a person with Taurus energy in their chart requires patience and gentle nurturing from their family.

Consequently, when anything disturbs or threatens that sense of continuity or security, the Taurean is thrown into a state of insecurity and fear. This is usually when the Taurean temper starts to manifest. Of the twelve signs, Taurus is probably the slowest moving. As a Taurus, when you are called upon to make a change that you do not want to make, or do not want to make at the present time, or if you are feeling the urgency to make a change at a faster rate than you feel is safe or comfortable, your sense of continuity and stability on the physical or emotional plane is threatened. This is when the bull sees red. This is when the Taurean explodes. Of the twelve signs, when the bull finally is brought to the point of rage, it has the most potentially destructive anger in the zodiac. There are two positive things about the Taurean temper: 1) It's relatively short-lived, and 2) Once the anger is expressed, it is also released. This is different from some of the other signs, such as Scorpio, which can vindictively hang onto anger until it evolves into a grudge. Taurus usually will not do that. There are a few minutes of absolute rage and in that moment there can be a great deal of destruction, especially to property. After awhile, things calm down and the Taurus continues as if nothing happened.

The expression of anger for the Taurean is much more of a defensive posture or expression than one of aggressiveness. Note again the difference between Aries and Taurus. Aries, a *yang* sign, is assertive and manifests energy from within the self outward. It can be very aggressive in initiating an offensive action. Taurus, a *yin* sign, is much more internal. It tends to manifest more in a reactive or protective rather than proactive manner when feeling threatened.

A mistake Taurus can make which exaggerates this tendency is to be too accepting, too patient. This can cause you to be lax or lazy about establishing limits and boundaries in relationships. Even if those lines exist, you may be slow to recognize that they are approaching. The Taurus gets pushed close to the limits, but either doesn't recognize that fact or doesn't act on it. You may be pushed to the limits and pride yourself on your perseverance so that again you don't say or do anything to alter the direction or flow of activity. By the time you are pushed beyond those limits, the explosive rage takes over. This is certainly unfair to the recipient, because they were unaware of anything being even slightly amiss. But is also unfair to the Taurus. This kind of anger is very draining, both physically and emotionally, and usually leaves confusion and hurt feelings all around.

Sometimes this Taurean tolerance of others can take the form of being generous to those who with whom you feel close. It could take the form of giving money, time, physical energy or possessions. As a Taurus, if you give beyond your means, you are putting yourself in a vulnerable position. You might have expectations of what you will receive as a result of your generosity. Those expectations could involve being in a position of power or control, or simply being appreciated by a grateful receiver. Without any return you may feel as if your good nature is being taken advantage of. This can also trigger an expression of anger. For Taurus to grow beyond these tendencies it is essential for you to become aware of how much you have to give in any situation. You need to monitor your responses and notice if they feel a limit or boundary being approached. If it is, communicate that fact or in some way act on it as a reality. In so doing, you put yourself back into a position of being under control and safe. Try to become aware of your expectations or underlying motivations for being so tolerant or giving. You might realize that they are unrealistic or not even things you truly want. In either case you can become more appropriate in your benevolence.

MODE AND ELEMENT

Taurus is a *fixed* and *earth* sign which implies that Taurus is oriented toward continuity, stability and security. As a Taurus you may also tend to be habit-bound or attached to your routines. There is nothing inherently wrong with that provided you are aware that you are doing something habitual, and you feel that the pattern works and is fulfilling to you. It's also important to understand why you have created and are maintaining those personal conventions. This awareness comes from paying attention, and noticing those patterns of your life that repeat.

The "why" requires a twofold answer. First, underlying the habit patterns and routines are values, assumptions and belief systems about the nature of life. All fixed signs, but especially Taurus, are very strongly attached to their value systems. The values may be out of date, however. They may no longer coincide with your needs, perceptions or experiences. It's also possible that the habits are based on someone else's values. This could be a parent, spouse, friend or teacher. Or they may represent family customs that you internalized as a child. These values may have been meaningful at some point in the past, but have long since grown old and stagnant. Prevalent patterns that are built on an outdated value system or on someone else's sense of significance, are not really going to bring the quality or degree of security or stability that brings fulfillment. They merely keep you stuck in a rut.

For the fixed sign Taurus, the prime orientation is toward creating continuity in a life that is safe and comfortable. This is achieved by clearly and consciously creating the building blocks of that security, which are values and belief systems that are up-to-date and accurate in describing the essence of what you find to be meaningful and significant. Sometimes the Taurus will maintain the old, decayed values, and subsequent habits, because they are easy and comfortable. Essentially there is a trade in the form of giving up growth and development in exchange for what is easy.

Once the values and beliefs have been updated, it is time to turn your attention to creating new modes of behavior. It is in this way that security is maintained and at the same time growth is insured.

One of the tools that the Taurean has to work with is willpower. The will of the Taurean is archetypal. If you are manifesting your will in a conscious and active way, you can be extremely creative in your life. If you are not using the will actively to update your values and habits, then the will turns around and manifests as "won't." I won't change, I won't develop, I won't do anything other than what I have always done because it's comfortable, because it's familiar, because it gives me a sense of stability and security. Of course, this is actually a form of addiction, but you are unaware of that while you continue to affirm and uphold those behaviors. It's as if the only way you define change is that it is what you receive after making a purchase.

Earth is the element of Taurus, indicating a fundamental connection to aspects of the material world. Like all the earth signs, Taurus is conservative and cautious, practical and hard-working. As the second sign in the zodiac Taurus is a young sign and can be satisfied with the simple pleasures of life. As a Taurus, being comfortable is important to you. Whether it's your material comforts in the form of possessions, the sensual coziness of your primary relationship, or your appreciation of a full stomach after a good home cooked meal. You can be patient and persevering in your attitude, but taken to the extreme, those qualities can become stubborn and willful.

Taurus is the most self-reliant of the twelve signs. You take pride in being able to take care of yourself and providing care and comfort for those closest to you. You maintain your autonomy by staying close to the most fundamental elements of life, avoiding that which is merely luxurious and unnecessary. There's an old expression that in dangerous times, Taurus guards the back door. This means that you are highly protective of those people and possessions that you value the most, and that you always have enough to get by when others may have to go without. But you can also value your autonomy to such an extent that you can have a hard time asking for help. This can keep you stuck in a limited framework of reality and prevent much personal growth from taking place.

Taurus is a builder. Sometimes this can actually take the form of an interest and ability to work in the building trades. Or this could simply manifest as being slow and deliberate in generating a life style that is safe and secure.

Fixed earth. The slowest mode and the densest element. As a Taurus, you must guard against becoming sluggish, phlegmatic, even boring. That may be how you are perceived by people who are familiar with your mode of being and acting. These are signs like Gemini, Sagittarius or Aquarius who adapt more readily to change and do so at a more accelerated rate.

In Nature something that is fixed and earthy is the planet itself. Your nature is to be slow and deliberate and you are probably the slowest of the twelve signs. It's been suggested that Taureans are clannish—if you know one, you probably know a dozen. This is because the other signs all move at a more rapid rate and are more prone to change. So when the other signs do get up and move, who's left? All the Taureans.

At a gathering I attended, several people were discussing this phenomenon. Two or three mentioned that they were Taureans, and that most of their family and best friends shared that same Sun sign. When one of the others asked what all these Taureans do when they get together, these people looked at each other, and simultaneously said, "Eat!"

As the sign of fixed-earth you may be slow, but nevertheless you move and change in a definite rhythm. Your rate of action can bring you into close connection with the cycles of the natural world. As a farmer or backyard gardener, you can intuitively feel the best time to till, plant and harvest. You relate well to animals, and can be a patient friend and guardian of both barnyard animals and pets. As a spring sign, Taurus represents fertility and is nurturing. The Moon, the planet that symbolizes motherhood, is strong when located in Taurus. It is stronger only in the sign that it rules, Cancer. When a planet is located in its second strongest sign, it is referred to as *exalted*.

Taking the analogy of Taurus to the Earth a little further, think of the actual physical manifestations of the annual cycle of nature. In Spring, the time of Taurus, the buds swell on the trees, followed soon by the leaves. Animals mate in time to birth and nurture the young during the growing season. Even though these external physical changes are slow and deliberate, they are only the ones that show on the surface. Other changes, equally important, take place in a less visible way. These are changes that start quite a while before anything appears. So it is with Taurus. Most changes Taurus makes are internal first. You slowly contemplate all your options, becoming aware of anything that could go wrong with each of those options, and what to do about it in case it does. When all this inner work is done the Taurean is ready to externalize the change. By the time Taurus acts, the changes have already been well thought out. The reason for the caution is that Taurus is charged with stabilizing and maintaining the vital life force. What Taurus contributes to the human experience is the drive, the will, the know-how to physically survive on this planet in a safe and comfortable way.

The image of fixed earth can be illustrated by a story using the image of a piece of the mineral carbon. Visualize this in the form of a piece of coal, something that is very dirty and that creates black smudges on your skin and clothes. It doesn't have much practical value. It might burn and provide heat for a while, but not for long, and even if it does, it pollutes the air while it is burning. Taurus is resourceful and hardworking, however, so it is going to find something pragmatic to do with that hunk of coal. It decides to dig a hole. Because Taurus is diligent, it's going to stay there and dig that hole for a long time, until it is perhaps a couple of miles deep. Then it will drop that lump of dirty carbon into that hole and cover it over. Because Taurus is so patient and persevering, it can afford to wait for long periods of time, several hundred years perhaps. Eventually it will unearth that piece of coal to find that it has crystallized and taken the form of a diamond. It is now many-faceted, clear, and radiant.

This is a good image to help understand the Taurean nature. The progress is very consistent. There is usually not a lot of backsliding. As a result, it's important not to goad a Taurus. Allow them to manifest and grow at the rate at which they feel comfortable. If something insistently presses the Taurus, either the bull will see red or the "won't power" will come up. Growth and progress will actually stop. By allowing the Taurus to function at their own pace—slow, safe and comfortable—eventually they can produce something valuable, beautiful and radiant.

Another realistic image depicting the preferred rate of the sign of fixed earth is a twelve-acre parcel of land. Let's assume that each acre is sold to a different sign. While the other signs are busy clearing the land, buying materials and erecting a house, Taurus is still excavating the property. Taking time to choose the best, most long lasting materials at the best price, Taureans will proceed in a cautious, deliberate manner. Being self-reliant, they may prefer to do most of the work themselves. This gives a deep sense of accomplishment and provides a more personal connection with the property. While Taurus is laying the foundation, the neighbors are moving furniture in and enjoying their new home. As winter sets in, when the weather limits the amount of work that can be done, Taurus will finally be ready to move in. When the neighbors are finding the flaws in the design, workmanship or materials of their houses, Taurus is sitting comfortably in an attractive and durable abode.

THE RULING PLANET

The ruling planet of Taurus is Venus. The glyph for Venus is the circle above the cross of the material plane (♀). Symbolically, this combines will and consciousness (the circle) with matter and practical application of energy (the cross). The fact that the cross supports the circle implies the primacy Venus places on things and activities of the Earth as the origin and support for the connection with Spirit.

Venus is one of the feminine planets and as such is receptive. It deals with the way in which an individual receives energy from the outer world and integrates it within the personal life. Socially, the function of Venus is to define patterns, behaviors and tendencies in relationship to others. The type and amount of social activity you need is defined by the sign and house position of Venus in your natal chart. It can indicate the relative ease or difficulty that you have in forming relationships. It can suggest the degree to which you are compulsive about relating and being part of a social situation, or to which you feel complete within yourself and prefer remaining aloof or independent. Venus in one of the security-oriented signs, such as Taurus, Cancer, Leo, Scorpio, or Capricorn, or in aspect to the Moon, Mars, or Pluto, has strong needs to connect consistently with one partner. Venus in Aries, Gemini, Sagittarius, Aquarius, or Virgo, or in aspect to

Uranus, may value their independence over relationship or feel content and complete within themselves without a primary partnership experience. Gemini and Sagittarius especially need variety in social situations. Depending on other factors in the chart (such as sign on the cusp of the seventh house) Venus in these two signs might prefer several relationships simultaneously. Serial monogamy is another realistic alternative for people who place higher value on independence than on intimacy. Serial monogamy is a pattern of committing yourself to one person but not necessarily with the intention of making it permanent. A relationship of this nature lasts as long as either or both partners feel comfortable there and want it to last. When the relationship grows stale or issues arise that need work and resolution the relationship might end. This pattern enables an integration of security with independence. It allows you to expand your social circle but also limits the degree of depth and intimacy you can experience in any one relationship.

Venus also indicates specific partnership needs and desires as well as your mode of expressing affection. Sometimes there can be conflict in relationship even though two people love each other because Venus indicates that their manner of expressing love—or their need to receive it—may be quite different. With Venus in Taurus or Aries for instance, you are affectionate and passionate. Venus in Capricorn or Aquarius would be much more cautious and reserved, even detached from demonstrations of love and affection. The Aquarius/Capricorn person might assume that their more affectionate partner is needy, controlling, possessive or demanding. On the other hand, the Aries/Taurus person may see the more detached Aquarius/Capricorn partner as cold, heartless and insensitive. In fact this is just the way the individuals express their love based on the sign placement of Venus.

To understand all your needs and patterns in social activities is based on more than just the house and sign placement of Venus and Mars and any aspects to them from other planets. The sign on the cusp of the Seventh House (partnership), any planets located in that house as well as any aspects of opposition (180 degrees) between any two or more planets, all have their place in determining your relationship needs and patterns. Venus and Mars are, however, the prime energies to pay attention to in this area. In addition to them, a subtle blending of all these influences is necessary before you can be fully aware of what you have to give and what you need to receive from a relationship.

Venus is the opposite of Mars. The energy emanating from within the self and being expressed externally in an assertive manner is Martian. The energy beginning externally and being internalized in a receptive manner is Venusian. Mars represents the male force, Venus the female. Even though each of us has chosen a male or female body, we each have both Venus and Mars in our natal chart. Even if you have no energy in either Aries or Taurus, you still have the influences of these archetypal expressions of masculine and feminine energy. If Mars is more powerfully placed, even if you are a woman, then it is important to integrate the assertive and direct qualities of that planet into your behavioral patterns in an obvious, yet comfortable way. If Venus is more significant, even if you are a man, self-acceptance and self-love require you to identify with and feel comfortable expressing the energy of harmony in your social nature. Ultimately we should strive to integrate both our Mars and Venus influences. Balance and use them in a way that is appropriate to the symbolism of their sign, house and aspect influence in your chart.

As the ruling planet of Taurus, Venus helps to define values. By house placement it indicates what area of life you value or within which you find experiences, possessions or people of value. Venus in the fourth house values home and family. Venus in the seventh house values one-to-one relationship. Venus in the tenth house values career and social status.

One of the things Venus calls your attention to as something of value is art, as Venus is the energy of beauty. One of the ways you have of connecting with Spirit and the awe of life is through beauty. This can manifest by being either an artist yourself or by appreciating the efforts of others. By sign placement it can imply whether you are more attracted to the classical or the *avant garde*. The earth signs are attracted to the classics, old standbys, that have stood the test of time. The air signs—especially Aquarius and Gemini—and the fire signs—especially Aries and Sagittarius—are more tempted to experiment and explore new modes of expression. Venus in Cancer or Taurus is oriented to the domestic arts like cooking and interior design. By connection to other planets you can gain insight into what art forms you could be more gifted in than others. For example, connections with Mercury indicate writing or working with the hands in activities like craftsmanship or playing an instrument. Aspects to Uranus could also imply writing or architecture. Aspects to Neptune imply music and dance. Mars is associated with the visual arts and movement. The Moon suggests photography. Several aspects to Venus support the possibility that you can express your creativity in several forms.

When Venus is retrograde, you tend to fixate on past relationships in which there has been rejection or negativity. This may have taken the form of unrequited love or a lack of fulfillment to the point that you mistrust offers of love. You could cut yourself off from a full expression of your love energy by choosing partners who don't really love you. You could recreate situations in which these deep hurts and rejections were experienced in previous incarnations. The re-creation of that pain can be an attempt to "get it right" this time, or may just be an attraction to something known and comfortable. This may be a self-fulfilling prophecy in which you undermine yourself and your relationship so that you are indeed rejected once again. It's the Brer Rabbit in the briar patch syndrome: it may hurt like hell, but at least it's home. You know what's coming and what to expect, and that knowledge brings a certain amount of security, even if the relationship provides no fulfillment. In a healthier and more conscious mode you might attempt to set up the dynamic again, but only to learn what your real mistakes or lessons were. By deliberately re-experiencing a situation, you can learn the underlying cause and motivation of the pattern, and work to change it.

This is a pattern that's called "fixed karma." Fixed karma manifests when you are attracted to someone who has a certain emotional or psychological blueprint. This other person is attracted to you because of your psychological and emotional blueprint. Soon after the relationship begins, many of those points of attraction become points of conflict. The mistake in these situations is to assume that it is the partner that is creating the tension or difficulty. All the two of you are doing is being who you each are. In the process of being yourselves, however, you are causing each other to become aware of aspects of your natures that need to be worked on and cleared. If you tend to be controlling or manipulative you may be attracted to someone else with the same pattern. The relationship becomes mired in a pattern of "who's trip are we going on." If you tend to be possessive and jealous you might be desperately in love with a freedom loving soul who refuses to be tied down. Or your tendency might be to become involved with someone who has such deep emotional or psychological needs that they are incapable of satisfying yours. The flow of energy is in one direction and you get drained. If any of these patterns are familiar to you because they illustrate a type of relationship you get in time after time, you are manifesting fixed karma. These are energy patterns which must be transformed so that you can release them and let them go.

With Venus retrograde, or with any fixed karmic pattern emanating from a different source (such as Venus in the twelfth house) learn to recognize those areas of conflict and try to clear them within yourself. For instance, eliminate tendencies to be overly sensitive to your partner's jealousy or possessiveness—two forms of control—by becoming more emotionally responsible. Avoid feelings of rejection from an independent partner by becoming more independent yourself—don't depend on your partner's recognition or feedback to feel secure. Work through patterns of being the "fixer" or "caretaker" by getting in touch with your internal sense of self-love, as well as your own needs in relationship. In any fixed karma pattern, take the responsibility to consciously express your needs and goals, your limits and boundaries in and of the relationship. Discuss these issues with your partner until you both become clear about the real connections and limits of the relationship.

If you are in a fixed karmic pattern of relationship remember that you can clear it unilaterally. It's not necessary for both of you to recognize these patterns to heal them. You can recognize your patterns and clear them within yourself even if your partner is not doing the same. This may lead to the break-up of the relationship, but it does free you to relate to a different type of person in a different kind of relationship. Your partner may be stuck relating to an individual very much like you used to be. Once you have done the work, it doesn't have to be you. Ideally, it would be nice if breaking a fixed karmic pattern can be done within the context of the relationship itself, thereby allowing the continuity of that relationship to be maintained. Realistically this rarely happens. Remember that one of the main points of attraction to this person was that they gave you the opportunity to become more aware of your negative patterns and stuck points. Assuming there is mutual consciousness, work and transformation, the relationship might evolve into a good friendship, or at least into mutual appreciation. But usually, once the pattern is cleared, it's time to move on.

THE SECOND HOUSE

The house, or area of life, associated with Taurus is the second house. At its most fundamental level it indicates your karmic credits, that is, those attributes that you have worked at, developed and earned the ability to work with in past lives. In a simpler sense, and more accessible, this translates as your tools and resources. Because this is an earth house, those qualities usually refer to practical applications of those attributes. Planets in the second house, as well as the planet ruling the sign on the cusp of the second and its location, indicate what tools will help give your life meaning. Furthermore, since the second is the first of the earth experiences, planets therein suggest how you can provide the basic comforts of life: food, clothing and shelter. They help you to survive. For example, with the Sun in the second house, or Leo on the cusp, you are your own greatest tool, and the best resource for providing meaning and physical functionality. The degree to which you value yourself, and feel autonomous, and have a positive sense of self-love and self-esteem, is fundamental if you are going to find meaning in your life and create a viable, comfortable existence on the earth plane.

In a broader context, these resources suggest what you value. It is not enough just to provide the material basics if the results of that process have little or no significance. The second house, and its residential planets, indicate what you value. If you have Mercury, the planet of communication, in your second house, or the signs Gemini or Virgo on the cusp, you find intrinsic value in the process of exchanging information. Furthermore, your tools and skills of communication will enable you to produce the physical comforts of life. Those skills could manifest through teaching, sales, writing, commerce, or travel. You may use several abilities at once, or different ones at different times.

Venus in the second house implies that you value aesthetics and that you have creative tools. You also value harmonious relationship and physical comfort. You apply Venusian tools in a way that enables you to create the attractive environment you need and the social harmony that is important to you.

Mars in the second house values activities in which you can be yourself. Ideally these situations would help you become more aware of who you are and provide the opportunity to develop your identity. With Mars in the second house you will display a strong drive for material self-reliance and prefer to work either on your own or in a creative field.

With the Moon in the second house you place high value on family. The Moon provides the ability to be emotionally self-reliant as well as be a caregiver and provider to others.

Jupiter is the planet of expansion, especially through the development of your consciousness. In the second house Jupiter values education and offers the tools to both learn and teach. Jupiter enjoys travel as a means of expansion. With Jupiter in your second house you would find that exploring different cultures and other areas of the world would be meaningful. Jupiter also suggest you are a good traveler.

Saturn in the second house emphasizes security. You have skills and tools of organization and the ability to structure your life to create long range security. You may value antiques and value systems that might seem dated to many of your peers.

If you have one of the outer planets in the second house, you find as much or more significance in the development of higher consciousness than you do in creating material comfort. Neptune in the second house would place more emphasis on spiritual growth, psychological insight, or creative inspiration than on material gain. However, you could use the tools of Neptune to become a psychotherapist or graphic artist, thereby doing something that has intrinsic meaning to you even as you provide for your material sustenance. Or you could apply one to the other. For example, if you have Jupiter in the second house, or Sagittarius or Pisces (the signs ruled by Jupiter) on the cusp, you could translate your love of travel into a practical form by working in the travel industry or in foreign service. So it isn't necessary to make an artificial distinction and assume that you should either value and pursue activities that develop the consciousness or those that produce security. The key is to integrate the two in ways that are coincident with the planet and sign that influence your second house.

Uranus in your second house suggests that you value your individuality, both its discovery and expression. You may choose unusual or unconventional ways to generate money, or it could come to you in unexpected ways. Technology or working with electronics or the media could be ways that provide you with income. However, your financial flow will tend to be erratic and inconsistent, so it's best to discipline yourself to budget and save.

Pluto in the second indicates that you have a profound connection to ancient wisdom. You also have both deep needs and resources to experience transformation. For example, it's important that periodically you transform your values. Release and let go those that are no longer meaningful to your present state in life. Then create new ones. As you engage in this process throughout your life, you will constantly be discovering new tools that were previously hidden from you, or new uses for old tools. Or you might realize that something you kept hidden from others, out of fear of rejection, is actually quite desirable and has value to you. So you resurrect it in a new way, and feel more comfortable exposing it by using it. If you are not updating periodically, you can become obsessed with certain aspects of the material plane. Eating, or at least eating certain foods, can take on a significance above and beyond mere sustenance. Feeling the need to amass large sums of money, investment holdings or possessions can take on a life of its own. Things and desires clog up your life with extraneous material. They block the process of transformation and keep you stuck at mundane and ultimately unfulfilling levels of existence.

In the most tangible sense, the second house is the house of money, specifically in the form of earned income. Jupiter or Venus in the second house, especially if well aspected, can indicate the potential to be financially successful. Jupiter implies success and generosity in past lives, so you have generated the potential for material abundance in this one. Jupiter in the second house or Sagittarius on the cusp can also impel you to be overly generous to both yourself and others. You may tend to spend freely and more than you can afford. Venus indicates both the ability to function well in the business world, and the potential to be creative in generating a comfortable and secure reality. Venus in the second also suggests the ability to appreciate beauty, whether in the form of Nature, works of art or fine gems. In fact, a lot of personal planets in the second house provide the skills of being creative in practical ways, such as through design. This could take the form of clothing, cars, landscapes, or whatever you define as important.

Mars in the second, or Aries on the cusp, indicates a drive to create a sense of security and survival. You possess an entrepreneurial, even pioneering spirit, and a powerful work ethic to help you manifest your needs in a creative way. The sign that Mars is in is significant as it can give you a key as to how to direct that Martian drive (through action-cardinal sign, service-mutable sign, the intellect-air signs, creativity-fire signs or the body-earth signs).

The Moon brings skills of nurturing, and strong needs for security. Either can be provided by family contact, either as a parent, or a dutiful child. The Moon in the second also gives the ability to work in the financial industry. In fact an abundance of three or more of any of the planets in any sign in the second indicates working with money in a professional context is something you might enjoy and do well. The Moon in the second house suggests the ability to earn your money in care-giving professions such as child care or those that involve nourishment such as the food industry.

Saturn could limit financial prospects primarily as a result of having a fear of poverty. Saturn in the second house tends to affirm the law of material scarcity. This creates a pattern that becomes a self-fulfilling prophecy. You fear that "since there isn't enough to go around, I probably won't get enough of what I need." It's an affirmation of the "cosmic law of poverty," which doesn't even exist. That affirmation creates a blockage to your earning potential. You can turn that around by using Saturn in a more positive way. It provides resources of organization, self-discipline and the ability to clearly define your financial goals. Saturn is also the energy of time. To apply the tools of Saturn over time suggests ultimate success in providing long range material security. The fear is gone.

A retrograde planet in the second house indicates that you have had access to that energy in a previous incarnation to create comfort and security. However, you may not have used it or taken full advantage of it. Or you may have been prevented from using it. If that planet receives hard aspects from other planets, you may have previously misused or misunderstood that energy. Now you are challenged to redefine its application, starting with what it implies in terms of values, and continuing to find new outlets for its expression. If that retrograde planet receives primarily supportive aspects from other planets, you probably underutilized that energy in the past. It's time now to become more deeply involved in the awareness and manifestation of the resources the planet provides. In any case, you need a period of reflection to help you consciously realize where you are with that energy. Spend some time reviewing what you find meaningful, what the primary needs of your security system are, and how you fulfill those needs. With retrograde energy in your second house, you may have developed one facet of that planet. Now you need to broaden your understanding of its potential, and update its application in your life.

If you have an abundance of energy in the second house, three or more planets, you may be extremely materialistic. You could place an inordinate amount of attention and resources on creating or maintaining your earth plane security. You may place so much emphasis on money, and the possessions that money can buy, that you limit yourself in two ways. First, is the limitation that comes from expecting the tools and toys of the material plane to provide you with deep and lasting fulfillment. Second is the limitation that you may not be open to deriving meaning from activities that the other houses provide.

With a lot of energy in the second house, especially the personal planets, a primary desire is to learn how to survive and provide for your security. These are the essential qualities of this house. To activate these potentials, learn these lessons and feel comfortable in your body. but not to the point of obsession or of restricting yourself to only those pursuits. If you become increasingly possessive, controlling and attached, especially to material objects, realize you are expressing your second house energy at a low octave and in an out of balance way. Explore the possibility that some of your second house energy suggests meaning in other areas. Perhaps the symbols of the planets in your second house, the sign on the cusp, or the house placement of the ruling planet of that sign suggest the importance of creative or spiritual pursuits. These influences will also provide tools that will help you find security in activities other than those of the material realm. By finding significance in providing both material survival and transcendent awareness, you create the personal balance necessary to find deep and lasting happiness in your life.

TAURUS AND THE BODY

Starting with Aries, which rules the head, each succeeding sign rules lower parts of the body. Taurus rules the part of the body that extends from just below the cranium to the top of the shoulders. This includes the jaw, the inner ear and the throat. Because of its connection with the inner ear, Taurus can tune into the inner voice, and derive wisdom and insight from this process. This is especially true with Mercury (communication) retrograde in Taurus. Taurus also rules the thyroid gland, whose function is to monitor metabolism and growth. The thyroid gland also has to do with the emotional state. Sometimes the thyroid will malfunction as the result of emotional stress or crisis, especially if you are neither in touch with your feelings nor expressing them.

Venus, the ruling planet of Taurus, rules the veins and the kidneys. The kidneys are major organs of elimination. If Venus receives hard aspects from other planets, especially Saturn, or is in a sign in which its energy may be discordant, such as Aries, or in the first house (body) or the sixth house (health) it could indicate the kidneys are under stress. Consequently, it can also indicate skin disorders because the skin is another major organ of elimination. If the poisons are not being released from one organ, they are bound to come out in another.

Venus is also the planet of beauty and grace. It is one of the prime feminine symbols. It can also deal with hair and complexion. A prominent Venus in the natal chart, such as in the first or tenth houses, could indicate a tendency to put a lot of time and energy into your appearance. You might even have a desire to work in the cosmetics industry. Venus in the first would also suggest being seen by others as being attractive. If Venus is in positive aspect to the Sun or Jupiter, it could indicate a particularly attractive complexion or hair.

Venus also rules the endocrine system and its balance. This is a system that contains eight glands, the function of which is to contribute hormones which regulate the metabolism. Each of the glands is associated with one astrological sign. Venus is the ruler of the whole system. If Venus is afflicted, weakened or under stress in the natal horoscope, there may be a tendency for the endocrine system to be out of balance and disorders of that system could set in.

The hormones of the endocrine system are mirrored by and connected to chemicals in the brain. These substances enable the brain to function properly in such activities as perception and cognition. Consequently, imbalance in the endocrine system can reflect or stimulate imbalances in the brain. As this happens, certain forms of mental illness, such as manic-depression (bipolar syndrome), can result.

CONCLUSIONS

"To everything there is a season and a time for every purpose under heaven." So does the Old Testament describe the cycles of Nature. As the sign of fixed-earth, Taurus can identify with and relate to that cycle in a direct and personal way. Through that connection Taurus can also feel a connection to Spirit. As a Taurus you are sensual. By tuning into your body you can become more aware of what you are feeling and how situations in your life are affecting you.

As the first sign of the zodiac Aries can be said to represent the earliest kind of human civilization, that of the hunter-gatherers. As an earth sign, Taurus symbolizes the next evolutionary step which is the formation of agrarian societies. In the beginning there was an overlap between the hunters and the early farmers. There weren't that many plants that had been domesticated, so that which was grown had to be supplemented with that which was hunted or found. Human needs were simple but also easy to satisfy: a reliable source of food and protective shelter for the tribe. This illustrates the simplicity of the Taurean reality. You work hard to create a viable livelihood for yourself and your family. Human effort must be accompanied by Divine Will, however, if the venture is to be a success. Regardless of how hard the early settlers worked tilling the soil, if there was too much or too little rain at the wrong part of the growing cycle the survival of the tribe was in doubt. For Taurus the concept of the Living God is one they can see and feel. It's the force that generates the heat of the Sun, that blows the wind and that keeps the planet moist. This awareness of the elements and understanding your kinship with it, is what can enable even the contemporary Taurus to rise above material attachments and get in tune with Spirit, the creative source of life. This connection can also help to clarify your priorities so that your life is both comfortable and significant.

As all farmers know, patience is required in allowing their crop to ripen for harvest. Often the lesson of patience is a hard, yet significant one for Taurus. As a Taurus your growth is slow and you build yourself and your life with caution and deliberateness. Trust in your process and your rate. In the process of developing patience you can create a place of inner peace. Real spiritual progress for Taurus comes from cultivating that serenity, not from external attachments.

If your tendency is to be more oriented toward possessions, being more object identified than self-identified, you will feel yourself to be alienated and insecure. This leads to attachment to either people or things. Through this clinging you are attempting to create a sense of permanence in a life in which chaos and uncertainty predominate. You become controlling of people and possessions as a cover-up for your internal emotional or spiritual lacks. Money and material objects are seen as tools of happiness and the instruments of security. Comfort and ease become the standards by which fulfillment is measured. Your sensuality can lead you to becoming compulsive about physical pleasure. This can be a form of laziness, whereby you are trading away stimulation and variation in exchange for the stagnation of sameness. This can also be an excuse to impose your powerful will on others. By controlling your world you try to limit your feelings of impermanence and insecurity. As an earth sign you are very sensual and enjoy the pleasures of the physical plane. That's realistic and appropriate. In an uncentered, unself-loving mode, however, those pleasures can become things in themselves and you can become addicted to the pursuit of comforts as that which provides you with meaning and satisfaction. It's as if the degree to which you try to control your physical relationship to life is directly proportional to the control that your appetites have over you. The more emphasis you place on controlling things the more you will also try to control people. The more compulsive you are about physical gratification and possessions, the more you'll try to subject others to your will. As an uncentered Taurus trying to realize this illusion of security-through-stuff, you would tend to be possessive and manipulative. This can lead to a desire to amass money, cars, houses or clothing or to a tendency to be bossy and tell other people what to do. It may appear as if being successful in these drives will lead to stability and security, but in reality those drives, even if you succeed in achieving those things, only serve to cover-up the inner fears. We live in a world of change, a dimension in which the only thing that is truly permanent is change itself.

Taurus is a sign of internal strength. The more you try to obtain security externally, the more your Taurean energy is actually being undermined and the less secure you will be. Houses can burn down, cars can be wrecked, clothes can go out of style. Excessive eating or drinking dissipate your vitality and good health, important factors that help determine the quality of life for an earth sign.

As you become more centered, you realize that possessions are external manifestations of feelings. The more emotionally clear and fulfilled you are, the less you need material props to help you feel good. The same is true for physical appetites. The deeper and more consistent your sense of inner self-worth the less prone you are to physical addictions. The more shallow and less consistent your internal relationship to yourself, the more you seek gratification by attempting to control your external world through money, possessions or people.

Taurus is an emotional sign, feeling things deeply. If you are overwhelmed by fears of vulnerability and loss of control, or if you are in the habit of hanging on and becoming attached, your emotional state is neither expressed nor satisfied. You feel a certain way about something because you always have, and probably always will. You get stuck in strong emotional states, and the physical manifestations that accompany them. When you hang on to your feelings you hang on to the objects that represent them. Break out of this inertia by getting more consciously in touch with your feelings, and learn when and how to feel safe expressing them. This will not only help you become more emotionally fulfilled and less fearful, but also less likely to become compulsive about your body and its satisfaction.

A similar pattern can develop mentally. You might stubbornly hold on to your opinions and point of view, refusing to review or change them. Your willfulness is an extension and expression of not updating values and habits in general. By remaining attached to your ideas you are trying to create a semblance of security. If you never perceive anything differently, there is no need to change anything. If things are constant, they must be secure. You may, however, be doing the work, but at a much slower rate than those around you so its appears nothing is changing. Your friends and family may be attached to you being a certain way and may not want you to change. Don't let others force you to continue to uphold a position if you have become unsure of it, but haven't yet found a functional replacement. Grow at your rate, and tell others you will let them know as soon the work is done.

To change this pattern, to find and utilize your core of strength, to become a centered, secure and unalienated Taurus, it's important that you keep your value system and priorities clear. Become aware of habit patterns and routines because these are the fundaments that help you create your sense of survival and maintain it in a secure way. Assess these qualities to make sure that they are appropriate to who you are, what your perceptions of life are and what your experiences in life have been. Are the values and priorities you are upholding truly yours or are they someone else's? Even if they were appropriate and meaningful earlier in life, are they now?

One of the most important parts of the centering process is to remain relatively close to the roots of your own survival in a way that enables you to feel a sense of control over your life. This is not to suggest that all Taureans have to go out in the woods and homestead a piece of land. But it does imply that one way for you to plug into your internal security, strength and power is to do something everyday that gives you a sense control over your life. This would be something that you can do easily and relatively effortlessly that provides an immediate sense of comfort, both physically and emotionally. This could take the form of having a small garden or some house plants, taking your dog for a walk, learning how to work on or at least make minor repairs on your house, your car or your clothing. Any or all of these activities help Taurus get centered. Music is often a significant part of life to those with energy in Taurus. Listening to a favorite piece, playing it as a hobby or even being a professional musician are all realistic outlets. They provide opportunity to tap into things that are meaningful and for which you may have specific gifts or talents. They provide ways of having quality alone time that is relaxing, comforting and useful. They provide opportunity to tap into your inner being and from within that place, access you inner strength. From that place of inner calm you can more accurately and clearly assess the fundamental building blocks of values and priorities that will combine to help you generate more meaning in your life and ultimately more security. As you maintain that secure and centered feeling, then you will become more clear about your needs as opposed to your wants. You keep in mind what really matters as opposed to what merely feels comfortable. Keep your life simple. Know what is enough. For most people with a lot of Taurus energy or planets in the second house, enough is what covers the basic needs of food, clothing and shelter. Avoid the trivial and inessential. In this context money becomes a tool and possessions are acquired as an outgrowth of your consciousness and your labor. But the money and objects are secondary in importance to the sense of fulfillment that accrues through the activation of your will in the pursuit of survival.

Taurus is a builder. For all Taureans, and people with energy in the second house, the most important project you are building is yourself. You must learn to value yourself. Realize that you are your own greatest tool and resource. This enables you to develop the most important and useful qualities of your potential: self-reliance, self-sufficiency and resourcefulness. As you grow through life at the time-honored, deliberate Taurean tempo you learn to overcome doubt about yourself and your ability to survive in the world. You can also overcome doubt about life itself and its ability and desire to support you. As you develop the habit of looking within the self to clarify what is meaningful, you strengthen your will. By developing your individual will you can access and identify with Universal Will, with the force of the

Eternal and the power of Oneness. You shift your point of attention away from attachment to the material plane and those things which are temporary. Use the sensuality of your body to learn how to tune in the ever-present flow of creative force. Objects are things in which the life force has become static, it is not involved with the creation of something new. By becoming aware of that energy as it flows through you, you can take advantage of it by being creative yourself. As a sign ruled by Venus, Taurus can be extremely creative. Use that creative connection to help you to develop an ever-deepening awe about the magnitude of Life. Real security is discovered in this point of awareness, and it becomes easy to surrender the need and tendency to control and impose. The *yin* nature of the earth energy enables you to feel eternally nurtured by Universal Love and supported by the presence of Eternal Being. True security at last.

♊ *GEMINI*

Gemini is the third sign of the zodiac. The first two signs, Aries and Taurus, represent archetypes of primal expression, action and stabilization; initiation and perseverance. The strengths of these signs are their ability to manifest qualities that are so fundamental to life. Their weaknesses are that they tend to get locked into those patterns and stuck in their insistence on keeping things at a simple, easy to control level. Gemini is more subtle. It serves as a vehicle for integration. As the third sign of the first quadrant, it is similar to Aries and Taurus in that it, too, is oriented toward the developing self. It, too, is internal and subjective in focus. It is not interested, however, in learning about the self in an independent or autonomous way, nor in keeping the conclusions of the process to itself or under its own dominion. To Gemini, those concepts are irrelevant, even boring. Gemini is the sign of dispersion and interaction. Much of its process of self-discovery, self-definition and self-expression comes from interacting with others. It represents the breath and mind of humanity. The breath is what connects the individual to the Life Force. The mind is what connects people to each other. Gemini says "I think." Its purpose is to act as a connector between ideas, between people, and between places.

Gemini concludes the first quadrant of the zodiac—the quadrant of self. The signs of this quadrant provide an opportunity to explore archetypes of consciousness and experience that are primary to life on Earth. Each is designed to help you become aware of who you are. Each represents ways of establishing yourself as a separate person. Each provides opportunities that serve to establish your identity, stabilize that identity and interact with others. To review the first three signs is to review three primary stages of consciousness. Aries represents the return of the individual soul to the Earth plane through the experience of "I am." Taurus sustains that emerging individual by providing physical nourishment to that being. It is the task of Taurus to learn how to be comfortable in the body, to survive on the material plane. The Taurean lesson involves "I have." Gemini grows beyond the primary experiences of beginning and sustaining. Gemini is oriented toward the manipulation of the environment socially, mentally and manually.

These signs also provide archetypes of the development of consciousness in the collective experience. For example, Aries suggests the pioneering individual, the nomadic hunter and gatherer. Very primitive, yet brave like those who traversed the Bering Strait and descended into the New World, what we call the Americas. Taurus represents the early settlers of the land, the first farmers. This is the instinct to preserve the tribe and provide for a secure and comfortable future. Gemini introduces the concept of the marketplace, the village. These are the artisans, craftspeople, merchants and traders, people who created with their hands the crafts of the culture. They are the travelers who exchange their creations for those made or grown or gathered by others. Not relying on the aggressiveness of the hunt, a masculine expression, nor on the patience of the farmer, a more feminine expression, Gemini makes a living by relying on the mind to create things to do and share with others. A written language, the codification of ideas, and the manual skills of the craftsperson help Gemini create objects of beauty and functionality that are the contributions it makes to society.

To grow beyond these basic experiences, either within your own consciousness or as part of a collective framework, is to partake of the experiences of the second quadrant.

In most years the Sun enters Gemini on May 20 and leaves on June 20. Because Gemini is more versatile and intricate in nature and orientation that the two earlier signs, this is a good place to introduce the concept of sign cusps. Planets can be on the cusp between any two signs and the richness of potential, or complexity, of both signs would be present.

THE MYTHS

The myths that help to illustrate the Geminian archetype are those that demonstrate versatility and the ability to interact with disparate phenomena or experience. Some of these myths depict

Gemini in terms of a duality. The Assyrians were an ancient Mesopotamian civilization. They worshipped twin deities: Nebo, whose function was to enlighten the eyes through his writing and literature (God as light) and Tasmet, his wife, who enlightened the ears through music (God as sound). Connecting and integrating. In the constellation (i.e., grouping of fixed stars) Gemini, the two brightest stars are named Castor and Pollux. The Greek gods Castor (the horse tamer) and his twin brother Pollux (the boxer) depict both the connections within the family and the potential to develop specific skills. They convey the idea that Gemini has to do with extended family (in this case siblings) and with crafts.

These stories also reveal the misconception that Gemini is two-faced, split or limited to a dualistic nature. That assumption is both limited and erroneous. If Gemini embodies both Nebo and Tasmet, or Castor and Pollux, then it can be just one or the other at different times, but can be both simultaneously. Thus it represents the ability to see a situation from many points of view.

The Hindus combine the versatility of Nebo and Tasmet, and Castor and Pollux in one archetype: Hanuman, the monkey god. Historically, the monkey was one of the earlier symbols and images associated with Gemini and one that more accurately represents its true nature: curious, clever and versatile. Hanuman is a compelling figure in mythology. He was the messenger of the gods and at their service in a variety of ways. Once, when the holy city was going to be attacked, Hanuman went out to challenge the enemy by himself. He expanded to the size of a mountain and single-handedly crushed the invading army. In another adventure he retrieved the queen's stolen crown by going to the castle of the thief. Once there, he reduced himself to the size of an ant. In that condition he sneaked beneath the door of the thief's house and retrieved the crown. He then leapt through the window, flew back to the holy city with his winged feet, and returned the crown to its rightful owner. The combination of the qualities of the clever messenger-servant with the versatile, mystical adept makes Hanuman a powerful image.

The Greek god Hermes was the master of sciences and craft. He was messenger of the gods. With his winged feet he guided souls to the underworld and protected athletes, businessmen and travelers. Portrayed in artistic renderings as a young man, he was thought of as the friendliest of the gods. He was considered the

inventor of the lyre, numbers and the alphabet. He was associated with the mineral quicksilver, "the spirit concealed in
matter." Another word for quicksilver is mercury, the name of
the ruling planet of Gemini, and the Roman name for Hermes.
The multi-faceted nature of Hermes enabled him to integrate
substances of seemingly opposite quality. For example, quicksilver is poisonous yet can be useful as a healing agent. It's a
metal, but in liquid form. Yet even as a liquid, it has the property
of adhering to precious metals, like gold. Quicksilver was valued
by alchemists in the Middle Ages and alchemy was a system said
to be invented by Hermes. Within that system, quicksilver was
used as an agent of turning base metals into gold. Its poisonous
nature was one reason alchemy was so dangerous. It had to be
heated in the transmutational process. If the fumes were inhaled,
or the beaker broken, it would mean death to the alchemist.

Metaphorically, quicksilver (Mercury/Hermes/Gemini) is the
guide to the gold, the guide to higher awareness. Metaphysically,
this concept of turning base metals into gold is analogous to
transmuting the lower qualities of human nature into the more
divine, the fundamental goal of alchemy. This is a more complex
extension of the concept of Hermes as a guide to souls. Not only
from one physical place to another (as the protector of travelers)
but also from one level of consciousness to another.

Hermes also represents the trickster, a universal archetype,
seen as the Coyote by the Native American culture, the Raven by
the Eskimo, and the Badger by the Japanese. It pertains to that
part of the human psyche that is cunning and clever. It can
manifest as the inspired inventor or insightful therapist in a
positive sense, or as an unscrupulous con-artist in the negative.
(Hermes was also the protector of theives.) Mythologically the
trickster is usually seen as one who has the power to change his
shape and, possibly, the intention with which he employs his
cleverness.

Pythagoras is another good archetype for Gemini. Although in
reality a man, he was of such monumental stature in his achievements, that, after his death, his life took on legendary properties
and he came to be thought of as a demi-god or god-man. He
traveled and studied in many countries. He learned about and
was initiated into the mystery schools of the Hebrews, the
Egyptians, the Babylonians and the Chaldeans. He was educated

in a way that enabled him to function as an embodiment of the Universal Mind in the sense that he studied and mastered an extensive array of subjects. He was the first person to define himself as a philosopher (one who finds out) rather than as a sage (one who knows), thus emphasizing his curiosity and desire to learn rather than his body of knowledge and prominence as a teacher.

His teachings demonstrate that universal quality. Basing his system of knowledge on mathematics and geometry, he used those disciplines to learn about God, humanity and nature. He was also a healer, relying on such varied methods as herbs, poultices, music and color to bring about successful healings.

These myths combine to portray certain qualities about the nature of Gemini. First is its potential for diversity. Hanuman and Hermes depict versatility. The images of Nebo and Tasmet, Castor and Pollux exemplify the desire and ability to perceive and experience situations from different points of view. They illustrate how to function on different levels of consciousness in a non-judgmental, non-competitive way. These myths also depict extended family relationships. Gemini represents the ability to change and be serviceful, as the messenger or communicator. It also demonstrates the potential to be curious, clever, sociable, and to relate to different people in many situations and places.

Pythagoras illustrates the human potential to integrate these mental, physical and social skills into a cohesive system that involves everything from philosophy to healing to the arts. At its highest level and most complex form, Gemini can embody and manifest this multi-faceted image.

THE GLYPH: Ⅱ

The symbol associated with Gemini is the Roman numeral Ⅱ. The Egyptians called Gemini Twin Stars, in honor of the two bright stars found in the constellation Gemini. The Babylonians used the appellation Great Twins. Each of these terms not only refers to the prominent stars we call Castor and Pollux, but also something about the inherent qualities of the sign. The concept of duality is introduced here for the first time in the zodiac. Aries and Taurus are archetypes of the pure masculine—expressive, forceful, independent—and the pure feminine internal, nurturing, receptive—respectively. With Gemini the concept of integration is introduced. The Ⅱ symbolizes that blending. The dualism of the Ⅱ suggests that Gemini is about exploring the vast array of phenomena and stimuli that life has to offer.

Gemini is also supposed to have been the patron of phallic worship in the ancient world. The Ⅱ may have originated as two phalluses. Gemini is a *yang* sign, and, as such, embodies the masculine principle. *Yang* energy is more oriented to the mental process. Thus the Ⅱ implies a constant dialogue, between the self and others, or just within the self. This dialogue can lead to sharing of ideas and learning, or can be experienced as the conflict between different points of view, between ideas and feelings, or between pure abstract concepts and pragmatic form. The interplay of information is central to the experience of Gemini. In this context, the Ⅱ may also signify two pillars standing in front of temples. In ancient times temples were not only places of worship, but also places of learning.

THE TOTEM: 🎐

The animal associated with Gemini is the twins. According to the ancients, the twins were two small children who were hatched from eggs. This implies a magical quality to these beings. The twins Romulus and Remus, the mythic founders of Rome illustrate this. The magic of the alchemist, or what seems like the magic of the person of knowledge when seen from the point of view of the ignorant and unschooled, also exemplify something fascinating. In fact, Pythagoras taught that the essence of learning was derived from combining divine wisdom with earthy wisdom. The interplay of these two forms, represent total knowledge.

This interplay also suggests that the twins do not simply represent a simple duality, but a blending of acquired knowledge for the purpose of understanding more clearly the nature of life. Each twin uses its own interests, ideas, and points of view to stimulate the mind of the other. The constant interaction between the twins, mentally as well as physically, represents the fact that Gemini is a very active sign.

Gemini is also the messenger. If the messenger is in the form of Hanuman, the totem is the monkey-god. In a Western framework, the messenger is Mercury, the god of winged-feet who carries a staff. The most important part of this image is the staff.

This is not a weapon-like baton, nor a stick that provides balance. This is a caduceus: a rod topped with wings and encircled by intertwining serpents. The serpents, in turn, imply three different meanings. First, each of the serpents represent one part of the primary duality of life: the masculine spirit and the feminine soul. Through the mystical-alchemical machinations of Hermes-Gemini, the two become united. Secondly, the twin snakes symbolize death and rebirth. In modern times this has come to represent the DNA double helix, through which coded genetic material is transformed into living matter.

Finally the serpents portray kundalini energy. This is the vital life force residing at the base of the human spine. It is referred to as serpent power, or as the sleeping serpent because for most people the awareness and usage of this energy is latent, existing in potential form only. To awaken the serpent is to bring the energy up the spine. On rare occasions this can happen spontaneously. The book *Kundalini* by Gopi Krishna is a record of a person whose kundalini suddenly shot through his system, with disastrous results. Kundalini energy, the vital energy of life, is fiery and hot. There are three channels in the spine. Like Hermes staff, there is a central canal, called the *Sushumna*, and two smaller, intertwining ones that weave around the *Sushumna*. They are called the *Ida* and the *Pingala*. Of the three only the *Sushumna* is capable of allowing the heat of the kundalini to pass through without causing harm. In an unprepared body, or uninitiated mind the kundalini can accidentally course through the smaller *Ida* or *Pingala* and literally burn out the physical body, especially the nervous system.

With the help of a consciously chosen spiritual path, usually connected with a spiritual teacher or master, and by following that path with purpose, dedication and consistency, the kundalini is raised in a gradual way, over a long period of time. The serpent activates the *chakras*, or energy centers of the body, one by one, raising consciousness as it goes. Although this process takes decades or lifetimes, the energy can eventually be raised all the way to the crown *chakra* at the top of the skull. The serpent is completely awake and we experience that state of being that has been variously called enlightenment, Christ consciousness, samadhi or self-realization. It is the potential to experience this level or form of the Universal Mind, that Gemini brings to the human experience.

MODE AND ELEMENT

Gemini's mode is mutable and its element is air. As a mutable sign, it is flexible, adaptable and places emphasis on gaining knowledge and wisdom for the purpose of expanding consciousness. Mutable signs enjoy being of service to others. Gemini provides service through communication and exchange of information. For this reason, Gemini can be considered one of the signs of healing. The healing could occur through a conversation about specific issues, such as would be provided by a counselor or psychotherapist. As a Gemini you could be of healing service simply by listening to others.

It is possible to over-use our mental and verbal skills, to the exclusion of our intuitive abilities. Words can be used to manipulate a situation so that internal signals are undermined or overridden. The demand for a logical explanation for all phenomena, the reliance upon the verifiable, quantifiable proof of something can be used as an excuse to be less expressive of feelings. Feelings are not logical, and by solely relying on the symbolic expression of logic—words—to define your reality and communicate with others, you can short-circuit parts of yourself that are illogical, but nonetheless true. However, being direct in sharing your feelings and your ideas can result in your becoming more integrated. As a healing tool, words can help to build bridges between people. This facilitates the sense of being more connected, less alienated and more a part of the greater human family. An extreme example of this came out in the news several years ago. A woman in Chicago was placed in a mental hospital in the 1930s, with the diagnosis that she was delusional and psychotic, unable to communicate with anyone. She remained there for over fifty years, often in solitary confinement. One day, quite by chance, some people, who were Russian immigrants came to the hospital to visit a relative. The patient overheard them speaking Russian in their unique dialect, and became overjoyed—at last someone to talk to. It seems that all along she hadn't been mentally ill. She too was an immigrant who was capable of speaking only an obscure dialect from a distant place.

The obstacles in making contact with others were so great that her alienation, and subsequent isolation, were quite real.

Healing can also occur for Gemini by listening and by being listened to. Gemini tends to identify with information—a "love me, love my ideas" approach to socialization. If others take the time to listen to those ideas, you would assume that they care about you. This may not always be the case, however, as sometimes people focus on your information and not on you as a person. But in a personal relationship, being heard is an important part of feeling appreciated.

Sometimes you can also be healed by listening. Instead of just idly carrying on a conversation with someone, try focusing on what is being said to you. Occasionally significant information may come to you in a seemingly random interchange. It's as if there are two levels of meaning to what is being said. By paying only tangential attention, you are aware of the superficial, or more obvious meaning, but gloss right over the subtleties. Often it will be that deeper strata of significance that provides you some key information that could be either healing or inspiring to you. The person delivering this message may not be particularly bright or even educated, let alone enlightened. In fact they may also be unaware of the underlying context of the conversation. So train yourself to pay attention to the truth or totality of what is being said. Your mind is certainly nimble enough to be aware of all the subtleties, the question is the motivation to focus and concentrate.

The strength of the Geminian tendency to be adaptable is that it allows you to have a wide range of interests. You not only can relate to many things in life, but you need the constant stimulation and change that this versatility allows: Gemini the Juggler. You like doing several things, sometimes simultaneously. A normal, healthy pattern for you is to do a lot of "messing around." You might begin a project, only to be side tracked by something else, from which you also might digress. Eventually you might finish the original activity, but the journey of getting from here to there is usually filled with interesting zigzags. Each time you meander from the main road, you create the opportunity to learn about life, or people or whatever you come across. In the long run, you can be just as productive as anybody else. But your path of achievement will tend to look less like a straight line, and more like a series of intersecting curves.

The weakness of this characteristic is that it can keep you from focusing in depth on anything. You impatiently jump from one activity or interest to another. You can know a little bit about a lot of things, but not very much about any one thing. It can be hard for you to do anything in a linear progression. You can become easily sidetracked and lose your main point of attention. You might also be so concerned with providing information that others are interested in, or expressing it the way they want to hear it, that you fail to identify those areas of interest or points of view that are truly yours.

Gemini is an air sign. The prime focus of the air signs is on ideas and people. You can manifest this orientation by being very sociable with a variety of people. Being able to relate to anybody, at any time, anywhere, to discuss any topic, is the mark of a Gemini. This versatility can be valuable in professions such as sales, public relations, or journalism. You enjoy connecting people with people, and people with ideas.

In the sharing of ideas, Gemini can be extremely witty and inspirational to others. You combine an insatiable curiosity with the ability to understand what you know from a number of perspectives. You are capable of pulling together information that other people either don't know about or don't make the connections between. This quality provides the tools to be a successful teacher, writer, or speaker. You can both instruct and excite an open and inquisitive mind. The image of Pythagoras is seen in the breadth of interests that is the best and highest quality of the Geminian potential.

Gemini's function is to learn and to grow through intellectual stimulation and/or social interaction. You may have a tendency to be a social butterfly, all sizzle, but no steak. Intellectually, you could be so flexible and adaptable as to be unable to make up your mind relative to your feelings or to your points of view. Regardless of how charming or stimulating you may appear to others, in your own mind you may feel confused. Your attention span may be short, your interests fragmented, and it may seem as if your life is too diffuse. It is as if you are a prisoner of your own curiosity: jumping randomly and impulsively from interest to interest, person to person, and place to place.

If this is a problem for you, try to be more defined in your activities and interests. Remember that it is the Gemini nature to be impatient and need constant stimulation. If you limit your activities too severely, you will get bored and probably return to your previous pattern of dissociation. Yet if you don't limit them enough, you never quiet your mind to the degree that you can take advantage of the inspiration and intelligence yourself, let alone function as an inspiring instructor to others.

THE RULING PLANET

The ruling planet of Gemini is Mercury (☿). The symbols for both Venus and Mars are comprised of only two of the three primary glyphs that make up the planetary symbols, the circle and the cross. Mercury uses all three. The semi-circle is above, the circle in the middle, and the cross of the material plane is below. This combination suggests that Mercury is a complex form of energy. The semi-circle represents inspiration which channels through spirit (the circle) and grounds through practical application (the cross). The flow can also manifest in reverse order: matter is supporting spirit such that inspirational concepts can be channeled. Just as Gemini offers a variety of interactive activities, so too, does its ruler Mercury provide outlet through several levels of awareness. It is up to the individual to decide how much time and energy is to be given to each level according to what is appropriate at any given time.

Mercury represents the principle of active intelligence or reason. It signifies communication, whether through the written word, the spoken word or even working with the hands through manual activity. This last facility can be expressed through craftsmanship, musicianship, massage or mechanical skill. When well aspected and well placed by sign and house, Mercury provides for a quick wit, an inspired mind and a love of ideas. For example, this occurs if Mercury is in an air or fire house or sign, or supported by conjunctions, sextiles, or trines to Jupiter or Uranus. When poorly placed, or aspected by sign or house, the mind can be restless, inconsistent, or superficial. Mercury squaring or opposed by Uranus or Neptune can indicate this pattern.

In general, Mercury is strongest in the air signs. This is the element that is oriented toward thinking and ideas anyway.

Mercury in Gemini provides the sharpest wit, potentially the clearest and most active and curious intellect. In Libra, Mercury is logical in its approach to information. This is an excellent placement for a debater. Libra is a sign that looks for and relies on feedback from others as a way of defining or validating its reality. With Mercury in Libra you could be indecisive trying to figure out which feedback source accurately reflects your point of view. The real question is: do any of them? Are you trying to see your opinion reflected by others, or trying to please others by coinciding your ideas with theirs? Mercury in Aquarius is the inventor. The mind is open to new ideas, progressive thinking and an overview perspective. Topics that are esoteric, like astrology, or that require expansive conceptual understanding, like radio astronomy, could be appealing to someone with Mercury in Aquarius.

Mercury is also comfortable in the fire signs. Here, the emphasis is more on the expression of ideas, rather than the conceptualization of information. Mercury in Aries or Sagittarius will be direct and honest in communication, sometimes to the point of being blunt or insensitive. They prefer the jack-hammer approach to verbalizing: put it out there assertively and with force. This is a good technique for initiating a debate, or for a teacher trying to make a point. But there can also be either a limited understanding of the topic, or a tendency to discount opinions that don't coincide with their own.

Mercury in Taurus or Leo is the mark of an orator. Taurus rules the throat, so there's a lot of energy in the parts of the body from which communication emanates. The quality of the voice can be harmonious, such that Mercury in Taurus can indicate a singer, or one who expresses themselves through music. One musical outlet that can be of double benefit is chanting. Not only is chanting a form of creative expression via the throat, but it is also a form of spiritual discipline that can aid the process of spiritual growth. In Leo, Mercury can manifest oratorical tendencies because it suggests a person who is confident in their ideas, loving the sound of their own voice, or who simply does not listen well to other people. Mercury in Leo also implies creative expression through writing, singing or crafts.

Mercury is also quite strong in the other sign that it rules, Virgo. Here, the analytical qualities of the mind are refined to their sharpest degree, although Mercury in either Scorpio or Pisces can also demonstrate good power of analysis. The drawback to excessive analysis can be a tendency to continually find fault with other people or external situations. Manual skills are also emphasized in the lives of people who have Mercury in Virgo.

Mercury in Capricorn is the serious minded detective, pursuing information in a deliberate, fact-finding, practical mode. At times this placement of Mercury can indicate the tendency to be skeptical of others' ideas, interests or truths, while tending to be rigid or dogmatic about maintaining their own. Mercury in Capricorn also provides a focused mind with the ability to concentrate on something long enough to obtain a deep, clear understanding of it.

The verbal skills associated with Mercury tend to be minimized when it is placed in a water sign. Sensitivity and intuition is heightened, but those qualities could also imply that Mercury in Cancer, Scorpio or Pisces is less likely to verbalize their ideas. With Mercury in any of these signs, you could assume that others have the same insight that you do, so why the need to openly express? Since most people are not particularly intuitive, and even if they are, they're not mind readers, failing to express your interests or feelings can create problems in a relationship. On the positive side, however, Mercury in any of the water signs can indicate the ability to work with numbers and have skills in the sciences.

Mercury symbolizes how and where connections to other people can be made. To pay attention to your Mercury is to affirm your desire to establish a definite, meaningful connection with others. For most people, the need for communicative interaction is fundamental. The ability to reach out and express yourself to others, to share your ideas, interests, and points of view are activities that are unique to human beings. The connections that are made by reaching out to others, or that are created when others reach out to us, can be healing in that they enable us to be more a part of the human family and, ultimately, part of the Oneness of Life.

By house placement Mercury indicates what area of life triggers your thinking and communication process. What you tend to think about and where you share those thoughts is a product of Mercury in the houses. In the first house you would focus on things that are taking place in your immediate environment. You would form opinions about those activities and want to express those points of view in a direct way to others. Mercury in the first house indicates a lot of communication skills as well as someone who is gifted in using their hands creatively or expressively. In the second house Mercury is more oriented toward thinking about security issues. You could use communication skills in business and be clever about ways of generating money. Tools of writing or dealing with commerce could also help you to stabilize your material security.

Mercury is the natural ruler of the third house and sixth houses. Located in either place Mercury is said to be accidentally dignified and would be strongly activated in your life. In the third house social skills and intellectual skills help to be constantly involved in the process of learning new information and sharing what you already know. Writing, journalism, teaching and sales might be potential areas of expressive outlet and fulfillment.

Mercury in the fourth house provides a more introspective mind. You would tend to focus on personal issues, especially those that pertain to home and family. You would prefer to converse with family members about issues that are of interest to them or that are shared by the family at large. By taking the time to listen to your own thoughts and creating a dialogue with yourself can help to make subtle ideas and feelings more conscious.

In the fifth house Mercury would be oriented toward creative ideas. Expressing your creativity through the written word such as creative writing, the spoken word through drama or oratory or through creative craftsmanship would come easily to you. Using your verbal skills in an entertaining way would also be appropriate with Mercury in your fifth house. Investments could also prove beneficial with Mercury here.

The sixth is an earth house like the second. Mercury in the sixth indicates that your mind would be oriented toward practical interests. You could use analytical abilities or mechanical skills in your work. Mercury in the sixth also provides the potential to be refined in your thinking and discriminating in your state of mind. Without developing this discernment, however, you could also be reductively critical of others. Thinking about health and healing or using your mind or hands as tools of healing could also define Mercury in the sixth house.

The seventh is the house of partnership. Mercury therein implies that your primary relationship and your partner occupy much of your mental energy. Communication would be an important part of relating. You love to share your ideas with a partner and communicate about shared experiences. These same tendencies and needs would also be present if Mercury were in your eighth house. Whereas Mercury in the seventh could be satisfied with sharing information with a partner that might be of a relatively general or superficial nature, Mercury in the eighth would rely on communication as a vehicle for deepening of the relationship to a point of intimacy. Mercury in the eighth could also be interested in science or any subject through which a deeper understanding about the nature of life could be learned. With Mercury in your eighth house you might be fascinated by death and the concept of eternal life. You could also be interested in the world of finance as an accountant or bookkeeper.

In the ninth house Mercury is stimulated to learn. This could take the form of learning more about one subject or finding new subjects to learn about. In the eighth house Mercury emphasizes *depth* of knowledge; in the ninth house Mercury values *breadth* of knowledge. Mercury in the eighth would tend to communicate in a more intense style. This position of Mercury also suggests someone who is such a deep thinker that they might not know how to or be interested in sharing their ideas. In the ninth house, however, Mercury would be more expansive and would prefer to share its information with others in an open-minded manner, possibly as a teacher.

Mercury in the tenth house is of a practical nature and is oriented toward conversations that help the individual to learn the "how to" of something. Mercury in the tenth also implies communications skills that are oriented toward commerce or helpful in your career in some way.

The eleventh is an air house, like the third and seventh. Air stimulates the intellect and social activities that facilitate the sharing of ideas. In the eleventh the mind would be open to new and progressive ideas, whether new to your experience or to humankind in general. Sharing this information in inspired ways with friends or within groups or organizations would prove fulfilling to Mercury in the eleventh house.

With Mercury in the twelfth house the mind becomes more introspective and less communicative. You might be intrigued by science, research or mysticism. Like the opposite house, the sixth, Mercury in the twelfth can be analytical. This can manifest in such activities as mathematics or music.

There may be problems in communication when Mercury is retrograde. Sometimes this can manifest as other people not really understanding what you are saying, and sometimes you could misunderstand them. This can be due to a highly personal or subjective way of perceiving situations, understanding information, thinking or communicating. For example, Mercury retrograde in Aries can create communication problems because your mind is too quick and impulsive. You tend not to be patient enough in choosing words that accurately represent the concepts you are trying to express. You may also be impatient as a listener, jumping to conclusions about what is about to be said rather than paying strict attention to the communicator. Mercury retrograde in Aquarius can render the mind too theoretical, entertaining only the most esoteric and far reaching, idealistic or scientific ideas and concepts. They may be ideas that most people are not interested in or have no previous experience with and which may seem foreign or frightening, causing communication breakdown. You may also tend to be bored by what others consider interesting. You could express that boredom by acting in an aloof manner or adopting a "know-it-all" attitude.

Mercury retrograde in Virgo has the opposite problem. As an earth sign Virgo is very practical. This position of retrograde Mercury promotes all mental and manual activities that involve detail and extreme analysis. Scientists and machinists with Mercury retrograde in Virgo excel in their fields as a result of their ability to be so mentally focused. But they also tend to be such perfectionists that it is hard for them to tolerate others' flaws and hard for others to tolerate their critical nature.

Similarly, Mercury retrograde in Scorpio tends to be so deep in its thinking that it fails to communicate at all. It may pursue data to a deeper level of understanding than most people. Or it may share the information in such a passionate, intense way, that the listener can be without a clue as to how to respond. Mercury retrograde in Capricorn could also have a similar tendency. Here, however, Mercury retrograde creates a desire to understand information at a deep level. But Mercury retrograde in Capricorn can imply rigid thought patterns and can lead to difficulty relating to information circulating in the outer world that does not coincide with the ideas that are so deeply understood by the individual. The mind is not very spontaneous, but can be focused and the degree of concentration can be excellent.

Sometimes the breakdown in communication is due to a simple lack of honesty. Mercury retrograde in Libra could have such a problem. If Mercury in Libra is indecisive, Mercury retrograde in Libra can carry that pattern to the extent that it becomes difficult for anyone, including the individual himself, to understand what he really thinks. Fear of being rejected, or at least undermining harmonious feedback for espousing their true ideas or opinions can exacerbate this problem. This can lead to someone valuing tact over truth.

Communication breakdown can also occur because we all tend to be more skilled in listening techniques than we are in patterns of honest communication. Our culture is very supportive of co-dependent patterns of communication that involve responding with "yes," "sure," "got it," and "I understand." But whether we actually are interested in what is being said or whether we really understand it is another matter. You may have had the experience of being listened to or listening to someone and either not receiving honest feedback or not giving honest feedback. When the conversation is finished, you get up and do something which is essentially very different than either of you thought you had agreed upon. Mercury retrograde in Gemini can create this confusion as a result of failing to take the time to find the words that accurately convey the concepts you are thinking about, or by failing to choose the way of expressing those concepts in a manner understandable to the listener, or failing to choose the right time to communicate. Mercury retrograde in Sagittarius has an encyclopedia for a brain. You can generate confusion in conversation by trying to provide such an excessive amount of information in the course of a conversation, background material, digressions, etc., that the listener is quickly lost.

Communication problems can also stem from failing to express your thoughts or mental interests. For example, Mercury retrograde in Taurus emphasizes the Taurean tendency to do things in a slow and complete manner by providing a deliberate and cautious mind. At times this can lead to fixation on certain ideas which can limit the ability to grow intellectually or to be open to new ideas. Although this placement of Mercury does not facilitate much verbalization, there is the ability to develop a deep understanding of whatever the mental interests are. Also, Mercury retrograde in Taurus symbolizes a very active, intuitive mind and the ability to tap into the "inner voice."

Mercury retrograde in Leo can think and communicate in grandiose ways. There can be a tendency to exaggerate the importance of one's ideas, or plan projects that are unrealistically large in scope. Often a sense of pride or fear of being embarrassed can impel one to hold the ideas inside and not express them at all.

In Cancer, Mercury retrograde can have a hard time distinguishing thoughts from feelings. There could be a tendency for ideas to generate feelings and for emotions to stimulate thoughts. This can lead to being overly analytical of emotions and seeking simultaneous emotional and mental fulfillment.

Similarly, Mercury retrograde in Pisces can create confusion as the individual struggles to separate thoughts from intuitions and ideas from fantasies. Failing to do so can lead to a sense of being mentally lost in trying to relate to the world. The key is to use the analytical ability of Mercury in Pisces to learn how to discriminate between these two qualities of perception and experience.

There are several techniques that resolve Mercury retrograde problems. One of these is writing. With Mercury retrograde in your natal chart, you can often make yourself understood more clearly through the written word than you can through speech. It may be that as you write down your ideas and concepts, you are taking the time to choose the words that accurately represent what you are thinking about. This can take the form of creative writing, keeping a diary or journal, or writing letters to resolve a problem or clarify an issue.

Mercury retrograde may have problems with verbal communication, but can be gifted in other areas of Mercury's domain, such as through the manual dexterity required of craftspeople or musicians.

Mercury also relates to members of the extended family, especially siblings. Mercury retrograde in a natal chart can indicate unresolved karma with regard to communication that sometimes involves the relationship to a brother or sister. You may have experienced blockage of your mental or verbal development as a direct result of your relationship to this person or as a result of the family dynamic created by that sibling. The birth of a younger sibling at a crucial time in the development of your verbal skills may have impelled you to retard that growth. As you saw all the attention you used to receive being given to the baby, you may have unconsciously sought to return to that pre-verbal state to compete with your new brother or sister, and reclaim that attention for yourself. Or if an older sibling were particularly bright, you may have seen your own mental and verbal skills pale in comparison, especially if you were always being compared to him or her.

Mercury retrograde in Scorpio, the eighth house, or in hard aspect to Pluto, can indicate that there could have been a death of a sibling when you were very young, and this too could have set you back in terms of verbal development. Mercury retrograde in Pisces or Virgo could suggest a health issue, or an institutional situation involving a sibling that impacted your development at an early age.

This is not a cause to blame the other person for your experience. You chose the familial dynamic because it gave you the necessary lessons, programming, or experiences you needed for your evolutionary journey. The key point for all of us, whether we have Mercury retrograde or direct, is that any factors that impede communication also limit the learning experience. Learning and sharing our knowledge with others is one of the basic reasons we are on the planet. Mercury in the natal chart suggests how we are prone to exchange information, in what ways and about what topics. Strengthening Mercury in your life helps to strengthen your connections with other people and to develop your ability to think and understand.

THE THIRD HOUSE

The house that is associated with Gemini is the third house. This is the area of life that deals with communication, education and transportation. Planets located in the third house of your natal chart will give you a lot of Gemini-type characteristics and tendencies such as being oriented toward journalism, radio work, sales or teaching. Activities that involve networking and data gathering in fields such as public relations also appeal to you.

The educational activities of the third house involve things that can be learned quickly. Phone calls, conversations reading, workshops, seminars and retreats are all third house educational modes. Any of those experiences may interact or connect with something more continuous in your life, such as a job-training seminar or a spiritual retreat that enhances your meditation. None of them, however, will provide you with a complete course of study or working knowledge of a field of expertise.

The aspect of the third house that involves transportation is oriented primarily to short journeys: traveling you can do that involves neither going great distances nor for long periods of time. People who take short trips for a living, such as sales representatives, truck, bus or cab drivers, or travel agents tend to have an activated third house. Activities that involve vehicles, such as making deliveries or that require mechanical skill can also be influenced by third house planets. The third house form of transportation can also involve recreational short journeys, such as bicycle riding.

The third house also can define or give insights into your state of mind. For example, Mercury in the third house indicates a curious person with a variety of mental interests, but one who may get involved in them only to a superficial degree. Uranus in the third is similar, but adds a tendency to be inventive and interested in esoteric subjects. Saturn in the third suggests a deep thinker with great powers of concentration, but also one who may tend to be a rigid thinker or tend to be of a dogmatic state of mind. Saturn in the third is someone who may have such a serious state of mind that it borders on depression. Neptune gives a very subtle and intuitive state of mind, but also one that may tend to be confused in thinking and evasive in communication. Pluto combines the mental depth and intensity of Saturn with the intuitive awareness of Neptune. Venus or Jupiter indicate a joyful state of mind and a "sunny disposition." These two planets, as well as the Moon, bring love of the social process, complete with appreciating the social graces and small talk.

Like the sign Gemini, the third house is an air house. It is not only oriented to the aforementioned ideas, but also to people. As the educational facet of the third house may be interested in variety, so does the social orientation of this area of life tend toward multiplicity. This is the house that deals with the random flow of social energy. In a personal sense, this is defined by your extended family: grandparents, aunts, uncles, cousins, and siblings. With personal planets in the third house, such as the Sun, Moon, Mercury, Venus or Mars, you may have been strongly influenced and imprinted by your extended family when you were a child. Your social life or emotional patterns as an adult will probably emulate or at least reflect your experiences with these people.

The Sun implies identifying with one particular member of the family, such as an older brother or sister, or a grandparent. The Moon suggests that much of your nurturing was received from a grandmother, sister or aunt. The Moon in the third house could also indicate that you provided the nurturing to younger siblings. Mars could indicate conflicts with siblings; Pluto that the conflict was hidden or that there was some betrayal or deception in the family. Pluto in the third house could also imply death of a sibling as a child. Saturn in the third, especially retrograde, seems to be present in the third house of people who experienced sexual abuse as children. Saturn here can also imply that your father was highly critical of your academic achievements, or that he demeaned your intelligence. If this was your experience and you internalized that negativity you could have doubts about your intelligence, your ability to learn or your communication skills. Uranus could indicate an eccentric sibling, in that he or she was brilliant, rebellious, or just weird.

Extended family can also include good friends. There could be a significant time spent with these people, such as on holidays and birthdays, and possibly even a desire to share a family or living situation with them.

In a less personal way, the third house encompasses your neighbors, immediate community and the general environment around your house. In the most impersonal sense, this house can indicate your tendencies and experiences in dealing with the "man on the street" type of casual, innocuous interchange. Usually they involve small talk and repartee exchanged in line at the market or with the gas station attendant. None of these people will necessarily have any sort of real relationship with you; possibly you will never even see them more than once in a lifetime. Yet that which can be learned from these people, or the information that can be channeled from them to you, can provide you provocative insights, or may be instructive or significant to you in terms of your personal life or spiritual growth. This does not have to be any sort of enlightened individual or a teacher of any kind. It can be just any person. It's as if he or she has been called upon—chosen if you will—to give you very important information. Pay attention to these random conversations. You might assume that because this is just an average person and not a teacher of some kind he or she will have nothing important to say. This is not necessarily true. Sometimes we can learn some very important aspects or features of life in general or our own life in particular, simply by paying attention to the conversations that go on around us on a daily or moment to moment level. This is especially true if you have the Moon or one of the higher consciousness planets, Uranus, Neptune, or Pluto in your third house.

The idea of the random flow of social energy also indicates that the third house is seen as the marketplace of life. This not only suggests just the immediate environment or the community, it also indicates the desire to exchange goods, services and ideas.

GEMINI AND THE BODY

Descending from the head, through the throat, the body begins to bifurcate (divide) into two branches—right and left. Anatomically Gemini rules this duality through the shoulders, arms, hands, fingers and lungs. As the messenger of the zodiac, Gemini also rules through the principle of "connectedness," connecting people to people, people to ideas, or ideas to ideas. By extension of this principle Gemini rules the tubes of the body such as the fallopian tubes, urethra, and the Eustachian tubes. Gemini also rules the thymus gland. Medical science has thought that the thymus gland served only to bring about the immune reaction in infants. As soon as the body was through creating antibodies the thymus gland became dormant. New theories are indicating that the thymus gland can also promote longevity.

As the ruler of the lungs, Gemini has dominion over the respiratory system, and can indicate problems with that system such as bronchitis or asthma. Consequently, Gemini rules the breath. The Eastern mystics use the term *prana* and the Chinese use *chi*; both are ways of referring to the vital life force, which includes the breath. As long as the body is breathing, the body is alive. One of the principles of certain techniques of meditation is the value of deep breathing. Sometimes this is a yogic form of breathing, which is a very slow and complete breath in followed by a very slow and complete breath out. Sometimes this can take the form of reciting a mantra or the repetition of a certain sound. Sometimes the mantra can even be chanted out loud as a form of singing, which can be a type of deep breathing in itself. The value of deep breathing is that it energizes the body. To inhale as much air, or *prana*, or *chi* as we can in one breath and to do this continually, breath after breath for a period of time each day, also energizes the mind and soul as well to the point where all the bodily processes and systems eventually slow down. This can be useful in calming the nerves, and ultimately prolonging life by giving the vital organs some time to rest.

Similarly, the breath is what connects the being to the body. If you have several planets in air signs in your chart, a strong Neptune, or significant planets in your twelfth house, deep and conscious breathing can be a way for you to stay in your body.

This type of exercise is especially important for people who have a lot of Gemini energy or a lot of third house energy or a very strong Mercury in the chart, because such people tend to have an overactive mind. It is continually going at all times, always taking in new ideas, new data. This information can be very fragmented. It pours in chaotically or at least in a very dispersed fashion to the point where it can't be taken full advantage of. To slow down the mind through the deep breathing enables you to control your mind and strengthens your ability to learn, understand, and gain knowledge from the raw data in a more efficient way. Your mind is what creates your life. To control your breath is to control your mind. To control your mind is to control your life.

The planet Mercury can also be an indicator of lung and speech disorders. Since it rules the central nervous system, too, it can also relate to nervous disorders. People with several planets in Gemini or who have a very strong Mercury can suffer from severe nervous tension. This is especially true if Mercury is in stressful aspect to the Moon or Uranus. Mercury in hard aspect to Uranus can also indicate diseases of the nervous system such as multiple sclerosis. The stressful aspects between these planets can also suggest the possibility of learning disorders. It's as if the mind is being electrified by Uranus, making it difficult for a person to concentrate and assimilate within the formal context of an educational system.

Finally, both Gemini and Mercury relate to the hands. In the positive sense, this can indicate excellent hand-eye coordination and the ability to perform delicate and intricate feats of manual dexterity, such as mechanical skill, playing instruments or working with crafts. The only potential drawback to this quality is the tendency to injure the hands as a result of frequent usage.

CONCLUSIONS

The strength of Gemini is its ability to absorb information and share that knowledge with others. Its highest potential is to embody the Universal Mind, having a vast array of information arranged in an intelligent, useful form. This enables you to excel as an educator, providing your students with a cohesive understanding of life from an infinite number of perspectives. As a networker you can serve as a link between people and resources that would benefit them.

Gemini's prime weakness is a tendency to be overwhelmed with too many ideas at once, and to be confused about who to share them with, at what time, in what way and for what reason. This can be partly due to a tendency to become too subjectively involved in your own ideas, a love me/love my ideas attitude about communication. This pattern of identifying with your mind and information is not necessarily conscious nor deliberate. Sometimes as a Gemini you can get so carried away by an idea or inspiration that you lose objectivity altogether. There is no critical awareness about an idea's relative importance to either yourself or to other people and you may tend to express the idea in a superficial manner.

One technique that can help you overcome this tendency is to visualize yourself as a switchboard operator. The switchboard operator sits, centered and grounded, waiting for the light to go on, then calmly connects the incoming call to the appropriate outgoing channel. As an ongoing methodology, and as a way to being able to make best use of the information, wait for the light (of inspiration) to go on, and plug into it. Then remain in your "seat" until every aspect, phase, or facet of the idea has been understood. You realize what part or parts of that information are valuable, pertinent or interesting to you. Then you can shift your focus to become aware of those elements of the information that are important to other people you know. Only after you have first learned and gained benefit from the knowledge yourself should you "plug into the other side of the board," the outgoing side. With clear understanding comes the critical discrimination of how you can use the information in a beneficial way. It becomes more obvious to you with whom to share that information, and which part of it would be most beneficial to which person.

From this visualization, you can become detached from your ideas and channel the data to others with a great deal of mental subtlety. This can also help you to see things from all sides, which is very appealing to your potentially inspired mind.

Gemini has to be careful not to get too fragmented with too much information. Sometimes your mind is very subtle, other times it can become confused. One of the reasons for this is that Gemini is so open to receiving information from such a variety of external sources. This can create problems in discriminating about the importance or quality of a piece of information. It is as if you get so overloaded by so much data, you need to have a warehouse to keep those ideas that haven't been thought through. At one time they may have seemed very fantastic, fascinating, or inspiring but for one reason or another you have been unable to integrate them within the context of your ongoing life. This information remains in potential to be learned at a deeper level, shared with other people or utilized in a practical way.

This pattern can serve as an illustration about the dualistic tendencies inherent in the image of the twins. If one twin is over here doing one thing, and the other twin is over there doing something else, the whole thing gets quite disjointed. If you allow yourself to be pulled in whatever direction you are receiving information from, your confusion level increases and your ability to interpret and utilize the energy decreases. One way to alter that pattern is by saying, "OK, twins, you are my children, and I am the responsible adult in charge. Twin number one you will do something that I have to do but am not now doing and twin number two, you will do something that I want to do but don't seem to have time for." The value of making each twin deal with something you have to do or something you want to do is that you are symbolically creating a way to empty out the warehouse, stop the confusion and get your life back in control.

A practical way to do this is to make contracts with yourself. Take something from the storehouse of ideas that relates to something you have to be doing and make a contract with yourself. Be easy in the beginning with these contracts. Don't necessarily string yourself out for weeks or months at a time because you don't really know if it is going to be valuable, interesting or stimulating once you have actually spent some quality time and paid some quality attention to the activity. The same thing would apply to something that you might want to do. You can take that activity or interest out of the storehouse and assign the other twin another contract. For instance, the initial contract could be for one hour, for one day, or for one hour a day for a week. If you find after getting involved with the idea that it has absolutely no meaning or interest for you, you can either break the contract on the spot, or finish it as a way to develop your self-discipline. If you find that the activity does have lasting interest for you, simply extend the life of the contract until eventually you have gotten all you can from the activity or have integrated it into the normal habits of your life. Then you can take on something else of that nature from the storeroom—either something you want to do or something you have to do. Try not to be too extreme in terms of extending the contracts, because you really don't know how far in the future this is going to continue to be a viable experience for you. A one hour contract may get you excited about a certain project, but at that point you may not know how long you will remain interested in it. By affirming that you will devote your next three week-ends to that activity may simply set you up for a feeling of failure. If you extend the contract from one hour to an hour a day for a week or to three hours on a Saturday you can be more realistic about that situation. Continue to extend the contract until you have learned all you can from it, or until it becomes part of the daily routine.

By visualizing the concept of the switchboard operator as well as affirming and actualizing contracts with yourself, you can become less dispersed and fragmented. These are techniques that can help you to become more directed in your mental and social activities so as to be able to take advantage of the curiosity, versatility and intelligence which are such primary elements of the Geminian potential. Remember that Gemini is a very inspired sign, which is a concept that has a multiplicity of ramifications. One is that inspiration can lead to or indicate genius potential. For inspiration to become genius, however, there needs to be control. For the Gemini, this definitely needs to be experienced through mental discipline. For without that discipline, inspiration leads to chaos.

CANCER

Cancer begins the second quadrant. This is comprised of houses four, five and six, and the signs Cancer, Leo, and Virgo. After the initial stages of experience and development represented by the signs and houses of the first quadrant, the focus shifts. The point of the first quadrant was to define, develop, and express the self. Now the orientation is to share the self with those closest to you. This sharing can be playful and creative or serviceful and productive.

The transition from Gemini to Cancer involves shifting from the element air to the element water. Air is oriented toward the expansion of the mind and the formation of relationships. As such it can tend toward variety and dispersion. Cancer is a water sign. It condenses the energy, focusing it in a more concentrated way. Cancer is potentially as versatile as Gemini, but prefers to center on one particular interest or activity. If Gemini represents the principle of the eternal youth seeking to satisfy its insatiable curiosity, Cancer signifies the eternal parent, focusing on the security needs of the child. Cancer is the sign of protection and nurturing.

Cancer is the first of the water signs. As such Cancer says, "I feel." Water provides lubrication, the ability to flow from experience to experience and from one condition to another. It is one of the two primal elements, the other being fire. The inherent contrast between these elements generated the tension and resulting explosion that created matter (earth) and wind (air). This stress is exhibited in the zodiac as each of the water signs is at right angles to a fire sign. This is a ninety-degree angular relationship, called a square ($\square$). The square is one of five major aspects that help to qualify the degree of harmony or tension that exists between two or more planets. The flow defined by the aspect indicates the way in which the energy defined by those planets will manifest. The square is an aspect that indicates internal tension. Two parts of the inner self are in conflict. The dynamic of the square is such that one part of you wants to remain within the self and function in a quieter or more practical way (water or earth). The other wants expression and the opportunity to share (fire or air). The square can be the most difficult of the aspects to resolve but, as such, offers the greatest opportunity for growth.

A good way to resolve a square is to focus on the mode of the signs involved. Usually the two signs will share a common mode. For example, Aries is cardinal by mode and fire by element. Cancer is also cardinal by mode but water by element. All cardinal signs are action-oriented. So if you have a planet in Aries square one in Cancer, resolve the conflict by a series of actions. Whether in the form of spontaneous trial and error or by devising a clear strategy eventually the right combination, or balance, between the fire and water will be realized and a new pattern begins. Finding the new pattern is the growth. If the square is between fixed signs, the question is how to integrate conflicting habits. Fixed signs base their habits on values. To find a common value system, that both the fixed signs share, or to create one that integrates something that has meaning to both signs, is to resolve the tension and grow. If the square is between mutable signs, which indicates that the energies in those signs are change-oriented, the result can be an amorphous, confusing, scattering of energy. The way out is to find a system that each sign can function within in a comfortable, effective way. It could be an external system that you connect with. Or a series of systems that you adapt to your needs. Or a system of your own creation. Whatever it is, it should provide the opportunity to learn, to raise your consciousness to a point of being able to integrate the curiosity and interests of the two mutable signs locked up in the square.

The Sun is in Cancer each year from June 21 to July 22. The first day of Cancer is the Summer Solstice, the first day of summer and the longest day of the year. The radiance of the Sun is at its peak. This could be mirrored by the individual born around that day. You can be filled with clear self-awareness, or tend to be so self-absorbed as to see others only as an extension of you. This is also similar to Hexagram 55 of the *I Ching*, the hexagram of Abundance. It counsels that as the Sun is at its peak each year, or even each day, its journey from that point is to descend. Don't deny that process, nor feel sad at the impending darkness. Internalize the light and imprint the radiance and joy of the season. As you flow with this radiance into the remainder of this season and on through the other seasons, you can experience your life feeling full from the inside out.

THE MYTHS

One of the qualities that makes water unique is its subtlety. As you will find with all three water signs, subtlety makes for a richly textured experience. That attribute is clearly seen through the myths associated with Cancer.

In Greek mythology Demeter is a symbol for Cancer. The Romans called her Ceres. She is the embodiment of the mother, the nurturer. She was the provider of food as the Goddess of Grain. Her most important relationship was with her daughter, Persephone. When Persephone was abducted by her uncle Hades, god of the underworld, Demeter grieved to such a degree that the grain, indeed all the crops failed, resulting in famine. Through the intervention of Zeus—Persephone's father—mother and daughter were reunited. Demeter is also a provider of spiritual sustenance as illustrated through her connection to the Eleusian Mysteries. These were religious ceremonies that re-enacted the cycle of loss (death of the child, removal from the light) and rebirth (return of the child to the parent, return of the individual to the light). These rituals taught the truth of eternal life. These were called mysteries in that they dealt with the eternal mystery of life and death. The rituals of this school were known only to the initiates of it; to the general public they were unknown. In that sense as well, they were mysteries.

The presence of Persephone in this myth is just as important as that of Demeter. Cancer is not only the sign of the mother, but also the parent-child relationship. Persephone was as devastated about being away from her mother as Demeter was about being separated from her daughter. But this devastation implies another side of the Cancerian nature. Beyond what point of caring and nurturing does the parent-child relationship become possessive, controlling, or co-dependent?

Demeter is actually a symbol of the Great Goddess, the all-nourishing Mother. She represents a universal archetype, variously called Isis, the Moon Goddess of Egypt, Ishtar, the Virgin Mother of the Semites, and *Inanna*, the Supreme Goddess of the Sumerians. Each of these Goddesses had dominion over the nurturing of the living, yet extended beyond the earth plane by descending to the realm of darkness, the realm of the dead. Consequently these archetypes enforce the concept of eternal life, and the nurturing available to everyone and needed by everyone in any condition of existence. These are all forms of validating the mysterious creative power which produced the Earth and every living thing on it. Metaphysically this is considered the primary feminine function. It is the maternal principle which nurtures new life to maturity, whatever the cost. Historically, the Goddess was conceived of as the originator of life. The independent feminine principle was the primary deity as worshipped by the emerging human race. Consequently it was a matrilineal society in which property was inherited through the mother.

Descending to the realm of darkness also symbolizes two other things. First is the blending of the conscious (above ground) with the subconscious (below ground). This is the path of wholeness as the individual making that journey is uniting the visible and the known with the invisible and the unknown. It is the unification of the seeming duality of life.

The second point is that the journey into the dark realm, the awareness of and conquering of the shadowy realm of the subconscious, is the road of the hero. The myths of Cancer suggest quite emphatically that this path is open to heroines as well. For example, in the Demeter-Persephone myth, just before mother and daughter were reunited, Persephone ate some pomegranate seeds. According to the law, as long as one in the underworld neither eats nor drinks, they can return to the realm of Light. Having partaken of sustenance, Persephone was allowed to go home only as part of a compromise engineered through Zeus' intervention. According to the compromise, she could return to her mother, but only for six months a year. After that she had to return to the realm of Hades, for the next six months. So ultimately, the Demeter-Persephone story represents a task that all humans experience. This myth illustrates how the potential to be aware of and work to unite the conscious-light with the subconscious-dark is a journey available to women as heroines as well as men as heroes. It is an experience necessary on the journey toward self-awareness.

THE SYMBOL: ♋

The symbol, the 69 laying on its side, is an obscure image. From one perspective it conveys a picture of the folded claws of the crab, the primary totem of Cancer. From another point of view, this glyph indicates the breasts, the organs of nourishment, prime symbols of nurturing, and a part of the body ruled by Cancer. The ♋ can also suggest the union of the female egg with the male sperm, the origin of life, and certainly appropriate for the sign of the mother. This can be seen as the long tail of the sperm cell is meeting and mating with the small, round egg.

Blending the two numbers into one glyph, it becomes the symbol for eternity. Again a significant mark of identification for the sign that deals with the beginning as well as ending of life. This is the first sign in which the sense of eternal life or the oneness of life has been present.

THE TOTEM: 🦀

Although the zodiac has grown and evolved, both in numbers of signs as well as in our understanding of the symbolism, the Cancerian archetype is one of the most ancient and universal. We associate the sign Cancer with the crab. Cancer is the Latin word for crab. In late June and early July when the Sun is in Cancer, it is transiting through the constellation of fixed stars that looked to the ancients like a crab. The northern-most point of the journey of the Sun is the Tropic of Cancer, approximately the 24th parallel. When the Sun reaches this point, it is the 21st of June, the first day of the sign Cancer. At a later date, people observing the development of a certain disease noted that it began as a cluster, then seemed to branch out in a manner similar to the claws of the crab. The name given to the disease reflected this similarity and was likewise called cancer.

In Babylon around 4,000 BC Cancer was referred to as the Tortoise. Turtles are hard shelled water animals, like the crab. Turtle Island is what certain tribes of Native Americans call the Earth. River turtles live in the Nile, and Egyptian pictures also exist which depict Cancer as the sign of Two Turtles. In Egypt around 2,000 BC, Cancer was also depicted as the Scarab, the symbol of eternal life. In Chaldea, an ancient Mesopotamian civilization, Cancer was referred to as the "Gate of Man," the portal through which the soul descends into the human body. A whole new quality of awareness is awakened here. There is a sense of connectedness to something much greater than the self.

Certain characteristics of the crab provide insight into the nature and behavior of the Cancerian experience. The crab takes his home with him at all times: a primary orientation of Cancer is the home and the family. It provides Cancer with the opportunity to create emotional security and experience the psychic bonding which it values. This bonding is necessary in the creation of a healthy family unit. Cancerians can, however, also be oriented toward travel. These are individuals who literally take their home with them wherever they go.

The fact that the crab has both a hard shell and a soft belly is also significant. It suggests that cancer is very sensitive and thus needs the security of a shell to withdraw into for the purpose of self-protection. Sometimes this can be misunderstood and seen by others as simply being crusty or unfeeling. Usually, quite the opposite is true.

Crabs walk sideways. It is as if they assume that the shortest distance between two points is around the block. This could indicate an awkwardness in its hard-shell body, the price for being so well-protected. In people, this suggests that to indulge in the self-protective mode too frequently or too consistently can make social interaction difficult. It can indicate a tendency to be self-conscious around other people. As a Cancer you may be so overly aware of yourself that your interactions are awkward and unpleasant.

The sideways motion and the inward drawn claws of the crab demonstrate its shyness and desire to avoid conflict. This is very much in the manner of the Cancerian who tends to be non-confrontational. Cancer is very indirect, primarily because it is so sensitive and emotional. As a Cancer, you can become blocked in expressing yourself or you can make it difficult for others to communicate with you. You might hide important, significant ideas within some seemingly innocuous dialogue, and assume that the listener will pick it up. On the other hand, Cancer may experience direct communication from others as confrontation and as such is likely either to ignore the point or leave. As a Cancer try to be more direct in your communication and for those having a conversation with a Cancer, try to be a little bit more subtle and sensitive.

The crab hiding within its shell also suggests a narrow outlook on life. Sometimes this can be in the form of a limited perspective on the outer world. It can also indicate a tendency to have blind spots about the self. With significant energy in Cancer you may tend to withdraw when confronted with information or situations that call upon you to take a look at some of those blind spots or confront sensitive issues within your life.

The claws of the crab pull into the self and indicates a high degree of tenacity. It implies that Cancer energy functions by drawing others to the self. If you have significant energy in Cancer this can manifest as possessiveness. If the clinging is done in a negative manner, with a self-serving intention, or if you are fearful or insecure, it is usually for the purpose of asserting more control and personal power in your life. If this drawing-in is done in a positive manner, however, it is motivated by a spirit of deep sympathy and compassion.

MODE AND ELEMENT

Cancer is the sign of cardinal water. The image is of rain, streams and rivers, water that is moving in one direction at a time. But rivers are changeable. Its been said that one never steps into the same river twice because conditions are always changing at any particular point. In different places along the same river, it can be narrow but deep and in other places wide but shallow. Sometimes there is sand on the bottom, sometimes sharp rocks, white water or calm current. This is indicative of the changes of mood or feelings of the Cancerian. Cancer can be so changeable in mood, that if you don't like the mood that you or your Cancerian friend is in, wait a few minutes because it is entirely possible and realistic to assume that during that time, the mood will change.

Rivers can contain waterfalls. To ride a raft down a cascading fall of white water is to be playfully pulled on a path from which there is no escape. Cancerian energy demonstrates this tendency through its social charm. As a Cancer your playfulness creates within you a certain compelling quality that can pull others to you in interest and curiosity. This is especially true of children who have significant Cancerian energy in their horoscope. It's as if they are ringmasters in social situations with other kids. They are always thinking up new games to play and fun things to do in a very spontaneous and joyful way. Others are drawn to them in a magnetic way so as to partake of the fun. Adult Cancers can manifest in a similar mode and have an analogous affect on their friends and family. Cancer is the sign of the eternal child. There is something very innocent, spontaneous and joyful about the Cancer child or adult.

Rivers also contain whirlpools. This suggests you may have a tendency to become too self-absorbed in your own activities or those of your family and live in a very small circle of awareness. The *I Ching* cautions against living your life as the eternal housewife, whose only perspective on the outer world is through a crack in her front door. It not only limits her awareness of what is outside, but also places unrealistic and unnecessary boundaries on her own potential experience and manifestation.

Water implies feelings and a connection to the mystical and the unconscious. The Demeter/Ceres myth demonstrates how this can be expressed through nurturing, maternal behavior. Inanna explored the inner world in a way that facilitated new birth of self in conscious awareness. Through mystical process we can connect with Creative Flow, that which generates all life. By tapping into that flow we connect with that which is greater than we are. We become part of the process of evolutionary development.

If you are manifesting your Cancer energy on a lower octave, it can create a different result. Too much reliance on family iden-tification can cause you to be dependent on the family or your role in it. Too much awareness of the feelings themselves can lead to being overwhelmed by your emotional reality. Too little expression of your feelings and emotional needs can create hypersensitivity and a tendency to take everything much too personally.

The cardinality of Cancer renders it a very active sign. As such you are extremely versatile and interested in many possibil-ities. You deal with them effectively and to your fulfillment. This encompasses lifestyle, career goals and family patterns—

anything that involves personal choice. In this way you are like the sign that directly precedes you, Gemini. For Gemini, however, versatility is not only a preference but also a way of life. For Cancer, enjoyment of the variety ceases at a certain point, and the desire and ability to focus takes over. You prefer to narrow your activity to one thing. You want to concentrate on that one interest that provides you with a sense of meaning, purpose and belonging.

Cancer is the second cardinal sign, the first being Aries. They have in common the desire and ability to be action-oriented and assertive. They both tend to act in ways that are oriented toward self. Aries is primarily involved in the process of self-awareness and self-development. Cancerian actions are more oriented toward taking care of that emerging self and protecting those closest to you. In that sense, Aries and Cancer are very different. The action of the Aries is direct; it asserts itself mentally and physically in the outer world, and in obvious ways. The energy of Cancer is more subtle; its assertiveness manifests through the expression of feelings and the discovery of the inner world.

THE RULING PLANET

When astrologers discuss the planets, they take into consideration eight planets of the solar system, plus the Sun and the Earth's Moon. The ruling planet of Cancer is the Moon (☽). The Moon is a very important planet in the astrological experience, second only to the Sun. The Moon is also important to the Earth, since its cycles affects the tides of the oceans. Its affects on people is demonstrated each month at the full Moon, as hospital emergency rooms and police precincts both report increased activity. The movement of the Moon affects the ebb and flow of human emotions even as it influences the tides.

There are a group of myths that help to define the function and significance of the Moon. Reflecting the light of the Sun, the Moon is often considered to be the female aspect of God or his consort, daughter or sister, the provider of the divine seed. In India, the deity Chandra Devi, was worshipped as the Moon Goddess. In Egypt, Isis was worshipped as the Goddess of the Moon and Magic. She was considered the loyal sister and wife of Osiris (god of the Nile). She was the embodiment of the dark, life-giving soil of the Nile Delta, enriching Egypt with her fecundity. She represents the mysterious creative power which produced the Earth and sustains all living things. She is the symbol of the original eminence and independence of the female principle, and the original leadership of women in tilling the soil. It was said that Isis discovered wheat and barley growing wild and revealed them to Osiris. She stands for the maternal quality of love. She nurtures and sustains her offspring until they reach maturity. In that sense she is said to have given birth to the Sun (the god Horus). In one myth about Isis, she was said to evoke from Ra (god of Eternity) the secret word with which she was able to command obedience from the unseen forces and power of Nature.

The Greeks called the Moon "Selene." She was the daughter of Theia, the Earth, and Hyperion, the Sun. The Greeks saw the Moon as having been born from the Earth, adding still another facet to the concept of the Moon as a symbol of nurturing.

These are similar to and extensions of the myths and images of Cancer. They remind us again of the fundamental quality of the female principle in the creation of physical life. These stories evoke reverence for women, and display honor for the contributions they made in the primary stages of the development of human experience and consciousness, and for the development of the individual child in the context of each family unit.

The Moon in the natal horoscope is symbolic of our most personal and primal experience. The Moon indicates our essence, the basic being or soul that we have been working to evolve throughout previous incarnations. By its sign and house position, as well as aspects to it from other planets, a fundamental connection to the inner self can be seen. The Moon in water and earth signs suggests a strong and comfortable interaction with the internal being. There is the potential to be in touch with your feelings and the desire to nurture others. Sometimes this can be too strong. For example, with the Moon in Capricorn (the sign of responsibility), you could tend to be concerned with taking responsibility for other people's emotional well being to the exclusion of your own.

The fire and air signs indicate more of a mental approach to the inner world. For example with the Moon in Aquarius, the eleventh house, or in hard aspect to Uranus, you could be detached from your feelings. In relationship with others there could be fear or expectation of emotional abandonment. With the Moon in the fire or air signs you could be more expressive of your feelings, but you could also tend to intellectualize them. You "think" that you are feeling, which isn't the same as registering a direct emotional experience. A way out from that pattern, and a way of getting more directly in touch with your emotional body is through your relationships with people. Whether they stimulate you to that end or provide you role models of how to express what you feel, you are using a strength, your sociability, to compensate for a weakness.

The condition of the Moon doesn't indicate your degree of evolutionary development, however. There is no way that I know of to determine either the spiritual growth you have attained or the philosophical perspective from which you are (or should be) working to develop yourself. The Moon can merely indicate your orientation to your soul, your comfort in relating to your inner being and the ease with which you share that part of yourself with others.

One of the functions of the Moon is to reflect the light of the Sun. Similarly, the Moon can reflect back to you this connection to your inner self. In childhood, the source of this mirroring is your family. The Moon indicates the form and quality of nurturing you received from your primary source. For most people, this would be the mother. For some, however, this could be the father, an older sibling, a grandparent or even an aunt or uncle. If your Moon is in a double-bodied sign like Gemini or Sagittarius, or in the third house, the house of the extended family, there may have been more than once source of nurturing, such as mother and grandmother, or mother and step-mother. You may have received conflicting signals from your nurturing sources either because there were different people, or the one person was confused or went through a significant change in her life while you were growing up. The value in analyzing the form and quality of your nurturing as well as the dynamic of the family as a whole is that it can help to assess your emotional and psychological roots. This information can help you to understand your potential for healthy relationships as adult. But this analysis can lead to a tendency to dwell on your childhood and blame your parents for your condition in life. Remember that the Moon is primarily an assessment of your own emotional and psychological development. It can indicate what you have developed, and what still needs work. You choose your family dynamic and your parents to experience what your being needs to evolve. The Moon indicates what work you need to do in this lifetime to become an emotionally and spiritually healthier, clearer being. Your parents are some of your first teachers. Whatever lessons they taught you were extensions of who they were and what they had learned. To blame them for your experience is to disavow any responsibility you had in choosing or creating it. Identifying as a victim keeps you stuck in the cycle of anger, blame, and denial. The first point of growth occurs when you notice the dysfunctional patterns that you imprinted as a child. To actually do the work of taking responsibility to heal those patterns and change those programs is the second point. In this way you take charge of creating your own emotional reality and furthering your own evolutionary development.

For example, Moon in Taurus or the second house can indicate that the mother was jealous of her offspring. To be aware of the controlling tendencies of your mother and the subsequent lack of nurturing that may have resulted, is healthy in several ways. It enables you to realize what you need but didn't get. It can also help you recognize your own tendencies to be jealous and controlling. Finally, and ultimately most important, you can understand that as a result of your childhood experience you had the opportunity to develop the qualities of emotional self-reliance and self-nurturing. From that point of awareness you can continue your own inner development and find within you the ability to care for others in healthy, supportive ways.

If your Moon is in Leo or the fifth house your mother may have been too preoccupied satisfying her own desires to provide adequate nurturing for you. She could have been involved in some type of creative expression or simply had too many children for her to cope with the demands and pressures she felt. Although you may have felt lost in the shuffle, this type of nurturing system provided a role model of someone who is aware of what she wants and some examples of how to manifest those desires. Even if certain nurturing needs went unmet, if you had several siblings you learned valuable lessons of socialization and perhaps learned how to play. A natal Moon in Gemini or the third house also implies a large extended family with meaningful and significant relationships with siblings. These were some of the specific needs that you came here to learn about or satisfy.

The Moon in Sagittarius or the ninth house suggests that education was stressed in your family. Perhaps one of your parents was an educator. Maybe your parents valued the importance of an education and helped provide you with what they considered the best. This could have been in the context of either an academic or religious training. Although supporting your mental growth, this type of environment could have stifled your emotional or creative nature. It was the need to develop your higher mind, however, that could have impelled you to incarnate with a Sagittarius or ninth house Moon.

If your Moon is in Virgo or the sixth house, your mother may have been task and chore-oriented but also fussy and critical. She may have seemed self-effacing at times, but resentful at others. She could have been in a health care profession and/or had severe health problems herself. In any case you would have been influenced and conditioned by any of those primary patterns had they persisted throughout childhood. You, too, are a service-oriented person. You had as a role model someone who may have been serviceful to a fault or to the point that her own needs became forgotten. You may have been inspired by your mother's physical condition to go into the health care field. Integrate that experience to maintain your desire to serve, but learn to do so in a way that allows you to blend your needs with those of others.

The Moon in Pisces or the twelfth house could reflect a similar situation to that of Moon in Virgo or the sixth house. In both cases the mother could have been a service-oriented, self-sacrificing type. Her health issues could have been part of your upbringing, although Pisces suggests emotional or psychological health problems more than physical. With a Pisces Moon, however, you could have received a double message. Pisces can be devoted and unconditional in its love and your mother may have reflected those feelings to you. Pisces can also be self-critical or self-defeating. She may have also given you signals that she was miserable or unhappy with her lot in life. She may even have questioned you when you put your needs or desires ahead of other people. In a healthy psyche both conditions can not co-exist. One does not unconditionally love the very thing that creates misery. One response to this dichotomy is to subtly undermine yourself by unconsciously vowing never to betray your mother by becoming more fulfilled in life than she. Whether in choices that pertain to partner, career or creativity you may make decisions that undermine your well-being and happiness. With a natal Moon in Pisces you are here to learn, among other things, how to distinguish love from pity. You need to realize where your emotional needs stop and where those of other people begin. You can understand that to help someone else you needn't get into the same condition that they are.

Libra is the sign of partnership. If your Moon is Libra or the seventh house, a partnership type relationship could have existed between you and your mother. In one scenario, she projected onto you who you are, which was often a reflection of who she wanted to be but for whatever reason couldn't be or wasn't. Your job was to carry out her unrealized dreams. Another possibility was that she brought you up as an ally against someone else in the family. You essentially became the mediator in the family, trying to placate everyone so that there was harmony in the home. In any of these possibilities your task is to learn how to separate yourself from others people's expectations. You came into this lifetime with the need to learn who you are and not to define yourself according to other people's needs or concepts of who you are.

If you are female, the Moon in your horoscope would indicate the cues or keys you imprinted from your female nurturing figure in terms of femininity, womanhood and motherhood. The Moon in positive aspect to Venus or the Ascendant can indicate being graceful and comfortable in expressing your self in receptive, care-giving ways. The Moon in Aries or in hard aspect to Mars, on the other hand, suggests a conflict with your mother over your identity. Are you who you think you are and want to be? Or are you who she told you to be? If the aspect is a square, you could internalize the conflict and be in continual battle with yourself over this issue without necessarily realizing what you are doing or why you are doing it. If the aspect between Moon-Mars in an opposition, the conflict would tend to be more acted out between you and her. The Moon in Aries or is aspect to Mars also suggests that your mother may have been angry when you were born. This anger was not directed at you but a condition in her life at that time. Often this anger was directed at her husband whom she felt betrayed her in some way. Nevertheless you could feel that anger and carry it with you throughout your life without realizing that it is there or what to do with it.

The Moon in a man's chart indicates his degree of familiarity with his own inner being. How in touch he is with his feelings and his receptivity. How comfortable he is expression his inner self to others. How aware he is of his soul. Since a man's natal Moon is indicative of the first relationship he had with a woman, it can also suggest his programming in relationship to women. What they offer and what they need. A Moon in Pisces, in the twelfth house or in aspect to Neptune, for example, can indicate a man who tends to idealize women or put them on a pedestal. He would relate to women as one who is a care-giver to them, assuming that they are fragile and in need of constant reassurance and reinforcement.

Certain sign-house-aspect patterns of the natal Moon suggest emotional-psychological challenges in the charts of both men and women. For example, if the Moon is in Scorpio, the eighth house, or in hard aspect to Pluto, the child could have felt emotionally deceived, betrayed or dominated in manipulative ways by the mother. These are probably very strong karmic, past life connections with that person. Nonetheless, the experiences associated with these patterns can be very painful and traumatic. They force you to look deeply within yourself, to become acquainted with part of yourself that heretofore was not conscious. They help you to feel more comfortable with your being in a way that allows clearer and more conscious expression of your inner self to others.

The Moon also is an indication of how you function moment-to-moment. It can portray how you react or respond to external stimuli. It's useful to define the differences between reaction and response. If you tend to be in "reaction mode," your initial point of awareness is to other people. You react to them, usually in ways that are oriented to doing or saying something that will satisfy their needs or contribute to their sense of well-being. By being in reaction mode you overlook your own feelings. You may be unaware of your own emotional experience or fail to act in accord with it. You may give to others beyond the realistic limits of your ability or desire, and feel frustrated, resentful or drained. The Moon in Capricorn, the tenth house, or in hard aspect to Saturn often orient you to reaction mode behavior.

To change that pattern, cultivate "response mode" behavior. When you are in response mode, your initial point of awareness is to yourself, your feelings, your needs and your limits. By orienting yourself in the here-and-now to your inner being, you are able to function in a healthier and more honest way. You become successful in letting people know who you are. You can still relate to others in sensitive, nurturing ways, but you do so within the context of your emotional reality, not the reality someone else lives in and may want you to join. In reaction mode you are allowing yourself to be an actor in someone else's movie. In response mode, you become the star of your own.

The phase of the Moon at the time of birth is also significant. Phases are determined by the Moon's relationship to the Sun. The cycle of the Moon lasts twenty-eight days. The key points of the cycle are the new Moon—when the Moon and Sun are conjunct—and the full Moon—when the Moon and Sun are in opposition. The conjunction between two planets marks the end of an old cycle and the beginning of a new one. The new cycle is characterized by certain patterns and influences which culminate at the time of the opposition between those same planets. The opposition allows one to develop perspective on the nature of the cycle and the way in which the opportunities of the patterns are being taken advantage of or not.

If you were born at the time of the new Moon this incarnation represents the beginning of the way in which you are defining and blending your soul (Moon) with your ego (Sun). This is a life in which the integration of your inner world and personal life (Moon) are creating new outlets for your creative self in the world. Being born at the dark of the Moon can also signify that you may have been your own source of primary nurturing as a child. Your sense of self (Sun) and your mother (Moon) were one. It can also suggest that your role and your mother's were reversed and you were at least as much a vehicle of emotional support and nurturing to her as she was to you.

A new Moon person can be subjective in dealing with life because one of your most important tasks is to nurture and create a new self. Spending time alone can be productive as it provides the opportunity to look within yourself for sustenance and clarity. New Moon rituals, celebrated by yourself or with others, can be useful to providing inspiration about how to proceed in your task. For all of us the dark of the Moon each month provides an opportunity for internal guidance. It is beneficial to mark that time each month with some activity that allows you to find direction from an inner source.

If you were born when the Moon was waxing, growing larger and moving from new to full, this incarnation is a building one for you. You will tend to be enthusiastic about your future and be concerned about developing something. Whatever you decide that "something" is, it is really just an externalization of the real building you are engaged in which is you. Even for those not born when the Moon is in this phase, the two weeks from new to full each month provide the energy for exuberant growth.

At the time of the full Moon we have more clarity and perspective of ourselves than at any other time of the Moon's cycle. The emotions which we have felt but tended to keep hidden during the new Moon phase may now come flooding out. We have the opportunity to become aware of what our emotional reality is both in terms of how we influence others and how they affect us. People tend to act out around the full Moon. It's as if they become overwhelmed by their feelings and can do nothing other put them out there, sometimes with unfortunate consequences. If you remain more consistently in tune with your emotions, however, the full Moon provides a time to be more objective about your internal reality. If you were born at the time of the full Moon, that clarity can be there almost all the time. You may feel as if your inner world is being played out on a huge movie screen with your secrets and sensitivities out there for all to see and take advantage of. You could feel vulnerable in unfamiliar situations. Regardless of how raw you feel, remember that although your feelings are obvious to you, that huge screen is in a very small screening room. It has one seat and that seat has your name on it. The purpose of an incarnation with a full Moon is to become more conscious of how your personal life affects your non-personal life and vice-versa.

Your relationship with your mother could have been adversarial if you were born at the time of the full Moon. You may have perceived her as working against you or what you wanted to do. You saw her as a reflection of your own inner struggles for expression and, as such, she could have been a valuable mirror. The full Moon provides perspective on what had been building. What was good or not so good about that phase of the process, what was or was not fulfilling. As the Moon is waning each month, moving from full to new, the emphasis is on learning from the previous two weeks. You can eliminate what didn't work and keep what did. This pattern is especially true for you if you were born when the Moon was in its waning phase. For anyone, however, this phase indicates a tendency to be more inclined to tear down structures that were previously built either by you in the preceding two weeks or by society itself. You will try to share with others the information you have gathered from the cycle now coming to a close. If the Moon was close to new in your natal chart, or as the Moon comes close to new each month, the orientation is to eliminate the old and decaying and prepare for the new birth.

For the Moon to be able to go through its entire cycle in twenty-eight days it must change sign every two to three days; as such it is the fastest moving of the planets. This changeable pattern is reflected in your degree of spontaneity and ability to flow with life. If you have a prominent Moon, such as conjunct an angle (house cusps one, four, seven or ten), or in the signs Aries, Gemini, Cancer, Libra, Sagittarius, or Pisces, or if you have a lot of planets in Cancer or Cancer rising, you tend to be very receptive to your environment. You can be spontaneous and immediate in your interactions or very moody and erratic. If this pattern is too strong, you may feel as if your whole life is spent in momentary flow. The Moon indicates the way in which you create the daily content of your life. If you are too much in the moment you may be all content with no form. No context of meaning within which to function. The Moon reminds you that life is lived in the here-and-now; all we really have is the eternal present. But it is important to create a balance between where you are and where you choose to go. This not only expands your perspective, but provides a sense of control and empowerment over your life that enables you to enjoy life even as you are growing within it.

THE FOURTH HOUSE

The area of life associated with Cancer is the fourth house. The fourth house is a water house just as Cancer is a water sign. The three water houses, four, eight and twelve, are each intricate and complex. Many astrologers assume that the first house is of greatest importance because it deals with the personality, or the expression of self to others. But the fourth house is also of fundamental significance because it pertains to your internal and primal relationship to yourself. As a water house it can indicate your thirst to get to know yourself in the deepest and most significant ways possible. The complexity of this house is evidenced by the fact that this relationship exists on several different levels of experience. The relationship you share with you can be physical, familial, emotional, psychological and spiritual. Physically, the fourth house is the home, the conditions you need and create in your residence. If you have an earth sign on the cusp, or Venus in the fourth, you may prefer rural to urban. If the Sun is in your fourth you want to be expressive and creative within your home. You could also be a builder of homes, a developer or a real estate agent. If Mercury is in your fourth, you may periodically change residences. Mars in the fourth implies that you have a strong drive to define and express yourself in your home. Jupiter in the fourth would see the home as a place to expand, to learn and have the potential to feel deep feelings of joy. Saturn in the fourth could cause you to want to own property, but you may also feel restricted by or overly responsible for your home. Neptune in the fourth wants the home to be a sanctuary, a place to go to be with the Higher Self, and tune out the mundane world. Uranus in the fourth implies a unique, unusual or unstable home. Pluto in the fourth sees the home as a place of transformation.

The fourth house is also representative of your relationship to your family, both in present time as well as family of origin. For example, with the Sun in the fourth you could strongly identify with the activity of both your childhood family as well as that of your adult life. The sign on the cusp of the fourth, the condition of the ruling planet of that sign, as well as any planets in that house, all define your needs and experiences within a family context. Your experience with your childhood family contained important programming about such things as how you feel about and relate to yourself and those closest to you. But just as we don't use the position of the Moon to blame or condemn Mom for who we are, so do we need to accept responsibility for our fourth house and childhood as being indicative of what our needs are for learning and personal growth in this most private of areas. With Mars in your fourth house, there might have been conflict in the childhood home, but with it came assertiveness. Neptune could indicate a dysfunctional family due to alcoholism by one or both parents. But with it came the opportunity to learn the importance of avoiding such patterns of escapism yourself. In many ways, it was this fundamental experience that created your emotional and psychological roots—your foundation in life. Feelings of emotional insecurity could result from Uranus in the fourth. You could have a sense of inner peace from the Sun in your fourth. Saturn implies a tendency to feel lonely and fearful as a response to a cold and controlling environment in childhood. If you feel confident, joyful and well-integrated you could have Jupiter in the fourth. The Sun or Moon in the fourth suggests a close bond with your family, a tendency to identify with your roots, and the conditioning of that time. Pluto also implies deep connections and strong, karmic ties with your family. But Pluto is the energy of transformation. It's an important part of your development that periodically you release and let go of those values, beliefs, and behaviors that you learned in the past, but which are no longer meaningful to you. It can be difficult to let go of that to which you are so attached. But failure to do so causes you to carry endless excess emotional and psychological baggage that is both weighing you down and blocking your growth. Even as an adult, with Pluto in the fourth, you must update what you are doing with your family, and how and why you are doing it that way.

Just as the Moon provides a reflected image of your soul, so the fourth house presents a picture of your past. Emotionally and psychologically, this past is configured by your family. Spiritually, the past includes past life experiences, especially those that you most identified with or were attached to, and have chosen to resolve this time around. So the condition of the fourth house is significant in illuminating who you are and where you're coming from in terms of your evolutionary experience.

Consequently it can provide insight into not only the condition of your childhood, but why you chose it and what your part in it was.

In a mundane sense, this orientation to the past can lead to being nostalgic for the "good old days and ways." You can enjoy the study of history or simply be a pack rat who has difficulty letting go of anything from your past, from possessions to programming to people.

The fourth house represents the spiritual river of life. Even as the first house overtly expresses "I am, this is me," the fourth questions, "who am I really?" As you look within, you can begin unwrapping the different levels of experience. In a most obvious sense, I am the resident of my house, the father or mother of my children. But that's not really who I am. I am my parents' child, the carrier of tribal programming. But who am I? I am the result of limitless previous incarnations, developing to the point I am now. But am I nothing more than the sum total of past personal experience? Am I nothing more than my place or role in my family? Who am I? As you keep digging in the fourth house, you eventually come to its deepest level which can be characterized as the spiritual river of life. This is the life force that emanates from Spirit and flows through everything. This river nurtures and sustains all beings. By becoming aware of the river, diving into it and swimming around from time to time, you realize your connection to all things that are, that have been, or that will be.

The Chaldeans of the ancient Middle East described the Cancerian experience as The Gate of Man, the portal through which the soul descends at birth. The Greeks maintained that it was the goddess Demeter who created the Eleusian Mysteries, which taught about eternal life, the cycle of death and rebirth. In this context, the fourth house conveys information about the circumstances of not only the beginning of your life but those at the end as well. Usually the conditions in which an incarnation ends, physically, emotionally and domestically, indicate the conditions under which the next life begins. Through exercise of free will, however, you can change the quality of those conditions. For example, Saturn in the fourth house suggests a childhood in which you may have felt very lonely and isolated from those around you. You may have had to take on responsibilities for yourself or others in your family at an early age. It may seem as if your old age will be spent in loneliness and isolation, restricted from enjoying the twilight years. But, if during this lifetime, you work on Saturn issues—if you become aware of limits and boundaries, develop self-control and self-discipline, and overcome your fears by conscientiously working to achieve specific goals—you create a different scenario. In it, you can become a wise and loving parent and grandparent, surrounded by your family in a mutually appreciative and supportive way. The next cycle of incarnation will reflect this picture and the growth it represents.

Uranus in the fourth house implies an unconventional family and a childhood in which extreme changes may have occurred suddenly, undermining your sense of emotional security. To overcome the potential to recreate those inconsistencies in your senior years, realize the lesson of Uranus in the fourth. Uranus is the energy of uniqueness. Much of what happened to you as a child threw you back on your unique self. Embrace that part of you—explore and express it within your family—to free yourself from the karma of the unexpected and undesired in your family life in later years. You are freed to create an environment in keeping with who you really are, while not undermining your security in the process.

The intricacy and complexity of the fourth house results from the fact that its energy can be experienced and expressed on four different levels. Spiritually, it represents the connection to life itself. It's the place to go to satisfy the deep thirst to know who you really are. At the cultural level, the fourth house expresses the foundation of civilization. It deals with the family in a tribal or clan sense. At the emotional or psychological level, the fourth house relates to your early childhood and environment. Your past can indicate your present needs for domestic or familial experience. Finally, at the physical level, the fourth house represents the home, the actual domestic structure itself and the type of domestic environment we need.

CANCER AND THE BODY

Cancer is the sign of nurturing and nourishment. It is significant that the parts of the body that it rules pertain to these experiences. The stomach, the womb, the breasts and bone marrow are Cancerian parts of the body. Cancer also rules the posterior lobe of the pituitary gland. The hormones secreted by this gland have several functions. One is to produce somatatrophic hormone that controls the rate of growth and has a relationship with the milk glands in the breasts. Cancer also rules according to the principle of containing, especially parts of the body that contain fluid. In addition to the parts of the body just named, Cancer also rules the sinuses and eyeballs. Cancer also functions in a protective way and as such it rules all coverings in the body. The membranes of the brain, the lungs, and the heart are Cancerian.

The Moon also has a function that pertains to health. Because its primary function is to deal with feelings, the position of the Moon gives indications of how easily this is done. The more stress or emotional anxiety is unconscious or unreleased the greater the tendency for physical ill-health to be a byproduct of that syndrome. The Moon also provides a picture of your childhood. Childhood or inherited diseases can be seen in the position of the natal Moon. These problems are often situations left over or unresolved from previous lives. They show up quickly to be finally dealt with or, in the case of conditions that become chronic, provide some of the major work or challenges of the incarnation. The Moon can also suggest the emotional and psychological state we function in, usually as a result of the relationship to family of origin and ways of being nurtured. Some people believe that emotional or psychological imbalances are the prime causes of physical ailments. If your relationship to your inner self is clear, there is no climate for illness to take hold.

The Moon also rules fluids in the body, excluding the blood and lymph which are covered by other signs. The Moon reflects disorders or imbalances which pertain to water and mucus membranes. Sometimes these problems manifest as allergies. The Moon in the sixth house, especially conjunct the Moon's south node, or the dragon's tail, can indicate allergies.

CONCLUSIONS

The first three signs provide the opportunity to create yourself, stabilize that self, and integrate new information within the self. Now the creation reaches out beyond the self to those who are closest to you. Aries defines the self according to what it *does*; Taurus defines it according to what it *has*; Gemini defines it according to what it *knows*. Cancer defines the self according to its connection to a unit of people greater than the individual. Cancer identifies with a family, a tribe, a clan. Cancer is the sign of nurturing, care-giving and the parent-child relationship. The signs of the first quadrant are "young signs" in that their function is to begin the process of life in three modes. Cancer continues that pattern of newness by adding the ingredient of water which provides energy for flow and lubrication. Water seeks a container, so a prime need for Cancer is security. To insure the continuity of that security, Cancer has the ability to remain very focused, concentrating on that which promotes the safety and well being of self, especially within the family unit.

Cancer contributes to the domestic reality by partaking of the roles of both child and parent. In its child-like mode it is present, spontaneous and expressive of emotional energy. If you are centered and self-loving in your child-like mode, you like to play. One form of recreation that is specifically Cancerian is collecting. Sometimes Cancer merely collects containers in case, at some point in the future, they have a collection of something that they want to save and protect. Similarly Cancer can collect and be protective of their memories. As a result they may have a collection of keepsakes and souvenirs. Being sentimental and nostalgic can generate interest in things created in the past like antiques. You could be interested in studying genealogy and pursuing your family history. These qualities can also cause you to reminisce about fond memories from your youthful, playful past. These interests can enable you to broaden what might otherwise be a narrow perspective or experience in life. With more information about the past you can extend your personal data bank about these things to the points of their origin. These tendencies can also, however, keep you attached to the past and stuck in situations that have little bearing on the present. If so, you will likely be limited in the awareness of life.

As a Cancer manifesting its childlike nature you are like a river flowing spontaneously through life. In your centered mode you would see people standing on the banks of the river and call out to them, "it's a hot day, why don't you jump in and play with me and together we can feel refreshed and happy!" In your uncentered childlike mode, however, you would demand "I'm bored and I'm lonely. I insist that you come in the river and play with me. I don't care if it is cold and rainy."

As the uncentered, self-absorbed, pouting child you would tend to avoid being confronted about anything that would hurt your feelings or call upon you to grow up and take some responsibility for yourself. You can be hyper sensitive and over-react, tending to take things too personally. Even if a comment made or action taken in your presence has nothing to do with you, you may lack that perspective and assume it was directed at you. You can be very subjective, relating to life strictly from your own personal point of view, and failing to see a broader range of possible interpretations of any here-and-now scenario.

In your centered and self-loving parental mode you are extremely receptive to others' needs. Your highest priority is your home and family, and you are capable of creating a comfortable, attractive residence for yourself and others to enjoy. You can be protective of your loved ones, and identify very strongly with your role as homemaker or provider. You can enjoy working in the domestic arena, whether you are male or female. There's an old expression that "every home needs a Cancer." This suggests that Cancer energy helps keep a residence clean and cozy, and the family feeling safe and secure.

If you have personal planets in Cancer or the Moon in the tenth house (of career) you might prefer working at home. If you have Venus, the planet of art, in Cancer or Taurus you can be very talented in, and oriented toward, domestic arts such as cooking. You could enjoy creating with food or simply enjoy spending a lot of time in the kitchen. Or if you have creative energy in the fourth house, perhaps Mars or the Sun, you can be interested in real estate, interior decoration or professions that involve the food or lodging industries. Careers related to young children or the elderly also provide realistic and fulfilling outlets.

If you are manifesting your parent-like Cancerian energy from an uncentered, unself-loving perspective you could be excessive in your care giving. Even though you may be motivated by sympathy for someone else's condition, feeling their needs in a deeply personal way, you could give more than is healthy for either of you. In a classic co-dependent pattern, you could sacrifice your own well being by trying to get someone else's life together for them. You become over protective, possibly to a point of smothering the ones you are trying so hard to help.

An equally uncentered pattern, but one not as well motivated, creates a tendency to be possessive and controlling. You can be very tenacious in hanging on to people in your domestic or familial situations to satisfy your need for emotional security. This is Demeter creating draught and famine because her daughter was no longer part of her life. It's a "Mother Knows Best" scenario in which you are always telling those closest to you what is best for them. In this mode you are actually using your nurturing as a tool or weapon. Only if others conform to your demands and expectations will you provide them the care they want or need. It's as if the primary decision that you have to make is whether your energy is going to be used to make others happy or to be used for the purpose of self-gratification.

One of the keys to creating a center for yourself and a loving attitude toward others is to balance the cardinality with the water. The cardinal part of your nature is action-oriented. The Cancerian traits of care-giving and nurturing are active expressions. They suggest that you have the potential to be assertive and demonstrate leadership in certain situations. Yet, contrasted with the sensitivity and receptivity of the water, the cardinal qualities seem paradoxical or out of place. If you are overly assertive, demanding that others allow you to take care of them, people will tend to push you away. If you are overly sensitive, you may withdraw from them. Sometimes your withdrawal could be a result of something your intuition is picking up. You could feel as if someone or some situation is not safe. To protect your feelings and your security just stay within yourself and away from them. As a highly intuitive sign you could be correct in your perceptions and this withdrawal is appropriate. You could, however, misread or misinterpret a situation and depart inappropriately. On the other hand, you might assume that other people have your intuitive ability to read people and your sensitivity to understand other people's needs. If they do and the other person is not meeting your unspoken needs, it may be that they simply don't like you. Of course, that might not be true. It may be that the person simply is not that sensitive or intuitively aware of who you are, how you feel or what you need. You might build a big "case" out of this slight, yet keep those feelings locked within you. To others with whom you relate, this can be confusing or even painful. It is important to use some of your cardinal-assertiveness at this point, and express what is going on inside. Communicate as directly as possible, stating to the other individual, "Well, excuse me, but these happen to be my feelings that you are stepping on. These are my points of sensitivity and I wish you would take them into consideration when relating to me." Of course, if the other person doesn't change their behavior after such a clear and simple statement, then you are certainly justified in withdrawing. But until your feelings and points of view have been made clear, withdrawing can be unfair to all concerned and lead to unfortunate consequences.

Cancer needs action to be centered and self-loving. You need to be assertive. Take initiative on the stage of life, but do it in as warm and loving a way as is possible and appropriate. This can be at the physical level, by providing food and a comfortable, hospitable home, or on the emotional level by responding sympathetically to others. Demonstrate your receptivity and nurturing through action, but combine that with a definite expression of your needs as well. Remember that *receptivity* is not the same as *passivity*—receptivity is an active state, passivity is not. By being actively receptive you are creating an environment within which you can function in a comfortable and secure way. You can fulfill your need to provide support as well as fulfill your own need to be supported.

As the first of the water signs, Cancer is the first sign that can be consciously aware of and cultivate spirituality. In fact, Cancer has been called the birth of spirituality. It can be extremely psychic and intuitive, drawing on the mystical forces of the unseen world. The myths that pertain to the archetype represented by Cancer contain numerous references to this. For example, when Demeter was mourning the loss of her daughter, she became aware of eternal life and created the Eleusian Mystery rites that taught about and celebrated this universal law.

Each sign contributes something special to the experience of life—something that helps transcend the mundane attachments to the material plane—so that by expanding awareness, evolution can take place. The Cancerian contribution is the awareness of, and the ability to live in, the eternal present. There is only the *Now*. Tomorrow never gets here, it just becomes the present.

Being-here-now, in a Cancerian sense, enables you to become aware of your feelings, sensitivities and emotional needs. It also brings up the warmth, sympathy and nurturing that can underlie your relationships with others. By balancing these two patterns, you realize how important it is to be aware of and share your inner world with those closest to you. Even if you don't have any Cancer energy in your horoscope, try to get in touch with your emotional state and express those feelings and emotions. Otherwise, the tendency is to hang on to them. This unreleased emotional energy is stored in the solar plexus area—the personal power center, the ego center. If you are not aware of your internal world, you tend to ego-identify with whatever emotional state you are not expressing. It's as if you allow the feelings to have dominion over you. As this energy builds up, it's blocked from rising up the spine to the higher centers and awaken spiritual consciousness. To be spontaneously and appropriately expressive of the feelings moment to moment, situation by situation, is to be focused in the present and keep the ego pure. You are more connected to the deeper rhythms of life, feel more comfortable within yourself and are more able to establish a sense of place and belonging in your social and familial context.

The *I Ching* counsels that the woman is the foundation of the family and that the family is the foundation of society. By developing the feminine qualities of care-giving, sympathy and receptivity we are each creating a secure base within ourselves. This base enables us to develop the ability to be self-nurturing. From a place of self-nurturing we can take care of those closest to us and allow them to demonstrate their care for us in healthy ways. We can become more conscious in our parenting. By establishing strong, healthy families we establish communities that reflect the condition of those families. Ultimately this can extend to the creation of conscious communities that function in tribal or clan-like ways in that each individual unit, person or group relates to each other in open, supportive, care-giving ways.

LEO

Each quadrant begins with a cardinal sign. These are the signs of action, of beginnings. They are followed by the fixed signs. These are the signs that stabilize and preserve what the cardinals have begun. Whereas the cardinal signs bring movement, the fixed signs offer continuity. Whereas the cardinal signs generate new growth, the fixed signs deepen the awareness and development of that growth.

Cancer, the water sign, led off the second quadrant with activity oriented toward the personal and family life. Its manifestation is creative, but internal and subtle. Leo is the second sign of the second quadrant. It continues the personal direction of activity, but as a fire sign it is more outgoing in its manifestation. Leo is the sign of creative self-expression. It is the sign of the exaltation of self. The Sun is in Leo every year from July 22 to August 23. Leo says, "I will."

The first fire sign is Aries, Leo is the second. These signs are 120 degrees away from each other, an angular relationship called trine. Energy moves the easiest and with the greatest harmony when in a trine formation. Signs that are trine to each other are also of the same element. The energy of planets that are in signs of the same element are able to flow smoothly because each of the elements represent a similar level of consciousness. Their manifestation is on a similar harmonic frequency. The energy is able to flow so smoothly because each of the elements gravitate to a similar level of consciousness. Fire, for example, is the creative, light giving expression of energy. Planets that are trine (Δ) to each other in fire signs find mutual support to manifest themselves in outgoing, dynamic ways. Karmically, planets are trine when you have worked to develop that positive connection in past lives. There are, however, potential drawbacks to this "good news." If you have already learned how to generate positive interaction in the past, what is your motivation to continue to learn how to use that combination in consistent harmony this time around? Often there isn't and that can result in the energy flowing at a relatively low octave. For example, with fire signs, you could submerge the enthusiasm and creativity within a self-serving, egocentric demeanor. Another potential problem with trines is that you might take the harmonic flow of energy for granted. Human beings seem to be more oriented toward noticing and complaining about what doesn't work rather than being aware of and feeling grateful for what does. It is beneficial to a peaceful state of mind to recognize harmony and appreciate the tools and strengths it offers. If you have trines, remember that you have them because you have worked for them in the past, and were successful in that work. Use the energy now, but continue to work with it in such a way that you take advantage of what has already been done, and strive to do more.

THE MYTHS

Leo is a *yang* sign, and as such its myths all pertain to male archetypes. Many of them relate to the image and concept of the king. For example, the ancient Ethiopian monarchy claimed to originate from the descendants of Solomon and Sheba. Sheba is said to be the daughter of the Sun, and the original empress of Ethiopia. This lineage emanates from the King of Kings himself, called *Jah* by the Ethiopians. The followers of *Jah* form the religious group known as the Rastafarians, found in Ethiopia and Jamaica.

In Egypt, statues were built in which Isis (the Great Mother) was suckling Horus, the god of the Sun. It is as if from Cancer, the female principle, emerges all things and demonstrates her power as the creator of all things including the Sun itself. This also connects Cancer with its succeedant sign, Leo.

The Middle Ages developed the myth of King Arthur, a young man of humble beginnings who was destined to rule his country. Many able-bodied men throughout England attempted to establish their right to the throne by pulling the sword *Excalibur* from a stone. All but Arthur failed. It was he who was able to draw the sword from the stone, thereby establishing his rightful place as monarch. This is the story of an individual who asserted himself and established a powerful position in the world. He gathered around him the illustrious and legendary Knights of the Round Table. The tales told about the Knights were exciting stories of heroes and heroines. There were long narratives about lonely vigils and dangerous quests. But they also instructed the listener about everything from chivalry—proper relations between men and women—to the quest for spiritual enlightenment—the story of the holy grail. In the center of this group of heroic figures stood Arthur, the leader and organizer, the one who established moral and ethical standards and who drew to him all who deserved to be counted among the ranks of the finest.

Perhaps the ultimate monarch was the Greek god Zeus. In the positive sense, he organized his peers, the other Olympian gods, to overthrow their oppressor and father, Cronus. On one level this is the tale of the emerging adolescent asserting himself against the power, values and behaviors of the older generation. In so doing, he established himself as the new power, free to create the new patterns for others to follow. He was artistically portrayed as a powerful man with a flowing beard, seated on a throne. His implements of power were thunder and lightning.

Another predominant feature of the Zeus myths involved his relationships with women. Many of the goddesses with whom he was involved—such as Metis and Themis—were archetypes of the Great Goddess. This is indicative of a fundamental shift in the cultural paradigm. It represents the union of the symbol of matrilineal society with that of the male-oriented. But his behavior in those relationships did not honor either the eminence of the goddesses, nor the significance of their union. Zeus was a philanderer. His first wife was Hera, like himself an Olympian, an equal and another archetype of the Goddess. After promising to marry and remain loyal, he betrayed her again and again, arousing her wrath and symbolically beginning the process of undermining female power in male-dominated society.

In the positive sense, Zeus represents the exaltation of reason, competence and will. He symbolizes the ability to control the outcome of external situations through the force of his presence and creativity. The negative side of this archetype is demonstrated through the blatant disregard for social mores and others' feelings. These actions may demonstrate power over others, but they do so at the expense of accessibility and connection to others.

The Old Testament hero Samson is also a mythic symbol for Leo. In Hebrew, the root of the word Samson means "belonging to the Sun" (the ruling planet of Leo). Similarly the root of the word Delilah, Samson's consort, is the same as the Hebrew word for Aquarius, the sign opposite Leo. The source of Samson's legendary strength was his hair. As long as it remained uncut it provided him with remarkable warrior power. The reference to hair evokes the image of the lion's mane. The lion is also in evidence in the Samson tale. On a journey with his parents, they were attacked by a lion, which Samson killed with his bare hands. Upon returning from their journey, they found that the carcass of the lion had become a beehive. At a party shortly after that, Samson challenged the guests to decipher this riddle: "Out of the eater came forth food, and out the strong came forth sweetness." He wagered thirty linen garments and thirty changes of clothing that no one would crack the code, an expansive and expensive gesture typical of a male Leo. And the riddle itself provides a good description of the sign—strong and powerful without and sweet and gentle within.

The negative side of Leo is also depicted in this myth. Samson was betrayed by his wife and, in retaliation, he burned the fields of the entire community of Philistines. Leo is a fire sign, and can be vengeful. When the Philistines retaliated by attacking the Hebrews, Samson killed thousands of them with the jawbone of an ass—royal retribution. Eventually he forgave his wife, visited her and offered tokens of his affection. Another typical act for a Leo—generosity and magnanimity.

THE GLYPH: ♌

There are several ways in which the glyph for Leo has been interpreted. The most simplistic is that it represents the tail of a lion or the outline of its flowing mane. It can suggest the rough outline of a heart, the part of the body Leo rules. In a more exalted context, it was used in ancient Dionysian mysteries to symbolize the phallus. By extension, it can be seen as an image of a single male sperm cell. What makes this interpretation most interesting is that it connects back to Cancer, the sign of the Eternal River of Life. As such, Cancer pertains to the feminine and the soul, Leo is oriented toward the masculine and the ego. Combining the essence of the female with the essence of the male, life is created. Cancer and Leo are the two signs for which the experience of procreation, children and parenting is most important. This is the marriage of soul with spirit, a union to be encountered several more times as we proceed through the zodiac.

The most esoteric meaning of this glyph is that it is purported to be a remnant of the royal coat of arms of the lost continent of Mu. According to legend, Mu was located somewhere in the Pacific Ocean. It disappeared, or at least became uninhabited, several thousand years ago. Mu was known to the ancients as the Empire of the Sun. Its crest was translated as meaning "the ruler." At its core is the symbol of the Sun, the symbol of power, creativity and eternal motion. If Mu existed was it a monarchy, and if it was, was this its coat of arms? These are interesting, provocative questions. Unfortunately, the answers are unknowable. More important are the symbols emphasized in the image. They certainly pertain to qualities of the Leonine nature, which are stylized in the simple curved line that represents Leo.

THE TOTEM: 🦁

We are all familiar with the idea that the lion is the king of the jungle. We project onto this beast human qualities of honor and dignity. Like the totems for the other signs, the lion was chosen for Leo by combining behavioral characteristics of people born at that time of year with a picture derived by connecting the fixed stars of a particular constellation—a kind of cosmic connecting the dots. Since the human imagination defines these pictures, it becomes a very subjective activity. For example, the constellation Leo was not always seen as the lion. In the third millennium BC, the Babylonians saw it as a sleeping or lying animal. They called it the Great Dog.

Most Western cultures have used the lion as a symbol for Leo. The Egyptians decorated their temples along the Nile with lion's whisker-like bristles. This was not only a way of showing reverence, but also a way of honoring the lion and raising it to an exalted and religious status. In meso-America, felines were artistically depicted as rulers and deities. In the Old Testament, the tribe of Judah was under the influence of the Lion. According to legend, Judah, the son of Jacob, was a Leo. In the story of Samson and Delilah, Samson's power came through his hair—hair like the mane of the lion. The Ethiopians, who traced the lineage of their monarchy back to Solomon and Sheba, referred to their king as the Lion of Judah, the "King of Kings."

Gautama the Buddha had a pet lion. It was said that the Buddha lay down in the position the lion assumed when resting. This Lion had miraculous powers and when the Buddha died, the lion did, too.

The Greek hero Hercules slew a Lion which had an invincible hide and then used the hide for his own armor. In Rome, the Lion symbolized the power of the Roman Empire. The practice of throwing Christians to the Lions was a symbol of power, indicating that they expected the Empire would be around long after the Christians ceased to exist. So much for expectations.

In the Middle Ages, the king of Britain, Richard the Lion Hearted led the West in their Crusades against the Moslems. In the Moslem faith, Mohammed's right hand man was named Ali who was called the Lion of God.

The image of the Lion is found in ancient times in the Old Testament, Greek, Roman and North African mythologies. It's also a totem common to the major religions—Buddhism, Islam and Christianity. In each era and in each culture, the lion was associated with positions of power and leadership. Depending on the values of the culture itself, this prominence was displayed either in a spiritual or secular context. If the society was a theocracy—as in England during the Middle Ages—the lion represented both. It is a totem attributed to notable leaders who have demonstrated great will and strength.

MODE AND ELEMENT

Leo is the sign of *fixed fire*. Its influence is hot and dry. The image of something fixed and fiery is the Sun, the ruling planet of Leo. This connection implies the radiance and dynamism that Leo can manifest. Leo's fixed nature provides an indomitable will. Your orientation is to protect, preserve and persist. Beginning the second third of the zodiac, there is the need to maintain all the work of self-awareness and development of the first four signs, and to grow still further. In this portion of the zodiac, there is movement beyond the self and the personal world into the realm of social interaction. You need to project yourself into new situations, but in a safe and secure manner.

Like the first fixed sign, Taurus, Leo is a creature of habit. Issues of consistency, stability and security usually rank high on the Leonine priority scale. Like Taurus, you are extremely loyal, especially to people or activities that have personal meaning to you. As such, your values are of great significance in defining and maintaining those habits and loyalties. Like Taurus, unexamined values and attitudes can keep you in stagnant behavioral patterns, with the attendant tendency to try to control others. As you investigate your values, pay attention to those activities in which you radiate and shine—situations that enable your leadership and organizational skill to manifest. The task of the Taurus is to stabilize the body and the self on the earthly plane. This promotes continuity and survival and provides a strong foundation upon which to grow. Leo is one of the signs building on that foundation. You seek to preserve and protect that defined, emerging self. Your task is to promote its flowering by doing things that you love to do and sharing that love with others.

While Taurus values practical things, Leo is more oriented toward luxuries. Taurus with its fixed quality must remember to update its needs; Leo must remember to update its desires and ensure that it does not become overly attached to inappropriate or outdated attitudes and possessions.

Your fire indicates that you are creative, and Leo is the sign of self-expression. You like to manifest what you feel, what you are inspired by or are interested in. This makes you tend to externalize yourself to others. Leo is the sign of illumination. Like the Sun you dynamically put out to others everything about yourself. The radiance of the fire also implies a sense of enthusiasm and exuberance that you bring with you to all your activities and that orient you to doing things that enhance and support those characteristics. Consequently, Leo is oriented to fun. Hobbies, sports, amusements and entertainment are some of the experiences which could be important to you and which you pursue just for the sake of doing them.

The fiery radiance can also render Leo a natural showperson who loves the limelight and center stage. Leo is one of the two signs that can be especially drawn to the theater. You could also demonstrate your dramatic inclinations in your own personal life, however, and be continually doing things that draw attention to yourself. With your fixed tendencies, make sure that you have not become overly identified with attributes and activities that put you in the limelight, in a place of prominence or prestige, to the extent that one of your needs becomes approval from others. This is a form of dependency that is preventing you from growing to new heights or levels of experience. Be careful as well to not become attached to desire itself.

The first fire sign, Aries, is oriented toward acting out the fire. It is independent and enjoys doing its own thing in its own way. Being fixed, Leo is more oriented toward being the center of things. In a positive sense this can manifest as radiating outward in dynamic, loving support of others. Being more socially-oriented than Aries you want your warmth to have a positive influence on others. This same radiance can also be motivated by the desire to be consistently demonstrating yourself through the expression of your own ideas and interests.

The combination of a fixed nature and fire suggests strong self-confidence, enabling you to burn through situations which block other signs. The negative side of the experience is a tendency to always be in this radiant, outgoing mode. This limits your ability to be aware of what is going on around you. This could take the form of not listening to feedback from others or being unaware of your affect on others. In other words, you may be blinded by your own light. You might burn other people by being too ebullient or through sheer force of will. You may not do this consciously and probably not maliciously. If you are stuck in rigid patterns, however, your failure to change could lead to a situation that is falling apart and needs renewal. You could try to control or dominate others simply as a way of maintaining a sense of stability and safety in that situation. Failure to do the work that precipitates change leads to power patterns. Otherwise, if you are updating yourself and your patterns periodically, the tendency to draw others away from their own paths and onto yours is either a result of your magnetism or overly abundant outgoing energy.

There are two results of this pattern. One is to be so oblivious of the interaction between yourself and others that you can unknowingly attract those who may drain you. They are attracted to your warmth, dynamism and light either because theirs pales in comparison or they are too confused or lazy to develop what they do have. Your failure to be aware of this can lead to being taken advantage of. On the other hand, the lack of insight or self-awareness can cause you to drain yourself. As the only sign ruled by the Sun, you may unconsciously assume that you possess an unlimited supply of energy. So you go and go, and do and do, not realizing where your limits are until you wake up depleted. You might call a halt to some or all of your activities until you regenerate or you may drag yourself through the experience. In either case you are wasting time, you are not enjoying life, and you are not functioning at your peak. In some ways, you share this problem with the other fire signs—Aries and Sagittarius. You must strive for a balance between the outgoing energy and the incoming energy. Without that balance, you can burn yourself out. This constant manifestation of self—this constant output of energy—can be coming from the need to protect yourself. It indicates that you are vulnerable. In that state, it may seem as if the best strategy is to strengthen your offense to compensate for what you may feel is a weak defense. You project and radiate a boundless energy, hoping that no one finds your vulnerable spots. Sometimes this can lead you to become a great braggart or excessively theatrical. It is important to realize that the obnoxious parts of Leo are coming from an internal sense of weakness and pain. Others may assume that the "Leo as showperson" is full of themselves to such a degree that their lives bog down in ego-mania. Leo feels the need to justify the self by always "being right" in a discussion. This tendency is not based on strength or self-love, but on weakness and fear. It is useful to distinguish between someone who is centered in a self-loving way, and selfish in a self-absorbed way.

The combination of fixed-fire energy connects you to the source of life itself—the limitless quality of love. That connection can influence your life in many ways. It can stimulate you do to things that you love to do. It can orient you toward relationships that are loving, playful and romantic. It can also draw you to a higher octave of experience by inspiring you to use the love energy to improve the quality of others' lives. As such, Leo is one of the healers of the zodiac. There are several signs oriented to healing—Gemini, for example, heals through communication. Leo, on the other hand, heals through the river of love. Through the expansion of the heart *chakra* or energy center you heal through your own radiant presence and by sharing your strong self-love and self-confidence with others. This isn't necessarily as a healing professional. It might be enough to visit a sick friend in the hospital, or to be with someone who feels down. Through your ability to project love energy—through who you are as much as what you do—you can catalyze others to feel better. To heal in a more structured, formal or professional mode you would need to feel a sense of personal direction, a mission or purpose in life. It's not going to just be a job. It's even more than an occupation.

THE RULING PLANET

Leo is ruled by the Sun (☉). It is the only sign ruled by the Sun as Cancer is the only sign ruled by the Moon. All the other planets either rule two signs and/or are co-ruling a sign with another planet. This is one factor that distinguishes the Sun and Moon as being of particular importance in the natal chart. This is one reason why Cancer and Leo are expressions of fundamental archetypal experiences.

The Sun is the source of life, light and energy in our solar system. Its influence is masculine in that it is outgoing, externalizing and individuating. The sign and house position of the Sun in your natal horoscope delineates a major way in which you tap into and manifest that energy. The Sun represents "I" consciousness, the awareness of self, who you view yourself to be. It defines your basic likes and dislikes, your sense of self-worth and your ability to love. This, in turn, defines your ability to respond to love.

The Sun represents the ego—the bridge between the body and the soul. This implies that you are simultaneously involved in two separate activities during an incarnation. The first requires being in your body. There are many subcategories of this grounding process. You are trained to do some of these things from childhood: discharge responsibilities in relationships, family and job. The other parts of grounding require awareness of your body and your specific needs for financial security, material comforts, health, affection, sex and a connection with nature. To be grounded doesn't require that your needs in each category be totally satisfied. But you at least need to be working at becoming aware of each of these categories in your life. What are your needs in each area? What can you do to fulfill those needs? As long as you are somewhere in that process, maybe becoming aware of certain things even as you are satisfying others, you are grounded.

If your being is in your body, if you are discharging your earth plane responsibilities, the next step is to give permission to your soul to sprout wings and fly. This can manifest through such activities as meditation or prayer, tapping into your creative imagination or participating in group ritual or ceremony. Any activity that helps you to connect with and relate to that which is greater than you is beneficial for spiritual growth. You are taking into consideration your temporary, physical, earth plane existence as well as your eternal spiritual plane existence. If you are involved in these two activities in a way that works for you, that enables you to be responsible and fulfilled materially as well as growing and evolving spiritually, internally you are centered and balanced. Your ego in this sense acts as a catalyst. It stimulates interaction between yourself and others, but doesn't get in the way of that process. As a result you feel positive about yourself, have a good self-image and feel lovable. In general, you will manifest the more positive qualities of your Sun sign. On the other hand, if you are taking neither the responsibility for your earth plane existence, nor for your spiritual growth, you are off center and out of balance. If you are strict about and dedicated to your spiritual practice, but materially irresponsible or very materially-oriented with no spiritual development, you will still be off center. Even with consistent inner work but only partial attention to the multi-faceted earth plane, you are out of balance. In this scenario the ego gets in the way in your interaction with life and you will feel neither lovable nor positive about yourself. Your self-image is poor. You will tend to express your solar energy of self in terms of the more negative qualities of your Sun sign.

As the Sun is the creative center of our solar system, so does your natal Sun indicate your creative tendencies and abilities. The house in which the Sun is located in the natal chart will indicate the area of life in which you enjoy expressing yourself and the area of life within which you have the potential to be creative. Whatever house your natal Sun is located in provides you with similar interests and inclinations as people born with their Sun in the sign associated with that house. For example, a first house Sun in any sign will have similar attributes to the Sun in Aries, in that identity and self-development are important. If your Sun is in the first house the manner in which you project yourself with others will coincide with your sense of self-worth. The more centered you are the more you will express the positive qualities of the sign. The less centered you are, the greater will be your tendency to manifest the unpleasant. Usually with Sun in the first house your Sun and ascendant will be the same, greatly emphasizing the nature and qualities of that sign. You will be more direct and authentic about expressing yourself in a "what you see is what you get" mode.

The Sun in the second house places emphasis on stability, resourcefulness and values. Just as the Sun in the sign Taurus symbolizes the need to establish a firm material base within which to survive and from which to grow, so does the Sun in the second house define you as a survivor. You are your own greatest resource, provided that you are centered, self-loving, and have a sense of your self-worth.

The Sun in the third house (communication, short journeys, extended family) indicates the potential to be creative in those ways. It also implies the fulfillment you experience through expressing yourself in them. Sun in the fourth house is similar to Sun in Cancer: home and family are of fundamental significance. You can be a nurturing, caregiving person, and those closest to you can provide you with great happiness and fulfillment. Be careful not to create a co-dependent relationship with your family, however, to the point that caring for others overrides your need to take care of yourself. Make sure you don't become dependent on your family to provide you with a sense of identity or security.

The Sun in the fifth house illuminates qualities that are essentially Leonine, even if your Sun is in another sign. You will be loving and generous to others, will enjoy sports and place high priority on self-expression. Your children will be important to you and you will tend to be a supportive, conscientious parent. You could also, however, have strong needs for personal recognition and spend too much time trying to be the center of attention.

The Sun in the sixth house can manifest certain Virgo qualities. You can be task-oriented, analytical and serviceful. You can identify with nature and enjoy such activities as gardening, hiking or camping. You may be concerned with your health, or be in a health-oriented profession. You can also be overly idealistic so be careful not to be too critical of others who don't measure up to your expectations.

The seventh house is oriented toward one-to-one relationship. If your Sun is in the seventh house, you have many of the same traits as a person with the Sun in Libra. You want harmony, equality and fairness in your life and your relationships. Striving for balance in your life is of utmost importance. This could be the balance between your professional and personal lives. It could also be the balance between being clear with others about who you are, yet remaining open to them sharing themselves with you. Avoid using cues in the form of feedback from others to define who you are. Try to avoid being judgmental of others or always seeing your problems as caused by others. This is a way of avoiding responsibility for who you are and what you need to do for growth.

With your Sun in the eighth house, the two most important experiences in your life will be personal transformation and intimate relationship. In Scorpio-like fashion you seek to understand life and people at the deepest level. Pursuing the fundamental truths of life catalyzes your consciousness and facilitates transformation in relationship. Failure to look within, both of yourself and what is around you, creates a dynamic whereby you can be deceitful and manipulative of others. You try to coerce them to be who you need them to be rather than working with them to breakthrough the barriers between you.

The Sun in the ninth house identifies with your higher mind and being a student of life. But just as people with the Sun in Sagittarius must remember to relate their ideas and concepts to real life, with your Sun in the ninth house, don't get lost in the ivory tower. You may become so idealistic or caught up in concepts and theories that you find yourself getting disappointed in the mundane affairs of life.

The tenth is the house of occupation. With the Sun in your natal tenth house, you tend to identify with your career and the public image and social status that accompany it. This is a wonderful placement for the Sun to manifest its creative leadership and organizational potential. If you are centered and self-loving, you should be successful and fulfilled in your profession. But uncentered, your ambition and competitiveness start to run the show. You become more concerned with demonstrating the trappings of success than really enjoying meaningful work.

With the Sun in the eleventh house, your friends are very important to you and you are a good friend to others. You shine in social situations involving both individuals and groups. With an eleventh house Sun, your independence is also important. Try to create a balance that enables you to feel comfortable and fulfilled in mutually beneficial social situations, while finding the time to experiment with your own uniqueness. Failure to create that balance can render you overly dependent on others to define you and the parameters of your life. Or you can take the alternate route and be a life-long rebel, one who is different for the sake of difference, to "prove" that you are unique.

The twelfth is the house of the subconscious mind. With the Sun here, you need to spend quality time alone each day. You could use that time in meditation practice, in creative pursuits or at peace in nature. These activities create an internal environment that enables you to have clear insights into your psyche and the spiritual nature of life. You could also feel called to a service field that is an extension and expression of your compassion or is of benefit to the world as a whole. Failure to cultivate the inner self can result in Pisces-like tendencies to undermine yourself through self-destructive attitudes or behavior.

The condition of the Sun can indicate your general state of vitality and health. This is further affected by aspects or angular relationships from other planets. For example, Mars trine the Sun indicates strong drive, assertiveness, and an action-orientation. You feel comfortable in the physical and athletic manifestation of yourself. Mars square the Sun, however, could render you too impulsive and risk-oriented to the extent that accidents or injuries could take place. You may struggle with self-expression, feeling repressed at some times, arrogant at others. On the other hand, Mars square or in opposition to Neptune suggests the possibility of feeling drained, especially by being too open and vulnerable to others. Saturn squared to or opposing the Sun can cause feelings of self-doubt or self-imposed limitation on the expression of your power and creativity. Physically, this aspect can cause you to feel inhibited or blocked.

As long as you operate from a centered and self-loving place, even the squares and oppositions can be turned into opportunities for growth. Neptune challenges you to look within and create a balance between the external manifestations of the Sun and the internal clarity of Neptune. By accepting the challenge you can learn how to integrate two aspects of yourself in a new way. Saturn squares and oppositions are about control. They teach you about the importance of overcoming your fear and taking responsibility for your life. Without doing that work, you would tend to give away your power to others or manipulate and usurp it from others. By doing the work the fear is overcome, you take responsibility for your own power and the physical or health obstacles are removed.

As a general rule, if there is a planet opposing the Sun in your natal chart, you will tend to identify with the energy symbolized by that planet. It's as if the Sun is illuminating that planet, making it easier for you to see. And it is incumbent on you to integrate that opposing planet into your sense of identity; but do it in a balanced, not extreme, way.

THE FIFTH HOUSE

The area of life that is associated with Leo is the fifth house. This is the "fun house" of the zodiac. At the most fundamental level, the fifth house, like Leo, is about love. It pertains to all the activities people love to do. Parties, hobbies, recreation and amusements are all examples of fifth house fun. All forms of entertainment fall into this category as well. Sports is also a fifth house activity and those who have significant energy there such as Mars, Jupiter or the Sun tend to be athletic.

The fifth is the house of creative self-expression. With Venus (art and beauty), Neptune (creative imagination), or the Sun (the creative force) in the fifth, the arts have a definite place in your life as a hobby or even as a profession. Neptune is especially oriented toward music, the theater and film. Mercury in the fifth provides the ability to create with words (writing) or the hands (crafts). Uranus brings originality and inspiration to the creative process, but it tends to be erratic with its energy. The inspiration may feel very strong for a short time and then dissipate suddenly.

Uranus in the fifth house also implies exploring new creative outlets, such as computer art, and forms of expression that are new to an individual's experience.

Pluto is the energy of transformation. It brings intensity and passion to the creative process. With Pluto in your fifth house you would want to generate a catharsis, a peak experience. You could be deliberate in developing a specific artistic skill and slow in expressing it. The act of creativity is, however, one that ideally would facilitate new realizations of awareness.

Saturn in the fifth is also cautious about creative expression, sometimes to the point of feeling too inhibited to do it all. As you learn to overcome those limits, Saturn can impel practical forms of art. You prefer to create things that are useful as well as attractive.

Creative self-expression can manifest in diverse ways, such as photography, poetry, dancing, singing, painting or sculpture. By combining your obvious interests and inclinations with the symbols of the planets in your fifth house and the sign on its cusp you can determine what art forms to pursue.

In personal relations, the fifth is the house of romance. With energy in this house you are looking for someone with whom to share a strong heart connection and with whom to play and enjoy life. Sexuality can be a form of that play and/or a way to generate and maintain the love bond. With Venus or Neptune in the fifth house, love and affection is more important than passion. Neptune especially would be a devoted lover. Mars, on the other hand, could place sex above love, or might confuse the two. Mars could assume that if you are sexually attracted to someone, or if you are lovers, then you must be in love. Pluto could combine the whole package. Pluto brings to relationships deep feelings, needs for emotional intimacy and a desire for powerful release of passion. Saturn could be fearful about expressing love and affection. With Saturn in the fifth house you have strong needs for recognition from others. You can be afraid that you are not worthy of receiving the love so you pull back and don't share your love openly. You equate approval from others with feelings of self-worth. As you grow to overcome this limitation you realize that what matters more than others' approval is your own sense of self-love. As you internalize and act on that realization you will function as a loyal lover who prefers traditional forms of expressing affection and sexuality.

One outcome of sex is children and the fifth is the house of procreation. The fourth house creates the emotional environment and domestic stability within which to bring a baby. The fifth creates the baby. The Moon in the fifth is especially oriented toward parenting, bringing the lunar qualities of nurturing and receptivity to this area. The Sun brings warmth, love, and the tendency to identify as a parent. Mercury or Jupiter in the fifth house emphasizes communication with your children and places high value on their education. Saturn in the fifth implies either not having children in this lifetime, or at least waiting until you are older. As a parent you could be either extremely conscientious or very controlling. In the former situation you would base the relationship with your children on mutual respect. Without that quality you would be inclined to demand respect from them by continually asserting your authority and dominion over them.

Uranus suggests step-children. If they are all yours, they would probably be unique in some way, or the relationship you share with them is unconventional. Neptune could imply adopting children. Pluto in the fifth house suggests that procreation and parenting could provide you with an opportunity for significant personal transformation. A catharsis of consciousness, or feelings of renewal and rebirth accompany your role as parent and the relationship to your children.

If you have significant energy in the fifth house, children are important to you. You can be a creative and conscientious parent, but you may have a tendency to identify too much with your children. Their successes are your successes; their failures are yours. With fifth house energy try to balance your role as parent with activities that are fun and expressive. By having creative and fulfilling activities, you will be less likely to live through your children.

The fifth is the house of hobbies and recreation. With energy in your fifth house, you like to play. Some people with planets there prefer not to have children so that they can be children themselves. They enjoy indulging in their games and their diversions. Look to the nature of the planets in your fifth house to provide guidance into the type of activity that would provide you with pleasure. Some planets are more inclined to physical pursuits (Mars or Jupiter) some to creative (Venus or Neptune), and some enjoy a variety (Mercury or Uranus). Saturn suggests a serious attitude toward your hobbies or that you prefer fun time to be structured and organized.

Finally, the fifth is the house of investments and financial speculation. This can be at the recreational level, such as playing cards with your friends or indulging in betting on sporting events. This can also manifest as a lifestyle. Certain planets in this house, such as Jupiter or Uranus, could find the stock market or other forms of financial speculation an appealing activity. These are energies that find the risk of speculation very exciting. Other planetary influences, such as Saturn, would prefer to avoid the risk altogether or at least make safe, cautious investments. The Moon in the fifth would be attracted to real estate. Venus in the fifth might prefer to invest in jewelry or in objects of fine art like paintings or sculpture.

The houses associated with the fixed signs are "succeedant" houses. The first succeedant house is the second house, associated with the fixed sign Taurus. In the context of money, the second house indicates earned income, both in terms of your orientation to it and the tools you have to create it. Manifesting energy from the second house implies working for your primary necessities: food, clothing and shelter. From the perspective of the fifth house, money is perceived as a tool for satisfying wants. A distinction can be made in defining the second house as the house of needs, the fifth as the house of luxuries.

The main drawback of the fifth house is a tendency to become so focused on your interests that you expect others to be equally enthralled both with the activities in general as well as your own endeavors and accomplishments in particular. This is a person who identifies so strongly with being a parent that the child's achievements are seen as their own. This is the artist who is always on stage or performing. This is the athlete who can only be excited by the field of competition. To avoid these traps, remember that the fifth house represents those activities that you love. By staying heart-centered, you can reach beyond personal interests that you love to do and share your love in a broader context with others in supportive and inclusive ways.

LEO AND THE BODY

Cancer and the moon rule the fluids in the body, not including blood or lymph. Leo and the Sun rule the blood. By extension, Leo has dominion over the entire circulatory system. The arteries that transport the blood and the spleen that stores the blood are Leonine parts of the body. The upper spine and the chest cavity, the chamber of the heart, are also ruled by Leo.

If a chart indicates tension in the fixed signs, such as squares or oppositions between planets in Taurus, Leo, Scorpio or Aquarius, the heart and circulatory system will tend to experience the stress more readily than if tension is produced by planets in other signs. This is especially true with a cluster of planets (called a *stellium*) in Leo itself. Strive to build up the strength of those parts of your body ruled by signs within which you have a lot of planets. Those planets activate those organs or systems and use up the energy required to maintain them.

The Sun indicates the basic vitality of the body. Aspects to the Sun, more than the sign placement of the Sun itself, provide the support to maintain health and vitality, or indicate where that vitality might break down and why. Trines or sextiles from Mars, Jupiter, and Saturn can all serve in this stabilizing or vitalizing role. On the other hand, squares or oppositions from Saturn or Neptune can deplete the body. Conjunctions to Mars or Uranus can create a tendency to be over-active or over-stimulated to a point of burning yourself out. With a lot of aspects to your Sun, or a lot of planets, including the Sun, in Leo, make sure your cardio-vascular system is getting appropriate exercise. Learn what foods help the heart to do its job most efficiently.

CONCLUSIONS

Dane Rudhyar, considered the father of modern astrology and the first person to combine traditional astrological concepts with modern humanistic psychology, defined Leo as: "The dramatic exteriorization of personality in order to gain social recognition and increase self-assurance as a social unit." Thus Leo is the first sign attempting to integrate a social persona which later becomes expressed and experienced as social relationships in the sign Libra. The rising sign is the self-defined persona that projects who you are to others. Depending on the rising sign you may or may not be inclined to share the self with others. Leo and the fifth house, however, strive for more interaction between the self and others. Leo begins the second third of the zodiac. Each third is begun by a fire sign followed by earth, air, and water. The first third started with Aries then progressed to Taurus (earth), Gemini (air) and Cancer (water). The pattern continues in the second group of signs starting with Leo, Virgo, Libra and Scorpio. This pattern is invariant. The signs always follow each other in the same order. This second third of the zodiac begins the portion of the zodiac which deals with relationships.

The first fire sign, Aries—a cardinal sign ruled by Mars— enjoys its independence. Leo, the fixed sign ruled by the Sun, needs more interaction with others and recognition from other's experience. As a Leo with all the love you have to give, and with as much joy as you experience in the giving, you can have fears of not being lovable yourself. You may have anxiety about not receiving enough love from others. Objectively, this is a result of being uncentered and unself-loving. You can't expect others to love you if you don't demonstrate that same love for yourself. Your need to be loved causes you to look outside to validate your ability to love and feel lovable. This can result in expressing your love conditionally. You tend to relate to love as a quantity of energy, rather than a quality of life.

In relationships in which you are not loved or recognized in a certain way, you may have a tendency to pull back from those situations. It is as if you profess to be willing to love someone forever, but they must love you back in a manner befitting your royal (lion-like) place in life. That posture limits your ability to give or receive love. In effect, you turn off your love light which is like cutting off your nose to spite your face. You are holding back your radiance and only hurting yourself. If the person you loved was not returning it in a form useful and fulfilling to you, to hold back and not give doesn't necessarily hurt them. They might even prefer less of your energy. But it does hurt you because Leo lives by the flow of love. To implode your light is to block other forms of expression, such as the creative or recreational. It is important for your growth that even as you acknowledge dissatisfaction with a relationship, you redirect the love energy. Don't turn it off entirely. For you that is neither desirable nor possible. Turn your attention to a hobby that you love, or to entertainment. Even if this form of love is not as romantic or as totally consuming, the important thing is to affirm that you are still alive and free to love. You can love yourself in the present and be open to sharing love with someone else in the future.

The energy of fixed fire is masculine. It tends toward extroversion, and can be extremely effective in positions of leadership. One of the most powerful images of Leo is that of the king. This is described in myth and expressed throughout human history. It is a man in an exalted and prominent position. He is able to express his individuality so that his desires are met and his wishes are acceded to by others. He carries himself with dignity, acknowledging by his demeanor his station in life. He is proud of his accomplishments and functions in a way that allows others to be benefited by them. We all have qualities of the king, whether we are male or female. We all have the need and the ability to radiate such that we see ourselves clearly, and create our lives with confidence and consciousness. We all have the need to be respected by others and be allowed to express our desires with the expectation that they will be acknowledged by others. The potential to be who we are is seen most clearly by becoming familiar with the nature and qualities of your Sun sign. Leo is ruled by the Sun. As such, it among all other signs is the most illuminating. It is charged with the task of creating the self by externalizing it, like the line in the Leon Russell song, "I acted out my love in stages, with ten thousand people watching." Sometimes these tendencies can be difficult. A person who doesn't feel lovable has the problem of needing to shine, yet fearing the feedback. One thing that Leo fears and avoids whenever possible is being embarrassed. With a lot of Leo energy you might resist making a change, even if you want to make it, for fear of trying something new and looking foolish. A Leo who is off center will hold a great deal of inner stress because of this. He could manifest this stress by being painfully shy to the point of being socially invisible. Or he could be so grossly demanding as to be overbearing. This pattern may cover up certain self-defined undesirable traits, but does so with behavior that may be worse.

For a woman, there is an additional dilemma. Our society, indeed most of the world, does not recognize or support women for being powerful, dynamic or self-expressive. A king can be exalted but a queen can be demeaned. One of the acceptable outlets given to women is the role of parent. In your quest to be loved and receive recognition, you might tend to accept societal expectations of who to be and what to do. Since Leo is the sign of procreation anyway, you can be comfortable identifying with that role. You love your children, and provide them with a loving foundation upon which they can grow and develop. Beyond that role you may feel stifled. You are caught between two needs. One is to be loved. The other is to be your radiant Leo self. When confronted with this dichotomy and in an unconscious and uncentered state, women with significant energy in Leo often don't see themselves or own their energy clearly. Leo is the sign of love, and that is your contribution to the human experience. Your ability to generate love and create heart-centered relationships is more important to you and potentially stronger than in any other sign. Never demean its significance or overlook it as something special that you have to offer. If you are aware of your loving nature, don't undermine yourself by assuming that everybody else is equally loving.

If you don't own your power to love you are giving away your energy and power. This will often be to a male partner, someone who society defines as acceptable to have power. It is as if you see yourself as an extension of him when in fact it is your light and love that is keeping him afloat. You may even be attracted to a person who does not have as much radiance and ability as you do. By giving him your energy you are propping him up, while defining yourself as his satellite, and vicariously basking in the glory he generates with your energy. This doesn't work. Giving away your power does not make you more lovable. If you are with a man who loves you as much as you love him and who is as generous with his energy as you are with yours, the relationship is balanced and workable. Otherwise you become drained, giving but not getting the recognition you desire. Remember, as a Leo you want recognition because of who you are, not because of what you do. In the long run, you feel resentful of the person and the situation. You get depleted and the relationship falls apart. In this scenario, growth for you comes from learning to develop perspective about who you are. Be who you are. You have the power to decide what you do with your energy, and learn how to own it, use it and feel comfortable and secure in its manifestation.

Whether female or male, as you develop more perspective on yourself, you can take better advantage of your strength of will in ways that let your inherent leadership and creativity shine. Your influence on others will be positive and supportive. Your honesty and integrity can bring clarity to others, helping them to access and utilize their creativity in a fulfilling way. With clarity and strength of will you leave behind the consuming need for recognition and approval from others. You become aware that your loveability is a true and inherent part of who you are. You conduct yourself with a highly developed sense of personal integrity. Among the attributes you value the most is a sense of honor in personal relationships. Integrate these qualities in your life, to avoid either the self-oriented need to be the constant center of attention, or conversely to deflect attention onto others at any cost. Much of your growth comes from learning how to make genuine expressions of self-offering to others. Not in a conditional way, but in a way that maintains your center at the heart level. Try to make connection with others who share with you both awareness of the importance of love and the ability and desire to share it. The clarity to do this comes from learning how to listen to others and allowing yourself to receive energy from them. Don't limit yourself unnecessarily by being only the giver.

Leo continually says, "I am beautiful." If this is done in an uncentered and unself-loving manner, it usually comes across like a petulant teenager. If Cancer is the eternal child of the zodiac, Leo is the eternal adolescent. In this mode, Leo can be obnoxious, egocentric and constantly demanding personal power. But, if Leo energy is expressed in a centered and self-loving manner, it manifests more as youthful innocence. Gemini, Cancer and Leo are all youthful and playful. Through this expression of youthful innocence, the Leo is likely to experience himself or herself in the following manner: "I love myself. God did a great job when he made me and you can love me too." At first, this might seem as self-absorbed as the uncentered Leo. But realize that one of the functions of Leo is to bring light and love to the earth plane; to teach us all how to tap into our heart and reach down always for a little more love energy. Mark Twain said that when we are sad, we must experience that feeling alone, but when we feel joy, we have to share it with others. Leo reminds and teaches us about the primacy of love.

The earth has been called the plane of love. This may be difficult to accept in the face of constant war, famine, disease and prejudice that has taken place throughout history and continue in today's current events. It is easy to become cynical and skeptical through life experiences. But whether your Sun sign is Leo or whether you have significant energy in the fifth house or not, you do have the ability to tap into your heart and feel love energy.

Everything in the universe is in constant motion. The energy of life is in constant flux and change. Energy on the physical plane is dense so events here move relatively slowly which enables human beings to have the opportunity to exercise their free will more consciously. You can choose whether to relate to yourself and others with cynicism or love, with animosity or generosity. It's been said that the purpose of life is to become more conscious. As you grow in that process, you periodically perceive glimpses of light and feelings of joy. You realize that there is always more. The destination of life is to merge back into the Wholeness, the center from which you were born and to which you return upon death. The center of a human being is the heart. Looking at the seven energy centers in the body called *chakras*, three are above the heart and three are below. The first three are oriented toward physical and emotional experience— survival and relationship. The upper three pertain to the develop- ment of higher consciousness. In the middle is the heart. To be centered is to be in touch with your heart *chakra*, to open your heart to the love energy that continually flows throughout all life. Use that energy as a basis to relate to yourself and others. It provides a firm foundation to continue your journey into higher levels of awareness, whether they are perceived and experienced on earth or other planes of existence.

To be self-loving does not mean to be self-centered. Loving yourself, even at the ego or individual level, helps to establish a pattern of being able to love others and to allow them to love you. This, in turn, creates a foundation upon which to learn how to grow beyond the self and feel love for Self, the in-dwelling Spirit of which we are all created manifestations. In the process of learning to love the self, it is important to consider the entire package of strengths and weaknesses, desirable and undesirable traits, parts of yourself of which you are proud and parts about which you may feel ashamed. To say that you should love all parts of yourself does not mean to be satisfied with them. Each time you discover a new part of yourself or see yourself from a new perspective you should try to love that new element even as you either strive to integrate or eliminate it from your nature. By allowing yourself to see yourself in totality you can develop true self-awareness. By eliminating those parts that are undesirable or that you don't love enables you to grow in a self-directed way as a self-defined person.

We are all manifestations of the Divine Source of Light, Love and Life. To actualize ourselves is to acknowledge that connection to the Creator and to see ourselves as beings of limitless creative potential. As an individual you can choose to grow into the fullness of your being and the totality of your potential. To see the influences of all the signs and planets as reflections of the Light and supportively accept them is to affirm the Oneness of which we are a part. As you work to become actualized you understand and accept the manifestations of all the various parts of the Whole. Internally you feel full and complete. To engage in the eternal flow of evolutionary growth will lift the species to more expanded levels of the consciousness of love.

VIRGO

Virgo is the sign of transition between the self-orientation of Leo and the social orientation of Libra. It ends the internal journey and helps to prepare for interactive experience with the outer world. The first six signs, and their attendant houses, comprise the Northern hemisphere. These are the signs that the Sun transits through during the spring and summer, when the days are longer and the nights shorter in the Northern hemisphere. At the Spring Equinox, the Sun enters Aries. It arrives at Cancer on the summer solstice, the first day of summer, and leaves the Northern hemisphere at the Autumnal Equinox, the first day of Libra. The Sun is in Virgo every year from approximately August 22 through September 23.

The first quadrant of the Northern hemisphere comprising Aries, Taurus and Gemini is oriented to initial contact of the soul to the body and the projection of self to the immediate environment. Cancer, Leo, and Virgo extend that experience to family and to the creative and functional interaction with those closest to the self. The task of Virgo, therefore, is to complete and bring closure to this internal and personal experience. As we journey out beyond our known world, life becomes more complex. In some ways, that complexity starts with Virgo in that it is an earth sign, like Taurus, but ruled by a mental planet, Mercury. It is the blending of those two qualities that helps make Virgo unique and complex. To meld those patterns, and help us make this transition, Virgo is called the sign of integration. To perform that task of integration Virgo says, "I analyze and discriminate."

THE MYTHS

The myths that illustrate the archetype Virgo fall into one of two categories. One group involves the harvest time in the yearly cycle. This emphasizes the earthy quality of Virgo. The second category pertains to images of the virgin. Many of the myths of the first theme emanate from the Middle East. One example is the Egyptian story of Isis, Goddess of the Moon who we initially encountered in the discussion of Cancer and the Moon. The Egyptians gave credit to Isis for inventing agriculture. In one story Isis is sailing through space, carrying a sheaf of wheat. She dropped the wheat, resulting in the formation of the Milky Way. This is a cosmogony tale, a way the ancient Egyptians had of explaining the origin of the universe. But it contains clear references to the harvest, as if the material universe as we know it is a result of a harvest or is itself a place to harvest. A harvest is a culmination, a completion of the growing season and Virgo represents the end of the growing season. Isis was also considered a great healer, a quality also associated with Virgo.

In Rome it was Ceres who was the goddess of the harvest. In Greek mythology, her counterpart was Demeter, whom we noted in the discussion of Cancer as the goddess of motherhood and nurturing. One of the ways she compelled the return of her daughter Persephone was to cause the crops to die, eliminating the harvest and creating the prospect of famine. It is significant to relate nurturing to the harvest, because a prime function of the maternal principle is to provide nourishment. These are *yin*, or feminine qualities and help forge a link between the signs Cancer and Virgo.

The image and concept of the virgin also describes characteristics of Virgo. In Catholic theology the Virgin Mary occupies a central and prominent place, combining the themes of both the mother and the virgin. In Sanskrit the word for Mary is *Maya* which refers to the illusion of matter and the world of phenomena. In Hebrew, Mary is *Mayam*, which means water. In Latin, Mary is *Mare*, the sea. The archetype of the Christian mother contains symbolic reference to water. Yet there is an implication from the Sanskrit that somehow water and anything else in the world of form is an illusion. This conveys a subtle suggestion to look beyond the physical and emotional worlds of self that the first five signs are so involved with discovering and defining. There is something more than the personal world, something which the last six signs will help us to discover.

It is interesting that the opposite sign of Virgo is Pisces, a water sign, symbolized by the fish. If Mary means water or the sea, then the Virgo-Pisces axis is about the interaction between an individual (Virgo) and its environment (Pisces). Water represents emotion and the inner feminine realm. The fish signifies the soul evolving through the integration of the personal emotions and impersonal universe. Opposite signs are those that are 180 degrees apart. They combine to form an axis. There are six such axes. Opposite signs are similar in that each of the pair is oriented toward the same general experience. What makes them different is that they are looking at the same situation from opposite points of view. Virgo and Pisces are opposite signs along the same axis. Mary, the virgin mother, is a symbolic expression of Virgo and is the source of material creation. She is the maternal source, the Divine Mother. She applies the love energy, so valued and developed by the previous sign Leo, in emotional devotion to the child. The child is, in turn, a symbol of the harvest, the result of previous acts of creation. Pisces is the sign of the fish, a symbol the Christians associate with Jesus. Virgo, the mother, is the opposite sign of Pisces, the son. Pisces is the product of Virgo as Jesus is the son of the Virgin. The child of God emerging into the plane of illusion, the world of form, from the Virgin. The consciousness of God is synonymous with Jesus. Water (Mare) is the symbolic vehicle for both the development of God-consciousness and the birth of the child through Virgin Mother. We come to the world of illusion, the earth plane, by being born. Jesus maintained, or regained his God-consciousness by not being attached to or deceived by this plane. He was as separate from it as the Virgin is separate from the male. He grew in consciousness beyond the world of matter as it is the function of Pisces to grow beyond the practical focus of the earth sign Virgo.

The image of the virgin can be misunderstood. At its highest level, the Virgin is one who is dedicated to being impregnated by the Divine Essence of the gods. The vestal virgins were women dedicated to a pure and chaste life. Historically vestal virgins were cultural institutions in Greece, Rome and Mexico. In the Aztec world, vestal virgins were offered as human sacrifices to the gods. Vestal virgins are also important people in modern religions, consecrating their lives to Krishna, Buddha or Jesus.

Part of the misconception of the virgin is that she is thought to be pristine in action and pure in body and mind. It would seem to be impossible to maintain this lifestyle and at the same time to live an active life that contributes to the community. To understand the basic meaning of this concept, however, realize that the term vestal virgin initially referred to the Roman goddess Vesta. Historically, vestal virgins were women dedicated to the archetype of this goddess. Vesta, whose antecedent was the Greek goddess Hestia, was the first offspring of Cronus (sky) and Rhea (earth), consequently one of the original Olympian deities. The name Vesta comes from the Sanskrit root vas which means shining. It was she who was given the responsibilities of keeping the sacred flame burning in daily lives of the people. Her presence sanctified each home and each temple through the the flame alive in the hearth. She brought a spiritual presence through the sacred fire that provided illumination, warmth and food. Yet there were never any paintings or statuary created that illumined her image. It was as if her energy was so personal and internal yet so fundamental within the collective consciousness that images were unnecessary, perhaps even considered profane. When a couple married, the bride's mother carried a torch, lit by the flame at the bride's childhood home, to the newlywed's residence, thereby creating a link to the family and sanctifying the new couple and consecrating their new home. A newborn child was carried around the hearth as a ceremonial welcoming into the family. If a new village was built, a torch lit by the flame at the temple in the old village was carried to the new temple, enlarging the community to include the new development.

As central an image as the hearth is, and as fundamental a deity as Vesta/Hestia was, she performed her tasks in a modest way. Girls who were chosen as her devotees were expected to live a chaste, pure life of devotional service to the goddess. They were expected to tend the sacred fire of the temple, and live modestly and anonymously. This conforms to the stereotypic concept of the virgin that has filtered down to contemporary society. To trace the concept of "the young woman in devotional service to the goddess" prior to the Greeks, is to discover a much different, much older definition of the virgin. In a time when people celebrated the prime deity in the form of the Great Goddess, women who spent their lives dedicated to Her were called "virgins," not because they were sexually chaste, but because they remained unmarried and belonged to no men. They were autonomous and complete within themselves. They offered themselves sexually to men who came to worship at the Temple of the Goddess as a spiritual act. Their lives centered around embodying and integrating the fertilizing power of the Goddess on the Earth plane.

This is quite a different picture from the later period in which both the concepts of the Goddess and the autonomous woman were eliminated from Western civilization. The spiritual monastics of both ages, however, do resemble each other in certain significant ways. It is those similarities that illustrate the Virgo archetype. Both groups were modest and self-effacing. They were service and task-oriented in devotional activity. They were central to the community as a group without individuation. Yet they were free to experience many facets of society usually denied women or allowed only to the people of the highest rank. Their significance is that they embodied the highest standards of their culture. They helped their society function effectively on the material plane even as they worked to develop their own consciousness and help their society to evolve.

THE GLYPH: ♍

The glyph for Virgo is derived from the Hebrew letter *Mem* (מ). and is very similar to the glyph for Scorpio. At one time, the signs Virgo, Libra and Scorpio were considered to be the same. As human awareness evolved, however, it became clear that those born in the early stages of the sign, what we now call Virgo, and those born at the end, Scorpio, were quite different. When it was acknowledged that these experiences were different, and, in fact, denoted different signs, it was decided to put another sign in between them—Libra, the sign of equality and balance. This not only maintains a distance between Virgo and Scorpio but enables them to function as equals.

The glyphs for Virgo and Scorpio also suggest the serpent power. Gemini, through the caduceus or baton of Mercury, brought to consciousness the potential of the kundalini power. Gemini symbolizes the universal mind. The symbol of its ruling planet, Mercury, indicates that a way to embody the universal mind is to awaken the serpent sleeping at the base of your spine.

The serpent is the kundalini. By awakening the serpent power, the kundalini energy begins to ascend the spine, facilitating the development of human consciousness. The Eastern and Western cultures have different ways of defining and appreciating this serpent. In the West the serpent is a key character in the Book of Genesis. It is the perpetrator of awakening awareness, who tempted Eve to eat the fruit of the tree of knowledge. It is at this point that humanity fell from grace and had to leave the Garden of Eden. This is a way of defining innocence as desirable and awareness as not. Considering that this myth is one of the primary foundations of the Judeo/Christian philosophy which has been dominant in the West for 2000 years, it says a lot about how our society defines the value of consciousness. It is the major justification for the primacy of original sin. This belief has helped to repress the development of individual power in general and the freedom and value of women in particular, because, after all, it was Eve who acted on the serpent's suggestion. Instead of praising her bravery and crediting her, and through her all women, for the beginning of conscious awareness in the human mind, Judeo/Christian theology has blamed her for the fall. It was her weakness, and through her all women, who are responsible for the human condition.

The Catholic theologian Matthew Fox has put forth the doctrine of "Original Blessing" to replace original sin as the cornerstone of Western philosophy. It espouses the celebration of the creation of life instead of the fall from grace. It is a liberating doctrine and enables each of us to pursue the development of consciousness. Through this growth we can become the embodiment of creation, instead of limiting our growth through fear and guilt. It also allows for a new interpretation of the Garden of Eden myth. If the Garden represents unconsciousness, it also represents being at one with the Creator. Humanity was inseparable from Spirit but didn't know it. But becoming conscious doesn't require the loss of this Unity. It can also imply the realization of our Oneness with the Divine and, through that, the realization of our connection to each other and all beings on the planet. The original interpretation of the garden of Eden tale equated loss of innocence with spiritual alienation. A new interpretation could equate our current condition with the opportunity for conscious awakening of our spiritual origin and the spiritual truth of life.

Eastern cultures, however acknowledge this definition. They equate the serpent with consciousness. It is the embodiment of awakening awareness and symbolizes kundalini energy. When the awakened serpent arrives at the top of the head, the energy center known as the crown *chakra*, enlightenment takes place. There is a return of a sense of oneness, of unity with all life. It is a return to the Garden of Eden. Western philosophy denotes consciousness as leading to expulsion from the Garden, clearly an undesirable occurrence. In Eastern philosophy its as if the development of consciousness leads to returning to the Garden, clearly a desirable occurrence. Eastern philosophies, such as Buddhism, Hinduism and Taoism espouse that we never left the garden, because it was never outside the human experience in the first place. It is always present within. By calming the mind and the emotions, by directing your attention and energy and by devoting yourself to the process, anyone can retrieve the garden and find within a place of joy and bliss.

This is a significant distinction of priorities. The evolution of social institutions, personal relationships and spiritual consciousness in the Western and Eastern worlds reflect that difference. Specifically in relation to Virgo, failure to consider its spiritual aspect, which in turn illuminates its devotional nature in a comprehensive, multi-dimensional way, limits the understanding and working knowledge of the archetype. The tail of the "M" is coiled, symbolizing the creativity as yet unreleased by the Virgin. This implies that the spiritual awakening is waiting in a potential state. The glyph for Virgo emphasizes the importance of aspiring for divine inspiration for it is that experience that awakens within us the realization of who we really are.

THE TOTEM:

The totem for Virgo is double-bodied, as it is with all of the mutable signs. The obvious totem is the virgin, one who aspires to higher awareness through purity and service. The virgin acts as a connection between practical functioning on the physical plane, and inspiration from the source of Being. In mythological terms, the creative spirit (the masculine principle) manifests in earthly experience by being transformed into form through the mother (the feminine principle). This primal female is a virgin because her spouse is the Invisible Unknown. Relative to the earth plane, she is autonomous and answers to no power greater than herself. Yet she has understanding of an obvious connection with Spirit. An example is the Egyptian virgin goddess Isis who was often depicted veiled. It was she who held the ancient knowledge and wisdom embodied in Hermeticism, yet would lift her veil and reveal the mysteries only to the initiated. Notice again the connection between the virgin and spiritual awareness.

A secondary totem for Virgo is the Sphinx. The Sphinx is an Egyptian statue built around 2990 BC. It is the representation of a lion's body with a human head. It symbolizes strength and intelligence. It is androgynous, indicating that the Egyptians recognized that their gods partook of both the masculine and feminine creative powers. It is thought that the wisdom and secrecy of the Hermetic philosophy of Egypt are epitomized in the Sphinx. Again we see the connections among the Sphinx, Hermetic teachings, the Virgin Isis, and the sign Virgo. The Sphinx symbolizes the need to integrate the individuation and emotional self-expression of Leo with the productive activity of Virgo. The Sphinx is the embodiment of one who has learned to tame the animal passions of Leo through the purposeful mental activity of Virgo. It represents the process of harmonizing the flow between purity and practicality. It depicts the evolution from the proud, individuated masculine monarch to the more refined integration of body, mind, and spirit.

MODE AND ELEMENT

Virgo is the sign of mutable earth. The earth quality of Virgo is symbolized by fields, pastures and meadows, all pastoral images. Like the other earth signs, Taurus and Capricorn, Virgo has a strong connection to nature. Perhaps more than the others, however, Virgo's connection is through being in and working with the natural elements. For example, those with their natal Moon in Virgo or in the sixth house, the house of Virgo, have an affinity for working with plants. As a mutable sign, Virgo is adaptable and therefore aware of the change of seasons. It is able to flow with those changes, and enjoys finding useful activities of different kinds. This contrasts with Taurus and Capricorn who may tend to seek control or to impose their will on a situation.

All three earth signs share the productive worker mantle, however, each in its own way representing an aspect of the salt of the earth.

Virgo is the sign of the servant, the employee, the apprentice and the technician. Each demonstrates the diligent task-orientation that Virgo brings to all of its endeavors. Each requires a period of learning followed by a period of refining the basic knowledge. The mutability of Virgo indicates that it prefers to work and serve within a given structure or system. Virgo is the skilled worker who seeks to become as technically proficient as possible within his or her field.

Mutability also implies learning. Its earthy nature orients Virgo to learn practical things. But it can also be referred to as the scholar of the zodiac. As a Virgo you can apprentice yourself to a deliberately chosen body of knowledge as well as to a specific manual skill. In a very detailed, analytical manner you will eventually understand all the aspects, phases and facets of that particular subject. Eventually, you can serve other people through that function or with that information.

A potential problem with this scholarly/experiential/practical approach to life is that Virgo can get lost in The Web. This is a labyrinthine, never-ending ordering of facts, information and ideas—universal knowledge, with limitless perspectives and levels of awareness. With its inherent curiosity and attention to detail, Virgo can master a particular part of that Web, becoming proficient in defining its reality from the point of view of whatever sector it is learning about and functioning within. After a while, however, the focus can change. Suddenly new perspectives and data can come flooding into your life as a whole new sector of the Web opens up to you. You could react with great anticipation of expanding the limits of your knowledge and experience, or react by feeling overwhelmed. Virgo tends to lose perspective and to relate to life in a very subjective way. Even if you aren't feeling overwhelmed by uncovering new aspects of the Web, your words and actions can confuse others to whom your changes seem illogical or arbitrary. It is almost as if Virgo seeks to create an understanding of the universe by building it atom by atom. If you are aware of the ever-expanding web of knowledge unfolding in your life, you can use it as a vehicle to continually bring your potential for inspiration and higher awareness into concrete and practical focus.

One of the specific areas where learning and practical service come together is the field of healing. The virgin totem indicates the orientation to purity. In the area of health this can be through purifying your own body through proper preventive care and/or involvement in a health care profession. Virgo is the third of the healing signs. Gemini heals through communication, Leo heals through love. Virgo heals more through technical understanding of the physiology or anatomy of the body. Professions such as physician, chiropractor and nurse can all appeal to the service-oriented, scientific Virgo.

Sometimes Virgo can be overly aware of the body to the point of being plagued by chronic aches and pains. In the extreme, this can result in hypochondriasis. You might make an issue out of something that other people would ignore as a minor physical problem. This is another example of Virgo's losing perspective. You can become compulsive about something relatively insignificant, and not be aware of it. As a Virgo, your best friend is your body. But this can be expressed by being overly concerned with the structure and condition of the body or by placing undue emphasis on adornments and cosmetic attractiveness.

This tendency to overemphasize the body can have deeper and more significant implications. As an earth sign, you are comfortable in your body. As a mutable sign, you are oriented toward learning, gaining practical knowledge so you are also comfortable functioning on the mental plane. But Virgo does not deal well with emotions. Sometimes you can have difficulty being in touch with what you are feeling. Sometimes you can have difficulty expressing those feelings to others. When there is unconscious emotional energy or unresolved psychological conflict you will first try to understand it logically. Since emotions are not logical, this process doesn't lead to clarity or resolution. So you tend to experience your emotional reality through your body. That doesn't work either and these feelings will often manifest as chronic aches and pains. If this tendency becomes a habit, you could follow the problem around from one system to another, from one part of the body to another, from one doctor to another, or one method of treatment to another. Always curing one ailment only to find another one occurring somewhere else. The real core cause of the difficulty isn't being dealt with. Your problem isn't just physical, but something much more subtle. By ignoring the internal nudges or suggestions you are creating a problem in much denser form.

Armed with this insight, realize that health maintenance for Virgo comes as a result of creating a proper balance between your emotional and physical nature. Physically, this means preventative medicine; paying attention ahead of time to the needs that the body has for proper exercise, diet and rest. This can come from understanding in an intellectual or scholarly manner, how the body works. What nutrients do different parts or systems of the body find necessary to keep the chemical factory of the body functioning and flowing as harmoniously as possible? You can also maintain physical health by simply tuning into your body. In addition to the objective, intellectual point of view, what does your body need right now? By looking at your horoscope as well as noting your own medical history you can find out what parts of your body break down most frequently. Because you body is your best friend, take the time to feed and nurture those parts of the body before they manifest disease. Make sure they are as resilient and as healthy as possible at all times. Even if you don't have significant energy in Virgo, any sign that has three or more planets in it in your natal chart will tend to feel stress. The parts or systems of the body associated with that sign need more preventive care so that they don't become depleted. The part of the body ruled by your rising sign or by the sign on the cusp of the sixth house also point to areas that should be strengthened prophylactically. Planets in the first or sixth houses also will provide clues as to body parts or systems that may be sensitive to stress. If you have planets in your sixth house you will tend to focus either on maintaining your own health, healing others or being constantly plagued with health issues.

Health maintenance for Virgo must involve more than the body, however. It also involves remembering to tune into your inner world. Become aware of your body, noticing any parts that are tense. This can be a vehicle for becoming aware of your feelings. This is a way of using your strength—connection to the body—to overcome your weakness—connection with emotions. Without touching your body, can you feel tightness in your solar plexus? Or a warm, relaxing feeling in your chest? In the former situation, you may be involved in an ego-oriented control dynamic. In the latter, you may be experiencing love and joy. It will take time to remember to tune into your body this way, and to develop the ability to be spontaneously aware of its condition. But it is a way to compensate for a problem which, for some Virgos is chronic.

Another more superficial way that Virgo is aware of the body is through adornment. This is especially true if Virgo is your ascendent or rising sign. Even if it is the Sun sign, Virgo often is a stylish dresser. Sometimes you can get carried away with the assumption that "you are what you look like." Then there can be a lot of self-criticism about personal appearance. Usually this comes up when comparing yourself to someone else, or to some arbitrary external standard of beauty. This is another way in which the mutability of Virgo can create an arbitrary, subjective point of view which is both detrimental and unnecessary.

Maintaining cleanliness, a positive attitude toward preventive medicine, and stylishness in appearance are basic parts of your nature. But remember that beauty is not only in the eye of the beholder, it also emanates from the eyes of the beheld. If you feel lovable within yourself, if you learn from Leo and its ruling planet, the Sun, about being centered and self-loving, you will be able to avoid some of Virgo's more negative tendencies. Express self-love through your eyes and with an ever-radiant smile. Others will pick that up and relate to you accordingly.

Ultimately the combination of mutability with earth puts fundamental significance on experience. Learning to do a variety of things, some mental, some physical, some an integration of the two is a way of having something to offer the world in a serviceful mode. As you help others you also learn about life, and yourself. This process of learning and serving is the positive manifestation of the Virgo nature.

THE RULING PLANET

The ruling planet of Virgo is Mercury ($\em07$), the planet of communication. Mercury is also the ruling planet of Gemini, indicating a similarity between the two archetypes. Both signs are oriented toward thinking, understanding and serving others by communicating what they know. Mercury provides a variety of ways to facilitate information from the spoken word to the written word. Also by using the hands in creative or productive acts of dexterity. Thus both Virgo and Gemini are adept at manual arts, with good hand-eye coordination. Activities such as crafts, playing instruments and mechanical skills are enjoyed in highly proficient ways by both signs.

But Virgo is an earth sign, whereas Gemini partakes of the element air, so there are also major differences in the way these signs apply the energy of Mercury. In terms of mental sensitivity, Gemini is more oriented toward inspiration, and is always open to being intellectually stimulated. Remember, Gemini represents the embodiment of the Universal Mind. This implies a versatility with respect to subject but also the ability to tap right into and be a conduit for information about limitless topics. Virgo is a worker. Its relationship to Mercury is practical. As a Virgo you seek to improve yourself through the mind. The virgin is one who waits in devotion for the presence of the Divine. Consequently, you are more oriented toward aspiration, toward being elevated in mind and spirit through rational activity.

Gemini can be excited by ideas alone. It can be purely intellectual, and comfortable traveling from one thought form to another. Virgo is more analytical and relates to ideas, concepts or data in a more concrete way. Virgo wants to be able to put information to practical use. Gemini enjoys using the verbal skills of Mercury in social situations and is capable of being charming and gregarious with a variety of people. Virgo is more oriented toward observation, tending to be socially shy and preferring less contact with people.

The Geminian tendency is to use its Mercurial energy to be witty and charming and has caused it to develop a reputation as the dilettante of the zodiac. Virgo uses Mercury to develop precise skills of the mind and hands. Virgo, a sign that values practical questioning and pragmatic application of ideas and data, is the scholar of the zodiac. As a scholar, you always strive to build a picture of life by amassing a limitless amount of detailed information about a particular subject. For this reason, Virgo can be a good scientist.

There are two potential drawbacks to your mental tendencies. The first one is The Web, mentioned before. Getting lost in the miasma of your eternally analytical tendencies can lead to defining your reality in an arbitrary and subjective way. Second is the expectation of perfect knowledge. Often a Virgo will hesitate to act until he or she has totally understood a subject and become a master at applying the information. In this trap, you stop yourself from learning more through the experience of doing. You can also simply lose perspective about what you already know by always concentrating on what you don't know. Realize that perfection may be a desirable goal but it's not realistic to expect yourself to already be there. As an earth sign, build your bank of information and apply it pragmatically as you go through life. Refine yourself by doing what you do best, focusing on the little things. As you change yourself gradually eventually you will at least approach and approximate perfection and be more productive and less hard on yourself in the process.

A discussion of Mercury's influence in each of the signs is contained in the Gemini chapter.

THE SIXTH HOUSE

The area of life that is associated with Virgo is the sixth house, a place of transition. It takes us through the process of moving from the inner world to the outer world, from the personal life to the impersonal. This is a journey that requires great subtlety and the ability to work hard with little overt recognition. There is an inherent modesty that can accompany sixth house energy as well as a strong work ethic. These qualities and tendencies combine to impel an orientation to service work. With significant energy in the sixth house you may be of service to others either in your personal life or be involved in a service-oriented profession. An abundance of planets herein could result in tendencies toward putting other people and their needs ahead of your own, even to the point of martyrdom and self-sacrifice. This pattern leads to resentment of those whom you are serving. You can become biting and reductive in your criticism of others who are doing what you would like to do if you didn't feel so compelled to do so much for others.

The sixth house is oriented toward home and hearth. Planets in your sixth house impel you to create an efficient, neat and clean home with everything in its place. It's also possible, however, to have a lot of sixth house energy and have a house that looks like a disaster area. No organization whatever, and a visitor may not be able to find a thing. But you've created that mess, and you know where everything is so, at least for you, there's no problem. With too much emphasis on orderliness you can become compulsive. This is the person who empties the ash tray each time a guest flicks an ash; or covers furniture with plastic to keep the upholstery clean. Broaden your focus and include things that take place out of doors. As an earth house, the sixth feels a strong connection to nature. Gardening, house plants, pets and other animals can provide profound pleasure as well as an outlet for productive energy. This can manifest in a professional context by working in a nursery, a park, a veterinary clinic or a farm. For other people, their sixth house energy impels them to camping, hiking and backpacking. Being close to nature in any direct and pure form can be very healing, relaxing and inspirational. The sixth is also the house of daily routine. Strive to create a routine that is varied, integrated and balanced between structure and spontaneity.

In the professional areas, you can express your inclination to serve through occupations that require technical skill. Tradesmen such as carpenters, electricians, mechanics, machinists, printers and those involved in the food and restaurant business tend to have significant sixth house emphasis in their natal charts. The personal planets, especially Mercury, Venus or Mars bring energy to be in these professions. But the one service function that is most closely associated with this house is healing. At the very least, one or more personal planets in the sixth, especially the Sun or Moon, promotes an interest in preventive medicine. You take pride in creating a daily routine that combines proper exercise, diet and rest to minimize the possibility of health problems. Notice the sign on the cusp of your sixth house and the planets located in that sign. The parts of the body associated with that sign and those planets tend to manifest health problems. Be especially oriented to strengthening those systems and avoid putting unnecessary strain on them.

The sixth house is like Virgo in many ways. You may have a tendency to be so focused on the body as to avoid being aware of your emotional or psychological reality. In that case, you could manifest psychosomatic symptoms. This could be in the form of hypochondria, in which supposed physical problems aren't really there, or psychogenic, in which they are. In either case, the cause is unresolved emotional issues. This can especially tend to manifest with Neptune in the sixth house.

Combining the interest in personal health with profession indicates the potential to be in a healing or health related field. Doctors, nurses, chiropractors, pharmacists and nutritionists could all tend to have significant energy in Virgo or the sixth house. Saturn in the sixth denotes someone for whom traditional medicine is more comfortable, whereas Uranus suggests being more oriented to the unconventional, even experimental, modes of healing. Pluto in the sixth or Scorpio on the cusp could also indicate the orientation to facilitate transformation for someone as a primary focus in your work. It can also suggest that one of the ways in which you might experience a major transformation in life is through a major illness or stress disease. There can also be a tendency to be overly dedicated to your work. With three or more planets in the sixth, or if the Moon is there by itself, you could tend to be a workaholic, either in and around the house or in your career. Your work may be fulfilling and cause you to feel good. But being overly focused on it can lead to a narrow perspective on life. This is a house of transition. Regardless of how important your work may be to you and despite how good you may be at it, to be overly concentrated on one thing prevents certain transitions from taking place.

Planets in the sixth house can indicate what parts of the body will tend to be afflicted or break down under stress. The Sun or planets in Leo emphasize the heart and circulatory system. The Moon or planets in Cancer suggest stomach problems. The Moon or Neptune can imply allergies. Neptune can also indicate a sensitivity to certain drugs. These variables also stress the importance of diet and the expression of feelings as important factors in maintaining good health.

Mercury or planets in Gemini or Virgo can place the fingers or hands in jeopardy and also point to the lungs and small intestine. Those variables or Uranus or planets in Aquarius can imply problems with the nervous system and difficulty relaxing. Deep, yogic breathing can be beneficial with these factors. Uranus or Neptune can also indicate illnesses which are hard to diagnose.

Venus or planets in Libra point to the kidneys as organs in which there could be problems. This in turn could indicate skin or complexion problems. The endocrine system is also ruled by these variables, so there may be hormone imbalances.

Mars indicates accidents, broken bones as well as pain in or injury to the head area. With Mars or Uranus in the sixth it's important to slow down, learn to be cautious in your activity and minimize the potential for injury.

Jupiter in the sixth indicates excellent health and vitality. It can also suggest a tendency to become lazy about maintaining that level of health or being over-indulgent. Saturn in the sixth or planets in Capricorn imply chronic illness and/or problems with the skeleton, especially the knees or spine. Pluto or planets in Scorpio in the sixth house suggests major stress disease. These illnesses create problems at the cellular level. They often can develop for long periods before they surface and the problem becomes known. Either the illness itself or the healing of it can generate a transformation for the patient. Just being sick and in bed for a long period can facilitate a sense of personal rebirth. Healing could require major revisions of lifestyle, not the least of which are new forms of diet and exercise, which are themselves forms of transformation. To heal the illness might lead to a sense of being reborn, feeling new and different in a fundamental way.

The sixth is the house of the apprentice and the employee. Always strive to learn more and become more adept at what you have already learned and put into practice. With energy in this house you are very process-oriented. Make sure that whatever you are working on that there is focus, a goal and that you are working within a system. Energy in the sixth house creates a strong pull to be of service to others in functional, practical ways. It is helpful to work within an ongoing structure or system to maximize your potential to be useful to others. This could be a system or mode of healing, a way of working within or for the environment or a specific trade that enables you to both serve others as well as provide a livelihood for yourself. Make sure that whatever that direction is that it is something you truly want to do, and not something you feel you "should" do. Thus you avoid the traps of martyrdom, resentment and compulsive behavior.

The transition of the sixth house is one that takes you from the first group of six houses to the second group. This is a journey in which the personal and inner life is becoming more oriented toward activities taking place outside the self, home and family. By remaining in touch with all you have accomplished, and who you have become, you can proceed to the next phase. To lose yourself and your focus is to keep you in a more limited context and prevent future growth.

VIRGO AND THE BODY

Virgo is the scholar of the zodiac. It is ruled by Mercury, the planet of communication. These facts combine to define Virgo as a sign that assimilates knowledge. Similarly, in the anatomical context, Virgo rules assimilation of food by the body. In general Virgo is associated with the abdomen and most of the organs and glands therein. The small intestine is ruled by Virgo. So, too, is the pancreas, that part of the endocrine system whose function it is to digest carbohydrates. The pancreas also secretes insulin and glycogen. Malfunctioning of the pancreas can lead to diabetes or hypoglycemia, both related to the digestion of sugar. It also has some dominion over the liver, which stores glycogen and is responsible for discriminating between useful nutrients and harmful toxins. The property of discrimination is specific to Virgo. The spleen, which creates and stores several types of blood cells, is ruled by Virgo.

Mercury controls the nervous system in general, and Virgo specifically rules the autonomic-sympathetic nervous system, which is responsible for vasoconstriction within the involuntary nervous system.

CONCLUSIONS

The transition from Leo to Virgo is one of the most difficult. There are no consecutive signs more dissimilar than these two. If you were born on the cusp between these two signs, or if you have planets in both, trying to blend influences from planets in each of these signs can generate a great deal of internal stress. Even as the Leo creates a very strong external self which is radiant, dynamic and expectant of recognition, Virgo's job is to refine that self. It tends to be very critical of that exalted Leo expression. It's as if the inner dialogue vacillates between the Leo-self saying, "Love me in my beauty," and the Virgo-self saying, "Why don't you climb down from your high horse.

What's so great about you anyhow, since there are so many flaws and imperfections in you that still need to be worked on."

Virgo's job is to complete the task started by Aries, that of creating a separate self. This process is one of refining that self by noticing all the rough edges and split ends. Paying attention to detail is the strength of the Virgo, and ultimately paves the way to integrate that completed self within the social context of a relationship to someone else, symbolized by Libra.

One lesson learned from Leo as it radiates in its self-glory, is the importance of becoming centered and maintaining a self-loving attitude throughout life. Indeed, that lesson needs to be internalized by everyone, regardless of Sun sign. Your degree of being centered and self-loving, the amount of time, energy, and work you put into grounding the body and growing in spirit will determine how you experience and express the creative energy of your Sun sign. In general, Virgo has the potential to manifest itself on three different levels, or through three different octaves of consciousness. These modes are not sequential. You are not necessarily born in phase one and die in phase three. Some start at the highest and stay there; for others the experience is opposite. It's even possible to begin this lifetime at level two or three and then regress due to wrong thoughts or actions.

The lowest level of Virgo manifests the characteristics most commonly associated with the sign. This is the most uncentered expression of the Virgo potential and causes it to receive its "bad press." It's not that these qualities aren't there, because they certainly can be. Most people with significant Virgo or sixth house energy are familiar with these traits even if they left them behind. No one is born centered and remains there for the duration. Even as you are in the process of personal development, you may occasionally slip a notch or two. But as a Virgo, if you have avoided working on yourself, you will be on this level most of the time. That is still only one-third of the total potential.

The first octave of Virgo is the critic—the nitpicker—who finds fault with everyone and everything. At a higher level Virgo feels a strong connection to nature. At the lowest level, however, you could abhor nature and natural bodily functions, considering them "dirty." You project unresolved parts of yourself onto others, see your flaws in them, and then criticize them for being that way. If you get stuck here, you aren't really constructive in your critiques of others. You are, in fact, hurting them though you may be unaware of doing so. Further, you aren't criticizing others in any way or for any reason different than you criticize yourself, but you may not be aware of that either. It's always so much easier to dump it on someone else and expect them to change instead of doing your own work. In reality that pattern is misleading. It generates conflict with others and you still have to resolve your problems anyway. Maybe you are aware of your faults but are too lazy to change. Or maybe you're aware of your problems but don't love yourself enough to feel worthy or capable of changing them.

There are several qualities of the Virgo nature that are exemplified by the first level. People stuck here tend to be highly idealistic and perfectionistic. Although there is certainly nothing wrong with ideals per se, when you are stuck in level one of your Virgo nature there is an unconscious expectation that the ideal should already be in place. You can worry incessantly about the imperfection of a situation. There is no sense of process or working over time to arrive at that ideal. Perfectionism can also be quite subjective. These Virgos don't realize that their ideas and points of view are unique to them and not universally accepted. This pattern is also arbitrary in that what may be your ideal now isn't what you defined as perfect a few months ago or what will be seen as perfect a few months from now. So even if you are doing the work and becoming the embodiment of the perfected image of last season, you don't realize it. You tend to always feel frustrated and disappointed in yourself.

As you become more centered and self-loving, you can exercise your free will to manifest your Virgo nature at the second level. Here, you raise the energy of criticism up an octave and it manifests as analysis. At this level you can function as the efficiency expert of the zodiac, highly organized and very scientific. The focus can be intellectual, through apprenticing to a particular body of knowledge. Or it could be something more concrete, such as becoming involved in a structured, systematic way of improving your health or learning a trade. It is at this level that the skill of critical thinking reaches a peak. It is through development of your analytical mind that you become adept at working in a practical, useful way. You can excel at working with details and be fastidious in your manner of being.

Like your lower octave potential you tend to be a purist, but not in a romanticized or critical way. You are willing to work for the desired goal whether that is by refining yourself or working on any external project that is important to you.

This phase of Virgo is also limited, however, as analysis can be a trap-like end in itself. You can go around and around analyzing something, yet never coming to any conclusion. You are stuck in the left brain. There is also a tendency to get mired in the details and fail to see the bigger picture. This can lead to confusion in thinking and compulsion in action.

Another way of trapping yourself in your analytical mind and losing perspective is by becoming overly focused on your tasks of the day. Virgos tend to make lists. Lists can be useful to help keep you organized and productive. You can see clearly what there is to do. But you become so concerned with the tasks still to be done that you never give yourself time to relax. You never think to look back at your accomplishments. It's as if when you finish something you don't think about it anymore. This can lead to endless frustration and constant self-criticism because you are continually confronted with work to do, but never derive any satisfaction from work already done. One way out of this pattern is to keep two lists. One is labeled "work to do" the other is "work already done." That way, at the end of the day you can look at the second list, realize a sense of accomplishment and feel better about yourself.

As you continue to work on the process of getting centered, you can eventually manifest your energy through the third and highest octave of Virgo consciousness. Here analysis is raised to discrimination, which is one of the two or three highest forms of rational activity the human mind is capable of at this time. Remember, that as a mutable sign, what truly matters more to Virgo than the idealized state or the perfection of knowledge is simply learning. Become aware of an entire spectrum of information. That way you can understand the various subtle shades and distinctions between the extremes of perfection and imperfection. By being open to a broad expanse of experience, you expand your perspective and avoid the mental traps. You can then manifest the mutable function of serving other people either at a scholarly level or in a more practical way such as healing, technology, craftsmanship or agriculture.

As you develop your ability to discriminate, you begin to use two of Virgo's subtler traits: refinement and awareness of quality. Through refinement, you work to improve yourself and get closer to the desired state of perfection. Pay attention to subtle tendencies and discern which should stay and which should go. Don't be afraid to eliminate something you've kept a long time. This does not happen overnight—it is the process of living—and you must be patient. Develop the habit of making self-discriminating statements, judgments and assessments. Try not to be judgmental or reductively self-critical but use a manner that both separates and unites. Separate from a trait, any habit of thought or action, that you wish to disclaim and no longer manifest. There are probably other characteristics that you want to emphasize more in your self or in your life or to develop as something new. As you develop this process, the quality of your being, your life, your work and your relationships improves. Noting the improved quality can provide great fulfillment. Your strength is in your ability to recognize and work with the little things, the minutiae of life. Working with them in a discerning way, developing a wider vision, you avoid the lower octave Virgo ruts of excessive analysis or terminal fussiness.

As this pattern becomes more a part of your daily routine, both mentally and behaviorally, you begin to understand that the highest quality of the Virgo is its spiritual nature. Remember the message of the virgin—to await Divine Inspiration. This part of your nature can manifest in a number of ways. The first is through purity of the body: cultivate your body as the temple of your soul through proper diet, exercise and rest. Purity of the mind is established through mental discrimination by being aware of the quality of your thoughts. If you are healthy in body and mind you can be of greater service. Virgo can also demonstrate its spiritual nature through the quality of devotion. This can be devotion to a partnership, family, business or spiritual discipleship. Divine Inspiration manifests in the form of expanded consciousness which can come as a direct result of devotion to a spiritual master or path.

Make sure, however, that your quality of devotional service doesn't go too far and manifest as martyrdom or self-sacrifice. As a mutable sign, you work best within a system. Learn the rules of that system, and use them to maintain limits to serve others in healthy ways and not undermine yourself in the effort. There can be wrong action even if the intention is good. There are two primary and obvious drawbacks to martyrdom. First, the flash is just too short. After you get all the abundant recognition and praise for having given up yourself, and after the feelings of self-satisfaction fade, you are left with nothing. Second, this leads to bitterness and resentment toward life and other people.

You can experience your evolving spirituality in a healthy way that is coincident with your basic nature through practicing karma yoga. Yoga means union and karma means action. So to be a practitioner of karma yoga means being aware that any act can bring you into Oneness with Spirit. From something as exalted as delivering a baby to something as mundane as doing the dishes, if you are aware of your state of mind and mental focus you realize that everything done with the intention of being in tune with God enables you to function as the Divine Essence on earth. This is the truest and highest form of service. It also conforms to a familiar pattern, because, even though you may be modest and adaptable as fits your mutable nature, you are very experiential about life. You enjoy going and doing, becoming familiar with life in a myriad of ways. Through karma yoga, you maximize your spiritual progress and the development of your consciousness as you learn to recognize the subtle beauty of life continuously and in a first hand way.

By practicing karma yoga and paying conscious attention to life, you can develop a new perspective on perfection. From an off-center point of view, looking at life in a narrow, egocentric way, you have a limited understanding of what is or could be perfect. You may project that image onto other people and life and criticize when your projections don't materialize. From a spiritual perspective, however, it becomes clear that life is already perfect. You realize that life is a coordinated continuum which functions in specific cycles operating at specific rates. You begin to understand that the universe is set up to maximize growth and creativity. From that point of view it becomes important to find your place in the continuum so that you take advantage of your potential both to maximize your own growth as well as make a viable contribution to totality.

Virgo corresponds to the Hebrew letter *Yod* (י), which stands for the hermit or the proselytizer. Even in a spiritual mode, these are patterns to avoid when taken to an extreme. Virgo is the sign of assimilation: it rules the small intestine and the liver. Virgo is oriented toward learning how to apply rational knowledge to practical functions. Ultimately, Virgo's job is to complete the task of forming and becoming a self by selectively integrating body, mind and spirit. Like the Greek goddess Hestia, Virgo functions in a modest, humble and dedicated way. You are task-oriented yet capable of functioning in a variety of life activities.

Paramahansa Yogananda was a God-realized master who came to the United States in 1920 to teach Kriya Yoga to the Western world. He said that there are two avenues open to us through which we can accelerate our spiritual evolution. One is meditation. This is a daily practice of a specific technique which is designed to help the practitioner grow beyond the ego-self and identify with God or Spirit. The other path is service. As we strive to provide for the well-being of others, we emulate the Universe itself. To expand Matthew Fox's concept of Original Blessing, the celebration of the creation of life, the Universe wants us to be happy. It provides all we need, in abundance, to allow us to be filled with peace, joy and happiness. It is merely waiting for each individual to define their path to fulfillment. When we function in a serviceful capacity toward others, we help them much as the Universe serves us.

Virgo represents the reintegration of spirit into matter, and from a state of self-contained matter to social sharing. The first *yin*—and earth—sign, Taurus, embodies stabilization of matter and survival in the physical state. The second *yin* sign, Cancer, embodies the spiritual river of life and emotional nurturing. Yet these signs can be involved in such an immediate way, that they might not look beyond to greater pursuits. Virgo contributes a mental subtlety that enables you to make a conscious decision to pursue social activity and spiritual awakening. By nature Virgo is shy and needs to learn how to look beyond the self. Virgo is the sign of transition from the signs of self—Aries through Virgo—to the signs of the other—Libra through Pisces. It is the sign of re-organizing desires, learning to take the needs of others into consideration. It is the sign of re-polarizing emotions, integrating feelings into social activities. And it is the sign of re-orienting impulses, learning to be aware and sensitive in social situations and learning to give and receive feedback.

LIBRA

The first day of Libra is the fall Equinox, one of the two points in the year when the lengths of day and night are the same. Light and darkness are in perfect balance. Libra initiates the Southern hemisphere which is comprised of quadrants three and four. The third quadrant begins at the third cardinal point or seventh house cusp. It is the southwest quadrant, focused in an objective way on external activities. Libra is the first sign of the third quadrant, which covers the signs Libra, Scorpio and Sagittarius and houses seven, eight and nine. This is the quadrant of relationship. The orientation is to the external world and learning how to relate to it in objective ways. It is the initial attempt to look beyond the self and the family and establish realistic, vital, fulfilling interactions with others. The first two quadrants, known as the Northern hemisphere, are oriented toward the inner world and the personal life. The first quadrant is northeast and consists of Aries, Taurus and Gemini plus houses one, two and three. It is the quadrant of *self.* They are archetypes oriented to the task of defining and developing the self, physically, socially, and mentally. The focus is internal and subjective. The second quadrant is northwest and contains the signs Cancer, Leo and Virgo plus houses four, five and six. It is internal and objective, oriented toward developing the core self in comfortable, safe and familiar surroundings.

The third cardinal point is opposite to the first cardinal point as the third quadrant is opposite the first. Oppositions create mirror images within which perspective can be learned and self-awareness can be more clearly defined. As the first quadrant is indicative of independent, resourceful activity, the third quadrant focuses on united action and social cooperation. The emphasis of the third quadrant is on building a society instead of nurturing the individual. Aries and Libra are the first pair of signs that are in polar opposition to each other. Each of the six pairs of opposite signs are oriented toward similar patterns, issues and experiences but they deal with those similarities from different points of view. In a chart in which there are planets that are in opposite signs and approximately 180 degrees apart, the planets are said to be in opposition ($\mathcal{S}$). Just as the square, or 90 degree angular, separation provides an internal challenge to grow, so does the opposition provides a challenge through the interaction between the self and the outer world. Often this will be in the form of a one-to-one relationship. The tension generated by an opposition not only provides an opportunity to develop a sense of self-awareness and perspective through feedback from others, it can also provide an important sense of direction. Oppositions indicate where there is tension between ourselves and others. The goal is to resolve that tension so that we can go through life in a harmonious way. To create and maintain harmony is a prime focus and function for Libra.

The balance of day and night—light and darkness—which occurs on the Equinox doesn't last. The nights grow longer for the next three months. The energy to manifest independently in a direct and forceful way diminishes and there is more of a need to rely upon the social, collective energy to define or manifest the self and to achieve goals. This is what the signs and houses of the Southern hemisphere, comprising the next two quadrants are all about. The sign that initiates this change is Libra. The Sun is in Libra from September 22 or 23 until October 22 or 23. It symbolizes the birth of the individual into the greater whole. Libra says, "I balance and harmonize."

THE MYTHS

Libra's prime focus is on relationship: the integration of the self into the greater social whole. Consequently, it is the sign of relationship, specifically a one-to-one primary partnership. The myths that illustrate the concept of primary relationship are in three categories. First is the relationship of husband and wife. One of the earliest myths of India is that of the marriage of Soma, the Moon-god and god of fecundity, to Sita, the daughter of the Sun. This is a harmonious and mutually beneficial union between two fundamental aspects of reality. There are other mythic tales in which the relationship was as equal but more stormy, or less equal and difficult to balance nonetheless. An example of an equal but conflicted relationship is that between the Hindu god Shiva and his consort Parvati. Shiva is one of the most ancient concepts of a deity that is still alive and worshipped in the modern world. He symbolizes the terror of destruction. His worshipers acknowledge the impermanence of all things, as well as the passion of creativity that lies beyond and behind death. Parvati is the female counterpart to Shiva. To some she is the physical embodiment of the spirit. Like Shiva she represents terrifying death but also the consequential renewal. There is a sense of equality about these deities, both in terms of focus and of power. There is also a sense of competition between them in terms of who has more power, or rights of manifestation in their relationship or in the world. The balance between them, their rights and their power is tenuous and always in flux.

A more recent, although still ancient, deity in India is Krishna. A physical incarnation of the Divine Eternal Principle, he is the manifestation of love and the Eastern equivalent of Christ. As a god, he was free to love all beings. In his embodiment of a man, he loved and married Radha. Yet he continued to love and be with other women, much to his wife's pain and mortification. There is less equality between Krishna and Radha than between Shiva and Parvati, but the difficulty in maintaining the harmonious balance in the relationship is similar. With love as a basis of the union, issues were resolved in ways other than competition and use of power.

Another example of marriage in mythic form is that between Zeus and Hera. Hera is the Greek goddess of marriage. She is depicted as the embodiment of loyalty in union, but she is also symbolic of the Great Goddess. She is left over from a period in human history that was primarily matriarchal, that is, female centered. During that period the prime deity was conceived of and depicted as female and in the form of the Goddess. When the patriarchal, dominator cultures descended upon the matriarchal and pastoral, men began to assert their dominion over women. The Great Goddess became subordinated to the god until she was eventually shattered into several concepts and images, thereby diluting her power. Hera is therefore a limited embodiment of the goddess, limited to her role of wife of or consort to the male principle. The story of how this came about is very instructive of a dynamic between men and women that is still being played out in our culture today. It is a story of cunning and manipulation as well as great public relations for what was at that time a new definition of spiritual reality. The story is that Zeus, symbol of the male principle, proposed marriage to Hera, promising loyalty and fidelity in return for her willingness to compromise her position as prime deity. After much thought and consternation, she accepted his offer. Soon after the marriage Zeus betrayed Hera not once, but countless times, becoming infamous for his relationships and sexual activities with women and other goddesses. These affairs bore witness to the emerging role of male dominance and its disregard for the female. By the time Zeus' pattern and plan became clear, it was too late for Hera; the compromise had been made and the new order was in place. What had been promised as a relationship of equals became in fact an out of control situation for Hera. From her place of primacy and power, she fell to become the symbol of the enraged, embittered, vengeful, powerless partner in an unequal relationship.

This is a story that symbolically illustrates the domination and subjugation of the resident pastoral and matrilineal society by the invading male dominated, authoritarian society. Maybe it was a story consciously designed to enlist the original culture in compliant acquiescence with the new, or perhaps a story that grew out of the experience of intermingling two societies of extremely different cosmologies. A cosmology is a system that attempts to define the nature of the Universe in an orderly way. All mythic tales emanate from such a system. They are a way of describing the Universe in a way that can be understood by people. In this way we can each feel a part of the big picture, less alienated, less fearful, and less out of control. In any case, the story of Hera and Zeus illustrates what can happen when relationship is entered into with unclear motivations, or a less than honest expression of what those motives are.

In the Middle Ages in Europe the story of Tristan and Isolde depicts another concept of relationship and one which, at that time represented a new concept in human experience. Feudal society of Europe was very rigid. In the upper class of royalty and nobility, marriages were arranged by families in what were usually relationships of political or economic significance. In the Tristan and Isolde myth, two young people came together and fell in love. They went against societal convention by wanting to be together in matrimony not for any reason other than their attraction and affection for each other. This initiated the idea that relationship could be based on individual choice.

The second category of relationship is the balance you create within yourself by uniting your masculine and feminine aspects. This is illustrated in the Greek myth of Tiresias. As he was walking through the woods one day, he came upon two serpents copulating. Fundamentally this is a symbol of kundalini energy being raised up the spine and illumining the Higher Being. Tiresias placed his staff (spine) between the serpents who, in anger, transformed him into a woman. He lived as a woman for many years until he once again came upon two copulating serpents. This time, a touch from his staff transformed him back into a man. An interpretation of this story is the potential each of us has to develop an actualized and expressed relationship with both our assertive/masculine and receptive/feminine natures. Thus, we create an inner balance through the relationship to ourselves.

The third category of relationship is expressed by the spiritual masters Buddha and Jesus who embody the relationship between our lower and higher beings. Buddha taught his followers to pursue the median path, neither too far to the left nor the right. This is the fastest course to enlightenment. It relies on the creation of internal balance, of equanimity, by the individual. Jesus is the Prince of Peace, the Supreme Incarnation of inner bliss and harmony. He taught us to strive to maintain contact with God, even as we went about making a contribution to improve the world for our fellow beings. One of his greatest contributions—perhaps the one which was most threatening to the political and spiritual power structure of his time—was to call attention to the low status of women. Stories abound about how he committed the heresy of seeking to raise women to the status of men, such as defending a prostitute being stoned by an unruly mob or allowing women in to his inner circle of advisors. By doing so he acted as an advocate of equality, a key need for Libra. In this case, equality as experienced in the relationship between men and women. This illustrates the spiritual truth that we are all children of God, manifestations of Divine Spirit, seen in an equal light.

THE GLYPH: ♎

The symbol for Libra is two parallel lines. The top one has a bulge-like semi-circle rising from its center. The bottom line is straight. This connotes three meanings. The first is equality; the idea that two things can be equal, yet separate and significant within themselves. The second is balance. It is almost as if the fulcrum of the balance is the bulge. It reminds us of how fundamental the state of equilibrium is and yet how fragile the balance. It is a task, a point of focus, to work at maintaining the balance in ones life. This balance could be between your higher and lower nature, your masculine and feminine nature, or the internal and external world in your relationships to yourself and others.

This is also a symbol of the Sun descending below the horizon. Libra is called the sign of the setting Sun for two reasons. First, it comes at that time each year when the days are becoming shorter than the nights. The light is decreasing in the Northern hemisphere during the time of year that the Sun transits through the signs of the third quadrant. The second reason is that in the course of a day, the Sun enters the seventh house, the area of life associated with Libra, just prior to sunset. The impending darkness symbolizes one reason why Libra has a hard time seeing the self, consequently why feedback from the outer world and other people is so important. It is also a reason why Libran energy carries with it the potential for a nostalgic melancholy for "the good old days" of youth, of warmth or of the recent day itself. The implication is of the need to balance the memory of the beauty and joy of the past with the anticipation of the new and as yet to be discovered.

THE TOTEM: ⚖

Libra is the only sign whose totem cannot be depicted in either human or animal form. The Greek philosopher Manilius assigned Vulcan, the blacksmith god and forger of metals, to rule Libra. But this never became accepted in popular usage. The totem for Libra is a concept which can be interpreted as balance, justice, and judgment. Justice is expressed both from the idea of the scales and the idea of the holder of the scales, blind justice. This implies a Universal Observer who continually weighs our acts against the balance beam and ordains our karmic debits and credits accordingly. Ultimately this corresponds to the Last Judgment when the cumulative actions of all souls will be weighed. This concept goes back to 2000 BC and the time of the Babylonian culture.

The idea of the scales also refers to the harvest in ancient Egypt. It was customary in that society for the harvest to be weighed and taxes to be assessed each year during the full Moon in the month of Libra.

The Scales of Justice also suggest that Libra evaluates people from a preconceived or previously defined social standard. This indicates that sometimes Libra can be highly idealistic and humanitarian but at other times opinionated and judgmental. For Libra, the concept of justice is meted out through the Old Testament concept of an "eye for an eye." In other words, for Libra, "You hit me, I hit you back and we are even." That's equal, that's balance, that's justice. As we will see later on when we talk about the sign Sagittarius, another sign very concerned with law and justice, that there are other ways of dealing with these concepts.

The Scales of Justice can also be experienced in a social context by Libra in the form of "I and thou." Libra is concerned and aware not only of self, but of other. The Scales signify the balance between individual expression and the traditions of society. Libra is a very moderate sign and is one of the more traditional and conservative of signs. Libra seeks moderation.

Ultimately, however, the scales symbolize the power of choice. They represent opportunity to express your free will by first weighing and balancing all your options. Libra strives to be logical and objective in its judgment. The ensuing decisions will either be correct in themselves, or fertile ground for learning and growth.

Although the sign Libra is universal, its concept and totem varied among the cultures of the ancient world. The Greeks called Libra the claws referring to the claws of the scorpion. At one time, the constellation Libra was seen as part of the constellation Scorpio, and was therefore considered to be part of the Scorpionic experience. In the second century AD it was agreed that the two were completely different experiences. It was at this time that the Greek astrologers Ptolemy, Hippocrates

and Erastothenes, called Libra *Zugon* which means yoke. They
were aware of the Libran tendency to join together as in
marriage. It's also interesting to note that *Zugon* is the basis for
the word zygote, which is the union of the sperm and the egg.
The Roman name for Libra is *Jugum*. The word *Libra* itself is
Latin for weight and measure. The Hindus refer to Libra as *Tula*,
which means balance. The Chinese call Libra *Tien Ching*, the
celestial balance. To the Hebrews, Libra is *Mosnyem*, which
means the scale beams.

By whatever name or symbol, the concepts of balance and
union are universal to the human experience regardless of time
frame or geography.

MODE AND ELEMENT

Libra is the cardinal air sign. Libra represents the atmosphere
around us, the environment that functions on the social level.
Libra's air nature indicates that it is intellectual and social. The
cardinality of Libra indicates that it is direct and action-oriented.
Putting the two together, Libra represents directed intellectual
activity in search of social interaction. Socially, this creates a
concept and behavioral dynamic of "I and Thou." Libra is the
archetypal experience of the sharing of the core self, defined,
refined and expressed through the first six signs. Libra seeks
clarity of self through harmonious relationship with others,
specifically in the form of one-to-one relationships. In this way,
Libra externalizes its internal harmony and internalizes its
external harmony. This flow of social energy is crucial to the
Libran sense of well-being.

With Libran energy, you are aware of and sensitive to
feedback from people with whom you have a meaningful
relationship. This feedback functions as a mirror. It provides a
sense of yourself from the perspective of the partner. Libra is the
sign of the setting Sun. It's as if the encroaching darkness makes
it difficult to see yourself clearly, so you look outside for more
information about who you are. One drawback to this pattern is
that the perspective you get from other people is based solely on
their subjective point of view, complete with their limitations
and prejudices. Nonetheless, your need for the feedback is
strong. The more consistently positive it is, the better you feel
about yourself. You have a stake in keeping a partner happy and

feeling good about you. As a result, you may placate your partner and function the way your partner wants you to, rather than as you want to. This could lead to a pattern of glossing over the negative or unfulfilled aspects of the relationship, or the parts of your partner that you don't like. Not only does this create a superficial relationship, it prevents you and your true thoughts, feelings and needs from being expressed and known. This pattern undermines the truth of the entire relationship and leads to dependencies on the partner. Ironically, this pattern of placation can also cause you to be seen as cold and unfeeling.

Growing beyond this pattern of dependency is to become aware of an entire social environment. From that point of view you become more concerned with creating an ambiance within which everyone can feel included. In this scenario you are more aware of how to externalize the harmony that you already feel within yourself. One of the finer social qualities of Libra is the ability to make others feel comfortable. The ability to do this comes from an understanding of what harmony is and how to manifest it. Harmony results from establishing within yourself a place of inner peace. From that point you can function in a cooperative way with others, thereby helping to create a peaceful environment. This quality can be useful in resolving disputes whether between family members or at a diplomatic post. As a cardinal sign you are an activist by nature. Use that tendency to establish harmony in your life in whatever areas are important to you, from the personal to the political.

Cardinal air also indicates that Libra is the sign of logic, a pattern of reasoning that leads to certain conclusions about a given subject. In the positive sense, this suggests a well-rounded mind that can engage in intelligent conversation on a variety of subjects. You can be an excellent debater, presenting your ideas in a clear, easily understood manner. In terms of personal relationships, Libra can usually identify with the Golden Rule: treat others as you want them to treat you. This is not solely to get positive feedback, but because it serves the cause of social unity. This is not only good diplomacy but also a way being a leader. By consistently putting out positive, thoughtful energy that is respectful and considerate of other people's needs and feelings, you can inspire others to learn how to relate in kind. In this mode you are also willing to compromise with others and understand the value and dynamics of compromise. Being a positive person and a generator of support to others increases self-confidence in others. Your reassurance promotes others to take positive actions which can benefit them, you, or a larger, more all-encompassing social structure. Sometimes you can be specific in your encouragement, inspiring someone to grow or do something that previously seemed impossible to them. You can also exude a buoyant optimism that can serve to hearten any who come your way.

The Libra love of logic can help you to become a good teacher. You have the potential to express an idea or point of view in a variety of ways until all your students understand the concept. Unlike Gemini, for whom the flow of information itself is the important thing, Libra is more oriented toward sharing information about a specific topic that is rendered in a cogent way. Similarly you can appreciate a well thought out argument presented by someone else even if you disagree with the premise. At times the rightness of your logic can help you and others to draw accurate conclusions about the topic at hand. Librans make good sales people because they can present a logical case and argument to the listener.

In the negative sense, however, this reliance on logic can cause you to be someone who is extremely opinionated and judgmental. Libra has been referred to as the sign of the judge. At other times you can be so caught up in trying to weigh and balance all the possibilities and points of view that you are unable to make a decision or formulate an opinion at all. You can also be very arbitrary in choosing a point of view. You may speak for a premise other than your true belief just for the sake of discussion. You could also use that tactic as a way of expressing anger at someone in a passive-aggressive way. On the surface, all is well, but you may have repressed feelings of anger and frustration which you fear expressing. Instead of being direct, you play the role of instigator. In one scenario you pretend to believe in something that is detestable to someone else. You use your power of logical persuasion to emphasize how much you truly believe in your point of view, that it is the right one and that they should believe it too. Your adversary might become enraged at your point of view, but not about your real feelings because they are unexpressed.

Instigation can also take the form of pitting one person against another. Instead of expressing your own feelings of alienation from or anger toward either of both or the other parties, you create problems between them. Even if they also begin to feel alienated or angry at each other, your original problem is unresolved, yet you have created difficulties for others that aren't even real.

The logical mind of Libra can also lead to a tendency to be rational all the time. If something isn't logical, it can't be true or real. Clinging to this point of view is a way to avoid dealing with the irrational elements of your life, such as feelings. This pattern certainly helps you avoid elements of life that might be ugly or upsetting. It keeps you functioning in a narrow band of reality and ultimately limits the truth and satisfaction of your relationships. There are also tendencies to rely on logic to such an extent that you rationalize that your opinions, points of view or social patterns are "right." Libra is the sign of rationalization. You can apply your logical abilities to the point that anything you want sounds good. You could be convincing yourself that a particular course of action or judgment is justified. You could convince others that something you want them to do is rational and appropriate even if a more objective argument would prove it to be otherwise. Sometimes you can get yourself or others into trouble simply by making something that is really not that good an idea sound very promising.

Combining the social and mental orientation of the element air with the action orientation of cardinality, Libra can go from one source of feedback to another trying to find the proper opinion or point of view. It's as if you assume that one of those people has the right answer, or at least the proper position for you to adopt, so you go from person to person trying to find your perspective in mirror image form. This can lead to vacillating between the mirrors, trying to decide which one is you. To avoid this confusion, realize that you can learn from each person you speak with. Instead of looking for the "right one," try to integrate information from each one in a way that enables you to build your own truth. In the end you can bounce that truth off a reliable partner, just to check its viability. In this way you use

your strengths of logic and social interaction to define yourself
and your reality in a clear and definite, but not dependent, way.

THE RULING PLANET

Venus (♀) is the ruling planet of Libra as well as of Taurus.
Through its rulership of Taurus, Venus symbolizes the energy of
sociability. It helps to define our social patterns, behaviors and
needs. Venus can also support the process of defining values. In
that sense, the association of Venus with Libra puts a high value
on art, beauty and aesthetics.

Venus' orientation toward people stimulates two types of
activities. In a personal sense, it can orient you to sharing
yourself through social activities with significant others in your
life. If Venus is prominent in your chart, such as conjunct one of
the angles or cardinal points or in Taurus or Libra, you will be a
giving, affectionate person. This is especially true if Venus is in
positive aspect (conjunction, sextile or trine), to the Sun, Mars or
Jupiter. These aspects also promote an ease in relating to others,
a sense of comfort with your sexuality and the potential to be
well liked by others. If Venus is sextile or trine to your ascendant
you will project yourself in a gracious manner and promote
harmony wherever you are. If Venus is squaring or opposing
Saturn or Uranus, it may be hard for you to either give or receive
affection. With Saturn you could be afraid of not being truly
lovable or be so concerned that you will be disappointed that you
block the flow of love between yourself and a prospective
partner. With Uranus the issue is more of maintaining your
independence. If you are concerned that being in a relationship
means you will merge with your partner and lose yourself, you
will react in an aloof way to offers of love. Squares or
oppositions from Venus to the Moon, Mars or Jupiter, however,
can indicate that your patterns of giving and needs to receive
love and affection may be too strong. These aspects suggest
tendencies to give more than you can afford or to be open to
people who don't really love you. As long as someone is there
who at least approximates a partner you feel satisfied, at least
temporarily. In the long run the relationships prove frustrating
and unfulfilling. The purpose of these squares and oppositions
are to help you become clearer about your needs, patterns and
tendencies in personal relationship. Don't confuse dissatisfaction

or disappointment with being unlovable or unable to "get it right." Learn from each experience and make changes in who you choose, how you share yourself and how you allow others to share with you. By becoming more conscious of yourself in this area you will be able to change your experience in relationship. Use the tension of the squares and oppositions to challenge you to do this work.

The specific patterns of the influence of Venus in each of the signs has been delineated in the Taurus chapter.

In an impersonal sense, the connection of Venus with Libra provides an external social focus. As Libra is the first sign above the horizon, it is oriented toward activities taking place outside yourself and your family. It represents the beginning stages of integrating the individual core self within a greater social context. This extends relationship beyond one-to-one, because Venus stimulates the development of a social conscience. The idealistic side of Venus can impel you to fight for social causes usually on the side of the underdog. If Venus is a significant planet in your chart, humanitarian social values are important to you. They are based on your drive for fairness and equality in social situations. Make sure, however, that your concern for others' welfare isn't just a cover-up of feelings of frustration in your personal life. You may be projecting anger that deserves to be directed at someone in your life, such as a partner or parent, onto external sources, such as governments or social systems. That may enable you to maintain a superficial harmony in your relationship and provide a lot of drive and impetus for your cause, but it doesn't relieve your own personal stress or improve the relationship.

Your social consciousness can also indicate an interest in current events as well as history. Noting where humanity has been, and where it is, can provide a sense of inspiration and direction about where to go from here. You can function as an activist who strives to implement a new philosophical or political paradigm. The concern for others can also impel you to relate to people in thoughtful, considerate and diplomatic ways. Even when you are taking problems into consideration and dealing openly with underlying feelings of frustration, anger or resentment, you maintain a tactfulness of expression, and a willingness to compromise. These qualities can combine in ways that enable you to excel as a mediator. Remember, however, to wait to be asked by the parties in question before you step in. Sometimes people need to resolve their problems by themselves. Some people are just attached to their misery. In either case you can be resented by the same people you are striving to help. By waiting to be invited in to resolve a dilemma, you avoid becoming the target. Don't supply an answer if nobody asks you a question.

Venus also represents the energy of art and beauty. If Venus is prominent in your chart, or if you have significant energy in Libra, you have a strong sense of aesthetics. You appreciate beauty, whether it is in and of the natural world or of human origin. The attractiveness of your surroundings is important to you. Your feeling about the color a room is painted can have a lot to do with enjoying the events taking place in that room. You are also sensitive to the colors and style of fabric used in furniture covering, carpet or clothing. Being stylish and wearing bright, cheerful colors will be your usual choice. You could also be attracted to a person more as a result of what they look like or what they wear than by who they are. There are limits beyond which it is dangerous to rely solely upon aesthetics.

THE SEVENTH HOUSE

The area of life associated with Libra is the seventh house. This is the house of partnership, the house of one-to-one relationship. Marriage or spousal relationship is one form of partnership. The seventh house can also manifest as business partnership, or with a student/teacher, a counselor/client, or spiritual master/disciple relationship. It can be experienced as a relationship between you and a good friend or between you and an advisor. The seventh house can also involve projecting yourself to the public. The primary stipulation of the seventh house social activity is that it is one-to-one.

With seventh house energy, as with Libra, you tend to seek validation, definition or justification of who you are from the mirror-like feedback you receive from a partner. You may have a tendency to internalize the feedback indiscriminately. If you internalize positive feedback, you might decide that you are such a wonderful person, that you don't have to grow or change or do anything differently. If you internalize negative feedback, you may think of yourself as a person who has nothing to offer. With significant energy in your seventh house, be selective about who you receive feedback from. Make sure it is from someone you admire, or from someone you can learn from, or someone who sees you in a positive, yet balanced way. Seeing yourself through a multiplicity of partnerships can help balance the equation. Some partners will see you more clearly and more positively in certain areas, while others may be more critical. In the long run both can provide you with a balanced perspective, offering the supportive strokes and the critical challenges that lead to a healthy, realistic sense of yourself.

You can create this balance either simultaneously or sequentially. In the former situation you spend time with a variety of feedback sources, none of which necessarily overlap. For example, you value your time with your primary partner, your good friend, your teacher and your business partner. Each sees you in a different way and values different aspects of your nature. You see yourself as a well-rounded person. In sequential partnerships, your image of yourself is derived from feedback over time from a number of similar sources. An example of this is serial monogamy. In this pattern, you immerse yourself in one personal partnership for a time and then move on to another. Each pattern is workable and valid. With a mutable sign on the cusp of your seventh house, you can adapt to several relationships at once; it also suggests more than one primary relationship or marriage. A cardinal sign would be more prone to one relationship at a time although sequential relationships are possible. A fixed sign on the cusp of the seventh house, however, implies the need for one enduring, stable partnership.

Sometimes the need for interactive feedback becomes too strong. You could become a relationship opportunist, always on the prowl for someone to hold up the mirror. This could lead to patterns of social manipulation or co-dependency. In either case, you seek personal harmony through relationship at any cost. This could be an addictive pattern. Although it's neither possible nor desirable to eliminate all one-to-one social interaction, you can certainly limit its extent so that you do not become dependent. To do this, either use multiple relationships or create other ways of seeing yourself.

The seventh house is oriented toward awareness of and interaction with the immediate environment. In that pattern it is similar to its opposite, the first house. One difference is that whereas planets in the first house tend to create an environment, those in the seventh are more affected by both the environment itself as well as the interaction of the energies of the individual with those of the environment. For example, with significant energy in your seventh house you could be strongly influenced by the aesthetics of a place. You are aware of and sensitive to qualities such as the color of a room. Your sense of internal harmony can be upset if the vibration of the external aesthetics does not coincide with your personal sense of beauty. Since the seventh is an angular house, it is action-oriented. With energy in your seventh house, you can do something that would contribute to the beauty of an environment. To eliminate the dependency on social feedback as well as create a more pleasing vibrational aesthetic, get more in touch with your artistic talents. The creative process itself can provide you with feedback. When you read the poem or story you wrote or step away from the easel to view your canvas or listen to yourself playing music or singing you have opportunity for a different type of self-awareness and self-image than another person can provide. It is neither possible nor desirable to eliminate social interaction and the feedback you receive from others. Through your artist efforts, however, you can limit the need for feedback, avoid falling into the dependency rut and create something that is a creative expression of yourself.

Although the seventh is the house of harmony, it can also be the house of open warfare. This can take many forms, from legal disputes to conflicts with a partner. You could act in a highly judgmental way toward someone or blame them for your problems. What are the underlying reasons for this? What causes the harmony-loving, balance-oriented seventh house person to create or become involved in this dynamic? Usually it is due to projection. Because your need for harmony is so fundamental, you may only see those parts of yourself that you like. If discordant elements are in your life, you assume they are being introduced by someone else. If don't have a partner to blame, you feel your problems are due to not having a relationship. This is a projection of your shadow, those murky parts of yourself which you either don't know or don't like, onto someone else. You are seeing your bad habits as caused by someone else. Or you don't see yourself at all and just assume that anything unpleasant in your life was brought there and deposited by someone else. Sometimes you can be most judgmental of people who openly manifest patterns that you also generate. Whatever this other person thinks about their actions, or whether they are even aware of them or not, you dislike those qualities. Rather than notice them within you and working to change them, you ridicule someone else. Nothing is ever your fault.

If someone calls you on these projection patterns, pointing out how you create your own disharmony, or questions you about some of your darker elements there might be real open warfare! Your attachment to harmony and to being okay is so strong that it can be difficult to admit to doing anything that might create stress. Listening to that feedback to the extent that you become aware of the blind spots of these patterns can produce growth. If you find that you are judging others, realize that it is those very qualities you judge that you need to work on within yourself. If you are attracted to someone who turns out to have tendencies you find intolerable, realize you need to own and work on those same patterns within yourself. Instead of responding in a hostile fashion if you are questioned about something uncomfortable, realize it is an opportunity to change and grow. Best of all is to recognize these things without needing the one-to-one dynamic to point them out. Even if you acknowledge what is brought up and are willing to work and change, if you always rely on the partner or relationship to challenge you, that, too, can be a form of dependency. Realistically, even in a healthy psyche and healthy relationship, strive to create a balance whereby you do as much work as you can on yourself by yourself. Balance can also be created as both you and partner gently and lovingly challenge each other to become more centered and conscious about yourselves, each other and the dynamic between you.

The seventh is an air house. The previous air house is the third, the area that deals with the random flow of social energy. But the sixth house, Virgo, teaches the lesson of discrimination. As applied to relationships, this suggests the importance of being selective not only about who to choose as a partner, but how to interact as well. With significant energy in your seventh house you would feel comfortable working in a situation that allowed you function within a one-to-one context. Professions such as therapist or consultant fall into this category. As an attorney you could draw inspiration from the seventh house' orientation toward fairness and social justice. As a teacher you could be most effective by working with students one at a time or in small groups.

The planets located in your natal seventh house indicate how you tend to relate and in the kind of energy you are looking for from a partner. What you offer, and what you need. With the Sun in your seventh, you tend to identify with both your partner and the relationship itself. You can be very creative in defining and functioning within the situation. The Sun in the seventh house indicates a strong tendency to look for your center in either the partner or the relationship. You may tend to rely too much on your partner's feedback to see or feel good about yourself.

The Moon emphasizes nurturing and family as qualities to share in partnership. Your strenghts include sensitivity to the emotional flow between the two of you, and receptivity to your partner's needs. You enjoy consistent togetherness and sharing the simple activities of the day. The danger is in projecting onto your partner expectations of behavior that applied to someone in your childhood family. You could unconsciously seek to recreate your parents relationship, or the one between you and one of your parents.

Mercury and Jupiter in the seventh both emphasize communication, exchange of information, and learning as important qualities to be experienced. Jupiter especially, places high value on emotional honesty and personal integrity. Either planet enjoys a student-teacher type relationship in which you are both open to listening to and learning from each other as well as sharing previously learned knowledge with each other.

Venus in the seventh brings the positive relationship qualities of diplomacy and tact, as well as the willingness and ability to compromise and cooperate in the co-creation of a harmonious, mutually beneficial union. But the downside is the "peace at any price" pattern of placation. Venus in the seventh house could also put a high priority on the attractiveness of the partner above qualities that have more substance and potential for depth. You also might prefer partners who simply go along and get along rather than those who are more process-oriented.

Mars in the seventh enjoys relating to an aggressive partner, one who enjoys taking the lead in the relationship. In the positive mode, Mars indicates passion and a lot of energy to put into relating. The negative tendency is to want the relationship contract to read: partner leads, you follow. But the fine print at the bottom of the page reads, "as long as you take it where I want it to go." By giving away too much of your own assertiveness, Mars in the seventh can lead to conflict based on this issues of leadership and direction.

Saturn in the seventh brings the element of control to relationship. There could be a tendency to give too much of your power to the partner or to try usurping too much from partner. The power-trip pattern is based on fear, an assumption that relationships are based on one person being in power, and the other person having none. The way out of that pattern is to take responsibility for what you offer to the partner and what you need to receive. Learn to be more open about your perceptions and feelings in the relationship as a whole. What are your goals in the relationship? What about timing, rate and rhythm? These are all Saturn in the seventh house issues. This is not to be rendered as a dictatorial demand. This is you sharing who you are with your partner. It's important to be open to partner sharing similar information with you. This openness is risky—something cautious Saturn prefers to avoid. Saturn in the seventh, however, brings lessons about life to and from relationship. This openness is also somewhat cold and dry. But through this process you learn what the realistic limits of the relationship are as well as the overlap and intersection of interests, needs and connections. The lessons require work, and are not necessarily easy. On the positive side, Saturn can bring a desire for commitment and the ability to remain loyal to a partner. It prefers to open up slowly and can indicate that it may take until after the Saturn return (age 28-30) before an enduring relationship is realistic for you. If you are male, you could be attracted to an older partner, being attracted to wisdom and experience. If you are female, you may prefer younger partners, offering your insight and grounding to an appreciative partner.

Uranus in the seventh prefers independence to commitment. With Uranus here, the most important quality to develop in a relationship is friendship. From that perspective you can give your partner the freedom to be who they are. Any attempt by your partner to possess or control and you're gone. You place value on tolerance, acceptance and unconditional love. These are the qualities you offer and what you demand in return. With this emphasis on personal freedom your relationships are likely to be made up as you go along relying more on inspiration and personal proclivity than on traditional forms. Without establishing friendship first, however, the commonality of interests, values and goals upon which to base a union isn't there. With Uranus in the seventh, your lesson is how to integrate your uniqueness into a mutually shared and beneficial relationship.

Neptune in the seventh is beneficial in the charts of therapists and counselors. In your personal life, strive to develop a relationship based on spirituality, in which both you and partner perceive and honor your respective higher beings. This is a type of union in which devotion and unconditional love are the overriding values. But make sure you're both on the same page, otherwise Neptune in the seventh house can create unworkable patterns, such as that of the savior/victim. You fall in love with the higher being of someone who doesn't even know what a higher being is. You are actually in love with love or confusing love with pity. Your pattern is to try to help, heal, fix or save someone whom you feel has been victimized by life. They could have drug or alcohol abuse problems, severe psychological problems, mental illness, or even be physically handicapped. Unappreciated and unrecognized artists can also fall into this category. Once you make them okay, your script is that this person will fall in love with you due to their undying gratitude. In reality, you become the victim. You either become drained by a relationship in which you do all the giving and receive nothing back at all, or the newly emerging partner blames you, the strong one, for being their problem in the first place. This is why it is so important to establish in a clear, mutually agreed upon and conscious way, a spiritual basis of relating, and save your healer tendencies for clients.

Pluto in the seventh brings the need for transformation to relationship. Your primary need is to experience personal renewal through a primary union. Secondarily, you need periodic rebirth of the relationship itself. To bring this about, there must be the willingness on your part to bring up and confront issues with your partner. These issues could address your deeper feelings, fears, or frustrations about yourself, the relationship or the partner's behavior. This also implies partner confronting you on a similar basis. These are not conversations that occur all the time, but they are necessary at least periodically. They can be somewhat scary, unpleasant, or even ruthless when they do occur. In the process the necessary transformation can take place and the negative options of Pluto in the seventh can be avoided. These involve a tendency to be deceitful, intimidating, or coercive of the partner, trying to manipulate the transformation you need instead of owning it and expressing it openly as a need. Or you might draw to you people who are acting out your negative Pluto energy. They could be powerful, intense and passionate. You might feel victimized by such a relationship or dominated and drained by such a person. You are setting up the scenario by not realizing that this energy is yours. By not being aware of this power as your own, or by not using it as a vehicle to experience transformation through relationship, it gets used against you. Whatever energy exists in your relationship that you don't like, is your energy. It may appear to be emanating from your partner, but it is really your own energy being reflected back to you from the partner.

By applying three primary rules, you can use the energy in your seventh house to create harmonious, growth-oriented and mutually fulfilling relationships. They are appropriate to any social relationship, from the most insignificant association to the most important primary union. Rule number one is that all relationships are based on a fifty-fifty principle. This is not meant as an absolute. In other words, don't keep score. Sometimes you give more than fifty percent of the energy, but at other times you will receive more. Or you consistently provide over half the energy in specific areas yet receive more than half in others. Overall, the amount and quality of time and energy you are putting into the relationship is balanced by that of your partner. If that is not the case, the exchange between you is unbalanced. The one who is consistently doing more of the giving could continue that pattern until it became more exaggerated over time. In the beginning it may be a slight difference, but as time goes by you will give more and more just to keep the relationship alive. The more out of balance the energy exchange, the more off centered you are. The more off centered you are, the more you will tend to be dependent on partner's feedback to feel good about yourself. You may hope that the pattern will change but realistically, it just gets worse. Don't automatically assume an inherent sense of fairness in your partner that will impel them to rectify the imbalance at some point.

To break this pattern, pull back to the fifty percent line. Give your partner a quality and quantity of energy similar to what you are receiving. When this happens, partner can respond in various ways. One is by saying nothing at all; not even realizing you are pulling back, which gives you a good idea of your partner's perspective on the relationship. Or, if partner does notice, he/she might ask why you have withdrawn. The realistic response is that you haven't withdrawn as much as simply created a more equal flow of energy between you. Partner can respond to this in several ways. One is by not changing at all. This indicates that you are already getting all there is to get, or that partner does not value you and the relationship enough to give more. Or your partner may increase his/her efforts, trying to put out more energy to you. If this is your experience, this new energy may or may not be fulfilling and meet your needs. Don't get so excited by partner's renewed enthusiasm that you forget what you want.

This brings us to the second useful rule of relationship: from each according to his ability, to each according to his need. Karl Marx expressed this concept as a basic tenet of his economic system, communism. As experience and world history have taught us, this is not a viable system, especially when applied to a large, heterogeneous industrial country. But when applied to individual human relationship, the concept of needs matching abilities is useful. It suggests that for a relationship to be viable, what you put out must match your partner's needs and vice versa. Even if your efforts and inclinations fulfill your partner, if he or she is putting out energy that does not fulfill you, it's not a viable relationship. This may be sad, and an unfortunate circumstance, but it isn't really anyone's fault. Although you are free to continue the relationship and learn from the process you are also free to let it go. Cultivate the concept of "no fault relationship." It's not an indication that you are unlovable if a particular partner can't meet your needs. Nor does it imply you are never going to be able to satisfy another person's needs just because a present relationship isn't working.

This leads to the third idea: no expectations. All relationships seek their own realistic energy level. If you try to force a relationship into a particular form, you are seeking to control the experience. Instead, spend more time working on yourself and the process of becoming centered and self-loving. From that place you can be open to interacting with people in a more spontaneous way. This process will certainly lead to greater self-awareness and personal growth, and quite possibly to a relationship which will prove to be continually viable, loving, and mutually satisfying.

LIBRA AND THE BODY

Libra extends the principle of balancing to the anatomical level. This principle manifests in several forms. Libra is partially responsible for balancing what is taken into the body and what is let go from it by its rulership of the kidneys. By eliminating poisonous waste material from the body, Libra is helping to maintain the body's homeostatic integrity. Libra is also one of the rulers of the lower back, because this is the area where the kidneys are. The kidneys are a major organ of elimination. If they are blocked or constricted, the body may try to eliminate its toxins through the skin, another organ of elimination also ruled by Libra. The skin is also under the dominion of the ruler of Libra, Venus, primarily due to the connection between Venus and beauty. There is therefore a dual association of Libra and Venus, one oriented toward health, the other toward appearance.

Libra also rules the basil metabolism, which monitors and maintains the acid/alkaline balance of the system. Imbalance here is often as a result of improper nutrition. An imbalance of foods, such as too much red meat or not enough fresh vegetables, can produce an imbalance in the pH of the body and diseases can be the result.

The most important association of Libra to the body is through its rulership of the endocrine system. Imbalances therein can not only result in physical problems but in mental illness as well. The hormones secreted by the endocrine system are duplicated in the chemistry of the brain. An imbalance in the endocrine system can be reflected in a similar imbalance in brain chemistry. This has been found to be a cause in such forms of mental illness as manic-depression (or as currently characterized, bi-polar syndrome).

The locations of each of the endocrine glands are also the locations of nerve matrixes. These glands and nerve centers are physical representatives of the *chakras* or energy centers. Each center resonates with a different level of energy. Some people can see or feel the *chakras* and claim that imbalances in these centers are the prime cause of ill health. Each *chakra* has a special purpose and a unique function. The lower *chakras* help us to function on the material plane, aware of our physical self and emotional connections to others. The higher *chakras* relate more to the development of consciousness. In the center is the heart *chakra*, which connects us to the divine source of love. To maintain the balance of the *chakras* is to maintain health and continue the evolutionary journey. The most obvious physical manifestation of the *chakras* is the endocrine system, ruled by Libra.

CONCLUSIONS

Libra is the archetype that represents the core self learning to function within relationship to the outer world. For many people its a hard job to develop a consistently good relationship with themselves. Once we look outside ourselves the task becomes that much harder and far more complex. We must continue to grow as an individual, support others in their process as well as work on whatever issues come up within the relationship itself. With this new complexity, however, comes new opportunity for awareness and growth.

Through relationship we have the opportunity for self-awareness. For example, the first sign of the zodiac Aries says, "First let me get going, then I'll know where I stand." Its opposite sign, Libra, the first sign of social consciousness says, "First let me know where I stand, then I'll get going." Being open to feedback and sharing develops a more objective sense of who you are. It is central to the Libran experience.

Libra is a *yang* sign. It tends to express energy to create a social ambiance and then wait for the feedback. That feedback tells them something about the degree to which they are accepted within that environment. Sometimes the expression of the energy is futile. Either the choice of partner is wrong or you put out an amount of energy to the partner that you can't maintain. Sometimes what you expect in return from the partner is unrealistic. In any of those scenarios, you can get drained. Your partner might take advantage of your energy output. Why should they put out anything when you're doing such a good job of doing it for both of you. In the long run this can lead to resentment and confusion on your end.

From the Virgo experience comes the lesson of discrimination. In this context, it is valuable to be selective in choosing who to rely on or look to for feedback. Learn to be discerning about how to relate and how much energy to give. Remember to pay attention to the fifty percent line and balance the energy output with the energy income to avoid being drained.

Librans will usually relate to others as they are related to by others. This is especially true of Libran children. People form their initial sense of self-worth as a result of how they are related to in childhood. This is especially true for Libran children because the parent-child relationship is a special kind of one-to-one interaction. As the young Libra is related to by their parents, so will they tend to project outward and relate to other people, not only as a child, but throughout life as well. For those of you who do have Libran children, make sure that you are putting out a great deal of positive, harmonious support and recognition to them. If there is need for criticism or discipline, make sure you explain to them what is happening. Remember, that they have good logical minds and can understand a discussion even at a relatively early age. If you demonstrate that you respect them by appealing to their sense of what is fair, they will mirror that pattern and explain to you what is important to them in a fair-minded way. As long as the lines of communication remain open the relationship remains strong. Try to avoid statements such as, "This is the way, period," because the Libran child is likely to turn that right around and say pretty much the same thing to you thus closing the communication.

In an uncentered unself-loving condition, Libra will tend to create superficial relationships that are based on a pattern of peace at any price. Placate the partner so as to maintain the harmonious, if artificial, flow of energy. This also leads to co-dependent relationships. These are situations in which you want your partner to be who you want them to be and do what you want them to do rather than be who they are or do what they do. Co-dependency can also exist if you consistently put your partner's needs ahead of your own and spend your time and energy trying to satisfy those needs. The uncentered Libra can also create symbiotic relationships in which you and partner feed off each other's weaknesses. It's a form of relationship based on a pattern of "I've got you covered." According to the rules of the game, because you love your partner so much, you take responsibility for him/her in such a way that you never confront them about underlying issues or call upon them to grow or change. They return the favor by never challenging you about your motivations and blind spots or their points of frustration. So the two of you create a relationship which is very secure and comfortable, but also very boring, stagnant and emotionally dishonest.

The Libra who has earned the reputation for being superficial, for being more concerned with how things look or appear than how things are or how they feel, is out of touch with their higher self. They tend to look outside themselves for identity, often defining their center as actually residing in someone else (their prime source of feedback) or as being between themselves and someone else. If partner sees you as being a certain way, the feedback is more consistently positive and you feel better about yourself. Whatever happens keep smiling, keep it light and make others happy. Libra, the sign of nice. Another dimension to this dynamic, however, is a tendency Libra has to match what the partner is doing. You reflect back to your partner who he or she is, matching both their energy level and behavioral patterns. As a result you become an extension of the partner. Your identity doesn't exist at all. You could block yourself from engaging in interests that your partner doesn't share or not express certain abilities that your partner doesn't like. You could lower your energy level or limit your creative output to reflect that of someone else.

As you become more centered, however, you become less susceptible to relating to others as they relate to you and less likely to define yourself based on what others think of you. You are less likely to imitate other people so you can fit in or be liked. You get more in touch with your cardinal energy of leadership. This enables you to establish the patterns of the relationship. You can use your ability to match behavioral patterns and energy levels with other people to perceive who they are, not who you should be. This enables you to create more harmony in that situation by being appropriately supportive of others without becoming drained or co-dependent.

To become centered you need to find an internal fulcrum, a base of operations within yourself. From this point you can maintain your identity and develop your higher potential. Growth begins when you acknowledge your inner self as you do your social self and harmonize your emotional truth with your social reality. As you become more centered you become more self-loving and develop the ability to harmonize your higher and lower selves. The lower self is not a negative part that needs to be purged. It just pertains to those aspects of life that are more oriented to the temporary world of the material plane. Being too focused on the lower self can create a sense of insecurity that impels you to reach out desperately to others for grounding. The higher self is oriented toward those elements of human nature which tap into the sublime. This is the realm of eternal Oneness and Love. True centeredness comes from combining your earth plane responsibilities with the growth and development of your Higher Self.

Libra is the point of balance between the autumn harvest (Virgo) and winter death (Scorpio). It can observe the equality between the light and the darkness without become attached or identified with either one. The truth that lies in the light is joy and abundance. The truth that lies in the darkness is the wisdom of inner truth and intuitive understanding. Libra represents the ability to objectively acknowledge and partake of both but also stand removed from both. Don't deny or try to suppress your physical or emotional needs or desires, however, trying to rise above them at all times in spiritual and mental detachment. Nor should you sacrifice the development of higher consciousness on the altar of sensuality. It is the higher octave of Libra that reminds us about the importance of giving equal attention to the light and the dark, to the intellectual/social and the physical/emotional.

Harmony is as much discovered as created. It shouldn't have to be forced because it exists as part of the natural flow of life. It can be perceived through eternal cycles of the physical universe and created through egalitarian social interaction. Thus it's important that you keep your vision and ideals high for the sake of the social unit, whether that be your primary partnership or society as a whole, not just for the self.

Libra also has the opportunity to unite both male and female characteristics. When the Bible tells us, "Male and female, made He them," was it talking about two different bodies, or about different characteristics within the same body? Libra obviously has the ability to unite with others. But it can also integrate its own masculine traits such as assertiveness and rationality with feminine traits such as receptivity and intuition.

Ultimately the internal fulcrum is forged by joining aspects of yourself that are seemingly polarized, such as your social with your idealistic, your emotional with your intellectual and your physical with your spiritual natures. Astrologically Libra is at the midpoint between Cancer which is oriented toward content, and Capricorn which is oriented toward form. Libra provides the potential to balance form with content. Libra is the experience which, at its most exalted level offers the opportunity to find within the self the ultimate point of resolution between all things that are seemingly in opposition to each other. From that point of perception comes the ability to develop your consciousness beyond duality, and become able to know the Oneness of Being.

Balance can be experienced as an exalted spiritual state. It helps to create a condition of inner calm and equanimity from which to relate to the world in a peaceful manner. It indicates the ability to develop self-control within which personal desires are fulfilled in a conscious, fair minded way.

In the *I Ching*, hexagram 22 is Grace. It speaks of perfection of form and reminds us that although a time in which there is perfected external harmony is rare and to be savored, it is not a time to make major decisions. In a Libran context, this suggests that the external beauty that you may tend to focus on is nice, but it does not represent your greatest power or potential. Native American tradition speaks of art and beauty as providing connections to Great Spirit. As the artist, you connect directly to the source of Creation and validate yourself as a direct link in the chain. Consequently, the spiritual Libran is one who takes advantage of their aesthetic sensitivities. Instead of focusing outward on beauty you become more aware of the creative flow of life energy manifesting through you as the artist. This enables you to provide a solid internal base from which to bridge the gap between that which is merely attractive and that which is of the creative essence.

As a cardinal sign, the inner fulcrum of the Libran is never stable. It requires constant action to maintain the point of balance. There is no time of permanent discovery or definition. You may be confronted with unpleasant challenges that disturb comfort zones in your life. The teaching that those situations offer can help you experience a degree of peace previously unknown. If you learn to understand the significance of a situation you can use it as an opportunity and take full advantage of its growth potential. Libra inherently possesses the tools necessary for this work. One of those is the ability to read the Cosmic Clock and to know when is the time for what action. Don't force issues, insisting or demanding that something conform to your expectations just because you think you are ready for it. All things come in their own time. The need for symmetry and equality within the various aspects of self and between the self and the world is the work of the Libran. Ultimately this work enables you create the healthiest integration of your free will with Universal Will. The awareness of the underlying harmony already present in the Universe, and potentially within the self, and how to work with those forces is the contribution that Libra makes to the human experience.

♏︎ *SCORPIO*

Scorpio is a succeedant sign. All fixed signs are also succeedant in that they follow the lead of the previous cardinal sign. What the cardinal sign initiates, the fixed sign can deepen and complete. Scorpio is preceded by Libra, the first sign that looks outside the core self and personal life to the greater whole. In the personal sense, Libra is oriented toward one-to-one relationship. In the impersonal sense, it is concerned with the development of a social conscience. Libra is concerned with the fundamental experiences of sharing in relationship—learning through trial and error the best ways to create a mutually harmonious and fulfilling union. Skills of diplomacy, tact, cooperation and grace are lessons to be learned, and characteristics to be utilized in the Libran experience. Scorpio deepens that experience in two ways. First, it goes beyond social relationship and seeks to define itself by understanding the whole of existence. Secondly, and in terms of personal interaction, Scorpio is more concerned with the underlying patterns of emotional and psychological union.

As Libra begins the third quadrant—the quadrant of relationship—Scorpio begins the process of exploring the interaction of the individual in its personal connection to all things. As a result it is a complex sign, a richly textured experience. Proceeding from Scorpio, each of the signs becomes more multi-faceted, sometimes in paradoxical ways. Because these signs are oriented toward the outer world, there is a continual process of external exploration followed by internal integration.

For Scorpio, this interactive flow leads to profound internal transformations, which in turn reflect and relate to the changes in the external world. The Sun transits Scorpio from approximately October 22 to November 21. At this time of year, in parts of the Northern hemisphere, the ground begins to freeze. Animals begin to hibernate. Leaves fall. The life force retreats for the winter. It is a time for the passing of the old. It is this seeming end of the light that can cause Scorpio to investigate reality and understand life at its deepest level. In the course of this process, Scorpio penetrates the apparent reality of the physical world and has the opportunity to experience and understand the truth and the mystery of life. Scorpio is sign of death and rebirth, the sign of regeneration and resurrection. Scorpio says, "I desire."

THE MYTHS

The myths of Scorpio reflect this dual connection to the deeper, darker elements of life and to the deeper levels of relationship. One of the archetypes of the Scorpionic experience is the Greek god Pluto, Lord of the Underworld. It is significant that the planet Pluto is considered the co-ruler of Scorpio. It was he who had dominion over that which is dark, cold and damp. It was said that people met Pluto when they experienced a death. It could have been the death of a hope, of a dream or of their body. Some, like the hero Odysseus, voluntarily descended to the realm of Pluto to gain information about things hidden. In a personal context, the house of Pluto contains individual thoughts, memories and experiences that are painful, shameful or repressed. On the collective level, Pluto represents everything known, experienced or dreamt by the human experience. It was Pluto who kidnapped the naive Persephone, and forced her to descend into his realm. Her mother Demeter pleaded with Zeus to intervene and allow her beloved daughter to return home. He agreed that Persephone could return, but before she did, Pluto tricked Persephone into eating some pomegranate seeds before going back. According to Olympian law, to partake of sustenance in the underworld is to be committed to staying there. Thus by eating the seeds, Persephone was bound to remain with Pluto. Zeus, however, as if knowing about the Libran experience, created a compromise. It was agreed that Persephone would live half the time above ground with her mother, and half the time below ground with her husband. So the life force and human awareness have two appropriate realms and orientations. One pertains to the conscious mind and things that are clear, logical and defined. The other is the subconscious mind in which things are murky, emotional and flowing.

In Judeo-Christian mythology the tendency is to value only the known, the illuminated and the orderly. In that context, the realm of Pluto is called Hell and the governor of that realm is Satan. Instead of realizing the importance of the balance between the external and the internal, the masculine and the feminine, it has evolved that only the former is seen as important and the latter has come to be demeaned. Yet it is ironic that the central figure of Christianity, Jesus himself, did not subscribe to that belief system. Jesus was dangerous to the movers and shakers of his day because he elevated women to equal status with men. The feminine experience is most connected to and identified with the inner realms. The world of the emotions and mystical attunement with life are derived from honoring the inward journey. Jesus' most heretical acts attacked the accepted ethos that kept women in a subservient status, with no power or importance. He invited women into his inner circle of advisors, he defended a prostitute, and he had a relationship with Mary Magdalene.

Another connection of Jesus to the underworld is seen through resurrection. His resurrection of Lazarus demonstrates an understanding of the life force and an ability to work with the universal law of death and rebirth. His own resurrection indicates his mystical attunement with eternal life and his ability to break the seeming inevitability of death. Yet the church fathers failed to follow his lead, either politically or sociologically. They preferred dogma to actualization, and separation to inclusion.

The Hindu trinity of Brahma the Creator, Vishnu the Preserver, and Shiva the destroyer also portrays the depth and complexity of Scorpio. The Hindu believes that the Absolute, the One-indivisible, manifests itself in these three modes. Brahma, as creator, represents the soul of the universe, the source and the essence of all things. Thus Brahma is known and worshipped only by those who aspire to identify with the consciousness of the creative source. Both Vishnu and Shiva have more devotees in India, since each represents a concept easier to experience and identify with. Vishnu can be experienced in three fiery manifestations: flame, lightning and the Sun. It is said that Vishnu creates a new cycle of life each time he exhales and ends it when he inhales. This reflects the endless cycle of death and rebirth experienced by human souls. Shiva is the annihilator of the individual, the god of death. He is depicted as dancing on dead bodies and celebrating in graveyards. His mythical/mystical function is to destroy the ego-identified individual and allow the soul to re-unite with the Infinite. To perceive Shiva from the ego is terrifying. To perceive Shiva from the more detached point of your Higher Being, is to recognize him as the transformer and redeemer. Over time, Brahma and Vishnu have merged into one, leaving Vishnu as the creator-preservor, and Shiva the world-destroyer. Ultimately, of course, even those are actually two aspects of the same thing. The sense, however, is that each of the gods has its own distinct function as the two experiences are separate from each other. Although there is no overt rivalry or competition, there is a feeling of an uneasy peace between these forces. Their domains are both primary yet dissimilar. For life to function, both of these archetypal experiences are required. The experience of Scorpio is to feel the interchange between these beings at all times.

Scorpio is a feminine, *yin* sign. The Hindu deity that best represents Scorpio in feminine form is Kali. She is one of the wives of Shiva, and the personification of the female aspect of the god. If Shiva is the spirit, Kali is the body. If Shiva is eternity, Kali is calculable time. Kali is called the "Ferry across the Ocean of Existence." The continuous interplay between these eternal forces combine to create the mystery of life. Kali is a manifestation of the Eternal Mother, yet is usually pictured in a terrifying pose. She has four arms, which symbolize her power. The upper left hand holds a bloody sword, in the lower left, a severed human head. The upper right hand is open and held up, in a "fear not" position, while the lower right is extended offering great generosity. She wears a necklace of human heads and a belt of human arms. She is the harmonizer of all pairs of opposites, birth and death, terror and reassurance. She is a symbol of Cosmic Power, yet is also called the Black One, the purveyor of the unknown. As a symbol of the eternal and powerful feminine, she represents the totality of what can be known from the perspective of the inner world, as seen through the internal eye. This is the realm of feeling, of passion and of the sensual. To refuse to include this perspective in your world view, or in your own sense of identity, is to attempt to eliminate the Kali-feminine. It can lead to defining feeling, nature and ultimately women as deficient, bad or the enemy. You undermine the awareness and expression of your own inner mystery, your connection to your inner being and your emotional reality. You become overwhelmed with terror at the prospect of the undeniable, the passage of your ego into the Eternal One. To acknowledge and accept the image if Kali is to explore your own inner being, and affirm your soul's mystical connection to Life. To accept the duality of your own nature—both the masculine and the feminine, the mental and the emotional, the spirit and the soul, birth and death—is to accept the Truth of Life. To accept that Truth is to look beyond the duality, identify with Oneness and accept yourself as a Being of Light and Eternal Life. This is the focus, work and challenge of the Scorpionic experience.

THE GLYPH: ♏

The glyph associated with Scorpio is derived from the same source as that of the glyph for Virgo, the Hebrew letter *Mem* (מ). In both signs the serpent power of creativity, the Divine Creative Force, is present. With Virgo, however, the fourth leg is crossed over the third suggesting the potential power. The Virgin awaits the Essence of Divine Creativity to awaken and inspire his/her own creative, serpent power. In the Scorpio glyph, the fourth leg is uncrossed. It propels outward, arrow tipped, and poised for action. The serpent-like kundalini force is manifesting in a thrusting, aggressive manner. The potential energy of Virgo has given way to the kinetic energy of Scorpio.

The serpent that the Bible describes in the Garden of Eden myth can be represented in the zodiac by Scorpio. In the definition and discussion of the caduceus—the symbol or baton of Mercury—it was noted that the serpent is the embodiment of creative power and offers liberation through its pursuit of knowledge, wisdom and consciousness. In Judeo-Christian theology the serpent is the symbol of sin—the instigator who induced Eve to eat the fruit of the tree of knowledge. By doing so Eve destroyed the ignorance and innocence of humanity which led to our eviction from the Garden of Eden. From unconscious non-individuation, humanity was thrust into a state of self-awareness. It is interesting to note how the concept of consciousness differs between the East and the West. To the Eastern philosopher, consciousness is desirable. It leads to power and liberation from the eternal cycle of death and rebirth. The origins of Western philosophy define this quest as bad. It was the female who initially sought the wisdom of the serpent. It would seem appropriate, therefore, that women be revered as brave pioneers seeking new levels of awareness. Instead, they are condemned for having yielded to the "temptation" (consciousness) of the serpent. This is part of the justification given by Western theologians for demeaning the female orientation to life in terms of their values, their bodies and their function in society.

THE TOTEM: 🦂

Unlike any other sign, Scorpio has four different images or totems that describe its nature and characteristics. These images are not sequential, and each has its own purpose and value. You are not automatically born in phase I and die in phase IV. Some people are born at the lowest octave and remain there, while others, born in phase I ascend through each of the levels of experience during their lives. Still others may begin at a higher octave and remain there, or continue to advance. The path you choose is an exercise in free will.

The first octave of Scorpionic consciousness, its lowest level of manifestation, is represented by the scorpion. The Egyptians, Arabs, Hebrews, Persians, Turks, Chinese and Hindus, all have a scorpion or a serpent in their zodiac. The Acadians refer to Scorpio as Girtab, the stinger. In the Greek myth of Orion the scorpion played an important role. Orion was a hunter who threatened to devour all the wild fauna of Crete. To defend the island the gods sent the scorpion who put an end to the hunter's marauding. In gratitude, the gods placed the scorpion in the sky, exactly 180 degrees away from Orion the Hunter. Thus as the scorpion rises, Orion sinks fearfully below the horizon. The scorpion is a symbol of warlike aggression.

The scorpion is an unpleasant creature. After mating, the female devours her mate. If she is around when her eggs hatch, she has been known to eat her young, too. The initial expression of social contact for the scorpion is the tail, the stinger, going over the head in a battle pose. People who function primarily from this level of Scorpio tend to be belligerent, suspicious, secretive, manipulative, domineering and pushy. They can be draining to others, using the resources or energy of other people for their own purposes. They don't ask, they just take, and often in a very conscious and malevolent way. The value of this level of Scorpio is that it can help you survive. If you are being threatened or intimidated by someone else you can just eliminate that person from your presence or your life in a very immediate and absolute way. Unfortunately, you can also use your stinger when your are not being threatened. You can be hurtful to others and walk away with no moral compunctions at all.

You aren't required to function in this way, however, and may rarely be in a position where it is necessary to be in this phase of Scorpion consciousness. You can raise the level of Scorpion consciousness to the second octave in which the totem is a human being. Scorpio, like Libra, is a sign of relationship. Libra is oriented to one-to-one relationships. Scorpio is more focused on deepening the nature, form and quality of relationship. In one-to-one experience Scorpio is oriented toward intimacy, a deep bonding and sharing of primary emotional, psychological, spiritual and sexual union. Beyond primary relationship, Scorpio can be identified with and attached to a group or a family. In this mode, Scorpio manifests as being very maternal, nurturing and care-giving. The danger at this level is dependency. The group's desires or values can become the Scorpio's desires and values. When you are experiencing your life from the second octave of Scorpio, support and protect those closest to you, but learn how to separate yourself from them.

The totem for the third octave of Scorpio is the serpent, specifically the serpent eating its tail. This is the symbol of Uorobos, and represents the pursuit of knowledge and wisdom. Relating the serpent to higher awareness is a theme common to many philosophical traditions and geographical areas. In Central and South America there are snakes carved of stone that decorate ancient temples. The snakes represent renewal. The serpent shedding its skin symbolizes rebirth. In Northern Europe there are the sacred serpents of the Druids and the Midgard snake of the Scandinavians. The Nagas of Southeast Asia and the snakes at the oracle of Delphi also connect this reptile to deepening awareness of the mysteries of life. Connecting this image to Scorpio defines it as being a highly inquisitive, potentially intellectual, experience. Scorpio's curiosity provides a penetrating drive to understand life in terms of universal knowledge. As a Scorpio, you are not satisfied with superficial information or an ordering of ideas. You go to prime sources for information and want to learn the most fundamental elements of the subjects in which you have interest. You penetrate the surface of a body of knowledge to learn the hidden principles.

The fourth octave of Scorpio symbolizes its highest potential, and is represented by the eagle or the phoenix. Winged creatures suggest transcendence. To the followers of the ancient Hermetic schools, religion, science and philosophy were three branches of the same thing. These scholars sought to study and understand the universal mind embodied by Hermes. During the Middle Ages the axioms of Hermetic wisdom were systematically codified. Out of this work the laws of alchemy were defined. In that system the eagle signified the secret process through which the low, and often mean-spirited infernal fire of the scorpion is transmuted into the spiritual fire of the gods. The eagle conveys a powerful spiritual image and suggests a strong sense of spiritual inspiration. In some cultures it has been thought that the eagle can look directly into the Sun without going blind. The eagle as a totem suggests that at its highest level, Scorpio has the desire and ability to eliminate all elements of its lower nature. As a Scorpio expressing your eagle-like nature you seek to purify your being, transforming any tendencies to possess, control or manipulate into qualities of Divine manifestation. This can be expressed through the creative or healing arts or through humanitarian acts of magnanimity and generosity.

The phoenix is a mythical bird. Legends from cultures as disparate as the ancient Greeks and the early Christians describe the life cycle of the phoenix lasting five-hundred years. This is exactly the same length of time that it takes the co-ruling planet of Scorpio—Pluto—to conjunct the planet Neptune (the energy of the subconscious mind), and is the longest cycle between any two planets.

The death of the phoenix gave birth to a worm. This was the germ of its new self. Thus it symbolizes the immortality of the soul and illustrates the universal law of eternal life. As the Hermetics saw the eagle representing the process of alchemical transformation, they regarded the phoenix as the symbol of the transmutation itself. To experience this transformation in your own life is to understand the meaning and mystery of life. Your greatest achievement becomes your conscious transcendence of the material plane. You transmute the limits of human life and live in the consciousness of the Eternal Oneness.

The nature of Scorpio is complex, as illustrated by its fourfold totem. From the murky depths of the internal swamp to the most expanded realms of human awareness Scorpio has the potential to experience life in a thorough, all-inclusive way.

MODE AND ELEMENT

Scorpio is the sign of fixed water. In nature this can take the form of ice. The scorpion-like Scorpio can be icy cold and insensitive toward others, as a result of being unself-loving in the first place. In the higher octaves the image of ice demonstrates that Scorpio can be like a glacier in that there is always more going on within than appears on the surface.

As a fixed sign, Scorpio has a powerful will. The will can be used to create and maintain habits that are designed to generate a sense of security. If you are centered in this pursuit this quality helps you to be persevering, sometimes relentless, in pursuit of anything that will help satisfy your desire to be safe. If you are uncentered, however, that desire can become so overwhelming that it becomes an obsession and takes on a life of its own. To satisfy a craving, Scorpio can resort to its lowest nature and become demanding, intimidating or manipulative.

As with all fixed signs, Scorpio creates its reality on a foundation of values. As a Scorpio, if you define something as valuable, you can become tenacious in that view. The tendency to obsess or control often arises when something you have valued and pursued for a long time ceases to work. To allow a habit to become an obsession is to forget what you valued and gave rise to the habit in the first place. You pursue something just because you "have to have it" and not because it brings real fulfillment. If you don't acknowledge this, your stubbornness creates more problems. You might become demanding and insist that others change their values to conform to yours. Or you might try subterfuges to manipulate them into doing so. Instead, let go of the old values and habits. And create new ones.

If you are functioning from the highest level of Scorpionic potential—eagle consciousness—you realize that the greatest value of your fixed nature is the ability to consciously maintain a place of internal security and from that point experience transformation in your life. Attaching to neither the sadness and grieving for the passing away of the old, nor to the joy and freshness of rebirth, you experience both with equanimity. Your strength of will enables you to be conscious in creating the cycle. Partaking of it, but not getting caught or stuck in any of its phases.

The water nature of Scorpio suggests that, like all water signs, it seeks a container within which it can feel secure. For Scorpio this container can be an intimate relationship, a deep connection to family or even a successful business. This need for security coupled with your fixed nature needing stability can render it difficult for you to willingly let go of what you have, even if you know it is decayed and dysfunctional. It's as if it's better to have something known and comfortable, even if it doesn't work, than to throw it away and maybe have nothing.

Water is in constant motion. Sometimes it can be quite calm, at others extremely turbulent. A good image for fixed water is the ocean. On the surface things may be calm and placid, while just under the surface life and death struggles occur continuously. For Scorpio, that pattern can be your normal daily routine and be reflected in your behavior. Even if there is no external expression you can emanate an intense passion just beneath the surface of your activity. Sometimes that intensity can boil over and spill out onto whatever you may be doing or whoever you are doing it with. This happens because you have been holding on to your feelings and holding in the expression of them. This idea also suggests that your emotions can be very deep and hidden. Scorpio is the sign of secrets. You can ignore the depth and significance of your feelings or, knowing what they are, you may hide them from others. You may fear that expression of your emotional depth and sensitivity can make you too vulnerable to others. Because of the constant inner churning of your feelings, you may hesitate to make a definite statement about them. Regardless of how intense the present emotion, you know it will change into a different, equally profound internal experience in the future. Remember, however, that the less you express, the deeper you bury the information. You might also assume that what is so deep and hidden is bad. Although the tendency to hide the emotional self is undesirable, that which you are secreting isn't necessarily bad, just unexamined. Spend time investigating and acknowledging your emotional truth and express it when, how and with whom it is appropriate to do so.

Another quality of water is that it flows along the line of least resistance. It fills up all cracks and crevices in the lower elevations before moving on to the higher. This translates into human experience as helping you to deepen your relationship to all things. You function in relationship from the bottom up. You start by becoming aware of the deepest, most subtle levels of emotion, then expand that awareness until you express the feelings. In the context of the transition from Libra to Scorpio you are moving away from the superficial social relationships based on Libran ideals and moving more into a cycle of unification through intensifying the emotional bond and penetrating to deeper levels of communion.

Within your own psyche, the process of deep discovery involves acknowledging and investigating your emotional truths. As you do this you become more aware of and comfortable with aspects of your inner being that you have had trouble dealing with. They could be old, terror-like fears that lurk in your psyche in a place that psychoanalyst Carl Jung called the "shadow." In the shadow are the unacknowledged and unexpressed parts of your inner self. These could include feelings such as anger or grief that had been repressed in your past. Or the shadow could hide parts of yourself that were undervalued or invalidated in childhood and that still wait for recognition and integration into your conscious mind and outer life. The shadow can submerge parts of your past that were painful or elements of your present life about which you feel ashamed. Desires, values or beliefs of which society disapproves may stay in your shadow. In fact any element of yourself that lives at the fundamental level of your being and which you don't understand, feel overwhelmed by, or you fear may cause social rejection, can be kept in the shadow.

If you are strongly attached to keeping things status quo, you will do almost anything to prevent your shadow from being exposed. You could act in threatening, intimidating or coercive ways to avoid expressing shadowy things. You could also see your own inner demons openly expressed by others. You can even be attracted to people who are openly expressive of those qualities you keep hidden. Those people might relate to you in a demanding, manipulative, deceitful way. Not only do these people not help you to become more aware of and resolve whatever similar patterns may be lurking within you, but you must also adjust to whatever forms of unpleasantness are coming from them. Sometimes these "shadowy" people may even be connected to the underworld in some way. This pattern of holding on and holding in can cause an implosion of energy, undermining not only personal relationships, but your physical and mental health as well. It can lead to an explosion or crisis within which your energy spews forth in an out of control manner destroying everything in its path.

If you are holding back hurt feelings, you could develop a deep vindictiveness toward the person who hurt you. An attitude of vengefulness is simply another way of covering your feelings and trying to protect yourself from further pain. It can also be a way of focusing on unpleasant things that other people are doing to you to avoid looking at the ways in which you might be negatively affecting others.

The fixed water combination can impel Scorpio to dependency and stagnation. You could become dependent on people, your own habits, or on deeply ingrained childhood imprints. As children we are all conditioned to behave in certain ways and believe in certain things. For a sensitive, impressionable Scorpio, childhood experiences can create a type of conditioning in which you make certain unconscious assumptions about the nature of life on Earth based on your family dynamics. You made these assumptions according to how your parents related to you, themselves, and each other. These assumptions can tell you about the nature of life and your place in it. Part of your process of discovery is to find which of those assumptions are incorrect: which ones had a deep impact on you based on a certain type of experience, or on a specific period that your parents or your family went through; or which ones were based on your own confusion and misperceptions at the time of the imprinting. Part of your renewal process is to become aware of how much of your reality is more assumption than reality. Challenge what you assume life to be, and you update your reality to conform with your life experience, perceptions and feelings. Unchallenged and outmoded assumptions can be a cause of dissatisfaction with your life. They can retard your growth and cause you to oscillate between stagnation and explosion.

The positive part of fixed water is the ability to tap into and understand deep undercurrents of ancient and eternal wisdom. You can use this understanding to nurture yourself and generate a sense of security. This also provides the insight to explore and investigate your shadow. You may be surprised that some of what you buried is quite beautiful and useful once exposed to the light of consciousness. Maybe some of your inner demons are old protectors from your childhood. A friendly monster who you created as a child to defend you against real or imagined threats may have evolved into unwanted or embarrassing baggage for the adolescent and adult.

The fixed water combination can also provide the perseverance to learn how to share your true feelings with others. This is a way of creating intimacy and depth in the relationship, even if it means admitting there are elements of yourself you don't like and are working to eliminate. To avoid communicating this truth leads to holding on to those undesirable qualities and stagnating in your own growth and the relationship. Remember that water is fluid. Even though you feel things as deeply and profoundly as you do, you can also choose to use the water to flush out your system. It is this ability to purge yourself of the undesirable elements of your life that allows you to regenerate that self. As you get comfortable with this process, inner darkness ceases to be perceived as negative. You realize that by immersing yourself into this realm you discover profound inspiration and understanding about the real nature of Life. If you pursue this quest in a centered way the Light of that energy can be seen and experienced even in the most difficult and terrifying realms. By making friends with this realm you overcome all fear. You become a powerful source of nurturing for others and understand the eternal truth of the cycle of life: birth, transformation and death.

THE RULING PLANETS

Scorpio is co-ruled by Mars (σ) and Pluto ($\mathcal{Q}$). Its rulership by Mars connects Scorpio with Aries, the other sign ruled by Mars. It indicates that Scorpio is a self-starter, as is Aries. It also suggests that, like Aries, Scorpio can be both creative and passionate on the positive side but rash, insensitive and possibly ruthless on the negative. Aries is an action-oriented cardinal sign, whereas Scorpio is fixed and prefers more depth, deliberation and stability. It uses the force of Mars in a more focused and continuous way. It doesn't just initiate situations and then impulsively move on. Scorpio has the potential to learn how to balance the intensity with control. The Mars influence also provides Scorpio with the pioneering spirit. As a water sign, the bravery of this energy should be used to explore the inner world in ever deepening cycles of awareness.

Aries is a fire and masculine sign, whereas Scorpio is a water and feminine sign. Both, however, are ruled by Mars, thus the force of aggression and initiation is present in the female principle as well as the male. Its purpose and manifestation, though, is different in each. Whereas the masculine Mars is obvious, direct and open, the feminine Mars is hidden. Uncentered, the feminine Mars can be imploded so as to direct your anger at yourself. Sometimes it can be hidden in that it manifests, but in a secretive, manipulative way. In a centered way, the feminine Mars activates the inner world, stimulating the deep feelings and realizations that they bring. It brings the quality of bravery to the internal quest of self-discovery and self-awareness. The feminine Mars lies within the self as power potential. It can activate creativity of home, family and children. It also implies an underlying potential of violence. When centered, this can manifest in a protective manner, preserving the safety of self or family. Uncentered, it can be an expression of hidden rage, lunging out at others in an indiscriminate way.

Mars can also make sexuality a driving force for Scorpio. The emotional depth of this sign suggests that what it truly seeks and needs in relationship is intimacy. Some Scorpios can become obsessed with sex, but this merely serves to cover over their real needs. Although it seemingly protects them from emotional vulnerability, it also prevents them from being fulfilled by touching and being touched at the deepest levels of emotional, psychic and spiritual union. Without emotional intimacy, sex for Scorpio can be at best boring and at worst draining. A centered, self-loving Scorpio can withdraw their need for sexual contact, sometimes for years, if necessary. But if the opportunity to expand an already deep, meaningful relationship into the sexual realm unfolds spontaneously, they can respond with passion.

The other co-ruler of Scorpio is Pluto. Pluto is the energy of transformation. It represents the principle of death and rebirth. It provides the impetus for everyone, whether you have planets in Scorpio in your horoscope or not, to plumb the nether reaches of your soul. Pluto is the redeemer, the energy of the purified golden light. Pluto was discovered when it was sitting at 19 degrees of Cancer in January of 1930. It was named Pluto after the Roman god of the underworld. As the farthest planet from the Sun, it seemed obvious to associate this planet with darkness. Prior to that, Mars was the sole ruler of Scorpio. Once Pluto was discovered, it was quickly assigned to Scorpio by astrologers of the day. The first book written about Pluto appeared in 1934 and direct correlations were made between the underworld realm of the god Pluto in mythology with the under the surface reality of Scorpio. It's also interesting to note the proliferation gangsters in the "underworld" in the 1930's in the United States.

Pluto is the slowest moving of the planets, taking from twelve to twenty-nine years to transit one sign. As a result, its placement in one sign can bind an entire generation of people together at deep levels. It can indicate desires, psychological orientations, and ways of dealing with death, sexuality and money. Pluto can also influence other planets for long periods of time. For example, Pluto has been in sextile ($\ast$) aspect (sixty degrees) to Neptune, the second slowest planet, since 1940. Operating at fundamental levels of the human psyche, this aspect has been stimulating a world-wide shift in consciousness. Spiritually, this period has seen numerous spiritual leaders from the East come to the West with their teachings and techniques. Psychologically, individual therapy and twelve step programs have proliferated. Western mystics such as Matthew Fox have either come forward or been rediscovered. The suggestion seems to be to go with what you know, start from where you are or what you need at your time of awakening. You can always change focus or path as time goes by and your needs and awareness changes.

Pluto, representing the energy of transformation, enables us to tap into the deepest realms and highest levels of life. It can help us break through the illusion of time. There are different kinds of time. Horizontal time is what we are most familiar with. It is chronological time, and takes into consideration events that take place sequentially. The planet Saturn has dominion over horizontal time.

Vertical time is a form of *synchronicity,* a focused expression of "be here now." The term synchronicity was coined by the psychoanalyst Carl Jung. Its theory is that all things that occur in a given moment of time share the properties and qualities of that moment. This concept is often cited as one reason why the natal horoscope is a map that accurately depicts a person's nature and tendencies. The pattern of the planets, their relationship to each other and the Earth, signify the patterns of internal experience and external expression of the person born under that configuration. According to the precepts of synchronicity, a person's behavior is not controlled by the planets, but rather shares the same qualities.

By being aware that vertical time exists, you can understand that there is a connection between the universal and the minute. One is a reflection of and is reflected by the other. Ultimately, they are one and the same thing, just seen from different points of view. By paying more attention to vertical time, you can realize that underlying these two perspectives is a Oneness, an entity that always exists and is always right here. Consequently, one aspect of Plutonian energy is to enable you to develop this perspective, this state of consciousness, and maintain the ability to be in the eternal present. In that sense Pluto is similar to the Moon. The difference is that the Moon's function is to bring your own emotional responses into here-and-now situations. Pluto's focus is more on the awareness of the Oneness from a more universal perspective.

The two concepts of time offer us the ability to be aware of two kinds of reality simultaneously, that which is *sequential* and that which just *is*. At the point of intersection between horizontal and vertical time lies the awareness of universal truth and the ability to feel the abundant flow of love, wisdom and joy. It's as if the intersection represents a crack in the cosmic egg through which our awareness extends beyond all deaths and rebirths and identifies with eternal flow of universal energy, that which is usually just below our thoughts, feelings and consciousness.

Pluto enables us to tap into our highest levels of neurological circuitry such as kundalini energy and the libido. The connection between the two suggests that there is a connection between expanded states of consciousness and sexual energy. The path to the expanded realms, the process of illumining the darkness, can be helped by proper use of sexual energy or impeded through wrong usage. Pluto, therefore, enables us to tap into the highest potentials of human nature as well as the lowest aspects of human nature such as violence, greed, lust and obsession. It's simply a matter of how you choose to express your Pluto energy.

There are two ways of relating to Pluto's energy. If you are doing it consciously, you are engaging in a continuous process of self-examination. What house is Pluto located in your natal chart? The activities that take place in that area of life are the ones that you should continuously be investigating. The house placement of Pluto can also indicate what personal or societal taboos you are working to breakdown in your life. What is the nature of life in that area? How do you influence or feel influenced by what goes on there? What are your habits in that area? What are the values upon which they are based? As long as you are asking these or similar questions, and finding meaningful answers, you are working with Pluto in a conscious way. You will be able to experience gradual transformations of yourself and your behaviors in and through your interaction with that area. Pluto helps you to sweep all artifice from your life in order to discover truth.

If you are not doing this consciously and regularly you could be obsessive about activities in the house of Pluto's placement in your natal chart. Pluto in the first house suggests obsession with your body or with the effect you have on others and the effect they have on you. Pluto in the seventh house implies obsession with a particular partner or just being in a relationship. It's as if you become addicted to the energy exchange in that area, even if the experience is not healthy, positive or fulfilling. Eventually the addiction-oriented Pluto generates a crisis. Think of this as a Plutonian wave or explosion, which can turn your life upside down. When you get hit by that wave, you may release and let go of a lot of old, stagnant values and patterns and even people with whom the relationship has become limiting, boring or draining. This can allow you to experience a certain amount of relief or release from the tension that had been building up. Realize, however, that in the moment of explosion you throw away a lot of things that were not only stagnant, but were also very much alive and well—things that you did not want to let go of now and maybe ever. You find that you are left with about the same ratio of garbage to goodies that you started out with. In other words, the Plutonian explosion is usually a waste of time. It gives a false sense of growth, an incomplete sense of change. You don't burn the house down because you don't like the living room furniture. You don't blow up your car's engine and think that you have bought a new car. Pluto is demanding. If you want to connect with the deepest strata of life and consciousness, you must be truthful with yourself and constantly vigilant with your internal process.

If you are not doing your Pluto work in a conscious and consistent way, its placement in your natal chart can indicate where you bring others into your life who will show you those parts of yourself that you don't see or don't accept. These could be positive or negative qualities which, for various reasons, you have a hard time integrating. Becoming aware of these things won't necessarily be easy and those relationships might not be particularly easy either. These "teachers" may relate to you in a domineering, draining or controlling way. You may feel betrayed or deceived by them. Whatever their pattern, or whatever your response may be, it is all designed to help you become more clear about some of your blind spots. Once aware you can transform it in some way, depending on what the trait is and what you choose to do with it.

Not dealing with Pluto consciously could also cause you to subtly undermine situations that occur in the area of its house placement. You could be withdrawn, demanding or manipulative in such a way that others with whom you come in contact break off the relationship. You could feel victimized by these people without realizing your own part in the drama. Whenever you feel that others are pushing you away, try to ascertain what you might have said or done—or not said or done—that helped to engender the result you experienced.

If Pluto is direct in your chart, you are learning how to use your transformational power constructively and interactively with those whom you connect with in that area of life. For example, Pluto in the fourth house can indicate very old, deep bonds with your family of origin. A healthy way of using Pluto energy here is to be engaged in the internal work of letting go of what they gave you in childhood in terms of values, acceptable behavioral patterns, and even a sense of your inner self that no longer work for you. Gradually you generate a new inner life that is more accurate in defining who you really are based on your inner drives and personal experiences. It's as if you periodically rebirth yourself into the context of your family. In turn this can catalyze your parents into an introspective mode as well leading to a regeneration of the entire family structure. But whether or not others respond positively and supportively to your process, it's important for you to do the work and benefit from the results.

With Pluto in your eleventh house, both people and social dynamics from past lives will manifest in the incarnation. You are learning about power in group situations. Experiencing what it is like and what happens when you are too domineering, or when you draw to you those who seek to dominate you, will help you understand more about your own magnetism and how to share it lovingly. Doing this is an open, even confrontational manner, catalyzes transformation for others in the group and possibly of the group dynamic as a whole.

If Pluto is retrograde in your natal chart, your primary work of transformation needs to be on yourself more than with others. To update yourself in the area of life relative to what you came into this incarnation with is fundamental to growth in this life. After you have become involved in this process in a consistent and dedicated way you can help facilitate or catalyze transformation for others.

THE EIGHTH HOUSE

The area of life associated with Scorpio is the eighth house, the house of transformation. As a water house it deals with complex issues which fall into one of two primary categories. One is as a house which helps contribute to consciousness development. The other is as a house of relationship which helps contribute to deepening of involvement. If you have a significant number of planets in the eighth house, or if only the Sun, Moon, or ruling planet of your rising sign is there, you might be interested in both of those avenues of experience.

Eighth house people are interested in the universal laws, the common denominators and the secret forces and mysteries of life. Consequently, people who have a lot of eighth house energy, can be interested in science and research. They could also have an interest in mysticism or the occult. On the mundane and recreational level, this can even manifest as sleight-of-hand magic.

Because the orientation of the eighth house is that which is hidden, it may seem as if energy in that area may be repressed. It's not necessarily repressed. It's just behind the scenes doing things in a very penetrating, if secretive and quiet, way.

The patterns you tend to manifest in the eighth house are deeply ingrained, karmically produced influences from past lives. If you expressed eighth house energy in a positive, loving way previously, you are seen as being so magnetic that others are drawn to you and want to share with you what they have. This could take the form of emotional support, providing you with security and nurturing. Or it could take a financial form. The second-eighth house axis is the axis of money. By being prudent and generous in past lives, you create a flow of money that returns to you. This can also take the form of financial support in business through loans or a business partnership.

The first house is the house of self. Its opposite is the seventh which is the house of partnership. Similarly, the second is the house of your resources and its opposite, the eighth, is the house of collective or joint resources. In an impersonal sense this implies taxes, the collective financial resources of a state or country. At a more individual level but in the realm of the family collective, the eighth house deals with inheritance and financial legacy. At the most personal level the eighth is the house of your partners resources. Planets in your eighth house indicate what you will tend to receive, how much you receive and the spirit with which it is given to you by your family or your partner. In an uncentered mode, this can manifest as becoming dependent on others' support emotionally, psychologically or financially. You may drain others of energy in various forms by being manipulative or coercive. You could take from others what you feel you need, but can't create for yourself, whether it is being offered to you or not. As you become centered, you become willing and capable of sharing your resources to mutual benefit. This sharing is on the deeper levels of relationship.

The second-eighth house axis is also the axis of values. The second is yours, the eighth is other peoples. Uncentered, you take on the value systems of those closest to you. What is meaningful to others seems important to you as well. If you are centered, you share your values with others. You and your partner influence each other to transform your respective values and integrate into your relationship some of what you both consider significant.

As a house of relationship, the eighth focuses on the deepest level of sharing: intimacy. To be vulnerable with your partner in an open and voluntary way enables the relationship to express a special dynamic, the ability to regenerate itself. Sometimes sharing in that way can be risky. You may be rejected if you express something about yourself that is objectionable to your partner. Opening up the deeper strata of your psyche can lead to a confrontation that is unpleasant to both of you. But without taking that risk, the relationship will break down. It could become so stagnant that it ends in a crisis, or it could just wither and die.

If you are willing to take the risk and open up, you enable the relationship to function at a profound level of union. You meet each other in deep emotional, psychological bonding. Sexuality can also be part of that sharing. Energy in the eighth house can be very passionate, but not without a more complete intimacy.

The fifth house also deals with sexuality, but from a different perspective. The fifth house bases sexuality on a strong heart connection with the lover. Qualities of romance, fun and pleasure pervade the experience and are valuable parts of it. With significant energy in the eighth house—such as the Sun, Venus, or Mars, or even with planets in Scorpio—sex is viewed more as a vehicle for personal transformation. Sexual intimacy between people who are strongly bonded emotionally and psychically provides an opportunity to transform energy. It can help raise the kundalini energy up the spine to the point where visions and transcendent images pervade the mind. There are many techniques—such as tantra yoga and sex magic—that can be very helpful in this process of transformation. This orientation to sexuality requires discrimination because there are relatively few people with whom one can be so open and trusting. Only by first establishing this kind of union can two people experience the transformation of consciousness through intimacy.

Intimacy is not easy—it takes courage, trust and patience. Courage comes with the conscious desire to share in this way. Trust comes by knowing what your needs are, expressing them, and noticing if your partner is able and willing to meet those needs. You need patience to descend the staircase of intimacy.

Visualize yourself as a small child, holding hands with another child. You are standing at the top of a very steep, dark and narrow stairway. It's scary to descend those steps. Since you are holding hands, you must tune in to each other to make sure you are going down at the same rate. If one of you is going faster than the other, you will pull each other down the stairs and get hurt. You must make sure that you are going step by step, skipping none. In this way you either arrive at the level at which the two of you should function, the limit of the relationship, or you make it all the way and share the bond of intimacy.

The key to understanding and working within the eighth house is transformation. This can take place through relationship as well as within yourself. Through the sometimes subtle, sometimes volatile process of becoming intimate, you question and challenge each other about who you each are and why you function the way you do. You share your secrets and expose yourselves to each other. Through sharing you can experience transformation. As you experience this personal renewal, the relationship transforms as well. Both personally and interpersonally, old, outmoded values, priorities, patterns, and expectations are purged. Then you can generate new ways of being, and new forms of relationship. This pattern of consistent renewal is a magical quality that helps to sustain you and bring periodic rebirth to your relationship. Through sexuality the physical, emotional, spiritual bodies can intertwine, become one, and feel a rebirth of the relationship.

Transformation can also take place through eighth house activities in ways other than primary relationship. As you deepen your awareness of the mysteries of life, your consciousness transforms. Aspects of reality you never saw before open up to you. Old attachments fall away as the realization of fundamental truths causes you to identify with elements of life that are eternal. With significant eighth house energy, the opportunity to experience personal death and rebirth occur periodically throughout your life. With the Sun in the eighth house, your lifestyle can resemble a perpetual identity crisis. Every time your values and their attending habit patterns seem to be just about right, something comes along to disturb the balance. It could be a new piece of information, a new relationship or a relationship opening at a new level that requires the updating of your values, habits and priorities.

The eighth is a succeedant house, indicating that it is oriented toward consistent activities taking place at a deep level, and to a point of completion. One of the activities that can enable eighth house energy to fulfill these requirements is ritual. This could be a Tantric ritual with a lover, a spiritual ritual of intense meditation or ceremonial celebration, or a scientific ritual in which a long period of research yields a breakthrough of realization. These activities can all help facilitate the primary eighth house experience.

SCORPIO AND THE BODY

Scorpio is all about releasing. Anatomically, this involves the excretory system, comprised of such parts of the body as the colon, nose, bladder and rectum. Problems or diseases afflicting these areas are usually a result of a blockage. Scorpio also rules the reproductive system and its organs, the genitals and gonads. Scorpio can also implicate diseases in parts of the body ruled by any of the other fixed signs. Malfunction of the thyroid (Taurus), heart (Leo), or eyes (Aquarius) could have an involvement from Scorpio.

Pluto rules activities that take place deep within the body. Diseases that affect cells and tissues, such as malignancies, infections or blood poisoning are influences of Pluto. Because Pluto is such a slow moving planet, affecting whole generations by its transit through one sign, it can also indicate epidemics.

Both Scorpio and Pluto have influence in the psychological realm, especially in relationship to sexual activity or dysfunction. Molestation, impotence or obsession can indicate the influence of Scorpio or Pluto. A relationship in which there is psychological dominance or manipulation, even if there is no overt abuse, can point to Scorpio or Pluto as a root cause.

CONCLUSIONS

In the transition from Libra to Scorpio, the shift is from Libra, a *yang* sign, to Scorpio, a *yin* sign. Libra gives first to receive the harmonious feedback. Scorpio wants to receive the energy first. Functioning at a lower octave of its potential a person with significant planets in Scorpio or a person with a prominent Pluto might be quite demanding or even coercive in wanting others to provide for them. Yet there be no intention to return what has been received. From the elevated consciousness of the eagle, however, a Scorpio could be so generous that they give back even more than they receive. From this point of view rather than be demanding of others, this type of Scorpionic manifestation tends to be highly demanding of themselves. They always look for ways to improve themselves, always trying harder to be purer in their actions and the ways in which they influence others. This type of extremism is typical in this sign. As a Scorpio going through a period in which you are less centered, you would be more grasping, intimidating or selfish. You would prefer to remain behind the scenes and keep your thoughts, feelings and motivations secret. When you are more centered, however, you can be equally excessive in being open, honest and loving.

Scorpio is fundamentally about identifying with the cycle of life and understanding the mystery of life. As a Scorpio you need to connect with that cycle and learn how to both give and receive. The experience of Libra has taught us the value and principles of balance. Use that knowledge to help you avoid the extreme swings of your pendulum, which can cause you to hold all your energy to yourself, or be too giving of the self.

Scorpio's opposite sign, Taurus, represents power expressed. Taurus wants to build from within the self and share the fruits of its labor. Scorpio can represent power internalized. This internalization can enable you to have a magnetic or charismatic influence on others. You can draw others to you for purposes that are beneficial to all concerned. You can also draw from your internalized power to provide nurturing, healing or protection for others. Internalized power can also lead to its misuse, however. Greed or lust for personal power can result when the energy is hoarded rather than shared. It can cause you to remain at the lowest level of Scorpionic consciousness. The holding on that Scorpio can do, at least as tenaciously as Taurus and Cancer if not more so, is often based on the fear of releasing and letting go. Consequently transformation does not occur. Without transformation Scorpio hangs on and resists rebirth. It also remains attached to emotional experiences, sometimes in the form of grudges or feelings of vindictiveness.

One of the tragic flaws that can confront Scorpio, is fear of visibility. This can manifest in your personal life as fearing emotional expression. It can show up in your professional life as fear of success. In the personal sense this fear is based on your extreme sensitivity and the depth to which you feel. As a fixed water sign your feelings can get stuck going around and around in a closed circle with no release point available. An image that describes Scorpio is that of a large mountain supported by and balancing on a delicate flower. The part of Scorpio that most people identify as being Scorpionic is the mountain: strong, impenetrable, imposing. That part which is less known is represented by the flower: sensitive and beautiful, but easy to overlook. Remember the Virgo lesson of discrimination. Use it and open up only to those with whom it is appropriate to do so. The lesson of Libra is balance. You will be treated by others as you have treated them. If both of these conditions have been met, you have little to fear. If neither have been met, it's time to transform some behavioral patterns.

Fear of success in your professional life can be based on the intuitive awareness that all things must die and pass away anyway. What is the point of being successful if that success is only going to be taken away? If you have completed the circuit and understood the cycle of life, you realize that your success leads to a peak experience after which new opportunity, awareness and energy are opened to you. The fear of death is replaced by the anticipation of a rebirth.

Scorpio embodies the cocoon principle. It represents the continual process of rebirth. Fear of surrendering the old prevents new generation and leads to stagnation. Embracing the process enables you to periodically emerge from your chrysalis with a new sense of self and new perspectives on life. One of the images for Scorpio is Uorobos, the serpent swallowing its tail. When it is time for the serpent to shed its skin, it is merely a process of assimilation and growth. The old skin, or awareness of the nature of life and your place in it, has become too small. It is time to expand your vision, to house the form of the emerging, expanding and evolving individual that you are becoming.

As a Scorpio when you finally decide that it is in your best interest to embrace the cycle of death and rebirth, it should be a deeply emotional cathartic experience. This creates a liberation that is very intense and involves passionate elements of your nature. A type of transformation can be experienced even on a mundane level through such activities as cleaning out the closets, garage and attic, updating your wardrobe or taking out the garbage. These activities could represent a conscious desire to update your life in material form or they could simply be a byproduct of your normal daily routine. There are other kinds of activities that can facilitate transformation that are more meaningful and techniques through which you can create a powerful catharsis. On the physical plane, you can participate in very intense physical activity. Rooting for your favorite ball team, screaming, yelling and carrying on can release a lot of tension and help provide transformation. Or you can actually become involved in an athletic activity itself such as playing ball on a team, solitary bike riding or even martial arts, the more intense the better. These activities can allow for a tremendous outpouring of emotional energy which may have been building up within you for a long time without having an outlet.

Scorpio is co-ruled by Mars, the energy of action, indicating that you are, potentially, a creative person. The creative process also offers an opportunity for transformation. By looking within for creative inspiration, you tap into deep levels of feeling. By manifesting that inspiration externally, you are creating an outlet for the feelings.

Social situations such as weddings or funerals can also stimulate the outpouring of emotion. Any kind of family gathering awakens the strong sense of tribal identification fundamental to the Scorpio nature and provides a safe and comfortable environment in which you can be yourself and express part of your deep and profound emotionality.

You can also experience transformation through spiritual activity. This can be of a consistent, devotional nature such as ritual, ceremony or meditation. It can also arise in the form of spontaneous spiritual experience such as suddenly being aware of a vision or the presence of a powerful or illumined being. It can even take the form of feeling surrounded by light or being filled by a deep sense of peace and well being. Whatever the form, there is an immediate relief from pressures that might have been building up, and a renewed sense that all is well.

As long as you are consciously and deliberately utilizing at least one of these techniques consistently throughout your life, you periodically create a peak experience for yourself. This is defined as a situation after which you are never the same. It is a rebirth, a catharsis of consciousness. This takes place as a result of engaging in some type of activity that stimulates you to tap into and release the deepest levels of feelings and passions. All Scorpios have a personal cycle that is unique to them. For some it could be as short as a few months. For most it is from two to five years in duration. If you are working consciously and consistently to create transformation in your life, at the end of each cycle you have a peak experience. Your awareness of life and your place in the world changes. If you have not been paying attention and doing your inner work, however, the end of the cycle tends to be more chaotic and crisis-oriented. During the crisis, you let go of things in a random way including parts of yourself and your life that were ready to go or that you wanted to release, as well as things that still had relevance and meaning. Yet you remain attached to as much of the old and the stagnant as you do to the positive and the desirable. No real growth, no qualitative change. For example, Scorpios are famous for uprooting themselves, giving away their possessions and moving only to repeat this pattern throughout their lives. Internally they feel frustrated, unfulfilled or fearful. They try to change that condition and rectify those feelings by altering conditions in their outer world. They neglect looking inward.

One way to determine the length of your personal cycle of transformation is to reflect back over your life. At what intervals have you had regenerating catharses or destructive crises? Although there could be a variance of several months one way or the other, over the decades a pattern should present itself. It is within the time frame of that pattern that you have the opportunity to be more conscious in creating your new self and new place in the world.

Scorpio is the sign of secrets. This could pertain to aspects of the self which you don't want to share with others. Or it could pertain to the secret forces of life. Scorpio, Pluto and the eighth house call upon you to recognize, deal with and learn from those mysteries. There are three main points of reference that will help you on this journey. They are birth, sex and death. Sometimes

Scorpio is incorrectly referred to as the death sign or the sex sign. It is neither of those things, although at times an uncentered Scorpio may be extreme in their obsessive attachment to only one or two of those points. For example, you could alternately be afraid of death and have a death wish. Or you could resist personal rebirth yet continuously be pregnant or go through so many rebirths that they are totally useless and counterproductive. You could be addicted to sex at one point only to abstain for lengthy periods at another. As you work at becoming centered, however, you realize that true universal knowledge comes through completing the circuit among all of these points. By consciously connecting with this cycle, Scorpio demonstrates its connection to the creative principle.

Scorpio has been called the sign of frozen fire. The fire in the ice. Scorpio's time is mid to late Autumn as the ground begins to freeze and the animals start to hibernate. Scorpio can emulate that part of the life cycle by wanting to be left alone. Sexually this can manifest as being dysfunctional in the sense that is difficult for Scorpio to open up and share the self with another. Sex can be significant in two ways. First is procreative and Scorpio can be a nurturing, family-oriented experience. Second is for intimacy. In the latter context, sex is a vehicle through which people who have already established a bond can physically express their union and trust.

As a vehicle for transformation sex can bring two lovers into such ecstatic union that it's as if the individuals dissolve into a oneness. This enables you to have a fleeting glimpse of what lies beyond the dualistic world we live in. Behind the day-night, male-female distinctions that are so basic to our world exists the fundamental energy that creates everything, destroys everything and is everything. As the anticipation and excitement builds to a peak, it is accompanied by the joy of generation. Immediately following the climax, even as the bliss of oneness begins to subside, a loss of self foreshadows the ultimate letting go, namely of the body at the time of death.

It has been suggested that one way to learn how to truly love life, is to understand and accept the reality of your own death. Through its mystical nature and intuitive perspective, Scorpio has the opportunity to realize that any death experience merely leads to a rebirth. This could be a rebirth of an identity, a rebirth through a new state of consciousness or a rebirth into a non-physical form. Life is eternal and once Scorpio completes the circuit of birth, sex and death, the awareness of that eternal cycle becomes clear. It also enables Scorpio to get in touch with its power. There is no sign in the zodiac with more potential power than Scorpio. There are two ways to manifest power. In the uncentered state, it is through the love of power for the sake of power and can be manifested as destructive, selfish and underhanded. In a centered state, it is based on the power of love and can be expressed through compassion, generosity and nurturing. With significant energy in Scorpio or the eighth house or with a prominent Pluto, it's important that you become clear about your motivation. What is your intention, to maximize power or to maximize love? Even after making a decision and expressing that choice through action, you could make mistakes. Your energy could be experienced by others as too demanding or invasive even if your intentions are good. Keep trying. You may need either further transformation to get your actions in alignment with your motivations or may need to simply refine and make more realistic the ones you've already experienced. Periodic purgation of that which doesn't work will eventually bring perspective about what does work.

Scorpio can be tuned into the dark side of life. Tendencies such as greed, jealousy and deceitfulness are part of this dark side. The extreme manifestations of this can be stealing, spying, even murder. Scorpio energy and people with strong Pluto or eighth house influence, can be fascinated by these behaviors and activities. Sometimes they partake in them, sometimes they merely attract others to them who act out these patterns. Others become obsessed with reading about people for whom these behaviors are facts of life. In the centered, self-loving mode, these tendencies are incorporated within the transformational process. You acknowledge your potential to engage in these actions even as you find them unacceptable. Use the awareness of that potential as motivation to facilitate a transformation and eventually transmute them to another form of expression.

If you are off center, you can get stuck in your own darkness, feeling overwhelmed by your fears, terrors and obsessions. You could choose to ignore your shadowy aspects because they pertain to feelings and as such are unknowable and illogical.

Unexamined feelings can lead to subterranean actions. As you acknowledge those aspects of yourself, you can liberate yourself from actions based on out of control emotions. Behaviors that can be defined as evil could actually be made in ignorance of either their underlying motivations or the ultimate ramifications of those actions. That which is kept in the unconscious state can contaminate the process of growth. You then become prey to the dark forces. As you accept all aspects of your nature your awareness penetrates beneath and beyond your feelings, passions and obsessions. You reconnect with the Light of Acceptance and Oneness and realize that the Light is always present. The darkness has even been defined as the hidden place where the Light dwells. It is lack of consciousness that keeps you unaware of the Light. When you remember that the Light of consciousness is the fundamental force of life, you will be able to shine that Light through the darkness and realize that the Light is ever-present in *all* phenomena.

The ultimate value of catharsis and transformation is in the opportunity to release attachments, such as to who you think you are. By breaking down the old, smaller self you can realize a new, more expanded reality. This involves diving into the abyss of the unknown. Not in fear, but in awe. As your new identity develops, it, too, eventually becomes worn out. A new rebirth takes place, enabling you to identify more with that which is permanent, immutable and indivisible, and less with the world of form, change and ego. Through this process, you eventually are able to realize who you really are and become aware of the omnipresence of the Light within. In turn you become more actively aware of the Oneness that is Life, and become more capable of seeing your true place in the Universal Reality.

SAGITTARIUS

The first two quadrants, comprising the Northern hemisphere, focus on self-development and self-expression. The third quadrant is part of the Southern hemisphere. Its orientation is toward the outer world, that which is apart from the self. Sagittarius is the third and final sign of the third quadrant—the quarter of the zodiac that pertains to relationship. The first sign of this quadrant, Libra, is primarily oriented toward relationship with people. The second sign, Scorpio, continues and deepens relationship with people and adds interaction with the greater whole, the eternal Oneness. Sagittarius seeks to develop and deepen the relationship with all things by being continuously involved with the process of consciousness development.

Sagittarius is also the last of the fire signs and consequently begins the final third of the zodiac. The last four signs are all oriented toward development of consciousness. Each has its own unique function in the material world as well. Because of the complexity and expanse of information and experience these four signs pertain to, each of the final signs is paradoxical in some way. It is through the delineation and manifestation of the qualities of these signs that much of the more expanded realms of awareness can open. The paradox emanates from the need to integrate the personal experience with that of the universal.

Sagittarius has been called the sign of the rainbow. The array of colors in the rainbow indicates that Sagittarius is a versatile sign. The elevation of the rainbow suggests that Sagittarius seeks to develop an overview of life. The myth about the pot of gold at the end of the rainbow implies something magical and lucky about Sagittarius.

Sagittarius says, "I seek and quest for a higher vision." The Sun is in Sagittarius between November 22 and December 21.

THE MYTHS

The myth that best depicts the nature of Sagittarius is that of the Greek god Apollo. He was pure and holy, the god of the sun and music. He was the lawgiver who could punish the breakers of those laws. He was the patron of medicine who could also initiate plagues. He had a twin sister, Artemis, and together they were noted for their archery skills. Apollo's color is gold, his sister's is silver. Together they comprise the *yang-yin* or masculine-feminine polarity, although in some of the myths they are seen to be in competition. All of these images imply duality. Apollo was a remote, independent, unapproachable figure, preferring a detached overview to an intimate relationship. His stories indicate his preference for objective reasoning over intuitive feeling. He was considered the god of prophecy and was given dominion over the oracle of Delphi, which was known throughout the ancient world as a place of prophetic divination. In the pre-Hellenic epoch, however, Delphi was ruled by a goddess whose symbol was a dragon or serpent. One of the Apollonian myths involves Apollo slaying a she-dragon and assuming rulership over Delphi. This seems to be another explanation/rationalization of the changing world order from matriarchal to patriarchal. It is interesting to conjecture where mythic stories come from. Is it an attempt to understand conflicting forces within the human psyche? Is it a story expressed in the language of the common people that explains what happened and why? Or is it political propaganda that justifies in popularized form the dominion of an indigenous culture by an invading one? Archeological data does indicate that the original pastoral cultures of Southern Europe were overtaken by more aggressive tribes from the north and south. Is Apollo a forerunner of the sky-god concept that has dominated Western civilization from before the time of Jesus to the present day? Is the competition between Apollo and Artemis a subtle reminder of the conflict between cultures that took place approximately 4000 years ago?

Another Greek god who represents the archetype Sagittarius is Chiron. Chiron was a centaur. A centaur is a mythical creature who has a human head, arms and torso which seems to emanate from the neck of a horse. His lower anatomy, body, legs and tail are that of a horse. Chiron was the wisest and most just of the Centaurs. A philosopher-king, he was adept at healing, hunting, warfare, prophecy and astrology. All the Greek mythic heroes, such as Jason, Achilles, Hercules, and Peleus were students of the great teacher Chiron. Chiron married a water goddess which suggests a union, not a competition, with the feminine. It implies the integration of the feminine/intuitive within the consciousness of the masculine/rational. This suggests that the mystical power of divination is present within the Chironic archetype as are the intellectual tools of education and healing.

Although an immortal god, Chiron became ill when he dropped one of Hercules' poisoned arrows on his foot. To end his suffering, he accepted death. Before doing so, however, he arranged a deal with Zeus whereby Prometheus, who gave the fire of life and creativity to humanity, was allowed to end his suffering. Thus Chiron provides an example of how to accept death in a way that promotes the welfare of others. It is through this act of generosity that Chiron healed himself and demonstrated the importance of being aware and considerate of others and the collective human experience. The lessons of Chiron help connect us with our Higher Being. They enable us to integrate all aspects of our nature into a pragmatic unit which, ultimately, can be a bridge to realization and liberation for both ourselves and others.

There are seven deities of Japan who are considered lucky. One of them is Hotei. Hotei was originally a real person in China, whose name was Kaishi. Kaishi was an itinerant Zen priest who cited the teachings of Buddha as he wandered around the countryside. The Chinese people referred to him as Ho-Tei-Shi. As he became deified by the Japanese and included in their pantheon, he was given attributes of wittiness, magnanimity and good fortune. He was considered to be the patron of fortune tellers. He was physically large which symbolically represented inner wealth and largesse of soul.

There are several gods of Japanese Shintoism who also embody part of the Sagittarius archetype. These are the Sae-no-kami, the gods of the road. After a journey to the nether world (the eighth house), they were pursued by the thunders. To protect themselves, they threw their walking sticks across the path announcing, "the thunders shall come no farther." Thus, the Sae-no-kami protect travelers and keep them from evil spirits.

Even in minor myths from relatively ancient civilizations there are myths pertaining to Sagittarius. For example, the Assyrians associated their ninth month, which equates with our November-December, with the archer god, Kislivu. The Babylonians called Sagittarius the "strong one," the one who personifies the archer god of war. Around 2000 BC the Hindus called Sagittarius "the horseman."

A contemporary myth that illustrates the Sagittarian nature is demonstrated by Captain Kirk, Mister Spock and the rest of the crew of the Starship Enterprise in the television and movie series *Star Trek.* This is a group of travelers who seek to make contact with intelligent human-type life forms throughout the universe. They are not only involved with the process of the journey, but also with the experience of learning from and teaching to others the knowledge of their respective civilizations. As a result, not only does the data bank of information of each group expand, but so, too, do the limits of the known universe.

THE GLYPH: ↗

The glyph associated with Sagittarius is an arrow. With the exception of the scales of justice which is the glyph for Libra, the arrow of Sagittarius is the only glyph that is a human artifact. This indicates a connection between these two signs. It also suggests that the consciousness developed by the Sagittarian experience is capable of generating things which benefit the general human condition. It is a symbol of aspiration, and is indicative of a strong desire for high achievement.

The arrow is a dualistic image. It can be a very positive concept. It illustrates the Sagittarian orientation to prophecy and the future by presenting an image that is looking up and is potentially in motion. It suggests that the experience of learning new concepts and understanding new thoughts are available to everyone and can be beneficial to all. Look up and go forward. It is the Apollonian arrow blazing new horizons of consciousness. In that sense it conveys a certain joyfulness of new, emerging images and manifestations of the human creative urge. It suggests a hopefulness about the potential these creations have to improve the human condition.

An arrow is usually thought of as an implement of destruction. It could be used by a warrior in battle, or by a hunter looking for fresh game to satisfy his family's hunger. These are primitive activities. These acts can be purely destructive, such as the imperialistic warlord who seeks to dominate his neighbors for the sake of his own greed and self-aggrandizement. Wanton aggression can also manifest as the sportsman, out on a weekend of trophy hunting with his friends. The one with the most heads at the end wins. The warrior and the hunter can also be positive, however. The warrior can be a soldier who defends his tribe from the invading warlord. The hunter can seek game and at the same time be in tune with the universal order. He acknowledges and honors the life of his prey, and uses every part of that animal to provide sustenance and comfort to his family.

The glyph for Sagittarius, therefore, suggests that there are potentials for two entirely different motivations and manifestations of the Sagittarius archetype.

THE TOTEM:

The totem associated with Sagittarius is the centaur, an animal that is half horse and half human. This represents the interplay between the emerging consciousness and the carnal instinct of conquest. The centaur suggests that Sagittarius embodies two distinct principles. One is the spiritual evolution of an individual. The human form is an archer who shoots his arrow into the sky as a symbol of aspiration and achievement. It suggests the inner human drive to aim at and manifest a higher degree of existence.

Second, the human torso is rising from the body and legs of the beast. The horse represents our physical form and our animal nature. In the natural state horses roam in herds. This suggests a desire to be free to move and travel. In their domesticated condition they have been used for everything from beasts of burden, to warfare, to jousting, to polo. This indicates a versatility to the Sagittarian nature. It can direct itself in the pursuit of travel, conquest or sport.

Mythologically, centaurs were considered to be wild and savage. They were known for their tendencies to rape, pillage and plunder. It was only due to the presence and wisdom of their leader Chiron that they were able to rise above these behaviors. From a more expansive perspective they could explore the realms of higher existence, and manifest behaviors that required more moral and ethical understanding.

Taken together, the two parts of the centaur represent the principle of expansion. The animal qualities suggest the physical and athletic. This can be warlike and aggressive or it can be more playful. In either case, the centaur suggests movement or travel. For the Sagittarian, this implies literally picking the body up and moving it around the planet. It also enjoys traveling through an exploration of ideas. This leads to the more human qualities of the centaur which represents the process of mental growth through learning. This can take several forms. One is learning in the form of raw data. Then there is applying the knowledge to physical activity. Finally, there is understanding of the implications and ramifications of those physical actions. The human-archer part of the centaur implies that Sagittarius can grow, not only through the physical or intellectual experiences, but also through consciousness development, eventually merging into a more divine state of being. The arrow is the key. It is pointed in the direction of the unseen and inexperienced. Flying through the air it symbolizes the quest to expand one's vision and learn more about life.

The image of the centaur implies that as a Sagittarius you have a choice. You can follow the lower drives of the ego-driven physical body, disregarding everything but your own satisfaction in the moment. You can also follow the plane of your arrow and seek a broader perspective. The arrow suggests the future and Sagittarius is the sign of the prophet. The arrow, which represents the spirit, can only reach stages of higher conscious-ness when it is not bound by the cord of the limited vision of self-interest.

MODE AND ELEMENT

Sagittarius is the sign of mutable-fire. This combination illustrates part of the paradox of this sign. Mutability is flexible and adaptable. It is oriented toward learning and service. Fire is direct, dynamic and expressive. It tends to forge and create rather than adjust and change. Mutability can also suggest a disposition to be easily influenced. A fire sign, however, would be more oriented to its own ideas and activities rather than those from external sources. It tends to do the influencing rather than being influenced. Mutable-fire suggests that Sagittarius has a tendency to be overextended. You combine the patterns of curiosity and open-mindedness with exuberant expression. These qualities can meld into a wide-eyed naiveté that can render you confused about what you are actually doing. As a Sagittarius you can be overwhelmed by having too many projects going on at one time. This can lead to confusion. Even if you feel good about all your various activities and are not bewildered by them, you could still ramble from situation to situation without manifesting anything in a practical or useful way. Like its fire-sign cousin Aries Sagittarius can also feel uplifted by the joy of a concept, but bored by the practicalities of its physical realization.

It's important to try to blend the mutability with the fire in a conscious and realistic way. Too much mutability can lead to mirthful good intentions followed by emptiness. Too much fire projects too much self and the tendency to do what you will regardless of the consequences.

The orientation of the final four signs is toward universal experience. As a mutable sign, Sagittarius' orientation to learning can take numerous, almost limitless forms. In general, there are two areas in which the mutable curiosity and desire to learn take shape. First is the academic. The study of any intellectual system can be fulfilling to Sagittarius. Sometimes you can enjoy learning within several systems at one time. Not enough mental stimulation can lead to boredom. Too much information can lead to confusion. You could direct some of the learning to a practical application, such as an occupation or job training. Some of the information might be more oriented toward satisfying your curiosity. Maybe this curiosity has always been there but you never took the time to satisfy it. Maybe this is something new that you just heard about. Maybe you want to study a subject because you know nothing about it at all. It might prove to be boring and useless, but at least it will expand your awareness beyond its present degree. The only stipulation about the subject matter is that it needs to be defined and presented in a systematic way. Random information learned in a spontaneous manner is less appealing to Sagittarius. If it is presented in an organized manner, however, it has a twofold benefit. First the information is useful unto itself as a body of knowledge. Sagittarius is always open to learning and understanding more about life. Second, the information can lead to further expansion elsewhere. It could lead to a degree or higher degree at the university. It could also lead to a broader understanding of your field of interest even if a degree or institution is not involved.

The second area in which your mutable "need to know" can be satisfied is by applying your time and energy directly to a system of consciousness development. In an academic context, this can take the form of philosophy and theology. At an early stage of this journey you should be true to your expansive nature by seeking to understand life from as many philosophical points of view as possible. From traditional thinkers of the West or East to the more radical ideologues, you can learn something from them all. From the former, you can understand how civilizations have been shaped by conceptual thinking. From the latter, you learn how the status quo is being challenged and consciousness is being pushed to new realizations. In the modern world, it is the Buckminster Fullers, the Malcolm Xs, the Matthew Foxs, who are making exciting contributions to the understanding of who we are and what our potential could be.

The most essential thing gained in a personal sense from the study of philosophy is the development of a system of morals and ethics. Morality is the socially accepted and acknowledged dos and don'ts. Morals describe how a civilization defines acceptable ways for people to relate to each other. Ethics are self-defined ways of being. You could live in a relatively immoral context, in which it is mutually understood that everyone is out for him or her self. As an individual, however, you could still be ethical in your dealings with others. The study of morals and ethics helps you to understand the cultural context within which you are living. An in depth study of these concepts will help you distinguish between expectations of your own or others' behavior that is idealistic and unreasonable or that which borders on amorality altogether.

From the philosophical, it is a short jump to the metaphysical. This is a form of philosophy that is concerned with the study of being in relationship to the entire structure of the universe. It tends to be speculative in nature, rather than scientific, and for this reason relies as much on the development of the intuitive mind as it does on the understanding of logic. Ultimately, the study of metaphysics can transform your awareness beyond the rational and into the mystical.

As a Sagittarius, when you begin to explore these exalted subjects, it is in your nature to do so in an expanded way. You might be interested to study all the great teachers or all the great teachings throughout the ages and all around the globe. After a certain point, however, to continue to broaden your search limits the depth of awareness that your quest will render. To grow beyond the limited logical mind, and begin the process of integrating the right brain with the left, a choice must be made. Decide on the path, teacher, philosophy or teaching that you resonate with the most. This is the one that not only gives you the intellectual understanding of who you are and why you are here, but also connects you in an inexplicable way with the Source of Life Itself. You can still pursue new topics on the intellectual and academic levels and be open to the experiences and paths of your friends and colleagues. To truly be involved in evolutionary expansion in a personal way, however, a specific path is strongly advised.

Mutability is not only oriented to receiving knowledge and information; it also includes a drive to share what it has learned. For Sagittarius this can take many forms. The most immediate is service to the community at large. Being a Big Brother or Big Sister, being active in a local community center or being active in a youth organization such as Little League or the Cub Scouts are vehicles of sharing. Charity work, such as The United Way or The Red Cross are also venues through which you can make a contribution to the community. Activity in organizations that go beyond your community to serve the world community—such as the Peace Corps, the World Wildlife Foundation or the Sierra Club—offer a direction for your service-oriented tendencies.

In a more practical sense, sharing your knowledge through your profession offers the opportunity to help others even as you take care of your own material needs. Teaching has an obvious appeal. From the primary grades through the university, the field of education has as many directions as even a multi-faceted Sagittarius would need. Even creating a philosophy of education, being a theoretician of new ideas about educating people and new techniques to use in that process, can be a Sagittarian pursuit.

If your higher mind pursuits tend more to the spiritual, the ministry is an occupation that provides the opportunity to be of service to the community, perform charitable work and educate others in uplifting ways.

The versatility of Sagittarius and its ability to perform simultaneous activities can make a career in administration realistic and rewarding. This could take the form of working within a business or a bureaucracy. You can find a rewarding occupation as an administrator. These are situations in which you would be performing many tasks within one context.

The fire quality of Sagittarius also has its dichotomous potential. As with Aries and Leo, Sagittarius can become blinded by its own light. You can become so concerned with your own well-being or the satisfaction of your own curiosity that you can be insensitive to other people. You can become so full of yourself that your actions are more oriented toward building up your ego than toward service to others. This is self-aggrandizement and your primary drive is to expand your dominion over others. This could take the form of a con-artist, who pretends concern for the welfare of others, when in fact the only consideration is the benefits you receive from your actions.

Fire can also generate a sense of limitless euphoria, a feeling that whatever you do will be successful. This can lead to various types of gambling, from card rooms to stock brokerages. It can also take the form of unsafe physical risks through such activities as mountain climbing, geographical exploration or select police and military teams.

In a more conscious and centered manner, Sagittarius can demonstrate its fiery nature in more positive ways. Fire is confident and enthusiastic. Sagittarius may even be the most optimistic, hopeful and joyful of the signs. For this reason, Sagittarius is known for its good fortune, sometimes being called the lucky sign, because luck is the power of positive thinking. Good fortune is not an accident or based on random chance. It is the marriage of opportunity meeting preparedness.

Fire illuminates. This could take the form of expanded awareness dispelling the darkness of ignorance. Sagittarius can also use this quality to be a seeker and speaker of truth. Although at times this quality can manifest as insensitive bluntness, the important thing to the fiery Sagittarius is the expression of their reality as they see it. Upholding definite principles and maintaining personal integrity, two byproducts of moral awareness and ethical development, are guideposts to Sagittarius in both word and action.

Fire also creates. For Sagittarius this can manifest through the expression of new ideas or combining old ideas in new ways. Careers that involve writing and publishing appeal to you as a Sagittarius because they provide the opportunity to explore new intellectual horizons as well as to share those vistas with others in ways that can be educational to them, and profitable to you.

Combining mutability with fire provides a vast array of areas to explore and modes of expression through which to explore them. Always seeking the new and more expanded within a framework or service can take you to various parts of the world. Opportunities in the travel industry or the foreign service are there if you can take advantage of them. Being able to relay ideas to people is useful in sales, public relations and advertising. The important thing is how you choose to express the energy of mutable fire. Don't be surprised if you choose more than one mode or path in your life, as that, too, fits Sagittarius. The key is to recognize the different options for expression, from those that are more physical in expression to those that are more sublime. The important thing is to always strive to learn more today than you knew yesterday while finding ways of sharing the knowledge that you already have.

THE RULING PLANET

The ruling planet of Sagittarius is Jupiter ($\u2643$). Jupiter represents the energy of expansion. It indicates how, by sign placement, you assimilate information and where, by house placement, mental and social development is available to you. In Vedic, or Hindu astrology, Jupiter is called Guru which means the teacher. In the Hindu scriptures spiritual progress is said to occur in twelve year cycles. The cycle of Jupiter is approximately twelve years. It takes almost one year for Jupiter to travel or transit through each of the signs of the zodiac. The Vedic texts suggest, therefore, that for every cycle of Jupiter that we live in physical form on the earth plane, we are experiencing one year of spiritual development. You can choose to accelerate that growth by consistently pursuing a specific spiritual discipline, such as a technique of meditation, prayer, ceremony or ritual. But merely by living a good life, and functioning as an honest, moral, ethical person, the transits of Jupiter promise a gradual growth of your consciousness.

There are two planets in the zodiac that are considered teachers. In addition to Jupiter, Saturn, the ruling planet of Capricorn, also has educational properties. They are, however, oriented toward different subjects and use different methodologies to get their lessons across. Saturn will be delineated in the next chapter. Jupiter is oriented toward subjects that are theoretical. It wants to take the mind into new territory. Philosophy is clearly a Jupiterian topic. From logic to ethics, from the pre-Socratics to the Existentialists, Jupiter loves to engage in discussion about the possibilities and probabilities of life. Subjects that involve people or that study the works of human beings are also under the dominion of Jupiter. History and literature are Jupiterian because they discuss the human experience and how that experience, measured through creative effort, expresses the evolution of consciousness at any time in any civilization.

The methodology of teaching that Jupiter represents is based on the joy of learning. This is demonstrated by the teacher who prefers the student not take notes, gives open book examinations and is more concerned with the process of learning than with the product of learning. This is the professor whose lectures are filled with humorous anecdotes. To engage the student in such a way that understanding takes precedence over memorization is the methodology of the Jupiterian teacher. This is not a judgment of other forms of instruction. Some students will take advantage of the openness and generosity of the Jupiterian teacher. They may need someone more strict or a curriculum that is more demanding. Others thrive in an environment that is pressure free and they take full advantage of opportunities afforded by the Jupiterian approach.

Jupiter represents what can come easily. It suggests where we can assimilate in a joyful state of mind, whether the assimilation is informational or social. Jupiter is computer-like in its ability to analyze, organize and categorize bits and pieces of information into larger thought forms and concepts. It moves from the specific to the general and prefers to work with the bigger picture than with isolated information.

In the social sense, Jupiter can suggest where, by house placement, opportunity exists for you to grow. It indicates where you can find reward or compensation for work done in other areas of life, or accomplished in previous incarnations. Some of these opportunities will arise as a result of the positive attitudes you possess in that area. People like positive people. You are attractive to others when you express your Jupiterian humor, joy, tolerance and generosity of spirit. Others want you to be part of their occupational or social experience, and will offer opportunities to you rather than to someone else who demonstrates a different attitude. This positive quality can be a byproduct of the confidence that Jupiter brings, a sense that you have of being capable of doing something.

Opportunities can also be available to you as a result of the integrity with which you conduct yourself. Principle and honesty are two important qualities of this energy. They help you to increase chances for success and reward. They also enable you to create a more honest experience and consequently to derive more intrinsic enjoyment from your efforts and actions.

Jupiter is also independent in thought and in action. With a prominent Jupiter in your natal chart, such as close to one of the four angles (house cusps one, four, seven or ten), conjunct the Sun or Moon, in the signs of its rulership, Sagittarius or Pisces, or in the ninth or twelfth houses, you will always strive for new information. Those experiences will be a priority for you and you will likely have the ability to understand and assimilate the new knowledge. The desire to disseminate information can also motivate a person with a strong Jupiter. This could manifest in professions that are oriented toward writing, education or publishing. With a prominent Jupiter, travel will also be a high priority for you. Depending on other factors in the chart, travel for you could be a recreational activity, a professional pursuit or even a life style,

The risk in all this mirthful expression is the possibility of being too idealistic. You could become extremely disappointed if expectations of yourself or others are unfulfilled. Unrealistic optimism can doom you to feelings of failure even if, objectively, the experience and the outcome are positive or successful. Hard aspects such as conjunctions, squares, or oppositions to Jupiter in your natal chart caution you to avoid this type of projecting. If Jupiter represents the principle of expansion, Jupiter under stress connotes too much expansion. In combination with Neptune, this could manifest as excessive idealism; with the Sun as too much confidence; with Mars as too much anger or too much self; with Venus as overindulgence or over-generosity; with Uranus as excessive change, with the Moon as extreme emotional reaction, with Saturn or Pluto as too much power or need to establish dominion or control

The house placement of Jupiter in your natal chart indicates where opportunities to learn and grow in an easy, joyful way will tend to be present in your life. In the first house of self, Jupiter provides an optimistic and enthusiastic attitude and outlook on life. That attitude and a wonderful, sometimes self-deprecating sense of humor helps to create positive experiences in your life. Planets in the first house can help describe the body type. Generally, the Jupiterian body tends to expand. This suggests either a large boned person or one who tends to gain weight easily. In either case with Jupiter in your first house consistent exercise is strongly recommended as a way of keeping a large body in shape or to avoid excessive weight gain.

The second house indicates what you value, what resources you have at your disposal, your level of earned income or your way of dealing with money. With Jupiter in your second house you put high priority on learning, both academic and philosophical. You could earn your living through any of the Jupiterian activities such as teaching, writing or administration. Jupiter in the second also implies the ability to generate more than enough money to meet basic needs for security and comfort. One potential problem with Jupiter in the second house, or Sagittarius on the cusp, is a tendency to spend money faster than you are making it.

The third house pertains to extended family and Jupiter in this house can indicate either a large extended family, and/or one that placed emphasis on education and from which you learned a lot as a child. The third house also can indicate your state of mind. Jupiter suggests a positive state of mind, one that is open to learning about life in a flowing way. Casual conversations with neighbors, newspapers and magazines, workshops and seminars can all provide opportunities to satisfy your thirst for information. Jupiter here has a spontaneous sense of humor which can be beneficial in dealing with the public (sales, public relations), teaching or writing. One potential drawback is a tendency to amass endless information that is either disorganized or doesn't have a central theme. Consequently the ideas can't be applied in a pragmatic way.

The fourth house represents your emotional, psychological and spiritual foundation. Jupiter herein suggests a deep well of internal joy that is always available to you to draw from. This is also the area of life that involves your home and family. Jupiter indicates a positive family situation. You offer an abundance of nurturing to those with whom you live and probably derive a similar quality from them as well. You might also use your home as a place to learn by reading there or by bringing people into your home for such activities as study groups. Jupiter in the fourth can also suggest that you enjoy traveling so much that your home could be on the road.

The fifth is the house of love, play and children. Jupiter in your fifth puts emphasis on education, both secular and spiritual, as a priority in parenting. Love can be expressed with expansiveness and joy. Jupiter in the fifth conveys athletic interest and skill in either competitive team-oriented sports or those that are more individual such as hiking and biking. Your self-confidence and self-esteem will usually be positive and consistent. One potential drawback, however, is a tendency to become too self-absorbed. You can be so interested in whatever creative or recreational outlets interest you that you can become oblivious of other things or other people.

The sixth house pertains to health and service work. With Jupiter in your sixth house your health should be good and you may be inclined to learn about your body so as to be able to maintain your health at a level of high quality throughout your life. Being of service to others, either in your home or through your job, can be a source of happiness and joy. You approach your work with integrity and thereby create a flow of new opportunities coming your way. Pay attention, however, to a tendency to be excessively idealistic. This can lead to being highly critical of others, especially employees or others with whom you connect in the workplace.

Jupiter in the seventh house indicates positive primary relationships. You approach relationship with a need for emotional honesty and personal integrity. You want a partner who is open to listening to you and learning from you and you would likewise be attracted to someone from whom you could learn as well. Generous, tolerant and open minded you create relationships that are always growing. With your orientation to sociability, you can also generate opportunities for new relationships if you choose.

Jupiter in the eighth house brings the desire and ability to deepen a relationship to a level of intimacy. You would also desire to learn and understand about life in a fundamental, bedrock context. You can be honest about expressing your deep inner feelings and challenging your partner about their patterns that may seem artificial to you. Make sure your inherent honesty doesn't generate hurt feelings and problems in the relationship, however. Science, metaphysics or the occult, learned from source material could all prove interesting in your quest for deep understanding about the meaning of life. You can appreciate the process of transformation, realizing the opportunities it offers for deepening awareness about life. Jupiter in the eighth house also indicates the possibility of an inheritance.

Jupiter is home in the ninth house. Whenever a planet in located in the house that it rules it is said to be accidentally dignified. Jupiter is accidentally dignified in both the ninth house (Sagittarius) and the twelfth house (Pisces). With Jupiter in the ninth house you approach learning and the process of consciousness development in an open minded way. Travel, school and independent study are activities that you are probably familiar with. One drawback to this pattern is a tendency to become a "professional student" who is always learning something new but never applying the information in a practical way that benefits you or anybody else.

The tenth is the house of career. Jupiter in the tenth house suggests success in your profession. The combination of positive attitude and personal integrity ensure opportunities for promotions and raises. You will generally have a positive reputation in your field which can help generate new opportunities both in your present position as well as in new ones, always coming your way. Don't let your successes cause you to develop an overblown concept of yourself, however. In that scenario you will likely alienate others by demonstrations of your power and displays of your achievements.

The eleventh is the house of friends. Jupiter in your eleventh house implies good, supportive friends always being in your life. You will enjoy each other's humor, learn a great deal from each other and genuinely enjoy each others' company. New friends coming into your life as old friendships continue to grow and expand help make this area one of great satisfaction. Watch out for a tendency to become socially over-extended by trying to relate to too many people and letting activities in other areas of life remain undeveloped.

In the twelfth house Jupiter expands the desire to look within the self. You can benefit from psychotherapy, finding clarity and insights from that process. You can find meditation or prayer extremely valuable in connecting to your higher being. You can feel so good during your alone time that you tend to be too reclusive. You can avoid that tendency, as well as experiencing deep feelings of joy and satisfaction from being of service to others either in a professional or volunteer capacity.

To understand how you assimilate information according to your natal chart, keep in mind that Jupiter works in polarity with Mercury. Their respective sign and house placements as well as aspects from other planets determine how well you integrate new information into the old computer data bank. They also indicate how readily and easily you integrate yourself into a larger social context. If Mercury and Jupiter are of relatively equal strength and importance by sign, house and aspect you should have an easy time learning. It would also be more obvious to you what your social group expects from you and what they offer to you as well.

If Mercury is much stronger than Jupiter in the chart, you may tend to have a backlog of information, more raw facts than you can understand. You may tend to have difficulty assimilating within your peer group or even deciding what group you feel comfortable being part of. It may be a case of too many people but not enough real connections. A strong Mercury with a weaker Jupiter can't function or adequately keep up with the inflow of data and people. Mercury is strong if it is angular, in one of the signs it rules, in Sagittarius or any of the cardinal signs. It is also strong when conjunct the Sun or in the third or ninth houses. In relationship to such a Mercury, Jupiter is considered weaker if it is in a succeedant house, an earth sign or in hard aspect to several other planets.

If Jupiter is much stronger than Mercury in the chart you may tend to be intellectually frustrated. It might be hard to take in enough data or information to keep you stimulated or growing mentally in a satisfying enough way. You may be socially frustrated or even isolated if Mercury, the data gatherer of the zodiac, is not capable of keeping up with the needs for expansion, learning and assimilation that Jupiter has. This condition would exist if Jupiter is angular or in a mutable sign, or supported by planetary aspect and Mercury is in a fixed sign or if it receives hard aspects from other planets.

When Jupiter is retrograde, there can be difficulty experiencing expansion in a clear way. The most fundamental way in which Jupiter promotes expansion is through learning. When it is retrograde, you may have difficulty validating what you know or in feeling comfortable with your degree of knowledge and understanding. You could even doubt your own intelligence or assume that most other people are brighter or better educated than you are. One reason to develop this perspective is that with Jupiter retrograde you may have a tendency to extrapolate a little information into an overly expanded thought. This leaves a residue of confusion and a potential assumption that others probably understand the bigger picture. The real problem is with the methodology itself. Instead of jumping to conclusions, try building up to a conclusion by amassing more data first. Another way out of this pattern is by utilizing archetypal symbols as ways of seeking expanded truths. Reading myths, understanding archetypes or studying the work of Carl Jung or Joseph Campbell can help you understand life through larger concepts. The symbols convey information in a way that combines as much right brain intuitive understanding as left brain facts. This integration can help you to avoid the Jupiter retrograde tendency to over think.

Jupiter also functions to bring abundance into your life. With Jupiter retrograde, there can difficulty with creating abundance possibly due to a feeling that you don't deserve to have all you need. This can be due to the fact that Jupiter retrograde tends to seek a higher or more exalted understanding of life. Your priorities are such that you prefer to seek expanded consciousness rather than material comforts. You may even tend to overlook and undervalue material plane activity altogether. It's as if you are making an unnecessary and artificial distinction about energy. The human body has seven energy centers, called *chakras*. Each one pertains to specific ways of interacting with life and it's important to activate them all in a balanced and appropriate way. With Jupiter retrograde there is a tendency to assume that you should choose only the four higher octaves, from the heart on up, through which to express your energy. In making this decision, you eliminate all information dealing with either the physical or emotional levels of reality. The *chakras* correspond to the glands of the endocrine system, and to major nexuses of the nervous system. The first *chakra* is at the base of the spine and deals with survival, your ability to know what your basic material needs are and to stay in your body long enough to satisfy them. The second *chakra* is slightly below the naval and deals with your emotional connection to life and to other people. This is the level that comes into play with sexuality. The third *chakra* is at the solar plexus and deals with personal power and ego. It contains the energy necessary to function in life as a separate, self-defined individual. The fourth *chakra* is at the heart and represents love energy. This is not only romantic love but also other, more exalted forms of heart expression such as compassion. By activating our fourth *chakra*, we open the heart. From this level we can feel the connection among all sentient beings. We learn how to relate to others as extensions of ourselves and to perceive ourselves as extensions of everyone else. This liberates us to relate to others as we relate to ourselves, and to know how we would like others to relate to us. The fifth *chakra* is at the throat and deals with communication. This can be shared, open, verbalized forms of expressions or the communication that is derived more from inner voice or clairaudient, modes. The sixth *chakra* is the point between the eyebrows, slightly above the eyes. This is the third or mind's eye. It pertains to the opening of higher awareness. It attunes our awareness of the intuitive, mystical and clairvoyant information. It is our opening to and a way of accessing Christ Consciousness. The crown *chakra*, the seventh *chakra*, is right at the crown or top of the head. Stimulating and awakening the crown connects you directly to the source of Life and Being. A fully realized spiritual master would have an open and active crown *chakra*. He or she acts as a fully functional expression of God and has full, conscious responsibility for their own evolution. This is a person who is the embodiment of Spirit and radiates endless Love, Joy and Light.

With Jupiter retrograde in your natal horoscope, you could tend to forget about the lower three *chakras*. You may be seeking only the love, higher communication and development at the conscious levels. It's as if you are assuming that the trick of life is to avoid the first three and concentrate only on the upper four. Having learned from the Libran experience about the importance of balance, it is important to apply this lesson to the *chakras*. Strive to activate all seven in a relatively balanced manner. Through the exercise of free will you can choose, emphasize and concentrate the greatest amount of your time and energy on those energy centers that you consider most important. The key is in the balance. Health problems are often caused by imbalance in the *chakras*.

With Jupiter retrograde you may need to focus more on the lower *chakras*, not only to remind yourself that they exist, perform vital functions, and have specific meaning and value in life, but also to integrate those levels of consciousness and activity into your life. In this way you can start to identify material things that you need and allow yourself to manifest them. You can begin to recognize your emotional needs and seek to satisfy them. By knowing what your real needs are, you will also realize what is enough for you and not get caught in the trap of empty materialism. You learn how to take responsibility for yourself on the physical and emotional levels yet still focus on consciousness development as your number one priority.

Finally, with Jupiter retrograde there can be tendencies to be excessively idealistic. This can especially manifest around situations involving people. You may tend to be too open and vulnerable around others, assuming that they are motivated from the same high ethical standards that you are. Starting with the process of early childhood socialization, you could have experienced disappointment and what felt like rejection. Even as a small child, you may have approached other children in an open, magnanimous, benevolent manner. Other children who do not have Jupiter retrograde might not have been relating in the same way. Children can be very cruel to each other, because they have not yet developed a social conscience. They are either unaware of the pain they can cause, or they just don't care. The child with Jupiter retrograde relates to others with openness and acceptance. That child might assume that because they are not being related to in the same way, that they are disliked and being rejected. The truth of the matter may be simply that you and the other children are following a different standard of behavior, but the assumption of rejection can follow you into adulthood. You may assume that this is the nature of other people. You look for that type of interaction to the point that you keep re-creating it. One possible response you could have to this dynamic is to become callous and less sensitive. That won't work though because by nature you tend to be open and generous. Another false way out is to stay by yourself and avoid the problem. That only prolongs the need for a solution. Another common response is to develop a better-than/less-than attitude toward people. A form of one-upsmanship, you become judgmental of others, always seeing them as better than you or not as good as you. This may avoid the feeling of being spurned by others, but merely evades the problem.

The best way out is through self-examination. Start by noticing if you tend to play one-upsmanship. If you do, try being less demanding or expectant of yourself and others. Another method of breaking down the feelings of rejection is through verbalization. In whatever situation you are experiencing what you assume to be peer group rejection, the best thing to do is ask if in fact the other people involved really don't like you or want you around. What you will probably discover is that the people are going to look at you blankly, as if they have no idea what you are talking about, because they really don't. This is really more a problem of style than substance. It is an extension of a tendency to be overly open, idealistic and uncritical on your part, rather than anything about you that is disdained by others. Over the years this confusion may have caused you to look for the wrong signals of acceptance or rejection. Learning to communicate in this way won't be easy. Learning new patterns can be difficult. By being selective about how, when and with whom you can bring this up will enable you to gradually learn who your real friends are and thus feel more accepted and less alienated.

There will, however, be those times when your feared rejection is real. Some people may simply dislike you. Often those difficulties will be easy to correct. Once you know what others dislike about you, you can decide if that is a quality you want to change or not. It might be preferable to just eliminate those people from your life. Their reasons for rejecting you might be so ridiculous that it is healthier and more appropriate to give up the relationship rather than compromising fundamental parts of your life. It may turn out that you are rejecting them even as they are rejecting you. It may also be more desirable, and a point of personal growth, to change some simple habits of socialization to feel more comfortable with others. For example, you may be in the habit of dropping in on friends unexpectedly. You come in smiling and present yourself in a positive, jovial and benevolent frame of mind while your friends feel intruded upon. That can be an easy enough habit to alter.

Which of these three possible manifestations of Jupiter retrograde will vary from sign to sign? Difficulty validating knowledge and intelligence might tend to result more from Jupiter retrograde in earth signs, where the emphasis is more on the material than mental planes. Problems manifesting things of the material plane might be a problem with Jupiter retrograde in air signs for exactly the opposite reason. And socialization/ rejection issues might be more of a problem with Jupiter retrograde in the sensitive water signs.

THE NINTH HOUSE

The ninth house, the area of life associated with Sagittarius, is the house of the higher mind. The process of expanding awareness can take place through several forms. One form is travel. As you expand your horizons, you expand your mind. A strong ninth house emphasis in your natal chart can indicate a drive to travel either professionally or recreationally. The Moon in the ninth house can even indicate a tendency to live in a country other than that of your birth. The third house can be oriented toward travel as well. But the third house takes short journeys. It enjoys going to places that can be reached by car, or places that require at most a night or two stay. The ninth house prefers longer journeys that can take a day or two just to arrive at your destination. If the third house is the bus station, the ninth is the airport.

Another focus of ninth house activity is higher education. As student or teacher, with planets in your ninth house you enjoy the process of learning and sharing the information with others. Some people with ninth house energy become eternal students, moving through the university catalogue amassing degrees as some people collect stamps. As professional students, their quest for higher knowledge is greater than their desire to apply the information.

Planets in the ninth house suggest what and how you enjoy learning. Venus indicates a love of learning and a preference for the arts. Saturn provides strong motivation to achieve in the academic arena, especially in the sciences. Saturn in the ninth can also indicate a fear of learning, an assumption that somehow you aren't intelligent enough to do the work or that you can't compete successfully in the academic arena. One way out of that fear is to clearly define a specific goal you want to achieve. Choose a structured learning situation that provides specific parameters and periodic measures of your progress. Far from being incompetent, with Saturn in the ninth house you have the ability to understand things at great depth and with great detail. Focusing and defining are the keys.

Pluto favors fields which require investigation and analysis. To work long and hard with Pluto in the ninth provides an eventual breakthrough or catharsis of understanding not only about the subject at hand, but also about the nature of life itself. Uranus can function well in a climate that allows the student to learn in an independent manner. Uranus is attracted to subjects that are unconventional or that are oriented toward technology and electronics. Neptune wants to learn about the psyche. Psychology and hypnotherapy rank high on the Neptunian priority list, although the fine arts also have an appeal. The Sun, Jupiter, Moon or Mercury in the ninth suggest a career in academia. The Moon would be attracted to working with younger children as a teacher.

The higher mind orientation of the ninth house can also be experienced through an interest in philosophy. At the secular level, classes involving logic and ethics can prove inspiring. In a more spiritual context an interest in theology, cosmology or metaphysics draws you. Choosing a particular religious framework or spiritual path or teacher can be very important. Living within the context of that system can be a way for someone with a lot of ninth house energy to remain grounded and stable even as they continue to develop their awareness. The problem is in making sure you avoid the traps of dogmatism or doctrinaire thinking. Saturn or Pluto in the ninth are particularly prone to this pattern, although Jupiter in a fixed sign can also do a lot of proselytizing or just get stuck in old patterns of thought and belief. With Saturn in the ninth, you may seek a sense of power, control or prestige by being "right" in your beliefs. Avoid this limitation by seeking a spiritual path that you can connect to in a deep, personally meaningful way. Saturn tends to be oriented toward the traditional. Pluto can avoid the trap of dogmatism by periodically uprooting, deeply analyzing and transforming those parts of the old belief system that are outmoded. With Pluto in your ninth house make sure that your experience in life or continued spiritual growth have not enabled you to outgrow a previously defined belief system. Jupiter in a fixed sign has provided you with lifetimes of security, but now it is time to update the philosophical framework that helped you manifest that security. Do it in as slow and comfortable a manner as you need to but you can avoid the dead-end of rigid beliefs by consciously making sure you are continuing to expand in this area.

Uranus would have the opposite tendency. It is attracted to new and contemporary, or at least unconventional paths to higher consciousness. Even if connecting to a traditional belief system, such as Buddhism, Hinduism or Christianity, a person with Uranus in the natal ninth house would want to practice the teachings in an independent way.

With the Moon, Neptune or Venus in the ninth house you would feel comfortable with spiritual traditions that are female centered. Paths that are oriented toward Nature, such as the Native-American or other type of indigenous people's system, would apply here. Rituals that celebrate the lunar cycle would coincide with the sensitive, intuitive, personal needs of any of these three planets in the ninth house.

The ninth house is oriented toward systems of thought. Your free will may incline you more to an academic system, a philosophical or spiritual system or an occupational system. All the systems, however, need to provide you with two things. The first is the opportunity to continually expand your mind in a way that can be shared with other people. Secondly, the system must provide a means of staying centered. Without adherence to such a system, your life could become confused and lack direction. You could also connect with more than one system, possibly one academic, another spiritual. It would also be helpful if you have already clearly defined your morals and ethics whether you ascribe to a particular spiritual or religious program or not. A fundamental, practical sense of right and wrong will make you more effective in your social relationships, and you will tend to be more fulfilled socially and emotionally.

SAGITTARIUS AND THE BODY

Anatomically, Sagittarius rules various parts of the middle area of the body, especially the upper parts of the lower extremities. The thighs, hips, lower spinal cord and the sciatic nerve are under the dominion of Sagittarius. The sciatic nerve is located in the lumbar region of the spine. Injury to that nerve can be felt in the lumbar area as well as the buttocks and down the legs to the thighs and calves. It's not uncommon for shooting pain in the legs to be traced to the sciatic nerve which in turn can be traced to problems in the lower back area.

Sagittarius also co-rules the liver in association with Virgo. Both of these signs are oriented toward absorbing information, just as the liver is the organ that helps the body to assimilate nutrients. Like Sagittarius, the liver takes in the material, and like Virgo, it discriminates about what is healthy and what is toxic.

Jupiter rules through the principle of expansion. Expansion can take place through a love of physical exercise. Generally, Sagittarius prefers physical activity that is non-competitive, such as hiking, back-backing, camping, skiing, bike riding, and horseback riding. Good health can also be maintained by expanding your vision of life. This helps you to develop the ability to maintain a positive, confident state of mind.

A prominent Jupiter or several planets in Sagittarius, especially if in the first or sixth houses, you can have a tendency to overindulge in food or drink. This proclivity to excess can lead to ill health. Ironically, this habit of overindulgence can be as a result of being in excellent health. You have a strong constitution and a lot of physical vitality and you may tend to take that condition for granted. You may assume that you can do whatever you want to your body and still be able to maintain your good health and high energy. If you abuse your body, your normal level of vitality is diminished and your physical constitution is eventually broken down.

Jupiter can cause disturbance by creating a tendency for the part of the body associated with Jupiter's sign placement to become enlarged, engorged or congested. For example, if Jupiter is in one of the three signs that deal with the legs—Sagittarius, Capricorn, or Aquarius—an individual can be plagued with varicose veins. With Jupiter in Leo, there could be a tendency to have an enlarged heart. With Jupiter in the first house you could be prone to gain weight. This could result from being indulgent, lazy about maintaining good health habits or simply not getting enough exercise. With a prominent Jupiter or Sagittarius energy, your strong, athletic nature provides the way out of this situation.

CONCLUSIONS

The sign that immediately precedes Sagittarius is Scorpio. Scorpio is involved with life at its deepest levels. It seeks to create a personal relationship with the universal laws and the mysteries of life. This is a personal and subjective experience. Because this type of realization is so deep and personal it can be hard to share it in a way that others would find meaningful, Sagittarius creates universal languages through which people can share their transformational experiences. By categorizing and organizing personally learned information that pertains to collective understanding into theoretical concepts, Sagittarius enables each of us to share our own insights with each other. Through that kind of sharing, we deepen our own awareness into the nature of life. Scorpio is an emotional, passionate, security-oriented archetype. Like its mythic ancestor Apollo Sagittarius is more independent. It prefers to relate more through the ideas and concepts than to the personal, emotional experiences of the journey. Sagittarius values its independence so much, it has been called the sign of the bachelor. It wants to be free to pursue whatever new situation or thought that is passing on the horizon.

The previous *yang* sign to Sagittarius is Libra. One of the lessons of Libra is balance. It is the first sign to develop social contact and a social conscience outside the framework of one's personal world. It seeks to create social relationships that are just and fair-minded. Libra conceives of justice in the biblical context of an "eye for an eye." For Sagittarius, there is a higher standard of justice based upon social ideals. Instead of relating behavior in terms of this action being retaliated by that action, Sagittarius relates to justice such that actions taken conform to clearly defined statutes of behavior. A highly developed sense of personal integrity motivates the Sagittarius, or anyone else for that matter, to make sure that they conform to those standards. In turn this sense of personal honesty is based on universal concepts of morality and ethics. Behavior is therefore matched against an archetypal ideal.

Sagittarius is also the last of the fire signs. As with Aries and Leo, fire indicates the need to develop receptivity. Without this quality their expansiveness can become unrealistic exuberance or self-serving conniving. The arrow of the archer is shot indiscriminately and brings neither expansion nor learning. Aries is cardinal. It builds up and initiates things, getting momentum going. Leo, the fixed sign, stabilizes that which the Aries has started. Sagittarius represents the ideal outcome of all the previous strivings. It is the archetype whose vision is to lift its mind into the freedom of the universal vision.

Like its opposite sign, Gemini, Sagittarius is double-bodied. Both signs can become confused, over-extended and lack direction. While Gemini can get lost in endless information or random social contacts, Sagittarius can become too theoretical. Sagittarius limits its ability either to serve others or to apply its ideas to its own pragmatic needs. Both signs benefit by finding the right number and the right kind of systems to apply their mental energies to. In this way they avoid the sinkholes of endless intellectualization and learn how to use their mental and verbal gifts to provide useful, inspirational information to others. They can present their ideas through teaching, writing or publishing. They can also be attracted to professions in which the meticulous study of a particular system is a necessity, such as the ministry, law or medicine. These fields are even more appealing to Sagittarius than to Gemini. Gemini can be more comfortable with spontaneity so it is attracted to professions that require versatility or the ability to integrate different systems.

The mutable sign at the midpoint between Sagittarius and Gemini is Virgo. One of the most important contributions Virgo makes to the human experience is learning about and working with the process of discrimination. As a Sagittarius, use that quality to discern the right system to which to apprentice your mind. It must be one that satisfies your endless curiosity, and also one which provides a long-range prospect of service. Remember, the myth of Apollo provides a connection to prophecy. Sagittarius has been called the sign of the prophet. Sometimes the ability to see the future is really the ability to understand the past. Prophecy can also be the clairvoyant ability to "see" through dreams or waking realizations, that which is about to take place. With this gift or even with a tendency to see and know beyond what is obvious or understandable logically, you need to be able to apply your systematically learned information to your vision of the future. The combination of the qualities of prophecy and "vision" help make Sagittarius ripe for a type of experience known as a vision quest. In the Native American tradition this meant to go off by oneself into the woods or out onto the plain with little if anything in the way of food, warmth or weaponry. The individual remained until a vision was perceived either in the waking state or asleep. The vision could be in the form of an animal or a person, sometimes a relative who has passed on. The information contained in the vision would tell the individual why they were here, what were they to do and gifts or talents they possessed to help them do it. Having perceived the vision, they returned to the tribe to take their rightful place in society.

In the contemporary world individuals, Native American or otherwise, are learning of and taking advantage of this form of vision questing. For others, who may be either less adventurous or lack access this mode, might prefer other techniques that are more coincident with twentieth century life. For example, years spent perusing various subjects and classes offered at a university, hours spent in libraries or possibly a week or two alone at home with no outside contact but with extensive reading and meditation could provide inspiration and insight into your nature and a vision of your future.

Sagittarius can also be inspired by one of its mythic ancestors, Chiron. Sagittarius seeks to serve others by helping to raise their condition, or vision, from one of mundane, self-centered behavior, to one that is more aware of and attentive to needs of the community. Chiron was a healer. Teaching or healing in any formalized context can be a way of performing selfless service and a context through which to improve the quality of the collective experience. The concept of freedom is very important to the Sagittarian. This can be in the literal sense of not wanting to make a commitment in a relationship, or more figuratively as in wanting to avoid rigid thinking and to keep an open mind. In a social context this pattern enables you to know many people but not necessarily at deep levels. Be wary of thinking that a large number of shallow relationships provides true connections or a real understanding of the universal human condition. As a Sagittarius you are by nature positive, benevolent, generous and have a wonderful sense of humor. Without a certain amount of emotion and depth in relationship, however, your social life can become superficial and tenuous.

Intellectually, too much movement from subject to subject tends to give you only a theoretical understanding, without any practical application of the material. You may have the best intentions and the highest ideals, but without a sense of direction you can be dogmatically pedantic. Too much independence, therefore, can render you a fanatic.

Like the traveling Zen priest Hotei, Sagittarius loves to travel. This can involve picking your body up and moving it around the planet as a lifestyle, a business or for a vacation. This can also involve, however, traveling the highways of higher conscious- ness. As a child in school if you heard your teacher remind you to, "stop, look and listen," you might have felt as if that sentence were incomplete. For you, the reason to stop, look and listen is to "learn." To you there is always more. Always a bigger picture, a greater perspective, an expanded level of understanding. As a fire sign, you have the potential to be in contact with the flame of inspiration. You have the ability to radiate the Light of that flame to others through your attitude, your actions or your professional direction. As a mutable sign, your desire is to serve. By teaching others about the Light, in whatever form you perceive it, you help them to see themselves and life in a new way. Ultimately, this helps them to become independent as well. It helps them to learn to do for themselves, and to expand their consciousness in learning about what opportunities exist for greater learning.

CAPRICORN

Capricorn begins the fourth and final quadrant. It leads us back into the Eastern hemisphere, where the orientation is toward a subjective interaction with life. Like the first quadrant, the fourth creates its own reality rather than reacting in a more objective way to someone else's. The first quadrant is focused on the creation of self. It's concerned with the awareness, definition and expression of personal identity. The fourth is more interested in testing and expanding that self through creating contact with the outer world. The signs of the fourth quadrant are Capricorn, Aquarius and Pisces. The houses are ten, eleven and twelve. The signs and houses of the Western hemisphere, comprised of quadrants two and three, are more concerned with an objective perspective. They often define themselves in relationship to something external, such as a family or partnership. Specifically, the signs and houses of the third quadrant begin the process of relating to and interacting with others, usually specific individuals. The signs and houses of the fourth quadrant, however, expand the social theater to focus on the group or collective process.

The beginning of this experience is cardinal point four, also called the tenth house cusp, or Mid-Heaven. It corresponds to the Winter Solstice. The Solstice was considered one of the most important days of the year by the ancients. It occurs on the day when the hours of light are at their shortest and the hours of darkness are at their longest. The time of darkness has achieved its most expanded degree. From this day forward for six months the hours of daylight will increase. The Solstice was considered among the most important holidays by early humans. They saw it as a point at which the bareness of winter was starting to be replaced by the potential for new growth. In ancient ritual temples, including Stonehenge and the Bronze Age stone circles of the Golan Heights, the front door is facing the point on the Eastern horizon where the Sun comes up on this day. The cold darkness is not yet past, but it is the promise, the vision, of the return of the dynamic life force that rekindles the feelings of warmth and joy. It is a time to go within the self to experience this shift. It is also a time to share this reaffirmation in ceremonial celebration with family and friends.

The fourth quadrant is the culmination of experience. If the first three quadrants help you to know who you are and how to relate to others, the fourth suggests why you are here. Depending on your values and perspectives, this could be defined as pertaining to either the spiritual or physical planes. Consequently, Capricorn is said to be the heaviest and the lightest of the signs. It is heaviest in that it is oriented toward taking responsibility to build with the dense energy of the material plane. It is the lightest in that it establishes concrete ways to complete the journey here and move on to other more sublime states of being. Capricorn can function as both the builder of the structure as well as the achiever of the more expanded realms.

As the first sign of the quadrant, Capricorn is an initiator. It constructs its reality from the experiences of the previous signs and houses. Capricorn says, "I use," which implies its orientation to the pragmatic and functional. The Sun is in Capricorn from December 22 to January 20.

THE MYTHS

Each of the signs of the fourth quadrant is paradoxical in some way. A Capricornian contradiction is that it is a *yin*, or feminine, sign that is associated with hierarchical male authority. Its mythic references include both feminine and masculine archetypes. Among the female, one of the best known is the Greek goddess Athena. She was the only Olympian goddess depicted wearing armor, suggesting an aggressive, self-protective nature. In times of battle, she developed strategy for her allies. In peacetime, she was the protector of cities, and the artisans who dwell therein such as weavers, goldsmiths and potters. She was also credited by the Greeks with helping to develop agriculture enabling the culture to become more agrarian. She taught humanity how to use the plow and rake, how to use a bridle to tame the horse, and to yoke and domesticate the ox. Intertwined snakes were the design on her shield, implying the kundalini force and the wisdom that accompanies it. Athena was associated with skills that require deliberate thought and willful action, such as organization and execution. She was commonly associated with male figures, especially her father, Zeus, from whose head she is said to have emerged fully formed and with whom she identified and considered her only parent. This was significant when she was called upon to sit as one of three judges impaneled to decide the fate of Odysseus. When this noble warrior had returned from the Trojan War, he discovered that his mother (Clytemnestra) had killed his father (Agamemnon) for having murdered their daughter (Iphigenia). In what may be the first case of a dysfunctional family in Western mythology, Odysseus avenged his father by murdering his mother. In his defense, it was claimed that he couldn't have murdered his mother, because the female only nourishes the seed planted by the father. The female has no dominion in procreation. Only the father contributes to the procreative process—there is no mother. One of the other two judges voted in favor of Odysseus' guilt, one for his innocence. The deciding vote fell to Athena. Because in her experience there was no mother, she voted to free Odysseus and absolve him of guilt. What is most significant about this myth is the precedent it set for Western civilization. It validates and legitimizes male dominance. Male-dominated tribes, which ascribed to a dominator principle in establishing their society, invaded from the north and south into the Tigris-Euphrates river valley. The indigenous people of that area were matrifocal and built their societies according to a partnership model. In a theme similar to the dethroning of the goddess by the god, as depicted in the Zeus-Hera marriage, Odysseus' trial is a symbolic way for new values to be impressed upon an invaded and dominated people. The message is clear: the male principle is the power, the female principle is merely an extension of it. When the seed of this abominating philosophy is planted within the institutions of marriage and procreation, it cuts as deeply as possible into the primacy of the female. It eliminates every vestige of power from women and establishes an out of balance society which is clearly out of touch with the natural order. This is a pattern that has persisted into modern times and is only now being altered both philosophically and behaviorally.

The male-dominator aspect of Capricorn is represented by Zeus. Driven by ambition and the need to establish a realm he could dominate, Zeus represents the archetype of the sky-god. He embodies the principle that there is some external source of power that controls everything and everybody. One of the consistent themes of Zeus' myths is *goals*. He was always striving to establish his authority, both in his personal life and in his activities out in the world. In the former scenario he would establish relationships, often for the purpose of procreation, but always with the attitude of the detached patriarch. To Zeus, the creation of a family was more as an expression of his power than of his feelings. He is the archetype of the father, especially the emotionally unavailable one who rules from afar, never coming close to the inner workings of the family or the individuals in it. He represents the suppression of emotions, both his own and others'. In his external activities, his goals usually involve putting himself in positions of leadership and control. The thunderbolt was his instrument of dominion, through which he acted decisively and often destructively in the satisfaction of his desires.

Another image of the father, this one illustrating his role as the teacher, is represented by the image of the Great Father Snake of the Murngin tribe of Australia. During initiation, the boys are taken from their mother's protection by the terrifying figure of the snake, portrayed by one of the male elders. Over several nights the boys are indoctrinated into the male world complete with its perspectives, values, behaviors and modes of being. The boys are taught about the order of the world. At the end of this time, they are ceremonially circumcised. Although alarming and physically uncomfortable, the Great Father Snake is the guide and initiator into the mysteries of the unknown.

The father-as-teacher archetype of Capricorn is also present in Moses. A charismatic leader, he ascended Mt Sinai and met Jehovah. He became the representative of God on Earth. God gave Moses the Law, and Moses, as the teacher, embodied and executed the Law. The images of Father Snake and Moses express the lighter aspects of the patriarch. More concerned with spiritual attunement to the universal order than with enforcing conformity to their own will, they inspire and instruct others to see life in a new way. Jehovah, the image of the Divine that inspired Moses, is more symbolic of the preserver of the eternal authoritarian order and the monolithic redresser of wrongs. The vengeful god of the Hebrews illustrates the demanding, fear producing patterns that are also contained within the Capricorn archetype.

In Brahmanic mythology in India, Indra functions as an illustration of Capricorn. He embraces the whole universe, and has the power to move and manipulate the material world. Like Zeus, the thunderbolt is his primary tool and weapon. He is the patron of nobility and the protector of warriors. For example, when darkness threatened to prevent his friends from having victory in combat it was said that he caused the chariot of the Sun to slow down by pulling off a wheel. Controlling the Sun and extending daylight is also a reference to the Solstice and the increase of light in the hemisphere that takes place after that event each year. It also illustrates that to his friends, Indra is good and generous. Even as he guarded his own herd of cattle, he helped his followers by watching over their herds as well. Capricorn is the manipulator of the material world, the organizer, protector and preserver of the established order. These are traits of Capricorn.

In China the deity Lei-kung, the Thunder god, embodies an aspect of Capricorn. Depicted as an owl, Lei-kung holds a hammer in his right hand to roll the thunder, and a dagger in his left to strike and punish the guilty persons he has been ordered to chastise. Even though considered a minor deity, he nonetheless possesses traits similar to those of Athena (wisdom), Zeus (thunder) and Jehovah (punishment).

THE GLYPH: ♑

The glyph for Capricorn is enigmatic. From left to right, it symbolizes the twisted horn, like that of a goat, with the tail of a fish. Originally this glyph was a Babylonian symbol called *aigerkeros* which means "creature with the horns of a goat." This can evoke the image of a mythical creature like a mermaid or sea-goat. It also resembles a narwhal which is a real sea creature.

The glyph combines earth and water, reminding us of the complexity of the nature of this sign, suggesting that it combines both physical as well as emotional and spiritual qualities. It wasn't until the astrologer Claudius Ptolemy limited Capricorn to a material orientation after the time of Christ that the more internal and mystical qualities of this sign became obscured.

In analyzing the meaning of the glyph, notice its two main parts. At the beginning is the horn of the goat. It extends straight up as if it were an antenna reaching for the Sun at the time of the Solstice. This suggests someone on a quest, striving to achieve an exalted goal. At the end of the glyph is the fish tail, evoking the image of one who is willing and capable of plunging to the depths of experience. This implies loyalty and persistence, sticking with something "to the end." It also conveys a connection to the inner world, both one's own inner being and the less visible, more mysterious elements of life.

THE TOTEM: ♑

The complexity of Capricorn is also illustrated by its totem. Capricorn is one of the five double-bodied signs. Capricorn is the only non-mutable sign with this feature; the other four are the mutable signs. The duality of the goat-fish suggests this. The symbolism of the goat draws out the material aspects of Capricorn. Wild goats are mountainous creatures who climb to the higher elevations to establish their domains. This corresponds with the ambition of the Capricorn, who strives to ascend to the higher levels. Whether in a Zeus-like manner of establishing absolute dominion, or a more benevolent Indra-mode that protects others, the focus is on elevated peaks. From there, you have the most expansive view. There are two types of goats that inhabit the world. There are wild goats who live in the mountains and are unlimited in their territory. They are free to choose their own path. In a manner reminiscent of the Dall sheep that helps depict the nature of Aries, mountain goats are proud and fierce. The first two syllables of Capricorn are identical to those in the word capricious. There is an element of playful abandon to Capricorn that is expressed in the sometimes erratic, inconsistent nature of the mountain goat. Domestic goats are limited by a tether or a pen. They are valued for their productivity and their abilities are used by those who have dominion over them. Their powerful and playful natures are sharply curtailed.

The fish's tail of the totem implies that Capricorn is oriented toward more than the mundane and the material. Fish live in water. Water is the element of the emotional, psychic and spiritual. There is a strong and basic element of Capricorn that can relate to those inner realms. The goat-fish implies that Capricorn is potentially as comfortable pursuing its drive for higher consciousness as it is in pursuing its pragmatic goals. In aspiring to climb the highest peaks of awareness, Capricorn shifts its drive and ambition from the external plane to the internal, with an equally strong sense of dedication and purpose to each.

The spiritual nature of Capricorn is illustrated by the totemic image of the mythical unicorn. Depicted variously as a horse or as a creature with the body of a horse, the feet of an elephant and the tail of a boar, it was always shown with a horn growing out of the forehead. The horn symbolizes the third eye, the center of spiritual cognition or Christ Consciousness. The unicorn was adopted by the medieval Christian mystics as a symbol of the illumined spiritual nature of the initiate. The horn represents the sword of spiritual truth against which nothing can prevail.

Symbolizing victory in any strenuous test, the unicorn satisfies the Capricorn need to work hard and to achieve. It can embody qualities of salvation and therefore pertains to the more spiritual elements of this sign. This implies the need and ability to penetrate the mysteries of life as a way of understanding and embodying Spirit. This requires both hard work and time, both of which are important characteristics of the Capricorn nature.

I would like to offer another possible image for Capricorn: the deer. The deer is similar to a goat in many ways. They both have cloven hooves. They are about the same size. Their gestation period is the same. They are browsers rather than grazers and prefer to live in the freedom of mountainous areas. The deer is also seen as being a spiritual animal, especially by many Native-American tribes. For instance, the Huichol Indians of Mexico relate to the deer as their elder brother, Kahyumadie who is the messenger between their own prayers and ears of the gods. Other Indians recognized the deer as a manifestation of spirit through the limitless ways that is serves to support human survival. Every part of the deer can be utilized for something. For some Indian tribes, even the hooves were used as rattles for babies. The

Indians recognized the power of the deer and the gifts that it provided by apologizing to it just prior to killing it. Hunters affirmed that at a future time, they would sacrifice their lives to benefit that of the deer. The deer is a Western Hemisphere totem for Capricorn, one that combines its earth plane, physical nature and its watery, spiritual plane nature.

The crocodile can also symbolize the Capricorn duality. An amphibious creature, it is at home both on the land and in the water. In Egypt and in India, the symbol of the crocodile was the five pointed star. This is an image that appears within the third-eye after years of diligent meditation. The opening of the third eye is associated with enlightenment: merging with Spirit in Universal Consciousness.

Totemic images from around the world and throughout time illustrate the Capricorn nature. From Egypt comes Denderah. Denderah is pictured as a man with a head of an ibex riding a mountain goat. The Assyrians called their tenth month, which equates with our December/January, *Dabhitu* the goat. The Chinese refer to Capricorn as *Mul-ki*, which translates as the goat/fish. The Hindus call Capricorn *Makaran* which is variously described as an antelope with a goat's head or a goat's head on a hippo's body. It's as if the more complex the image, the more obscure the point of reference. A richly textured symbol implies a multi-faceted nature, and a great potential to synthesize all its possibilities.

MODE AND ELEMENT

Capricorn is the cardinal earth sign: directed activity on the mundane plane. An image in nature associated with Capricorn is mountains. To climb the mountain is to manifest energy in a direct way on the earth. This suggests that the action of Capricorn is to achieve. Capricorns are ambitious climbers and organizers socially, politically or professionally. As a Capricorn your ambition is to establish a goal, then work diligently in a controlled and structured manner until it has been accomplished. You are circumspect in your planning and deliberate in your action. This is not the impulsive rush of Aries or the accommo-dating action of Libra. It isn't the personal expression of Cancer. Capricorn is more specific, even to a point of being calculating. If you are off centered in your approach to this pattern, you tend to allow the ends to justify the means. You can be manipulative of people and situations until you get what you want. Deceit and deception can accompany your actions. Your focus is to control others. This pattern appears in despots and dictators. The tyrannical Josef Stalin was a Capricorn of this nature. Even duplicitous politicians in democratic societies, such as Richard Nixon in the United States, can utilize this lowest potential of their Capricornian nature.

In a more centered and self-loving manner, the political leader functions as a true, honorable statesman. A leader like President Woodrow Wilson, who was instrumental in creating the League of Nations, was a Capricorn of this type. This is an individual who acts in a self-controlled, self-disciplined way. The pattern of thoughtful consideration remains, but its resulting action is oriented to benefit other members of the group as well as the self. There is little concern to act in a way that only benefits the standing of the individual performing the action.

The earth quality of the Capricorn implies the ability to work hard. Like the other earth signs Capricorn is a builder. As a Capricorn, the most important thing you are building is your own reputation. If you are off center in this quest, you do whatever is necessary to increase your social prestige and maximize the recognition you receive from others. This is similar to the Libran pattern of placating a partner to receive positive feedback and a positive self-image. Capricorn finds out what others require for their approval and then acts accordingly. In this manner you allow others to make your rules. You allow others to have dominion over you, giving away your power. If you are successful in building your sense of self-worth within that frame-work, you will ultimately desire the authoritarian role, seeking in turn to impose your judgment on others.

If you are centered, however, your primary objective is self-respect. You function in an empowered way by reassuring yourself that you are the prime authority figure in your own life. You do what you do and how you do it because it satisfies your requirements, and not because it conforms to someone else's. If the two happen to coincide you could still receive high accolades from others, and ascend to an exalted position in a particular situation. That's fine. But that is not your primary objective.

This is not to imply that as a centered Capricorn you may tend to be lazy and irresponsible. Your fellow earth sign Virgo tends to be a perfectionist in thought. You tend to be a perfectionist in action. As a result, you could be far more demanding of yourself than others are either of themselves or of you. Your actions must conform to your high standards and you are very resolute in defining what they are as well as judging the results of your actions against them.

Your climb to the exalted peaks of your personally chosen mountain tends to be formal and you will pursue your goals with great seriousness. Once arriving near your destination, you are capable of a vast perspective and can realize that your actions and what you are building may have ramifications far beyond your awareness. There are many points of foundation to a mountain, but only one peak. This is quite different from the other earthy builder Taurus. The Taurean prefers to construct that which will provide the most comfortable and stable life for both the individual Taurus and those closest to him or her. Capricorn's perspective is more on the collective. Consequently you function well within the context of a group or organization. Your cardinality can drive you to a position of leadership. You can function comfortably as an organizer of both the people within the group as well as the collective activities around which the group functions. The CEO of the multi-national corporation, the union organizer, the priest or priestess could all have significant energy in Capricorn.

You might also express your drive to build in a more literal or concrete way by being an entrepreneur. People with Mars in Capricorn have an especially powerful sense of ambition and drive to get ahead. An example of this is someone working in the building trades. The personal drive could lead to learning several skills and eventually becoming a contractor. As the leader you organize others by hiring them to perform specific tasks. You could even strive to become a developer, whose vision is not just one structure, but an entire housing tract, industrial village or mall complex.

If you are off center in this quest, your goal could be limited to making as much money as possible. You may even maintain a controlling interest in the project to the extent that only *you* will receive the income for decades to come. More centered, you are conscientious in creating a structure within which everyone benefits. You would take into consideration the way in which your project would enhance the quality of life of the people working, living or playing in the facility. You would pay attention to the environmental impact not because by law you had to, but because you were aware how everything impacts everything else. You would be aware of the aesthetics of the project and would consider not just the money in your pocket, but how the buildings would affect the lives of generations to come.

If your orientation is less physical and more spiritual, or if you are working at integrating the two, you would bring the same sense of deliberation, discipline and dedication to your spiritual path as you would to the construction of a mall or the running of a corporation. You would be selective about choosing your path, making sure that your values and beliefs closely paralleled those of your spiritual teacher or the teachings that you adhere to. You would apply yourself to practicing the techniques with great personal honor and resolve. As a Capricorn you are comfortable with ritual, and oriented toward ceremony, even to a point of putting yourself in the role of the leader or teacher. This inner quest, this desire to ascend the spiritual peaks of wisdom, knowledge and bliss is pursued in a practical and functional way with the same clarity of purpose and concentration on goal that you have in your everyday work. Ultimately, the material success and promotions that you earn in a concrete way on the job are mirrored by the slow but real fulfillment of inner peace and joy.

THE RULING PLANET

The ruling planet of Capricorn is Saturn (♄). It's symbol consists of a cross that is supported by a semi-circle. This indicates the pre-eminence of the physical over the spiritual and suggests that the mundane world of form is that which is significant to Saturn. It also illustrates, however, that the soul and subconscious mind (the semi-circle) supports and sustains the material world.

The ruling planet of Sagittarius is Jupiter, the teacher. The ruler of Capricorn, Saturn, is also a teacher. But the Jupiterian and Saturnine teachers are quite different. The Jupiterian teacher is supportive, and tries to get the student to learn in a positive way. The Jupiterian teacher is oriented to the joy of learning. He or she would tend toward subjects in which theory and concept are important and in which people are central to the curriculum. Philosophy and psychology would appeal more to a Jupiterian type teacher. The Saturnine teacher, however, is much more strict. There may be more demanded of the student or a more rigid way of explaining the material. The Saturnine teacher would be more inclined to math or the sciences, subjects that had definite rules and parameters.

Saturn is the energy that mediates between your higher self and that which still must be resolved on a material plane. It can be a teacher in that it is your conscience, your guide to constructing your life in a realistic and pragmatic way. If Jupiter supplies the philosophy Saturn provides the form to put the concepts to work. Saturn is the energy of responsibility and indicates where (by house) and how (by sign) we need to develop accountability for our actions.

Saturn pertains to the world of form and structure. It is oriented toward using the elements of the material plane to construct a meaningful reality. It is the energy of authority and control. Without a sense of personal authority or a feeling of control over your life, or without doing the work necessary to reaffirm your power, Saturn manifests as fear. It can frustrate you with feelings of repression, isolation and an unsettling, and sometimes overly constrained sense of your limits. It can also, however, take you to the point of personal liberation. It depends entirely on whether or not you chose to use its energy and do the work.

Saturn can also teach you about limits by helping you learn how to establish and consistently enforce your realistic limits and desirable boundaries. Limits represent what you can give to someone else. Whether it is a result of the amount of time, energy, interest, motivation, ability or expertise, you can only provide others that which you realistically have. Boundaries are what you establish for others in their relationship to you. You let others know what is unacceptable to you in terms of their behavior, expectations or demands on your time and energy. Failure to establish limits and boundaries can result in over-whelming fear or in being dominated or drained by the other person.

Emotionally and psychologically, Saturn is the symbolic representative of your father in your natal chart. The house and sign placement of Saturn as well as aspects from other planets indicate what the emotional and psychological impact of that relationship meant to you. It is your subjective evaluation of him both as a father and as a man. Your perspective of your father is based on your experience with him. This picture reflects much of your own patterns in dealing with the energy and influence of Saturn. The lacks in the relationship with your father indicate what is lacking in your utilization of Saturn's potential. For example, a harsh, domineering father might suggest you need more work on defining limits and boundaries in this lifetime. An absent or emotionally unavailable father might suggest the need for you to pay more attention to self-discipline. An inconsistent or ineffectual father could imply your need to work on defining your goals and organizing your time and resources so as to be able to attain them.

Saturn is also important in your natal horoscope because it provides two ways out from anxiety and stress. One way is to ground and connect with the earth plane in concrete, useful ways. Saturn also provides a way out by providing you with a clear sense of direction, a goal, something to be achieved in this lifetime. For example, Saturn in the first house enables you to ground by taking responsibility for your actions in the world. Your goal is to learn how to integrate yourself in the world in an honorable and productive manner. In the second house Saturn provides the energy to take a functional approach to meeting your financial needs. Saturn in the second teaches you about how to organize your resources in a manner that allows you to sustain your life and provide comfort and security for you family. Saturn in the third fosters a cautious, deliberate way of communicating. to the extent that you gain information that helps you learn how to do something useful. Your goal is to learn to take responsibility for both what you say to others as well as being aware of the state of mind within which you communicate.

Saturn in the fourth house provides grounding through home ownership and by taking responsibility for household chores and tasks. Find the balance between doing everything for everyone with whom you live, or being excessively demanding of others and trying to control the domestic arena.

Saturn in the fifth house implies the need to take your creativity and hobbies seriously and ground through the pleasure those activities provide. Saturn in the fifth takes parenting quite seriously. Do not allow your role as a conscientious parent to prevent you from enjoying the lighter sides of life; neither allow yourself to become an overly-controlling, over-protective parent.

Saturn in the sixth house suggests the importance of maintaining a good health program. You can also ground by striving to become highly efficient and productive in your work. Don't allow occupational responsibilities and the desire to be indispensable to make you a workaholic. Patterns of that nature bring with them a high stress level that can ultimately undermine your health.

Saturn in the seventh house defines one-to-one relationship as a place to ground by learning to be clear in defining what you offer, what you need, and what your limits and boundaries are. Avoid tendencies of covering up any fear of relating by giving away your power to your partner or usurping power from your partner. By staying clear within yourself and open with partner you can avoid these traps.

Saturn in the eighth can ground through a deeply bonded, intimate relationship. It also offers the energy to deeply probe the meaning of life through science, mysticism or the occult. The use of ritual, daily, weekly or seasonally, can help you to deepen your connection to and understanding of life. Any tendency to avoid deepening your connection to life and other people can cause you be coercive and manipulative in getting what you want.

In the ninth house Saturn takes the theoretical concepts of higher mind development and organizes them in such a way as to be able to apply them to practical activity. Failure to do so can lead to patterns of being dogmatic and rigid about maintaining your ideas and points of view.

Saturn in the tenth house grounds through professional activities that help you to achieve a desirable public image. Saturn suggests leadership potential. Don't abuse that ability by being dictatorial or authoritarian in your relations with others. Provide the organization and structure that allows everyone to benefit from their occupational situation.

The eleventh is the house of friends. Saturn in the eleventh provides the desire and ability to develop stable loyal relationships. Avoid patterns of becoming overly responsible either for your friends or the relationships themselves. Similarly don't allow others to make inappropriate demands on you that limit your freedom in life.

The twelfth house is oriented toward inner development. Saturn therein can help you to ground yourself through a consistently pursued program of spiritual discipline. The twelfth is the house of the subconscious mind. Saturn herein provides the energy to pursue psychological clarity through an organized activity such as psychotherapy or hypnotherapy. The twelfth house indicates our karmic debts. Saturn in the twelfth suggests the need to work on developing your own sense of empowerment and authority.

Saturn tells you where your work lies. If you resist the message Saturn functions in a limiting, inhibiting, fear-producing way. If you accept the message, it brings you to freedom. To fully understand the significance of this energy, it's useful to understand how this archetype has been perceived and used throughout human history. At each stage, it reflects the development of consciousness of the people of that period. You can notice the development of your own consciousness as you learn the ways in which you feel comfortable with this important influence.

In Greek mythology, Saturn was the eldest born of Uranus. Saturn was seen at that time to be the god of agriculture. The Saturnine age was called the Golden Age. In those days people were industrious. Their lives were simple and austere, but they were essentially happy and peaceful. Saturn was called the planet of limits because it represented the limit of the known solar system. Saturn was it, beyond it was nothing. That nothingness produced fear in the minds and psyches of the masses. In the Middle Ages of Europe, Saturn became confused with Satan and it became associated with time and death. Its energy supposedly led to weariness, heaviness, old age and ill will to others.

In the contemporary world there are three octaves of Saturnine consciousness and their respective manifestations. These are not sequential. Like the octaves of Virgo or Scorpio, they are based upon free will and individual perceptions and choices. On the lowest level Saturn represents limitation, repression and fear. At this level, you are responding to the repressive external demands of authority figures. As a child, these people are your parents, but as an adult you could transfer the role of authority onto teachers or government officials. You respond to these external demands by giving in to them. You refuse to set limits or take responsibility for yourself. You accept whatever comes along in life with no sense of direction or assumption of control in your life. Perhaps the form of repression you experienced as a child was parental fear. You get stuck in the "I can'ts." In other words, "I can't do that because my father told me not to." Or, "We don't do things like that in our family." Or, "Girls don't do things like that." Regardless of the restrictive conditioning that was internalized in childhood, you can feel stuck in being unable or incapable of doing things for yourself. You may also feel as if you always need someone else's permission to do something, or that you need their approval of what you have already done. You tend to senior others to you. You project your personal power or give up your personal power to others. Feeling out of control you might tend to look for someone else to do what you can't or someone to blame for being stuck. You are accepting no blame and no responsibility. You are not doing your Saturn work.

The second octave of Saturn is experienced through organization, structure and control. On this level, the power of Saturn is internalized but not personalized. You could become aware that Saturn influences personal power and authority, but assume that this gives you the right to dominate others. You could force yourself on others, demanding that they accede to your authority and limiting the expression of their own. Sometimes this could be exactly what it appears: an exercise in asserting your will over others. At other times, it can be a genuine offer of aid and assistance to someone who is unable to organize their own lives and who feels incapable of resolving their own fears and limitations. This is a form of well intentioned wrong action. You are taking on too much responsibility for others. Even though you may be trying to resolve other people's pain or confusion you are nonetheless trying to control someone else's life. It doesn't work.

Saturn is a teacher. As you develop your own skills at living you can instruct others how to do the same for themselves.

Sometimes a high form of love is to say no. You are not here to take responsibility for anyone other than yourself and your children. Even with your children responsibility is taken only for a relatively short period of time in their lives and in relatively limited ways.

Beware of getting stuck at the second octave of Saturn by creating symbiotic relationships. This occurs when two people base their relationship on, "because I love you so much, I will do certain things for you that you are not going to have to worry about doing for yourself anymore, and of course, because you love me so much, you will do certain things for me that I'm not going to have to worry about doing for myself anymore. As a result, we will feel safe and secure. Our relationship will be comfortable, easy, stagnant and boring." Even if you go into the relationship in a centered self-loving mode, you could get lazy. This pattern is similar to co-dependency, in which your concern for your partner's needs and feelings supersedes your concern for your own

To break this pattern and raise the level of Saturnine consciousness to its highest octave, you must develop a sense of personal responsibility through self-discipline. Realize that all life is conditioned and unfree. You are limited by the need to provide for your body. To be free in any given area of life, you must voluntarily choose how you will be limited. By being willing to restrict yourself in certain ways and areas or at certain times you are ensuring that parts of your life that are of a higher priority can remain intact. You are free to continue to pursue and enjoy them. Ultimately this leads to taking total responsibility for all of your feelings, thoughts and actions. This is a full time job. You really don't have time to take on a lot of tasks or responsibilities for other people. In the process of taking this responsibility for yourself, however, you become centered and self-actualized. By taking complete responsibility for yourself and your life you empower yourself to become your own primary source of authority. By this you accept who you are and where you are in your life as a result of past actions and decisions. If you don't like those current conditions you are free to change them, but at least you don't blame others for your situation and fall into the victim role. Nor do you beat yourself up when you realize you are unhappy with your life. The choices you made in the past reflect the lessons you needed at those times. What may seem obvious in hindsight is something of which you were previously ignorant. Furthermore, it probably took a long time to create the current conditions of your life. It will therefore take time, and patience on your part to change the present conditions and create new ones. By working in a Saturn-like way—slow, deliberate but relentlessly moving toward your goal—demonstrate your freedom by making consciously defined, concrete changes in your life. In a sense you are completing the image of the king or queen, first expressed by Leo in its quest for individuation. That quest can reach fruition in Capricorn, or through the conscious expression of Saturn, as you affirm your power to make self-directed changes of you who are and what you do. You are the liberated monarch sitting peacefully and effectively on the throne of your reality, directing and overseeing the activities of your life.

You can also organize and structure your life by defining personal goals. These goals could involve cultivating your public image through job, career or profession, or through becoming familiar with "the myth of myself." The "myth of myself" represents a person who does not exist at this time. It represents a collection of all the heroes or heroines that you have ever had; the people you have known in person, read about in books, seen on TV or in the movies, or learn of through current events. Little bits and pieces of each of those people sparkle out at you as if to say, "be like me in this way, or be like me in that way." As you gather together all these qualities and define this mythic figure, you're one third of the way to realizing it. As you start a program of conscientious, consistent, step-by-step, day-by-day working to become that myth, you are another third of the way there. The final third is the process. It's the living commitment to becoming the embodiment of the image. As time goes by, you will internalize some of those desirable qualities, just as some will be eliminated and others may be added through new experiences. Through the realization of "the myth of myself" and your embodiment of it you are freed from the demands and expectations of others. Your parents, society or friends stuck in octaves one or two will no longer have dominion over you. You are empowered and you are free. You realize that you are the prime authority figure of your reality. You are the source of permission, recognition and approval; the definer of the shoulds and shouldn'ts by which you live, and the sole judge of your actions. You get in control of your material world to the extent that it functions smoothly and appropriately, and you are free to move into the higher realms of awareness symbolized by the trans-Saturnian planets.

Saturn is retrograde every year for approximately four months. From the standpoint of the natal chart, this affects about one-third of us. Retrogrades remind us to review our past and to see where we have been and what we have done. When Saturn is retrograde, there is the sense of needing to complete what was left over. The lessons that Saturn had to teach you were not internalized in past lives. Usually they revolve around issues of power and control. With Saturn retrograde you may not have been given much control over your life or felt a sense of power to make your own decisions when you were a child. This implies a difficult relationship with your father. Sometimes it's because he was not there physically or emotionally. At other times he was there, but set a very poor example, being too hard, too much the disciplinarian or too authoritarian. Perhaps he was exactly the opposite; too loving but over protective, preventing you from having your own experiences and learning about your strengths. Women with Saturn retrograde, tend to choose men to relate to in their earlier relationships who are very much like their father. This gives them an opportunity to return to their past. By being involved with someone who has an emotional and psychological blueprint similar to your father's can enable you to re-experience the childhood relationship with more consciousness. As a child you were limited by the dependencies of a child. You were also under the control of a domineering father figure. As an adult you are free from both restraints. You can take back your power and the control over your life by working through feelings of fear and limitation by relating to a peer who tends toward authoritarian behavior. This would not necessarily be a relationship to remain in unless your partner transmutes and resolves his patterns. It can, however, be a valuable therapeutic experience, enabling you to do the work necessary to reclaim your power and start learning to establish limits and boundaries.

For men with Saturn retrograde, the issues are similar. There is a need to work on defining a structure within which to achieve goals. Sometimes there can be an overly developed sense of responsibility that can keep you in a repressed or inhibited state. For men and women, Saturn retrograde in the natal chart reminds you that goals, responsibility, and a balance in the give and take of power and control are issues to work on.

THE TENTH HOUSE

In most house systems, the tenth house cusp is also called the mid-heaven. Sometimes this is labeled "MC" on your chart, the abbreviation for *Median Coeli*. This is a Latin term meaning "directly overhead." The mid-heaven, MC and tenth house cusp are synonymous. Even in house systems in which the mid-heaven and tenth house cusps are not at the same point, they refer to a similar part of life. They are almost always in the same sign with the mid-heaven given more emphasis. The mid-heaven has certain similarities to the ascendant, or sign on the cusp of the first house. Both indicate a primary way that you project yourself to the outer world. The ascendant, however, is more comprehensive. It indicates your attitude about life as well as the actual mode of expressing that attitude in your immediate environment. It can also delineate your physical projection, from body type to body image. The ascendent is an immediate, spontaneous way to let others know who you are in both personal or impersonal activities. The mid-heaven is more limited in scope. Its function is to determine how you express yourself in public, especially in the workplace. The mid-heaven is restricted to the manner in which you want others to perceive you. Consequently, the mid-heaven is less spontaneous and more deliberate. There is more forethought given to how you want to function in the world, and the type of situation you want to cultivate.

The mid-heaven helps to define your public image. This can be the way you project yourself in career, or with people in groups, institutions, or the body politic. The tenth house cusp also deals with the societal demonic: the underlying moral and ethical program of our civilization, the accepted do's and don'ts, shoulds and shouldn'ts. The sign on the cusp of your tenth house as well as the planets in the tenth, can help determine how and to what degree the societal demonic influences you. For example, with an air sign on the cusp, or planets such as Venus or the Moon in the tenth, you would tend to be more oriented toward working with people and more inclined to fit into a social framework. Air signs also suggest perceiving societal values more objectively and being more detached from them. Aquarius can be so detached that its projection may be quite unconventional altogether. Pluto in the tenth or Scorpio on the cusp might want to look beyond the acceptable and be comfortable with the role of taboo breaker. Fire signs and the Sun or Mars suggest more need for creative expression and independence in your work. Uranus in the tenth projects a more individuated public image. Earth and water signs project a more traditional image and feel more comfortable acceding to the mores of the day to achieve a sense of security through interaction with life.

Similarly, planets in the tenth house can provide some indication of the type of work you would enjoy and in which you would be successful. For example, Mars in the tenth implies a pioneer, someone who enjoys starting new jobs or businesses. Venus or Neptune suggest professions in the arts. Neptune, as well as Pluto, could indicate a pull to a healing profession. Mercury or Saturn point to business and commerce. Jupiter suggests education or work in the ministry. These rules are general tendencies, and can be stronger or weaker as determined by other factors such as planets in the second and sixth houses. The sign on the cusp of the tenth and aspects to the tenth house cusp from other natal planets are also important here.

Another significator of career interest and talent is indicated by the house position of the ruling planet of the sign on the cusp of the tenth house. If Capricorn is the sign on your tenth, for example, what house is Saturn (the ruling planet of Capricorn) in your natal chart? If Taurus or Libra are on the cusp, where is Venus? If the ruler of the tenth is in your fourth, you could work at home, or be involved with families or property. If the ruler of your tenth is in your fifth, working with children or sports could be implicated. A connection between career and creativity could also be seen. The ruler of your tenth in an earth house suggests business, although the sixth house also points to healing or careers in the food industry. In air houses, activities are people oriented such as in sales or education.

The tenth house cusp relates to situations which are objective and external. It deals with the future. The fourth house cusp, opposite the tenth, pertains to where you've been in terms of past lives as well as earlier in this one. The tenth house describes where you are going. The past provides the foundation upon which you build your experience. The area of life associated with Capricorn represents your goals, your ascended peaks. Your social status is a byproduct of what you do as well as how and where you do it. As with Capricorn, if you have significant energy in your tenth house, your need for recognition can be a strong motivating factor. You may tend to be ambitious, competitive and achievement-oriented. Taking this drive to its logical extreme, you might strive for a position of leadership in your company or in your field. You might strive for political office, being seen by a wide audience within the public arena. Politics is a tenth house experience. It functions in a structured context and usually in a traditional framework. It functions within and for the public. Depending on the sign on the cusp, and the planets within, you could aspire to a position of organizer (Virgo, Capricorn or Saturn), leader (Sun, Mars, Leo or Aries), functionary (Mercury, Gemini or Virgo), or behind-the-scenes power broker (Pluto, Scorpio or Taurus).

The significant point is that all tenth house energy involves directed, goal-oriented activity that functions in an organized way to achieve something. Whether that is for yourself or for the group or public good depends on the expression of your free will as well as the specific combination of variables that affect that house and its cusp in your natal chart.

CAPRICORN AND THE BODY

Capricorn is the sign of limitation. Its ruling planet Saturn was considered the energy of limitation because it represented the end of the known solar system at that time. Anatomically, Capricorn rules the skin, the limit of the body. Capricorn is also an earth sign and, as such, is a builder. Capricorn rules the most solid parts of the body, those that provide it with structure such as cartilage, knees, bones and teeth.

Capricorn is connected to the digestive system, with specific rulership over the gall bladder, the organ which secretes bile into the duodenum. This helps digestion by breaking down fats and promoting peristaltic movement in the intestines. Problems with the gall bladder can produce difficulties with elimination—such as constipation, diarrhea or colitis.

Capricorn can be controlling and set in its ways which can cause chronic physiological problems. Diseases such as arthritis, especially in the knees or spine (both ruled by Capricorn and Saturn), are prevalent in people who have significant energy in Capricorn or a powerful placement of Saturn. If the Sun and two or three other planets in Capricorn are located in the first or sixth houses, the tendency for these ailments would be greater.

It's as if problems in the body occur when you have allowed your Capricorn tendencies to be magnified in an uncentered way. Too much control, concentration or lack of change can lead to blockages in movement or structure. Your body is the external manifestation of your internal attitudes.

Saturn can also bring blockage or contraction. It will specifically affect the part of the body ruled by its sign placement. In other words, if Saturn is in Gemini, which rules the lungs, there might be blockage there. Sometimes people with Saturn in Gemini tend to be very shallow breathers, restricting the amount of *prana* or air that they take into their lungs. With Saturn in Leo, there can be a tendency to have a fear of opening up the heart and loving or a fear of expressing themselves creatively. The way out of this fear is by taking responsibility to set in motion a structured, directed and goal-oriented program that is designed to overcome these fears. Such activities as creative arts, sports or hobbies can be useful to this end.

CONCLUSIONS

Capricorn is the experience of controlled organization for the purpose of achieving a goal. As an earth sign, Capricorn likes to compete in the material world, demonstrating its ambition by establishing itself in positions of leadership. The first earth sign, Taurus, says, "I have." The second earth sign, Virgo, says, "I analyze what I have." The final earth sign, Capricorn says, "I use what I have," thereby seeking to establish its dominion over the world of form. Capricorn is more action-oriented than Taurus, sees more of an overview than Virgo and is possibly the most circumspect of the twelve signs. If your Capricorn energy is in the Northern hemisphere (houses one through six), you tend to structure the personal areas of your life, such as your finances (second house), ideas (third house), family (fourth house), or creativity and children (fifth house). If your Capricorn energy is in the Southern hemisphere (houses seven through twelve), your focus is more on asserting control over aspects of the outer world, such as primary relationship (seventh house), career (tenth), or groups (eleventh).

Capricorn is in polarity with its opposite sign, Cancer. Together, they are the two most focused signs in the zodiac. They have a natural ability to concentrate on a specific project or situation and block out interference. They are both conservative, traditional experiences that value security. Cancer, however, is more oriented toward the past. Capricorn deals with the future. Cancer is concerned with the personal meaning and content of an experience. Capricorn focuses on creating the form within which the experience takes place. Cancer is spontaneous, Capricorn is formal. Cancer is the sign of feeling, Capricorn is the sign of authority. Cancer represents the family, Capricorn represents the State.

Capricorn follows Sagittarius, a somewhat difficult transition between apparently disharmonious signs. For example, Sagittarius is known for its joyful optimism, whereas Capricorn has a reputation for being serious to a point of pessimism. Sagittarius deals with theoretical concepts, Capricorn with pragmatic action. In the economic sense, Sagittarius can be said to symbolize a bull market. This is one that is very expansive and positive. Capricorn, however, would seemingly identify more with the bear market, one that is more contracted. Relative to the law, Sagittarius is the law giver and definer, Capricorn is the law executor and enforcer. This is not a complete definition of the sign of the goat-fish, however. Although these qualities can be expressed by someone with significant energy in Capricorn, these tendencies are not the totality of its potential.

There are two phases of the Capricorn experience. If your primary emphasis is on the material plane and you tend to be uncentered and unself-loving, Capricorn can be opportunistic, blind to scruples and suspicious of others' motives and actions. Your philosophy of action may be that the ends justify the means. This is like the reputation of politicians, whether they function in the government, in board rooms or in offices. In your relationships you may tend to manipulate others into conforming to your expectations. You may use others to help your goals, which often involve dominion over others.

If, however, you are working to center yourself, the earth emphasis of the Capricorn can impel you to be very honest and exemplary in your relations with others. In this case your self-respect is of the highest priority and you measure your self-worth by your ability to cope with practical situations in a virtuous and honorable way.

If you seek to honor the double-bodied nature inherent in Capricorn, embracing your fish tail with the goat body, you balance the material side of your life with the spiritual side. In this way you build on the lesson of the previous cardinal sign, Libra, whose primary lesson is the importance of balance. By internalizing that concept, you can integrate the earth with the water. For example, since you are highly goal-oriented you can define destinations that are focused on both practical projects as well as those that enhance your spiritual growth. As a Capricorn, if you put all your time, energy and attention on the world of form, you could eventually feel loss of vitality, dissatisfaction with your endeavors, even depression. All of your worldly accomplishments may not bring a deep sense of meaning regardless of your intentions. Without creating an internal fulcrum that enables you to balance your accomplishments in the physical world with those of the spiritual, your most consistent effort and integrity may prove unfulfilling.

Capricorn is the first *yin* sign after Scorpio. One of the functions of Scorpio is to learn about the mysteries and universal laws of life. With the awareness and understanding of these laws comes a great deal of personal power. As a fixed sign, Scorpio tends to use its power in a stable or habitual way. The primary options for Scorpio are to either accumulate more personal power at the expense of others or to use their strength to continue the development of their own higher awareness and to facilitate transformation for others. Much of the experience is internal, or at least behind the scenes. As the next *yin* sign, Capricorn has similar choices about utilizing power. As a cardinal sign, however, it is to be used in a more direct and active way. As a Capricorn, if your focus is primarily material, you can use your depth to discover hidden facts. In this sense Capricorn has been called the detective of the zodiac. If you function consciously in a spiritual context, if you are on a spiritual path, this same energy can enable you to develop to the point that you become initiated into the higher states of being and consciousness. You are an initiate when you apply your concentration, diligence, and dedication to the task of understanding the mysteries and universal laws of life and applying that information in a grounded way to control your life. It's as if you function as a scientist in a spiritual context, applying your power of concentration to know and use the secrets of Spirit. You are relying on your earth nature to bring the secrets of the Scorpionic depths up to a point of concrete, practical development.

The Capricornian ability to concentrate, your love of order and discipline and your tendency to take your interests seriously are all qualities that can help you benefit from formal meditation. Through consistent practice of a specific technique you develop your inner vision, your intuition. You sharpen your power of concentration to the degree that you achieve single-pointed consciousness, a prime requisite for spiritual advancement. Through this single-pointedness, you still the restlessness of your mind and partake of a clearer vision of Oneness. It's as if the structure of the ritual frees you to look deeply within the self both for emotional clarity as well as for spiritual growth. Through this journey, you pass various tests posed by life and are eventually allowed to be initiated into the higher realms of realization. Capricorn is a sign that relates to the group experience. This spiritual passage enables you to join with like-minded souls who have chosen similar goals in life. In this way members of the group provide each other with mutual support with which to continue the journey.

As you become more dedicated to your inner growth you achieve your spiritual goals as well as your material ones. You can create personal laws that help you to achieve your goals. Law is important to Capricorn. There are man-made laws and Capricorn is the executor of the law. There are also God's Laws, the cosmic laws. As you set your mind on the higher goals, you sometimes have to use the Virgo quality of discrimination to discern which goals or laws are worth following.

Your ruling planet, Saturn, symbolizes the father in your natal horoscope. In an ultimate sense, who is the father? Who is the fundamental authority? He could be your biological father who proscribes laws for the family or the governmental authority that defines laws for the common good. As a spiritually-oriented

Capricorn, the father could be God the Father. Relying upon the image of the Holy Spirit as the giver of the law enables you to be more dedicated to your path.

Capricorn is the sign of authority. As such you identify with people in positions of power. You can work hard to gain recognition from those people. You will be a dutiful offspring, a loyal employee, an obedient spouse. There can be a danger if your need for approval from others is greater than your ability to feel good about yourself. You can give away your power, allowing someone else to dominate or control your life. As a consciously defined spiritual being, you identify with Spirit. You try to emulate the Supreme Being in words and by being a faithful follower of the Universal Laws. You replace recognition from others with respect for yourself. If you are being conscientious about defining your goals and you are pursuing those ends with right motivation and right effort, you know that you are doing the best you can. The results will follow and that's what is important. Others may approve of your work, and that's fine as a secondary issue, but not as a prime cause or reason to do it in the first place.

As you become more aware of Universal Law and prioritize self-respect above recognition, you deepen your sense of responsibility. Capricorn is the sign of responsibility. To not accept any is to create a life filled with fear and inhibition. To take on too much is to limit yourself by others' needs and desires. In this mode you can also be too demanding or controlling. Sometimes this is just a cover-up for your own fears. You give your power to a person or to the social shoulds and shouldn'ts of your culture. To affirm your own power, accept total responsibility for yourself. This starts by defining the limits of what you are willing to do for others and what they may demand of you. You elucidate the material work you choose to do and the spiritual path you choose to follow. Through the acceptance of those tasks, you create a path to empowerment and personal freedom.

If you feel stuck, unable to liberate yourself from years of limiting patterns, realize that the cause of these patterns is a combination of fear and lack of imagination. You can be so serious, formal and reserved that you block yourself from changing the causes of your frustration. There is no one external to you who has power over you. Conquer your fear through deepening and broadening the responsibility you take for yourself, striving to become empowered by learning how to take total responsibility for all phases and aspects of your life. You can stimulate your imagination by being more playful. Capricorn can be a late bloomer, an old age sign. You can act younger the older you become. That is because Capricorn needs a track record. As you lengthen your list of accomplishments, your prestige in your field increases and you create comfort in your life. You can relax and enjoy life more. Your capricious nature begins to be expressed and you access your playful side. Develop your imagination by developing your creativity and deepening your faith. That faith enables you to feel part of the universal plan. As a cardinal sign, Capricorn is an activist on the stage of life. Don't wait for these things to happen, take the initiative yourself.

A good image for Capricorn is the mountain. You are the climber, the one who ascends the peaks of accomplishment both on the physical and spiritual planes. Your faith can impel you to higher and higher peaks of achievement and consciousness. One primary aspect of your nature is to be enterprising. On the material plane, your strength comes from your ability to be persistent and diligent in your work. You can be dedicated and resolute in problem solving. Capricorn is also one of the most intense signs on the spiritual level. It has the interest and ability to discover and understand issues of universal consequence and manifesting these concepts in a practical, useful way.

Capricorn can also be considered the lightest sign. On the material plane you can work in an honorable and dedicated way to benefit everyone within the group. The group could be a political body, a social institution, your family or coworkers. In the spiritual sense, Capricorn is the lightest sign through its ability to deal consciously and conscientiously with a path of spiritual realization and enlightenment. Spiritual masters teach that you can determine what is important to you by what aspects of yourself you develop. If you are mainly concerned with sensual gratification, your body is your primary concern. If you are more concerned with reading, taking classes and developing the mind, your fundamental priority is your intellect. If you are more concerned with meditation, spiritual service and being in compliance with the universal laws, then you are striving for the highest goals, the ascended peaks of life. Your eventual destination is self-mastery and self-realization. You are self-realized when you accept your true nature as a manifestation of Divine Light. As an initiate your goals and actions conform to that nature and you radiate the Divine Light in all your acts and achievements.

AQUARIUS

Aquarius is at the midpoint of the fourth quadrant. Midpoints can act as triggers by focusing and releasing energy. What was initiated by the action-orientation of the cardinal sign Capricorn or by the activity in the angular tenth house, can be deepened and broadened by Aquarius or energy in the eleventh house. This is preparation for the consciousness development and transition to come in the sign Pisces or in the twelfth house.

The expanded focus of Aquarius enables it to be the sign with potentially the greatest overview of life experience. How can a sign be oriented to both a deepening of experience and a broadening of perspective? Welcome to Aquarius, perhaps the most paradoxical of the twelve archetypes. As a sign that seeks an overview of life, it is aware of the collective situation of humanity. As a sign of the Eastern hemisphere, however, it is self-defined. Following a cardinal sign, it tries to stabilize what was previously initiated, while as a midpoint, it likes action and change. Where Capricorn tends to be conservative and conventional, Aquarius enjoys challenging the time-honored and tradition-bound. Even though the totem is the Water Bearer, Aquarius is an air sign, not a water sign. It seeks an objective framework within which to develop a conceptual understanding of all that it becomes aware of. The awareness is a result of a continually growing expanse of perception and experience. The tendency for Aquarius to identify with its awareness causes it to say, "I know." The sun is in Aquarius from January 21 to February 18.

THE MYTHS

Aquarius is the eleventh sign of the zodiac. The Babylonians called their eleventh month *Shabatu*, the curse of the rain. The Babylonian god *Ea*, the deity of streams and fresh water, has been associated with Aquarius. The ancient Egyptian god *Hapi*, depicted as dispensing water from two jars, also represents this archetype. The Acadians called Aquarius *Ku-ur-ku*, the seat of flowing waters. Why are all these images of water connected with an air sign? A myth from the beginning of Christianity can best answer this question. For the early Christians, Aquarius represented the ritual of baptism. This is a process in which a person is immersed in consecrated water. It is a ceremony that symbolizes the union of humanity, water and spiritual consciousness. The Aquarian focus is not on water *per se*. It uses the element water to stimulate the internal awakening of the inspirational and the intuitive. Water is seen as a vehicle that can aid in the broadening of the Aquarian awareness and as a link between all people and all of life.

The concept of One-ness has appeared in various cultures around the globe and is embodied in several significant myths. One such concept was embodied in Jehovah, in which the inherent authority of one entity creates a hierarchical universe. The Aquarian concept of One-ness can incorporate that image, such as in the early and primitive embodiment of the sky as depicted by the Greeks as Uranus (Heaven). In this myth, Uranus mates with Earth (Gaia) and together they create the race of Titans. The father figure, the all-powerful Uranus condemned his children to the underworld. They were saved and led to escape by their mother. They then overthrew and killed their father. The leader of the Titans, Cronus, married his sister, Rhea. Together they created the deities who were to become the Olympian gods and goddesses. Like his father, Cronus sought to destroy his children. But Rhea saved them through a clever ruse. Eventually the youngest child, Zeus, led his siblings in rebellion against the patriarchal authority and together they slew their father and ascended to the thrones of power. These tales illustrate the authoritarian potential of Aquarius, and those who use their overview to define their values or needs as right and all others as wrong. These myths also imply that part of the inherent duality or paradox of the Aquarian nature is to engage in cycles of repression and rebellion.

Another Greek myth that illustrates the more freedom loving and rebellious nature of Aquarius is that of Prometheus. The word Prometheus means forethought. It was his idea to steal fire from the gods, knowledge from heaven, and bring it to humanity. Through this act he was able to teach the people all of the useful arts as well as the power to think and create for themselves. By this act he committed hubris, rebuking the absolute right and power of the previously supreme gods and goddesses and rebelling from their dominion. Prometheus is the archetypal iconoclast, breaking from tradition in such a way as to inspire others both by his actions as well as through the information gained by the actions.

Aquarius can also expand beyond the images of limitation and destruction illustrated by Uranus or the rebellion of Prometheus. It can represent the One-ness that is an inherent interlocking unity of all things which mirror each other. Taken as a whole, these individual things comprise Life. There is no hierarchy, no better-than-less-than, just *us*. Myths that pertain to the sky, that which surrounds everything and which can perceive life from the broadest of perspectives, are illustrative of Aquarius. Such a mythic figure is Ahura-Mazda, the Lord of Light and Heaven. Ahura-Mazda appeared to the Persian prophet Zoroaster and presented him with the *Avesta,* or *Book of Wisdom and Knowledge.* Ahura-Mazda was said to embody all that is. His clothes were the material world itself, his body was the Light, and his eyes were the Sun and Moon. No longer is the universe divided into the deities of water, plants, clouds or wind. All manifestations are now embodied in one form, one concept.

From India, the origins of Hindu thought also contain clear reference to the concept of Unity. It is contained primarily in the myth of Brahman, the one pervading, impersonal, all-embracing, understanding, intangible essence of the world. Brahman is the "Real of the Real." the unborn, undecaying, undying, the "Soul of all Things." The concept of Brahman emanated from the Vedas which are ancient, sacred books which combine pagan philosophies such as animism, anthropomorphism and pantheism to create a philosophical understanding of life. Brahman incorporates all that preceded it with the additional realization that none of these exist apart from each other. They are all included within Being. The concept of Brahman is that behind all form and beyond all subjective and objective interpretations of life is the de-individualized reality, the essence of all things, the One. The spiritual discipline of yoga is designed to enable the practitioner to calm the mind, control the body and to separate from any identification with it. Ultimately there is a union (yoga means union) with Brahman, the spiritual base of all things, the selfless, immortal, immaterial spirit. Both Brahman and the devotee who attains union with it remain detached from the finite world of the material plane.

The concepts of Ahura-Mazda and Brahman are beyond physical imaging. They represent a clear break with myths that depict the previous signs and suggest a new consciousness. This new awareness develops within a society or an individual to relate to, identify with, and internalize the abstraction of Pure Being. These deities indicate a new world view, which leads to the invention of new ways of relating to life and to one another.

THE GLYPH: ♒

The glyph for Aquarius consists of two parallel wavy lines, one above the other. There are four levels of meaning and interpretation of this glyph. On the physical plane, it represents lines of force. This can be expressed scientifically as waves of energy, such as electricity. Politically it represents the people in charge of governing others as being of equal power to those whom they govern. Metaphysically, these wavy lines can represent serpents, symbols of knowledge and wisdom, signifying the ongoing development and unfolding of consciousness. Spiritually, these parallel lines suggest "as above, so below." There is no difference, no separation, regardless of what appears to be.

In circular fashion, this leads back to the physical and the definition of the lines as waves of water. The water represents knowledge that serves to quench the thirst for understanding about the nature of life.

THE TOTEM: ♒

The totem of Aquarius is the water bearer. It can be depicted in several specific ways. One is as a man with a jug of water on his shoulder. Another is of an angelic or androgynous figure dispensing water from an urn. It has also been suggested by some scholars of Eastern religions that the totem for Aquarius is a simple pot or urn that stands by itself and it not held by a human-like figure. The most commonly accepted totem for

Aquarius, however, is that of a human figure holding or carrying a large container.

Aquarius, Gemini and Virgo are the only signs whose totem is a human figure. For Aquarius, what is more important than the person carrying the jar, more important even than the jar itself, is the contents of the jar. The fluid contained within and emanating from within the vessel is the water of eternal life. The water represents the consciousness that unfolds in the evolving human mind. The confusion that underlies thinking of Aquarius as a water sign comes from emphasizing the substance itself rather than realizing it is only a gross or materialized manifestation of something far more subtle, significant and sublime.

In the physical sense water is life. Carrying water to a thirsty person helps prolong physical existence. In this sense is one of the two most humanitarian signs in the zodiac, the other being Pisces. The difference in how these signs express their humanitarianism can be illustrated by an economic theory. Aquarius manifests humanitarianism through the "trickle down theory" in which wealthy people are left with most of their money; taxes are reduced for the wealthy with the idea that this will enable them to create new businesses and jobs and opportunities for those with less capital to join in the world of comfort and security. According to this theory, the money will "trickle down" to the hands of the masses. In other words, Aquarius is humanitarian in a top-down manner. It has a higher understanding of the order of things that prioritizes the Oneness of all things. To help all things co-exist in that spirit of community fellowship, it strives to create an ethos of mutual generosity and a sharing of material resources.

Water is a symbol for consciousness. To dispense water to others implies the intention of raising the consciousness of others. This is analogous to the Christian rite of baptism. This is a ceremony in which immersion in a body of water is used to symbolize a new connection to Spirit. This spiritual baptism in turn suggests the dawning of a new consciousness. The image of the water bearer defines Aquarius as a facilitator and catalyst of inspiration. It depicts one who brings the higher awareness of wisdom and the understanding of a higher ideal to the people. In this way, the totem of the carrier of consciousness depicts the

Aquarius archetype as one that seeks to inspire, stimulate and uplift humanity.

MODE AND ELEMENT

Aquarius is the sign of fixed air. As an air sign, Aquarius is oriented toward perceiving and relating to life through the logical, rational process. It is attracted to, and inspired by, conceptual thinking. These could be abstract thought forms that deal with advanced levels of thinking in various systems of thought. Scientifically, this could relate to new theories of quantum physics, radio astronomy or breakthroughs in computer technology. Innovative thinking is a highlight of the Aquarian mind. Artistically, this could include new architectural visions, new musical forms or multi-media renderings of the creative impulse. As an air sign, Aquarius likes people. The intellectual focus can include politics and sociology. In either system, Aquarius would tend to be aware of how people relate in groups. They like to experiment with new and progressive theories of how different groups could interact. Utopian experiments stimulate the Aquarian mind. Aquarius would typically be the one to both conceive of the social experiment as well as being the first to sign up to implement it.

This type of perception and thinking is valuable to the human experience because it pushes us into more open-minded discussions and forms of relationship with each other. This type of communication can bring about more understanding between groups and among individuals. It makes the world smaller, more unified. Through the Aquarian openness and ability to conceptualize on a grand scale, we realize that we all have a lot more in common than we do differences. As an Aquarius you strive for an objective overview that enables you to understand how life relates to all people, and how people create the quality of life.

There can also be a danger in this type of thinking. As an Aquarian you can become isolated within your own theories, limited by your own originality. You could disavow any ideas that do not coincide with your own and eliminate any people who don't share your world view. This works against your desire for unity by creating more stratified divisions both in your own world as well as any part of the outer world over which you have dominion. You could feel isolated from your family and previously close friends if the evolution of your thinking brings you to a life style other than theirs. You could distance yourself from people altogether, preferring to remain in the purity of your idealism. It's as if you relate to life as an experiment within which nothing is real but your own conceptual analysis.

As an air sign, however, you are more than just a walking idea factory. People do play an important part in your life. Aquarius is a friendly sign and can be defined as the sign of friendship. As an Aquarian you tend to be generous and good hearted. One focus of your social awareness is, in typical Aquarian fashion, oriented toward the overview. This implies the ability and desire to relate to groups. These could be groups of friends, people congregating in organizations, or even relating to others through computer networks. You can be concerned with the quality of life for all people. The breadth of this perspective enables you to be aware of the collective experience of humanity, and to see how different groups affect each other and the earth. Being at the forefront of thinking and awareness helps stimulate behavioral changes within the human family and helps break down patterns of social prejudice such as racism, sexism and ageism. If you are too extreme in your thinking, and excessive in espousing your ideas, you run the danger of being seen as revolutionary. You could become a target of conservative elements in society with a vested interest in maintaining the status quo. If your ideas and realizations are good ones there will be a positive and responsive resonance from the community. It may take a while, but eventually many of your realizations will become the standard. Just as your understanding came suddenly and inspirationally, however, so may you lack the perseverance to wait for your new theories to take root within a broad range of the community.

Impatience is not a quality usually associated with a fixed sign, but like most things connected with Aquarius, you tend toward the unconventional or the unexpected. In your fixed quest for consistency, you demonstrate the principle that there is nothing so permanent as change. As a fixed sign, you are concerned with security. Security for you is a byproduct of your thinking, knowledge and understanding. With your tendency to seek an overview, your sense of security is predicated upon defining a concept of universal law. With your orientation to social consciousness, you extend that understanding to include a corresponding desire to bring all things into harmony with that law. It's as if you identify as a vehicle for bringing a higher truth to social activity. This truth is ever changing, as a result of your various experiences and degrees of expanded awareness. Your Aquarian mind refuses to sit still. Your conception of Universal Truth and the plan whereby you seek to implement it, is always in flux.

This combination of constant change of both mind and behavior can render it difficult to relate to you. Your changes are often very unexpected or extreme to the outside observer. Even your periods of relative stability can be erratic or inconsistent. It's as if you seek to weave the fabric of truth by your words and actions. You can be insightful about life and convincing to others about what your conceptual understanding of life is, and why they should agree with you. Because of the expansiveness of your awareness, and the progressiveness of your thinking, it may take awhile for your associates to understand you. Even after they do and assuming they come to agree with your truth they will probably find that you have changed the fabric of your reality, changed your conception of the truth or changed your universal vision. You may be aware of being so changeable but have a difficult time admitting that fact. To you it's just part of the ongoing series of changes in your consciousness, a new unfolding of your awareness. Others can find this very frustrating. Trying to pin the Aquarian down, whether it's in defining themselves or their concept of reality can be a difficult and frustrating task.

The combination of mode and element in each of the other signs is seen in natural phenomenon. For instance, Capricorn, cardinal-earth, can be depicted as the mountains, Sagittarius, mutable-fire, as the rainbow. One of the ways in which Aquarius demonstrates its uniqueness is by challenging us to find a natural phenomenon in which air is fixed. Clouds don't count because they combine air with water. Inert gases like neon come close. To find something in nature that truly combines these qualities requires that we expand our previous understanding of life and that we look in unusual or unexpected places. In this way we are emulating qualities of the sign itself. Aquarius seeks to expand its consciousness and perceive an overview of life. That quest can lead to some out-of-the-way and esoteric places. Trying to discover fixed air in a natural setting without a broad and unique perspective will undoubtedly prove futile.

THE RULING PLANETS

Aquarius has co-ruling planets, Saturn (♄) and Uranus (♅). The influence of each can be experienced and expressed productively or contentiously. As a sign of social awareness, Saturn can enable you to realize the importance of laws and social order even in the most utopian of social experiments. This can also be true for anyone with a prominent Saturn influence in the natal chart. Without some sort of organization, focus or goal, even the most egalitarian system will devolve into anarchy. The laws and forms of social structure may be new and help to define new forms of confederation among groups of people, but they still need to be generated in an orderly fashion. People with a prominent Saturn tend to organize.

By emphasizing the darker side of Saturn you can be an inhibitor of the personal freedom of other people. This can manifest in social situations that are repressive rather than humanitarian, fascistic rather than altruistic. This can result from remaining too aloof from others or by being more attached to the idea of something than to the quality of its implementation. Your detachment can be defined by others as self-righteousness. Your austerity can be seen as coldness and lack of caring. You become more focused on the letter rather than the spirit of the law.

To begin to understand the influence and nature of Uranus, notice its glyph. It resembles a TV antenna. This implies that Uranus can pertain to technology, especially forms of technology that are used by the mass media. This enhances and reinforces the collective experience we all share. It enables people from all parts of the world to tune into each other, experience some of our respective cultures and lifestyles, and can help bring about more understanding among the nations.

In the upper portion of the glyph consists of two semi-circles connected by a horizontal line. These symbols are like moons which, in turn, represent two aspects of the subconscious mind. Like waxing and waning moons, they suggest that Uranus is oriented toward both spiritual awakening and scientific inspiration.

Uranus is the energy that inspires you to move out into uncharted territory of thought, understanding and behavior. The house placement of Uranus in your natal chart indicates where you explore and experiment, where you are challenged to wake up and become more conscious in some way. Activities taking place in that area can challenge you to become more aware of yourself and to break out of old patterns. People will often tend to do something a certain way just because it's comfortable to do so. Uranus won't allow that. If the activity isn't stimulating, Uranus wants a change. These changes are designed to help you to progress in your personal growth as well as to develop interests in the esoteric and the unconventional. Uranus serves to awaken you to new possibilities or to seeing things in new ways.

Uranus is the planet of genius and originality. If you don't allow your Uranian energy to manifest in your life, its repression can lead to feelings of frustration, restlessness, dissatisfaction or impatience. Excessive nervousness can also be present and can manifest as sleep disorders, facial tics or sudden outbursts. In a more general context, it can create a continuous pattern of change for the sake of change and in a manner that is self-consuming and self-oriented.

Uranus was discovered in 1771, a singular and unique time in human history. The Benjamin Franklin experiment that validated lightning to be a manifestation of electricity took place in 1752. Many historians mark 1760 as the approximate beginning of the industrial revolution which altered the social order. In a positive way, it opened society up. From all over the world the expanded technology furthered manufacturing and trade in ways that are still evolving: creating a global market which will include the resources and talents of all races and ethnic groups. The changes of the industrial revolution also led to two types of change which were not so positive. First, families left the land to work in factories, breaking the connection between the human race and the rest of the natural order. Men became alienated from their families. Boys lost the constant contact with their male elders and role models. Detaching from nature, being separated from their wives and daughters, influenced men to lose contact with the feminine principle, and its inherent qualities of receptivity, care-giving and intuition. Women became undervalued and unempowered as the world of family, feeling and soul became subordinate to possessions, conveniences, and labor-saving devices. Profit became a new way for the few to dominate the many.

A second unfortunate consequence of the industrial revolution was the exploitation of certain cultures and ethnic groups by others. In terms of labor and natural resources, the owners of the tools of manufacturing and the leaders of the corporate structures have gone beyond their own countries to take what they needed from others. In promoting the value of consumerism, this pattern has not only maintained a rigid separation between cultures and races, but created a class structure within each culture as well. These are the negative more self-oriented manifestations of the Uranian impulse. These tendencies toward separation, loneliness and alienation are inherent within Uranus. It is not enough just to have access to its energy. Without a conscious awareness of its tendencies and potential, it can create a one-step-forward-one-step-back progression. A lot of energy expended, but little progress gained.

Uranus was also discovered during a period of political revolution. In 1775 the American Revolution, in 1789 the French Revolution, in 1808 the Spanish Revolution all heralded the birth of a new type of governmental concept. It's a concept that is oriented toward political consciousness as it affects the masses. A useful way to define the qualities and characteristics of Uranian energy is through the slogan of the French Revolution and it keywords; *Liberté, Fraternité, Egalité. Liberté* implies that Uranus represents the urge to change in a willful and rebellious manner. Uranus symbolizes unconventionality, personal freedom and uniqueness. This is the energy that helps to define that part of you that is different from everybody else. It represents "the weirdo within." Since we all have Uranian energy, we all have to assume that there is some part of us that is different and unique. This impels us to engage in a process of becoming aware of and accepting our uniqueness. Explore it, experiment with it and express in ways that are exciting to you and, hopefully, stimulating to others.

Fraternité indicates that Uranus represents friendship. Social activities stimulated by Uranus could be with associates, friends or colleagues. By extension, Uranus also represents the group mind, the collective consciousness and group karma. It calls upon you to notice to what degree you are influenced by or independent of the changes that your group, your community or even your generation are perpetrating. Your membership in the fraternity or sorority of life reminds you that you are part of a greater whole.

Egalité means that Uranus represents the concept of the universality of all things. It represents one of the forms of higher consciousness through which love is experienced as a quality of energy. It is a principle of consciousness. It is something to be shared equally and distributed universally among and throughout all of humanity. In this sense Aquarius, ruled by Uranus, is quite different from its opposite sign Leo. If you remember from our discussion of Leo, one of its tragic flaws is a tendency to manifest its indomitable love and heart energy in a very personal, yet often conditional way, almost as if love were a quantity of energy. The Uranian energy, through its openness to higher consciousness, teaches that there is a never ending supply of Love energy that exists for everyone. Some spiritual masters even instruct that Love is the very substance and foundation of Life, the essential energy of Creation. Aquarians and people with a prominent Uranus in their chart tend to be aware of this principle and to use that awareness as a vehicle for relating to themselves, others and life.

Uranus is retrograde five out of twelve months. This can trigger different kinds of patterns depending on what sign and house Uranus occupies in the natal chart. In Taurus, Virgo, Libra or Scorpio you could difficulty defining, developing or demonstrating your sense of uniqueness. Those qualities may feel uncomfortable, even embarrassing. With Uranus in Aries, Sagittarius, Aquarius or Pisces the opposite tendency may prevail. You could feel so unique and so much of an individual, that you may have a hard time integrating that energy within any sort of social setting. You could fear the of loss of your freedom, thus being uncomfortable with others. You could also be seen as so rebellious and challenging, that others feel uncomfortable with you. Uranus retrograde in Aries, Gemini, Sagittarius, Aquarius, or Pisces could have certain visionary qualities. Your lifestyle, consciousness, and interests surpass most of your peers. Socialization for you can be frustrating. You may find yourself a reformist, years ahead of everyone else. When your peers finally do catch up, you will still be more progressive in thinking and understanding. If you have Uranus retrograde in Cancer, Leo, Virgo, Capricorn, Aquarius, or Pisces, you could feel a very deep and personal sense of responsibility for the evolutionary progress of humanity. You may even sacrifice your personal satisfaction for the betterment of the planet or your fellow beings.

A retrograde planet in your natal chart can indicate something that was misused in the past. The retrograde symbol (℞) can function as a prescription to both higher consciousness and freedom from your karma from the past. With Uranus retrograde, this freedom can come through learning to validate ones' own sense of independence and uniqueness and in learning how to incorporate that into social situations.

Uranian energy is unstable, unpredictable and volatile. It is electrical energy that provides a spark of new awareness and realization. It can challenge you to become aware of where you may have become stuck manifesting old patterns and rigid values. Once aware, you can make whatever changes are desirable, necessary or appropriate to liberate you. Uranus prevents you from becoming bored, It stimulates change. The house placement of Uranus indicates the area of life in which you tend to seek expression for your uniqueness. It is not an influence that helps prolong things or to manifest them in persistent or practical modes. For example, if Uranus is in any of the houses of the first quadrant, its influence is to stimulate you to become more aware of your inherent uniqueness. In the first house this could manifest through affecting an unconventional mode of dress, social manner or attitude on life. You would tend to project a friendly and accepting manner to others. In the second house Uranus suggests unique values, ones that put higher priority on personal freedom than on security. Your flow of income could be inconsistent and you might even make your living in unconventional ways. You could generate money at unexpected times or from unexpected sources. Uranus in the third house provides a quick, open and inspired mind. You could find relationships to members of your extended family challenging and perhaps at least one sibling who is a social rebel or from whom you feel alienated. You could be friendly to neighbors and your good friends are important to you even if your relationship with them is inconsistent.

In the second quadrant Uranus implies a unique quality to your family life and to your mode of self-expression. Uranus in the fourth house suggests an unconventional early childhood. Your family might have moved a lot or there may have been other patterns that resulted in emotional inconsistencies. Your parents may have been lenient and tolerant of your behavior or simply negligent and erratic in nurturing you. As an adult you might prefer living alone for a period of time followed by a desire to be part of a commune or other type of experimental living situation. In the fifth house Uranus suggests unconventional and sometimes risky hobbies and recreational outlets such as hang gliding or sky diving. You can feel periodically inspired to be creative and would tend to be attracted to unique forms of expression. Your children will be challenging and you might be part of a blended family. Your children could also be unusual in some way. Most parents feel their children are special. With Uranus in your fifth house there may others who agree with you based on their objective experience of your son or daughter.

Uranus in the sixth house implies unexpected changes in your health. Sometimes the symptoms will appear and disappear suddenly. Seeking alternative methods of healing could prove beneficial. Uranus in your sixth house could also affect your work experience. You could change jobs frequently and prefer working in technical fields. Your relationship with your co-workers would also be important to you. As an employer, you could have unreliable employees or find them to be interesting and stimulating, even if they seem a little odd in some way.

If you have Uranus in the houses of the Southern hemisphere your experience would differ depending on whether you felt comfortable with that energy or not. If you are consciously integrating Uranian qualities into your activities in the outer world, your uniqueness and freedom-loving tendencies would be obvious. If those qualities are uncomfortable for you to express, you will tend to attract others to you who will be challenging and stimulating in some ways and unreliable and erratic in others. Uranus in the third quadrant affects the nature and form of your relationships. With Uranus in the seventh house your emphasis would be on patterns of relating. If you are conscious of and comfortable with Uranus, you would look for someone who could be your best friend. You prefer relating to someone who inspires and stimulates, but who also tolerates and accepts you as you are. You want to feel free to be yourself in the relationship and to work with your partner to experiment with different forms of relating. If you aren't owning and expressing your Uranian energy, you are likely to have a series of short-term, erratic relationships with people who can be exciting one day and cold the next. This type of person may help to awaken within you a part of yourself of which you were previously unaware, but emotionally they may be distant and unavailable.

If you have Uranus in your eighth house you could be drawn to unconventional ways of learning about the deeper qualities of life. Science and the occult—the exoteric and esoteric—could provide both insight and inspiration. You might also choose to express your uniqueness through your intimate relationships. This could manifest as only allowing your primary partner to see and experience your unique self. Or you might seek unconventional and adventurous ways of sharing intimately, especially in your sex life.

The ninth house pertains to higher mind. Uranus therein implies being attracted to esoteric subjects or studying them in unorthodox ways. Independent learning might be your method of choice. You could be excited by subjects as varied as technology and astrology. In travel you would prefer going to out-of-the-way places and taking unusual routes to get there. You could also have unusual, mind-expanding experiences while you are on the road. Expanding your mind in any context would have an awakening, inspirational effect. If you're not connecting with your Uranian energy, your mind may be too scattered to learn anything in depth. Your experiences while traveling would be unsettling rather than exciting.

If Uranus is in your fourth quadrant its effects would be manifested in your career and social activities. In the tenth house of profession, Uranus would orient you to work that you find challenging. Ideally you would be in a position where your bosses and co-workers were friendly, accepting people who would allow you to do your job in your own way. If you are in touch with and comfortable with your Uranian energy you could be drawn to something that enables you to inspire and awaken others. A career in media, working with technology or anything that stimulates and supports your inventiveness would all be attractive to you. If you are not manifesting Uranus in a conscious way you could feel frustrated and dissatisfied in your chosen profession. You could move from job to job or career path to career path, never really finding your niche. With Uranus in the tenth house your career niche would probably be outside the conventional.

The eleventh is the house of friends, groups and organizations. With Uranus in your eleventh house, you would be attracted to groups of people who came together in loose-knit ways. Their common interests could range from esoteric subjects like astrology to topics that had a progressive, humanitarian orientation. The more free-form the better. A lot of rules and organization would deter you from joining. If you are aware of Uranus' influence you could be seen as a role model by your friends and acquaintances. You would also prefer to be friends with people whom you saw as unique and unconventional in a way that inspired you to liberate yourself from patterns of being that kept you stuck in convention or fear. You may not see these people often, or the relationships with them might be short lived, but whenever you do get together and for however long the association lasts you would find that they have an awakening affect on you in that they would help you perceive parts of yourself of which you were previously unaware. If you not aware of your Uranian energy your friendships could seem chaotic, here today and gone tomorrow. The people you are drawn to could prove unreliable and unavailable when you need them the most.

The twelfth house pertains to the subconscious and superconscious mind. Uranus in the twelfth house suggests an interest in unconventional ways to develop your higher consciousness. You might even enjoy getting together with small groups of people who all have that same esoteric interest. In this type of pattern you are aware of your uniqueness but keep it hidden from most people, sharing it only with specifically chosen individuals. If you are not in touch with or oriented toward developing your consciousness, however, your sense of yourself as a unique person may be locked up in your subconscious mind. To others you may appear rebellious and willful, but you are unaware of those parts of yourself or unaware that others perceive those qualities in you. With Uranus in the twelfth house it is incumbent upon you to own, explore and experiment with your individuality to liberate yourself from pre-conditioned habit patterns and minimize the possibilities of unconsciously alienating others.

Saturn and Uranus co-rule Aquarius. Saturn is considered the traditional ruler because it has been associated with Aquarius since Babylonian times. Uranus was discovered a little over 200 years ago and was subsequently realized to be similar in influence to Aquarius. In this context, Aquarius and its rulers Saturn and Uranus are similar to the other two signs that have co-rulerships, Scorpio (Mars and Pluto) and Pisces (Jupiter and Neptune). The traditional rulers are the inner planets, Mars in the case of Scorpio, Saturn for Aquarius, and Jupiter for Pisces. The trans-Saturnian planets—Uranus, Neptune, and Pluto—are all of recent discovery. Assigning their rulerships was a problem and how this was done is open to question. If it was partially based on observation, what was going on at the time of discovery? What major, obvious and significant changes were people and the planet experiencing that were coincident with the first obser- vation of these bodies? Astrology correlates events on earth to planetary cycles. In all likelihood, however, there is no basis in a cause-and-affect sense that validates astrology and makes it work. It is a system that notices the one-ness of life and the inherent interconnection of all things. An event on earth is not caused by planetary influence, its existence is mirrored by a combination of planetary configurations.

Understanding the nature of these new planets and under- standing their implication and influence on human life could also have been partially based on inspiration and intuition. That seems appropriate since the energy of these planets call upon humanity to open our collective psyche to new forms of awareness. One of the more interesting debates in astrology pertains to where these planets were prior to our discovery of them. Were they always there and we just discovered them or, did they just come into the solar system at approximately the time they were discovered? And if that's the case, where did they come from and how did they get here? Certainly we had the telescopes and the technical ability to see these planets long before they were discovered. Could it be that it took the growth and development of human consciousness into new levels before these planets could actually be seen and measured in a physical sense? Remember, Uranus represents revolution, whether it be technological, political or sociological. Could it be that Uranus was not discovered until human consciousness had evolved to a point where it could handle that type of progressive thinking that led to the startling social and political changes of the last two hundred years?

Although there are no clear answers that resolve the questions of why and from where, the more interesting and significant point is how can we use these energies? What are the new emerging states of consciousness? How are they inspiring us to enter and create the future? Sociological and political experiments of democratic egalitarianism still need to be expanded and refined. Sexual and gender liberation and equality are in the process of becoming more acceptable. We are also still striving for racial equality, relating to people based on the quality of their character, integrity and contribution to the community, not on the basis of skin tone. Scientifically, we are still discovering how to benefit more people with medical and health breakthroughs. Most important, however, is the underlying consciousness. The changes of the 21st Century will dwarf those of the past. They won't be legislated, coerced or demanded. They will come about only as each of us continues to pursue our own path of realization. By devoting ourselves to internal awakening and sharing the results openly, lovingly, and in the spirit of One-ness, the potential of the energies represented by Uranus, Neptune and Pluto can come to fruition in ways that can only be thought, discussed and speculated about today.

THE ELEVENTH HOUSE

The area of life associated with Aquarius is the eleventh house. An air house, it pertains to people and ideas. Sometimes the people you associate with through your eleventh house energy awaken new ideas in you. It can also work the other way, whereby a certain set of ideas and concepts about life can cause you to perceive and relate to people in new ways.

Following the tenth house, the eleventh extends some of the tenth house activity. As a succeedant house, the eleventh also deepens and completes the activity of the tenth. The tenth house, for example, works within a clearly defined structure to achieve certain goals. It may be the planets in your eleventh that help you to complete the job or having completed it to bring reward and recognition for a job well done. One of the ways in which you might be rewarded is by being given more personal freedom on the job. A more desirable office, a raise in salary or better benefits can all be ways of being rewarded. The eleventh house also pertains to those people with whom you work. As you become more successful, your reputation grows among your peers. Sometimes they may tell you about a new or better position, sometimes they will even hire you themselves. The eleventh house also includes any job related groups or organizations. Labor unions are an eleventh house activity. So are business groups such as Women in Business and the American Medical Association. Fraternal groups such as The Odd Fellows and The Boy Scouts, and service-oriented political groups such as The League of Women Voters are also included within the experience of the eleventh house.

The eleventh is said to be the house of hopes and wishes. This can pertain to what you get to do because of personal proclivity. Once more practical and concrete things have been accomplished, you become more aware of new options. These can involve doing things that are interesting and satisfying to you. They are activities that you get to do as a result of what you have previously accomplished. The choice could be oriented toward either that which is personally exciting or which enables you to be part of something that involves a larger, more collective context. The eleventh house can raise the practical productivity of the tenth house to a more ideal utopian or idealistic manifestation. The eleventh house is open and progressive in its orientation. With significant energy in your eleventh house you tend to be tolerant and accepting of other people. You perceive humanity in collective contexts and have an inherent overview of the human condition. Being part of a social experiment that would be beneficial to groups or the masses can be exciting and meaningful.

The eleventh is also the house of the group mind and collective consciousness. This can be experienced in three different ways. On a personal level the group mind is your friends. If you have significant energy in your eleventh house, friendship is important to you. The planets in your eleventh house indicate the interests you would want to share with your friends. The sign those planets are in would suggest how you prefer to share. If the Moon or Venus were in your eleventh house, you would feel comfortable with women friends. With the Moon there you would be attracted to people who were nurturing or who you could nurture. You would want to share your family's interests with other families and might even think of members of your family as your friends. If it were Venus, you would enjoy the harmony and sharing of the interaction and would be attracted to creative people as friends. You might even want some aspect of the art world to be the point of connection between yourself and others. Venus in the eleventh also points out the importance of establishing a good friendship with someone before becoming lovers or partners. The Sun, Mars or Saturn implies male friends. Mars in the eleventh suggests being competitive with friends in athletic or recreational contexts. With Saturn you could become involved in power struggles with others you thought were your friends. You could also discover that they are very critical or repressive to you in some way. They might make demands on your time or insist that you take primary responsibility to keep the relationship alive. Or you could be the one relating in a overly domineering way, seeking to control others to the degree that they and the relationship conform to your expectations. Saturn could also distance you from other people, causing you to feel isolated or to feel unclear as to who your friends are. You could have many acquaintances but very few real friends. Once you do make a friend, however, you will be very loyal and work to make the relationship endure.

Pluto in the eleventh can bring up power issues. With Pluto in your eleventh you need to learn about power specifically in group situations. You may tend to be manipulative or to create adversarial factions within the group or to allow others to coerce and drain you. Pluto in the eleventh can generate a series of crises with friends or with groups. Those explosions could be emotionally painful for you, but they could also stimulate a personal transformation, a peak experience. Through this process you could see through some of your negative patterns of socialization, understand what you do and why, let go of those behaviors and create new ones to take their place.

Mercury, Jupiter and Uranus in the eleventh are more oriented toward learning. Mercury brings a curiosity about people and the ability to have many friends in many contexts. You enjoy having debates and discussions or exchanging ideas with associates. Young people might seem attractive as friends because they tend to be curious and open-minded. Jupiter is similar, but, as you might assume with the planet of expansion, it adds more. In addition to enjoying the give and take of learning, Jupiter also suggests an abundance of opportunities to socialize and to make friends. You will probably experience your friends as generous, humorous and fun to be around. Learning from them is fun and they probably feel the same way about you. Uranus implies attraction to unusual people as friends and having interesting, even challenging experiences with them. The relationships may not be particularly long or consistent, but they will provide you with inspiration and opportunities to explore different parts of yourself.

Neptune in the eleventh house indicates a desire to be involved with others in a spiritual or creative context. You tend to feel devoted to your friends, relating to them with compassion and unconditional acceptance. Be careful, however, that you are not seeing others as you want them to be, rather than as who they are. You could be taken advantage of as a result. You could even allow a sense of pity to be the foundation of your relationship. People with alcohol or drug problems or those with severe psychological problems may evoke a strong feeling of sympathy within you, but be careful not to confuse pity with love or mistake someone in need as being a worthwhile candidate for friendship. Strive to develop friendships with those who provide a realistic feeling of inspiration. This good feeling shouldn't be there only when in their presence, or as a result of what you do for them, but as a byproduct of the relationship itself. That sense of inspiration should remain even after you are no longer in each other's presence. People who identify with their spiritual path and their higher being yet share experiences in a humble way could provide you with satisfying social activity. Meeting with people in psychological support groups, meditation groups or twelve step groups could all be beneficial with Neptune in your eleventh house.

With any of the previous planets in the eleventh house, but especially the Sun, the experience will differ depending on the consistency of your centeredness and your degree of self-love.

The less centered you are, the more you depend on others to create your experience of friendship. If the Moon or Venus are there, you can become emotionally dependent on friends. Mars indicates that you need and allow others to initiate both the experience and the quality of the experience that you share with them. Saturn or Pluto can bring in controlling, draining or domineering types of people and situations. With the Sun, however, you could allow your friends, individually or as a group, to define, validate or justify yourself or your reality. You see yourself as an extension of others and seek to fit into their social framework.

The Sun in the eleventh house of an uncentered person can also create a strong drive to rebel. It may seem as if by continually separating from others you are defining yourself. In fact all you're doing is maintaining a detached aloofness that prevents real sharing or friendship from taking place. If you really know who you are and feel comfortable with that knowledge, you can integrate into any type of situation without losing your inherent self or being limited by others.

If your eleventh house energy manifests in a more centered and self-loving mode, you will have an inspiring effect on others. You will be seen as a leader of your group and a role model to your friends. Your manifestation within the group will be positive, supportive and creative. Your thinking will be progressive, with a tendency to seek the overview and to be concerned with the welfare of a broad range of humanity. You will relate to others in an altruistic, humanitarian manner.

In addition to friends, you can be influenced by the group mind through role models. In a positive context, these could be people who help you to develop your potential. You may not know these people personally, they could be community leaders, political leaders, spiritual teachers, or just people who inspire you to maximize who you are. If you do know people such as this in your life your relationship to them could be close. Your awareness of who they are, what they do and how they do it can galvanize you to grow beyond what you had previously assumed was your limit. Sometimes you could find a quality demonstrated by a role model that is so exemplary that you want to emulate it. Other times it's exciting just to know someone who is so great just being themselves. You may not want to do the same thing or be the same way, but you may become enthralled by the possibility of being as true to yourself as they are to themselves.

There are some drawbacks to being influenced by role models. There is the danger of relying on their influence to inspire you to change or grow. That dependency can prevent you from looking within yourself for guidance. There is also the possibility that you may admire a person for certain reasons, but allow yourself to be influenced by them in a lot of different ways, some of which may not be so admirable. You may try to model yourself after someone else to the extent that you exclude those parts of yourself that need to be developed further. Don't lose your ability to discriminate.

The group mind can also influence you through the media. From advertisements to comments made, topics discussed and styles worn there is constant bombardment of what to look like, what to read, what to think, what to say and how to say it. If you are unclear about who you are, you could find yourself influenced by this type of subtle programming. You change your habits, values and style to conform to the mode of the day.

The level at which you relate to the group mind can indicate your degree of centeredness. As a centered eleventh house person, you would be more oriented to friends and positive role models and less likely to be influenced by negative models or patterns of role modeling. You would have very little, if any, interest in the media hypes. The less centered you were, the more vulnerable you would be to any external influences. You could live a vicarious life in which others peoples' experiences and reality were more important, and more real, than your own.

AQUARIUS AND THE BODY

Structurally, Aquarius rules the calves and ankles. More subtly Aquarius also rules the oxidization of gases, the release of oxygen to the cells. As the opposite sign of Leo, the ruler of the heart and circulatory system, Aquarius also influences the circulation of blood. With a lot of energy in Aquarius you may tend to have less oxygen in the blood, especially if your Aquarian energy receives squares from planets in Taurus or Scorpio, or oppositions from planets in Leo. As a result, you might suffer from poor circulation and feel chronically fatigued or be chronically cold. To counteract this tendency, work to bring more oxygen to the blood by watching your intake of starch, as starch robs the body of oxygen during the digestion process. Get plenty of exercise and sleep near an open window so that there is fresh air circulating in the room. Deep breathing while walking or through *Pranayama* (deep, yogic type breathing) can also bring more oxygen and energy in general to the body to counteract these problems.

Aquarius also regulates the retina, and the rods and cones of the eye, which deal with color vision. In a pathological sense, this can lead to general weakness of the eyes, color blindness or even glaucoma or cataracts. In a more positive sense, this same influence can produce the ability to see auras.

Uranus can bring sudden and unexpected disorders such as spasms, strokes, sudden paralysis or shooting pains. Sometimes Uranus can indicate a situation that could cause you to go into shock, or experience unusual kinds of maladies that appear suddenly, are difficult to diagnose and also disappear suddenly. With Uranus in your sixth house, or ruling your sixth, you would be open to alternative, non-traditional forms of healing.

Uranus in hard aspect to Mercury in your natal chart, indicates an over-active nervous system. In addition to high levels of stress and anxiety, this combination can produce learning disabilities or damage to the nervous system itself through such diseases as multiple sclerosis.

CONCLUSIONS

Aleister Crowley called Aquarius the energy of the magician, the ability to call forth the unseen dream of universal dominion for his or her idea. This implies that Aquarius is an archetype that can perceive a utopian vision of a paradigm of reality that establishes a world in which life is oriented toward the greatest good for the greatest number of people. It could also suggest, however, a program of power wherein the many were dominated by the few. Whether this is in the form of a fascist state or a family controlled by authoritarian parents, some have power and others don't. It's a situation in which the vision of one person or a small group of people dominates the ideas and experiences of others.

If the vision is an inspiration that is motivated by the desire to benefit others and executed with a true humanitarian spirit, it can manifest intellectually as new scientific hypotheses or occult inspiration. It can be expressed sociologically as new forms of social relationship or ways of bringing about radical reform of social and political institutions. This orientation toward the progressive defines a clear difference from the previous sign, Capricorn, which is more oriented toward the preservation of existing forms. Capricorn is traditional, conservative and cautious. It sets goals and works to achieve them in an organized, disciplined way. Aquarius is more oriented toward change and spontaneity. It is the sign of uniqueness and personal liberation; it is the Bohemian or beatnik of the zodiac.

Aquarians tend to be idealistic. They are similar to both preceding *yang* signs of the Southern hemisphere, Libra and Sagittarius. Like Sagittarius, Aquarians can have a hard time grounding their ideals in pragmatic action, preferring to remain in the rarefied air of theories, thought forms, universal languages and concepts. Aquarius is the sign of the inventor and the innovator.

As the third of the air signs, Aquarius offers a final perspective to the ways in which we can use our intellect to understand the best ways to socially interact. For the first air sign, Gemini, ideas and relationship can be random as long as they are interesting. Data gathering and networking are prime experiences for Gemini. The second air sign, Libra, refines the social experience to a quality, one-to-one, primary relationship. The Libran mind is logical, and Libra enjoys the give and take of debating. There is more definition and direction in both the social and mental experience of Libra than of Gemini. Libra is cardinal, Gemini mutable. Aquarius is a fixed sign and brings completion to the experience and activities of the other two. It broadens the social orientation of Libra beyond the one-to-one to include the group. It expands the mental approach so as to incorporate new, exciting ideas and ways of thinking from a vast array of interests. Libra tends to be conventional, Aquarius unconventional. Libra will try to solve problems within an acceptable context. Aquarius goes beyond the known and seeks solutions in a more experimental way. Aquarius also differs from Gemini in that it provides a context within which to learn, relate and share. As a result, it may not be as spontaneous as Gemini and also may tend to become attached to a particular idea or point of view. Like Gemini, Aquarius enjoys relating to a variety of people. Whereas Gemini enjoys a constantly changing variety, however, Aquarius prefers more consistency, as within a particular group. Aquarius is also the last of the fixed signs. In the Bible, in the Book of Ezekiel, Chapter 1, the Hebrew prophet talks about a vision of God. In verse ten, he describes the face of his vision: "As for the likeness of their faces, they four had the face of a man and the face of a lion, on the right side: and they four had the face of an ox on the left side; they four also had the face of an eagle." In verses 15-16, he says, "Now as I beheld the living creatures, behold one wheel upon the earth by the living creatures with his four faces. The appearance of the wheels and their work was like unto the color of a beryl: and they four had one likeness: and their appearance and their work was as if it were a wheel in the middle of a wheel." The wheel Ezekiel is referring to is the zodiac (wheel of animals). The four fixed signs of the zodiac according to their totem are the ox (similar to the bull) = Taurus, the lion = Leo, the eagle (one of the four totems) = Scorpio, and the man = Aquarius. The four fixed signs each represent different aspects of Divine Will and that, when taken together, they can manifest unlimited creation through the exercise of that Will. Ezekiel equates strength of will, a primary characteristic of the fixed cross, with the creative principle.

As an individual sign, Aquarius is an archetype that represents two aspects of creative will. It recognizes its oneness with others; it is humanitarian, altruistic and friendly. It defines love as a quality of energy that exists for all beings and is to be shared among all beings. This is different from Aquarius' opposite sign Leo. Leo is oriented to love more as a quantity of energy that one has. Although it can be generous in sharing its measure of love, it does have a need to receive a like amount in return. It's orientation toward love is usually based on a heart connection with specific people like lover and children.

Aquarius feels comfortable with groups and organizations, especially those oriented toward a cause or an uplifting purpose. Aquarius can also be concerned with ultimate self-awareness and the development and demonstration of uniqueness, individuality and personal liberty. Aquarius is a paradox.

The negative characteristics of the Aquarian nature manifest as tendencies to be inconsistent and aloof or to make change for the sake of change. You might be rebellious and act against various forms of authority as a way of seemingly establishing your independence. In reality, you are using the structure provided by that authoritarian figure or institution as something to bounce off of. You are defining "them" as wrong and "you" as right without stopping to consider you may agree with them in certain ways or be similar to at least some of what the authority represents. You are actually giving the external symbols of power the right to define your reality, then rebelling against it. You are playing the "prove-it" game. By acting out as a way of establishing your identity, you are hoping to prove to others that the act is really who you are. You assume that the more extreme the behavior the more others will tend to believe that that is the real you. Your tendency to shock others into noticing who you are is a way of obscuring who you really are, both from them and from you. You are avoiding the work of defining your unique self.

It's as if you are living your life by looking in a rear view mirror. You know where you've been and what you don't like about it, but you have no vision or inspiration about where to go or how to get there. Changes of this nature tend to be trade-offs. You trade off one set of positives and negatives for another without really improving your situation in a qualitative way.

As an uncentered Aquarian, you rely too much on feedback and support from the group mind. You become dependent on others until you feel the urge for independence. Then suddenly, and unexpectedly, you disappear. Adopting a cold and aloof attitude, you ask all these "others" to give you some space. After being alone for a while, you remember that you are an air sign, a social animal, and you call your friends, asking where they've been and why they don't come around anymore.

You run the gamut from being overly-accommodating and friendly to being self-righteous and distant. You can recognize yourself in this phase if you feel a lot of nervous energy and have a hard time grounding and getting things done. This type of Aquarian energy tends to be a media-junkie, always tuning in to the latest fads or cultivating a couch potato life style by staying up to date with the latest sit-coms and soap operas. You are living a vicarious life, being excited by things that concern other people but are not really pertinent to you. Any of these patterns could also be present if you have a lot of significant energy in your eleventh house, even if in a sign other than Aquarius.

If, however, you work on yourself and remain centered and balanced most of the time, your Aquarian-eleventh house patterns will be different. First of all, working on self for an Aquarian involves learning about, accepting, owning, exploring and experimenting with your uniqueness. You recognize and feel comfortable with that part of yourself that's different from everybody else—the weirdo within. You pay attention to and respond to your inner light or internal inspiration. You feel excited about life, and are seen as a role model by others, inspiring them to get more in touch with their own uniqueness simply by your example.

By becoming more aware and tolerant of yourself, you duplicate those patterns in your relationships. You are aware of who you want to associate with. You feel free to be yourself, to do what you will, independently of others. If you don't appreciate who you are, you may not allow yourself to express your uniqueness. You will tend to be intolerant of others. You will probably relate to others with a "holier than thou" attitude of disdain. Learning to honor your unorthodox qualities enables you to transform disdain into true detachment. You enjoy your life, but don't try to hang on to what it is. Your interest lies more in what it is *becoming.* You are in the world, but not of it. A problem with this attitude is that you may have difficulty relating to others in a close, personal way. You are more aware of, and concerned with, the utopian ideal than with your fellow beings. It's as if, in your inimical outlook, your affirmation of life becomes, "I love humanity, it's people I can't stand."

The work that you are doing to integrate your personal and impersonal selves and realities is mirroring what is taking place within the consciousness of collective humanity as well. We are entering the Age of Aquarius. This refers to the wobble of the Earth on its axis. Our Earth acts like a gyroscope, rotating in space while maintaining a centrifugal force. The Earth also exerts a gravitational pull on its axis, trying to pull it down, even while the centrifugal force keeps it going. The interplay between these two forces is called precession. It is the precession of the axis that keeps the axis moving in a small circle. As the axis moves, it causes the Earth to change its position relative to the groupings of fixed stars, called constellations or signs of the zodiac. Using the first day of spring as a reference point, and looking from a geocentric perspective, during the last 2000 years, the Sun was in the sign Pisces on that day. Due to the precession, the Earth is gradually changing so that it will soon see the Sun moving into the sign Aquarius on the first day of spring, marking the beginning the Aquarian Age. There is, of course, some debate within the astrological community as to when the official first day of this epoch is to take place. Some well thought out theories claim it has already begun, others that it is still to happen. Whenever the discussion is about a cycle that lasts approximately 2000 years, however, it is best to assume a relatively long period of transition that may even last several hundred years. Assuming the discovery of Uranus 200 years ago, the co-ruler of Aquarius, marked the beginning of the cuspal or transitional period, there may be an additional 200 years before we are truly in and of the new age. During this last 200 years, the industrialization of the world has brought humanity many things: transportation devices like automobiles, airplanes and space vehicles; labor-saving devices like vacuum cleaners, washing machines and central heating units; and communication devices like telephones, television sets and computers. These inventions have made the world more comfortable for those who have access to them. They have made the world seem smaller. And they have also threatened the survival of the human race. Medical breakthroughs that help alleviate suffering and prolong life have also helped create the problem of overpopulation. The byproducts of the manufacturing of the new products have polluted the air, water and soil. The alienation that has become accepted in the Twentieth Century has cut us off from each other. This pattern has elevated the value of the individual above the welfare of the community. This is a classic manifestation of the Aquarius paradox.

What has been lacking in this proliferation of new products is the development of a new consciousness that provides a perspective on the ramifications of what we are doing. How are these material advances affecting each other, our communities and our planet?

Two thousand years ago was the beginning of the Piscean Age. It was helped in its initiation by a great teacher, a being who achieved a state of awareness called Christ Consciousness. His name was Jesus. He prophesied a renewal of his teachings that came to be called the Second Coming. Did this refer to the reincarnation of Jesus? Or did it presage a time when the consciousness of the Christ would dawn in a new, collective way?

Christ Consciousness is not about one person. It is about a state of being, a mode of perceiving reality. It is a way of seeing the Life Force permeating all things. It enables us to realize that we all have a lot more in common than we have differences. We are all part of the same Oneness, the same Experience, the same Being.

Aquarius is the sign of the human being. The Aquarian Age is the Age of Humanity. It is an epoch in which the Second Coming can manifest within the minds, hearts and souls of all beings who choose to seek that mode of perception, that state of awareness, that level of relationship. This is the ultimate resolution to the Aquarian paradox. It is initiated by each individual, claiming their birthright as Beings of Light and Transmitters of Love. By engaging in this process, we eventually realize the beauty of the Human Family. We alter our behavior and collective values based on the realization that we are all reflections of each other, facets of the same radiant light, manifestations of the same creative force. Even as we take into consideration the differences in our rates of growth, our levels of development in any area at any time, and disparate philosophical or theological reference points, we work to bring the welfare of the Whole into greater, healthier balance with the welfare of the individual. It is this level of consciousness, this perspective on life, that is the most exalted contribution that Aquarius makes to the human experience.

PISCES

Pisces is the final sign of the final quadrant. The fourth quadrant is oriented toward collective experience as a vehicle for developing higher consciousness. Pisces is the astrological archetype that provides the most unifying perception of life. Pisces stimulates and facilitates the relationship to one's Higher Being. It is also the sign of dispersion, dissolving the ego of the personal self. It challenges us to learn how to be aware of and feel comfortable in "the real world that isn't there." The only way that the essence of the Piscean archetype can be appreciated is by allowing all of the seemingly firm boundaries of the physical world to dissolve. Pisces says, "I intuit and believe." As this becomes more a part of your daily awareness, distinctions of class, race, and nationality begin to disappear as well. They are replaced by a growing sense of connection to all things.

There are also some traps that can accompany this experience. To enter the Piscean realm without realizing what this archetypal experience is about can lead to overwhelming feelings of confusion, fear, and being out of control. You can become plagued by terrifying demons that seemingly invade and erode your existence. The trick is to allow yourself to be open to the vastness of the Piscean reality, to be filled with the awe of realization, yet not be undermined by feelings and perceptions that are either illusions or byproducts of your imagination.

As a sign of the Eastern hemisphere, Pisces is a subjective sign, defining its reality and creating its own experience. Because it is capable of vast breadth and depth of understanding, the sense of being in charge of what is taking place in your life is ephemeral. If, as a Pisces, you insist upon relating to life just from the ego perspective of your personal self, you can feel lost amidst a myriad of perceptions and levels of awareness. If, however, you can learn how to identify more with your Spirit

Self, your Pisces energy may provide the most all-inclusive spectrum of life. For that reason, it can also be most confused about what is going on in any particular situation.

To be fully functional within this archetype involves opening all the doors of perception, allowing previously defined expectations to fall away and to remain firmly grounded in the Light.

The Sun is in Pisces from February 18 through March 20.

THE MYTHS

The myths that help describe Pisces and define its characteristics come from all the main cultures of the world. If the nature of Pisces is subtle, it is also universal.

The Buddha provides an archetypal image of the Piscean nature. Even as the Buddha shares his wisdom with others, there remains a core of inner strength nurtured by silence. This defines the spiritual path as solitary. Whether before or after enlightenment, the inner journey is fundamental and needs to be followed consistently. Even if practiced within a group context, it is still up to the individual to work at developing a personal relationship with the Divine Essence. For Buddha, that relationship comes through focusing on the empty mind and feeling compassion for all beings. The empty mind enables connection with "Ground Luminosity" or grounding in the Light and Nature and realizing the primary experience that we all share. Compassion results from opening the heart to the flow of Love and Acceptance that is present at all times for all of us. To identify with it, to nurture it as a state of being and consciousness is to become an expressor of compassion yourself.

Buddhism provides the concept of the *Boddhisatva*. This is a person who has finished his or her earth plane experience. There are no more desires to be fulfilled, no more mistakes to be rectified. However, Boddhisatvas take a vow to not completely sever their connection to this plane until all sentient beings are enlightened. They put off their own entry into higher realms of being, nirvana for example, to be of selfless service to those still working through the trials of the physical realm. One of the dangers of this path is that in returning to earth, they create new karma by engaging in wrong actions or doing something born of ignorance. Their task is not only to help others—as teachers, healers, friends or relatives—but to remember at all times to be aware of their own actions, thoughts and motivations.

In India there are numerous stories about the *Jatakas* or virtues that are developed by those men and women who have consciously sought to evolve into Buddhahood through the path of the Boddhisatva. Unlimited generosity, unbroken devotion and unremitting right action help to comprise the path of *Jataka*. Ultimately it provides a way to reverse all past negative, or self-serving, karma (actions) and merge with the godhead.

Such a being is *Avalokiteshvara*, the Boddhisatva of Compassion. He protects against shipwrecks, assassins, robbers and savage beasts. Buddhist iconography has depicted this being in one hundred eight forms. They range from human to "the shape with a thousand arms." In Tibet, the thousand armed and thousand eyed Boddhisatva sees all the pain in the Universe and reaches everywhere to extend his help. His image was placed in temples at the entrance to the sanctuary. His right hand makes a gesture of charity and in his headdress is a figure of the Buddha.

The feminine energy of Avalokiteshvara is represented by Tara. Like the male image, she is compassionate and is referred to as the "Savior," the "Giver of Favors" and "She who brings [others] through evil passes" (places). She is the protector of navigation, travel and of all those on a path of emancipation. At times she is depicted in terrifying form, to illustrate the pain and suffering required to rid the self of a personal identity and to be able to identify with and merge with the Oneness.

Another female myth that represents traits of Pisces is the Greek goddess Aphrodite. The Romans called this goddess Venus, and it is significant that the planet Venus is said to be exalted in Pisces. It is stronger in Pisces than in any sign other than Taurus or Libra, both of which it rules. Like the qualities of the planet Venus, the goddess Aphrodite represents love and beauty. To the Greeks, Aphrodite was extremely beautiful and irresistibly charming. Most Greek iconography that depicts doves, roses and apples signify a connection with or the experience of romantic love. Unlike other prominent goddesses—such as Hera, Demeter and Persephone—Aphrodite had the freedom to choose her own lovers and to create her own relationships. Among her paramours were the gods Hephaestus the blacksmith, Ares, the god of war and Hermes, god of the universal mind.

Pisces

Each of these relationships symbolizes an important union of human experiences. Aphrodite and Hephaestus represents the marriage between beauty and craft which is art. Aphrodite and Ares combine love and war. Aphrodite and Hermes integrate intuition with logic.

Aphrodite is a good model for the feminine, water sign Pisces. She embodies the subtle awareness of the inner realms expressed by romantic love and art. She also feels comfortable with herself and comfortable expressing her nature in a self-assured, powerful way. Rather than being overwhelmed by her need for love, she manifests a variety of lovers. Rather than being used for her beauty, she uses it to inspire the creative muse in other deities as well as in humans. Complexity, independence and intrigue are all compelling qualities of the mythic archetype of Aphrodite.

Christianity is abundant with mythic references to Pisces. Aquarius taught that it is through the water and the rite of baptism, that we are purified and released from attachment to past negative karma. Pisces continues and extends references to water as a vehicle for transmutation of consciousness. Pisces is the sign of the fish. Jesus chose his twelve disciples from among fisherman saying, "Henceforth, thou shall catch souls." Pisces the water sign is analogous to the parable about walking on water. This is similar to the higher spiritual qualities of Pisces. It indicates the potential for emotional and spiritual self-mastery as control is developed over the body (physical self) enabling the individual essence to rise above the water (emotional self) and have dominion over the soul (spiritual self).

In the story of the loaves and fishes, Pisces is connected to its opposite sign, Virgo, the sign of wheat and the harvest. Virgo/Pisces is the axis of service. This is a story about how to provide for others by developing compassion and remaining in touch with Universal Spirit.

Pisces rules the feet. Washing the feet of others is a supreme act of service. It is recognized not only by Jesus, but also by the 20th Century Avatar, Meher Baba. It is symbolic of two things. First, it is a recognition of the God or Spirit within. Any person, regardless of circumstance, has the potential for God-realization because we are all inseparable manifestations of the Divine. Second, washing the feet is a physical expression of the internal process of cleansing and transformation that the spiritual master is performing on the disciple. It's also interesting that Meher Baba himself was a Pisces.

Perhaps more significant an illustration of Piscean qualities than any of these anecdotal parables, is Jesus' relationship to the downtrodden. As an itinerant teacher and healer or through his political defiance he was always seeking to be of service to the alienated and dispossessed. His intention was to manifest love and compassion both in his words and actions as well as in social institutions. Probably the most heretical and threatening to the ruling hierarchy, was his support of women. As an early feminist, he brought women such as Mary Magdalene into his inner circle, allowing them to occupy important positions of counsel and leadership. This was in a time and culture when stoning a woman to death for assumed transgressions was commonplace. Allowing creditors to have their way with one's daughter as payment for a debt was acceptable. To recognize women as equal to men in the eyes of God, to affirm that we are all of One Spirit, was not only a revolutionary thought in Jesus' day, but is a concept still demanding acceptance and institutional change in our culture today. It may also have been the reason the authorities put him to death; the threat of insurrection from women was absolutely unacceptable and unforgivable.

THE GLYPH: ♓

The glyph for Pisces contains two semi-circles, symbols of the soul and the subconscious mind, linked together by a horizontal line. The semi-circles are back to back, suggesting a dichotomy of nature and of the potential manifestation of energy. Like the other mutable signs, Gemini, Virgo and Sagittarius, Pisces is double bodied. Cancer relies on one such symbol, which suggests that it relies on one focused path through which to relate to the inner self and function in life. Pisces utilizes two circles implying that it has more potential for variety of interests and versatility of focus. Also like Cancer, the semi-circle indicates that Pisces represents experience on the inner planes. Spiritually it can connect to the highest realms of consciousness. Psychologically this glyph suggests the potential to develop insight into the deepest levels of the subconscious mind.

The horizontal line that joins the hemispheres is significant in two ways. First, energy along the horizon enables interaction with the world. It allows us to share our energy with others and allows them to share with us. This prevents the Pisces from disappearing into their own internal isolation tank. Second, this line signifies the ability to be infinitely receptive, of both internal information and other people's experience. It helps Pisces to serve the needs of others from a point of clarity and inspiration.

THE TOTEM:

Pisces is the sign of the fish. The Babylonians called Pisces *Nunu*, which means fish. This is a symbolic reference to those who spend significant and quality time in the deeper, more internal areas of life. Water implies emotion. The fish, therefore, symbolizes one who is surrounded and supported by this ever present quality. One way this totem is depicted is as two fish. The fish resemble each other but are looking at and swimming in opposite directions. Here we see another reference to the duality of the Piscean nature. It refers to the Pisces dilemma of functioning for self—leading to personal growth and fulfillment, but which at times puts too much emphasis on individuality—or functioning for others—which promotes service but can also lead to self-sacrifice and resentment. The struggle between pure soul or spiritual experience, and the need to remain within a body and function in a practical way is the Piscean dilemma.

The fish can also be rendered such that they are intertwined, or at least swimming in the same circle. They can still be going in opposite directions, but are involved in the same experience. This symbolizes the wheel of life, the process of death and rebirth. This can also be characterized as the eternal cycle of rebirth. Every ending is a new beginning. From a spiritual point of view there is no death. Just a letting go of various forms or bardos of temporary experience. By opening to the inner realms, there can be conscious choices made about when, where and why to integrate your ever-evolving new awareness into new circumstances. The fish represents one who lives in the cosmic sea of emotional, psychic and spiritual energy.

It's ironic that Pisces rules the feet, yet fish have no feet! This implies that although Pisces may be comfortable in the emotional and intuitive realms, they can also be ungrounded when it comes to practical matters. Floating along with the strongest streams of feeling, or simply the current of their own daydreams and fantasies, Pisces often needs to concentrate on functioning in the body.

It's interesting that St. Augustine claimed that the initial letters of the Greek words that form the title, "Jesus Christ, Son of God, Savior and Cross," spell the word *fish* in Greek. To live on the Earth within the state of Christ Consciousness is to be continually drawing inspiration from your higher being and remaining pure—free from sin or karma.

MODE AND ELEMENT

Pisces is the sign of mutable water. Fog is a good image of amorphous water floating in a free-form state, an apt description of Piscean energy which can be subtle and camouflaging or confused and indefinite. Mutability indicates the ability to respond and adapt to one's surroundings. This can be so extreme that, as a Pisces, you may be unduly influenced by others as to what you feel, what you think and even who you are. Your vulnerability suggests that you may lack a clear sense of your own identity. It is easier for you to blend in with what is happening around you, or with what others want you to do or to be, than to define and assert your true self. Pisces is the most ego-less of the signs. A beneficial effect of the lack of clear self-definition is that it makes it easier to see life as it is. A clear sense of identity can create a tendency to project your subjective evaluation of who you are, what you believe, how you perceive life and to assume that that is really what's going on. Because Pisces doesn't have clear definitions, the projections are fewer and the scope of life is broader. In this sense it is the wisest of the signs and is most open and most likely to fulfill the mutable desire and need to learn, understand and develop consciousness.

Partaking of the element water defines Pisces as a sensitive, intuitive sign. Sometimes the emotionality can be overwhelming. As a Pisces, not only are you open to having your own feelings hurt but your watery nature renders you extremely sensitive to others' pain as well. Suffering that others are experiencing can be felt as your own. It could be the individual unhappiness of friends or family, or the collective misery and tragedy that pervades the human condition. You can even be strongly influenced by people you pass on the street. Like a mass of walking psychic Velcro, you attract other people's unowned and unexpressed emotional pain and psychological confusion. Being around strangers can be uncomfortable, and being in a crowd can be overwhelming. This is one reason why Pisces is humanitarian. To heal or resolve the situation for others can also relieve your own. Unlike Aquarius, who is humanitarian because it "knows and understands the right way to be," Pisces is humanitarian based on a gut-reaction to life and to people. If Aquarian humanitarianism is based on the "trickle-down" economic theory, Piscean humanitarianism is based on the "pump-priming" principle. In trickle-down economics the wealthy remain in control of a vast majority of their money, by increasing use taxes instead of income taxes, and by providing tax breaks as incentives for new investments. This in turn will create new businesses, more jobs, increase the tax base and promote the general welfare. Pump-priming is an economic theory through which the poorer classes are taxed less, either by lowering sales taxes or by altering payroll and income tax. As a result, they have more money in their pockets, which they then spend on products and services. This increases the demand for those goods which, through the law of supply and demand, generates more jobs, a stronger tax base and a healthier economy. Instead of stimulating from the top (the head, logical understanding), you stimulate from the bottom (soul, emotional reaction).

The manifestation of this economic theory in terms of human behavior is service. As a mutable sign, Pisces is one of the two most serviceful of the twelve signs, the other being its polar opposite, Virgo. Like Virgo, Pisces can carry the act of service to the point of self-sacrifice. The lack of clear identity makes it even easier for Pisces to undermine or lose the self than it is for Virgo.

To counteract tendencies toward martyrdom, Pisces can function best when serving within a structured system. Hospitals, prisons or the police force can all provide you with opportunities to satisfy your need to be of service, yet also provide limits that prevent your good intentions from becoming extreme and self-defeating.

The combination of mutable-water can also render you extremely intuitive. As a result of having little ego-attachment, you tend to have fewer expectations and are more accepting of other people. It's as if you have the ability to get inside other people's heads and see the world from their point of view. If you can maintain some objectivity and detachment about what you are experiencing, this insight can teach you a great deal about specific individuals as well as the nature of the human condition. This can prove useful in such healing modes as psychotherapy, psychic or shamanic healing or just being a sympathetic good friend.

Make sure that your compassion has limits, however. Otherwise, your could feel plagued by a lack of fulfillment or satisfaction in your life, because you are overly concerned with others. Sometimes your insight into others and your understanding of their motivations can override your best interests. If someone hurts you, for instance, your tendency is to try to understand why—and you usually can. Then it's "I understand why that person hurt me, so it's okay." Compassion for the other becomes more important than compassion for yourself. However, it's not an either/or situation. The situation doesn't have to be experienced in terms of "It's okay that you hurt me because I understand why you did it." It is also possible to affirm your intuitive insights and at the same time establish a boundary that enables you to express your feelings and prevent you from being hurt again.

In your personal life, your watery nature defines you as being emotional in the sense of being devotional and romantic. Sometimes those qualities can cause you to be idealistic about relationships. You could fantasize about being with someone whom you idolize but don't really know. You could relate only to the positive, desirable parts of a person, pretending the other, less comfortable parts aren't there. You could overlook the reality of the partner altogether, and make the mistake of falling in love with love. You romanticize the relationship but are not really in touch with your true feelings about the partner.

Your sense of compassion can cause you to confuse pity with love. Feeling sorry for a person, you want to be the helper, healer or fixer. This pattern also suggests difficulty with your own sense of being lovable. It's as if you feel you must do something special to be worthy of being noticed, appreciated or loved. In the long run, your partner could resent you for being so good and so self-less and reject you anyway.

Obviously all of these patterns can be well intended, yet lead to deep feelings of disillusionment and disappointment. This can eventually lead to resentment. You are likely to express your resentment by being unfairly and unrealistically critical of both yourself and your partner. There are several possible ways out. The first is working on self-love. For Pisces this usually involves developing a strong spiritual path, through which you learn faith. Faith is not wishing and hoping, but true knowledge. It is a way of taking advantage of your wisdom to guide you through life and relationships. Through the spiritual journey you realize that you are an intrinsic, inseparable part of Life. As such you come to understand that Love is not just what we feel for someone else, but a state of consciousness, a part of the human condition. To be "in love" is to acknowledge that concept as a reality and work to live in it daily. Being "in love" has nothing to do with someone else. It is a state of mind, a quality of consciousness. Any type of spiritual discipline can teach you the truth of this concept. Meditation, yoga or prayer when practiced regularly with dedication, direction and discipline, can help to develop your intuition. As you develop spiritually your intuitive growth follows along automatically. Developing your psychic potential does not necessarily support your spiritual growth, however. With spiritual advancement comes awareness of, and identification with, the Love energy; intuition simply becomes a tool to understanding life. For example, instead of allowing your empathetic nature to cause confusion between pity and love, use your intuition to notice your reaction to someone and then to ask yourself why that person is in such a condition. You may or may not be able to derive hard facts just from your inner being, but you can at least get glimpses of what that person's lessons are, or what work they still need to do for themselves. You could get some clues as to why they aren't doing their work. Is something blocking them or are they merely ignorant of what to do and how to do it? These realizations can prevent you from opening up too much and lead to excessive vulnerability or being drained and disappointed.

Strive to develop a relationship based on spiritual values. You have the ability to see goodness, beauty and truth in everybody. Don't make the mistake, however, of relating from your higher being to the higher being of someone who doesn't know what a higher being is. Make sure a potential partner is spiritually aware and is working to develop both psychologically as well as spiritually. Find another part of your life to express your service. Occupationally, or through volunteer work, you can feel as if you "gave at the office" and remain clear about your more personal needs and feelings in your primary relationship.

Instead of using your imagination to create an illusory relationship, you can use fantasy as a vehicle for play. Fantasy can help you and your partner to get clear about your respective feelings or patterns that might otherwise be uncomfortable to communicate about. Role playing, each acting out the partner's persona as you experience it, is useful as a means of seeing yourself through your partner's eyes. This can bring a real change or breakthrough of issues that talking about may have confused.

By making your relationships more spiritual, being aware of and verbalizing your feelings and needs, you can avoid other traps too. For example, you might use your ability to find goodness and beauty in others as a convenient excuse to flirt with them, causing your partner to become jealous. This pattern can be redirected to healthy, open friendships that threaten nobody. Becoming emotionally dependent on your partner can be eliminated.

As a Pisces, your watery nature can render you so sensitive and vulnerable that you become a psychic sponge. This can cause you to have difficulty figuring out where you stop and other people begin. By working on the inner planes, spiritually and psychologically, you can start to see yourself clearly. You can then use your openness as a vehicle for embracing life in a more joyful, all-encompassing way. Sharing yourself and your love with others in safe, appropriate ways serve to bring harmony to your relationships and fulfillment to you.

THE RULING PLANETS

Like Scorpio and Aquarius, Pisces has co-rulers: Jupiter (♃), its traditional ruler, and Neptune (♆), its modern ruler. For each of these three signs, learning to integrate the energies of their rulers is a different experience. For Scorpio, it's learning how to combine planets of a similar nature that function at different levels, with Pluto functioning as a higher octave of Mars. In some ways, Aquarius' job is harder. It has to combine influences that are almost diametrically different; Saturn, the conservative planet of form, and Uranus, the progressive planet of change. Pisces' problem is not as obvious as that of Scorpio, but is more harmonious than that of Aquarius. Jupiter and Neptune have differences, but are united by a significant theme: both represent forces that further the development of higher consciousness.

The rulership of Jupiter implies that Pisces can be very independent. Although Aries, Sagittarius and Aquarius are generally considered the most freedom-oriented signs, Pisces also appreciates its autonomy when it feels the influence of Jupiter. This independence can manifest in many ways, but one area in which Pisces especially feels the need to be free is spiritually. This can manifest through the feeling and expression of joy and optimism, while being careful to avoid the Jupiterian traps of abundant idealism or excessive expectation. Spiritual freedom can also be expressed by being of service to others or by pursuing educational goals. Like Jupiter's other sign, Sagittarius, Pisces is oriented toward community service. This can manifest in such activities as a neighborhood center, Big Brother or Sister programs or volunteer work within institutions like hospitals or prisons. Pisces can also be comfortable as an educator in many different systems, from public schools to Sunday schools. Here they can function as philosophers and theoreticians, whether in developing new modalities of classroom instruction, or by clarifying a theological vision. The rulership of Jupiter also suggests a strong affinity for travel. Pisces seeks the opportunity to develop a cross-cultural perspective to more completely understand the nature of life.

The glyph of Neptune is indicative of what it represents. The semi-circles of the subconscious mind are elevated above the material plane, indicating matter dropping away from the soul or the formless rising above the form. It also suggests that spiritual growth can take place on the material plane by functioning in a grounded, yet conscious way. Neptune was discovered in 1846, the first year that ether was used for surgery and the first year that gas was used for lighting. Neptune has been associated with chemicals, drugs and petroleum products.

In the context of human experience, Neptune is the energy that opens awareness to the subconscious mind and the Spiritual

Being. Getting in touch with the subconscious mind can be accomplished through monitoring the psychological process with such tools as psychotherapy, hypnotherapy or paying attention to dreams. Any of these can help you become more aware of your underlying feelings and motivations. Therapy could be verbal. Forms of verbal therapy could be traditional or contemporary and experimental. Massage can also be used as a valid form of therapy. There are many different schools and techniques of massage therapy as well. For emotional release, the more physically intense the more therapeutic.

Hypnotherapy is also a Neptunian form of healing and a technique for getting in touch with, even exerting control over the subconscious mind. Bypassing the logical mind, you have the opportunity to experience in a conscious way what your underlying thoughts and feelings are that may be holding you back. Past life regression is a form of hypnotherapy that enables you to extend your data bank of experiences further back than even early childhood so you may explore the origins of patterns that you feel stuck in.

Dreams can also serve as a doorway to get in contact with feelings or to see with a clearer perspective what the importance of a particular part of your life is. Taking the time to write dreams down is another way to decode the subconscious and learn to work with the energy of Neptune.

Exploring and expanding your Higher Spiritual Being is more subtle and, in the West, less accepted. One of the best vehicles to do this is meditation. In the Far East, meditation has been known about and practiced for thousands of years. In some countries, such as India and Tibet, meditation and other forms of spiritual ceremony are the cornerstone of life for much of the population. Meditation techniques are taught in such disparate traditions as Buddhism, Hinduism and Islam. In Buddhism alone there are a variety of meditation techniques, each designed and oriented toward a different function. There is also an extensive variety of forms of yoga, any of which can be, and are, practiced by devotees of religions from Catholicism to Judaism and from Buddhism to Hinduism. Yoga is not a religion, although certain masters and teachers of it espouse a philosophy. Yoga means union. It is a series of techniques that are so precise as to be scientific. These techniques produce noticeable changes in your body, mind and soul. Any form of meditation, if practiced with dedication, concentration and openness, will help you to make direct contact with your Higher Being, thereby utilizing Neptune's influence in a sublime and supportive way.

You can also access Neptune by activating your creative imagination. Imagination is comprised of two root words: image and nation. Reverse their order, and Neptune can open your mind to a brand new realm, a nation of images from which you can draw limitless creative ideas. Use your imagination to help you to notice visions or sounds of beauty for yourself and others to enjoy. Use the images as a vehicle to enhance your psychic sensitivity through which you can more clearly perceive and understand other people and the world around you.

However you choose to tap into Neptunian consciousness, its energy is quite subtle. It's as if we're all blocked from even being aware of these inner realms by a veil, as hidden from us as the information it conceals. There are two ways of relating to Neptune: to allow the veil to remain or work to remove it. If you are not taking advantage of at least one of the aforementioned tools, Neptune will continue to be veiled and will manifest in your life unconsciously. When Neptune is veiled, it manifests as the energy of illusion and fantasy. It lacks the means to discriminate between where individual illusion stops and where the reality that everyone else relates to begins. This can lead to unrealistic expectations of yourself and others. You could believe that what you want is achievable and fulfilling when it's not. You could assume that who you think you are is the same person that others perceive you to be when that may not be the case at all. Ultimately these are patterns of self-deception and lead to undermining yourself by being self-critical and self-denigrating. A veiled Neptune can prevent you from seeing yourself or what will truly be fulfilling to you with clear perspective. Even if you get glimpses of your true self from time to time you may feel as if you don't deserve to be that person. You may fool yourself into believing that what you have is what you really want. Escapism through abuse of drugs and alcohol, extensive watching of television or withdrawing into fiction and fantasy are all expressions and byproducts of the veil of Neptune being allowed to remain in place. In any of these scenarios, you are left in a state of vagueness, confusion and fog. Your activities in the house of Neptune's placement will be nebulous and without solid form. As you express the energy from your veiled Neptune, others could accuse you of being evasive even if you think you are being clear.

As you work with these practices to lift the veil, you become familiar with yourself on the inner planes. You make friends with all the influences that could otherwise function as inner-demons, undermining your health and well-being. Your Higher Being flowers with ever-present joy and peace. Your psychic ability starts to develop. In this context, Neptune functions as a higher octave of Venus. It can bring relationships to a higher realm of devotion and unconditional love. It can help facilitate creative inspiration, especially through music. Often, people who are attracted to music as musicians also understand and function well in areas of higher mathematics, another aspect of Neptune.

The most exciting, and significant, function of Neptune is to help you connect in a clear and consciousness way with that which is greater than you are. Neptune teaches faith. Not just hoping or wishing that something is true, but a deep, abiding certainty about life. It's a different type of perception, one that looks through and beyond the three dimensional limits of the physical universe, and sees the underlying unity of all things. Neptune offers the energy to surrender to the omnipresent current of life. By consciously and willingly swimming in that current your will and individual self merge with the Self of Oneness of which we are all a part.

The Bhagavad-Gita offers a wonderful story that depicts the Neptunian experience. The Gita is an ancient Hindu text that is comparable in that culture to the Bible in the West. It is said to contain all of the most important spiritual precepts that must be known and practiced to develop spiritually and evolve. It can be read and interpreted on several different levels. On one level, it depicts a kingdom in India in which the king has recently died and there are two factions vying for the throne. On one side is the late king's brother with his supporters and friends. On the other side are the late king's sons with their supporters and friends. One of the sons is named Arjuna. As the two sides prepare to do battle, Arjuna sits in soliloquy wondering what the proper course of action is. He is afraid of having to do battle with his teachers, with people he has known his whole life, people who used to be his friends. He is afraid that fighting against these people will create negative karma and cause his ancestors to look upon him with ill favor. Here he is, however, facing the battle. Can he be a coward? Does he really want to run away and let down his brothers and friends? While he is thinking out loud in this fashion, his charioteer comes to him. In those days, the noblemen rode in chariots, protected by lower-caste drivers. Arjuna thought his charioteer was his cousin, when in fact it was Lord Krishna, an incarnation of Divine Spirit. Upon hearing Arjuna's dilemma, Lord Krishna approached the young man and eased his confusion by saying, "Arjuna you were born into the warrior caste. It is your karma to fight and do battle. It is your karma at this time, to do battle with the side that opposes you. You would create negative karma if you did not respond to this challenge. That is when the ancestors would look with ill favor upon you. To go into battle and do the best that you can, even under trying and confusing circumstances is the highest option for you to take." Arjuna liked this line of reasoning since it helped resolve his dilemma. However, because he thought these words came from someone he considered inferior, he was unsure if they were true, and if they were, should he listen? To check out the source, Arjuna demanded that the slave (Krishna) tell him why he was so sure. At that point, Krishna lifts the veil of illusion from Arjuna's eyes and Arjuna is literally thrown out the back of the chariot as all kinds of sounds, visions and images come cascading through his consciousness.

Aldous Huxley has called the brain a reducing chamber because it filters out all the data that cannot be understood, or that does not in some way pertain to an individual's life. When Neptune's veil is lifted, however, especially if suddenly or unexpectedly, the consequences can be overwhelming. There is no way to understand what is taking place, let alone control it or shut it down. Arjuna begged Krishna to stop the nightmare, which he did by replacing the veil of illusion over Arjuna's eyes. But he had seen. He had realized and understood the wisdom and power of his charioteer's words and consequently the true power, nature and intention of the universe.

This story illustrates the nature of Neptune in two ways. Most obviously is the necessity of lifting the veil of illusion in a gradual manner. Second, and perhaps more important, is that beyond the world that we call reality, the three dimensional world of form, the realm of Saturn, is something so vast that it defies description. It is so grand that it cannot be comprehended. It is the dimension of Oneness and Truth and shows that this plane that appears to be solid is, in fact, the illusion. Beyond this world exists one beyond space and time and which embraces the Totality of Existence. This is the place that Neptune can impel you to become aware of, if you take the time to lift its veil. Like Arjuna when Krishna ripped his veil away, you develop the ability to perceive all facets of reality simultaneously. To look God in the face with love and understanding, you realize the endless love, compassion and acceptance from the Divine Source of Light present in your life at all times. Krishna counsels Arjuna that "pleasure and pain, gain and loss, victory and defeat are the same." Life is neutral; we make of it what we will. The natal chart is the basic framework within which to create the content of experience. It is a personal map to help guide each person to greater awareness of the nature of reality and the potential of life. Sometimes when you are in a natural environment, the veil might lift for a moment. You recognize this when you feel the tides of the ocean rise and fall in your body, when you blend with the scent of the flowers or your body sways in the wind with the trees. Nature, the Goddess/Divine Mother, is a universal pass key that can lift Neptune's veil of illusion.

When Neptune is retrograde, there is usually a tendency to perceive all things in terms of their deepest significance. If you have Neptune retrograde in your natal chart, you have a hot line to God. You have a very personal sense of religion and can make direct contact with Spirit. This may be in a conscious and formal manner, such as through prayer, affirmation or meditation. It could be something unique that puts you into immediate contact with that which is greater than you are. Activities like dancing, wind surfing or gardening can be useful vehicles having direct communion. With Neptune retrograde you have little need for organized religion. The scriptures and dogmas of traditional religion can stifle your spiritual progress.

A problem with Neptune retrograde is similar to that of Jupiter retrograde in that everything tends to be experienced in its highest or most spiritual form, to the point where you can become idealistic and ungrounded. You tend to confuse your personal needs with your ideals for humanity. You may have difficulty separating your fantasy about someone from who that person really is. This can create a *naiveté* or vulnerability in social situations if you open yourself up too much to people who don't warrant that trust. You become a well-intended dreamer for whom nothing of substance ever materializes.

With Neptune retrograde, you need to learn discrimination. Your intentions in relating to others can be good, but you have a tendency to not be in touch enough with your own personal reality and the needs and feelings that accompany it. Strive to balance your active and evolving spiritual awareness with a grounded connection with yourself and realistic perceptions and expectations of others.

If you allow Neptune to remain veiled, its house placement can indicate where your life has no form. You could relate to that area with little or no confidence. If you are developing your inner life, the house placement of Neptune indicates the area of life where spiritual inspiration is likely to come. If Neptune is in your first house of self, your identity or self-concept could be vague. You could see yourself as a savior of some kind without realizing it. You could lack self-confidence and be susceptible to self-undermining habits that involve the excessive use of drugs or alcohol. You can change those patterns by working to lift the veil in which case your ability to identify with your Higher Being provides you with a clear, positive self-image. You can still be empathetic, humanitarian and service-oriented, but you are realistic about what you can and cannot do.

Neptune in the second suggests feeling confused about how to generate money and feeling undeserving of comfort and security. Or you may buy into the illusion that possession of material objects can lead to fulfillment. By doing your inner work you develop faith and intuition as tools to build a stable, comfortable life. Service, healing and the arts are all viable ways of making your living. You can also use affirmations of faith and reliance on the law of prosperity to help generate what you need on the material plane. Experiencing the fulfillment of these affirmations can provide further spiritual inspiration.

Neptune in the third can bring spiritual inspiration in spontaneous ways. Pay attention to what is happening around you at all times. Sometimes you will derive a message of sublime significance, that can have deep meaning and lasting importance in your life. The source of that information isn't necessarily someone you know well, or even someone you consider educated, wise or evolved. He or she is merely being a channel for you. Without developing your intuition, however, you could be confused in your thinking and evasive or vague in your communication with others.

Neptune in the fourth house can bring spiritual inspiration from family members, or from within your home itself, sometimes by creating a sacred time and space for daily renewal and lifting of the veil. Not taking the time to lift the veil, however, can create confusion in your personal life ranging from childhood experience to present time family needs and patterns. There could have been drug or alcohol abuse in your family or simply no structure and discipline in your home life. You could address those experiences by idealizing who your family was and what actually took place. By doing your inner work you build the internal strength even as you allow yourself to see the truth of your past in an unadulterated way. This also clears a path for being honest with yourself and developing insights into others with whom you live in present time.

Neptune in the fifth offers inspiration through your own creative process and through children. You can bring the humanitarian quality of Neptune into your child-oriented experiences by adopting a child or feeling truly devoted to a step-child. Music, photography, dance, poetry and the theater could provide stimulating outlet for your creative imagination. If Neptune is still veiled in your life, however, you could fail to see your creative tools at all. You might undermine yourself by assuming that your efforts aren't good enough or worthy of being exposed to others.

The sixth is the house of service work and health. Neptune in the sixth implies being drawn to the health field. Through your work you can experience a feeling of being spiritual uplifted which can in turn provide a deep sense of devotion to the work itself. To maintain your own health requires a balance of inner work, to keep your emotional and psychological energies clear and flowing, and physical activity to stay grounded. Without the inner work you could be unsure of what to do as well as your abilities to fulfill the job description. Your own health could suffer as you could be plagued by allergies, be sensitive to certain drugs or experience illnesses that are psychogenic in origin.

Neptune in the seventh house can bring inspiration through a partnership, either personal or between you and a spiritual teacher. You could be devoted and unconditional in your love of that individual. If Neptune is veiled in your life, however, you could idealize the partner and romanticize the relationship. You see the person as you fantasize or project them to be rather than as they truly are. You could be attracted to someone whom you feel compelled to heal or save in some way. If you are doing the inner work, you could still be attracted to someone as a partner who is disabled in some way, but you would see them and experience the relationship with realistic expectations.

In the eighth, Neptune brings wisdom through intimate relationships and through such sexual practices as tantra yoga. You could also feel inspired by a thorough scientific penetration into the universal laws of life. You could enjoy spiritual ceremonies or rituals as ways of getting more deeply connected to life. If Neptune is veiled, however, you can get lost in sexual fantasies about people whom you may not even know or be relating to. You could also tend to drift off into illusory expectations or assumptions about life and your place in it.

The ninth is the house of expansion. If you have Neptune there, and you are working to lift the veil, travel, reading or the study of spiritual treatises will uplift. You could be attracted to mathematics, accounting, psychology, pharmacology, chemistry or one of the fine arts. Your dream life is filled with clarifying and uplifting symbols and images. You could be drawn to and find some benefit in psychedelic drugs as vehicles for self-awareness and consciousness development. Spiritually you could be attracted to charismatic paths that enable you to connect directly with Spirit. If you are not working to lift the veil, however, you could be confused about what to study and undermine yourself by not believing you are intelligent enough to do the work. You could also be vague about your spiritual path and unclear about your philosophy of life. You might be so idealistic about your own behavior that you are continually criticizing yourself for failing to live up to your own expectations without realizing how unrealistic they might be.

Neptune in the tenth house of occupation impels you to be serviceful to others, especially by working in health care or the arts. These activities can also facilitate developing your own higher awareness. If you are not working to lift Neptune's veil, however, you could be confused about what you want to do. You could chase fantasy careers that are not right for you or that will not bring fulfillment. In either case you can become discouraged and disillusioned in the professional area of life if this pattern becomes chronic.

The eleventh is the house of friends, groups and organizations. If you have Neptune in your eleventh house and you are working consciously to lift its veil, you will find help in doing so from individual friends or groups such as a meditation group, a dream workshop or a twelve step group. If you are not doing the inner work, however, you will attract people who drain and take advantage of you, people who are emotionally disturbed or psychically manipulative. You will allow yourself to become involved with these people out of a sense of pity for them, but will come to discover that their presence in your life is toxic. You tend to be devoted and unconditionally supportive to your friends, so make sure you choose those who can relate to you in the same way.

In the twelfth house, Neptune inspires through the act of meditation itself. Look within, find your path and go forward. Dreams, hypnotherapy, spiritual retreats and certain forms of psychic development training can prove beneficial in the quest for higher consciousness. You are empathetic, compassionate and humanitarian. Your creative imagination is also strong and clear, especially if you are using the arts as another vehicle for inner development. The only difficulty that Neptune in the twelfth house can bring, if the inner work is not being done, is an overactive imagination. This can keep you stuck in realms of fantasy and cause you to periodically drift off in a private reverie or daydream when you should be focusing on something external.

THE TWELFTH HOUSE

The area of life associated with Pisces is the twelfth house. British astrologer Vivian Robson has called this area of life "the dust bin of the zodiac." He puts everything that doesn't fit anywhere else in here. Although that concept is as misleading as it is demeaning, the twelfth house is nevertheless complex and subtle.

The traditional definitions of the twelfth house contain such threatening terms as karmic debts, secret enemies and situations over which one has no control. Any of these conditions could manifest if you have planets in your natal twelfth house, but not necessarily in an undermining or overwhelming way. It's not a requirement of this house that any of them will be your experience at all. The determining factors were probably decided in the first few weeks or months or your life.

The twelfth house is the area of life that the planets enter upon ascending and moving above the horizon in the East. Spiritual masters maintain that energy from the East has the greatest impact on consciousness and behavior. Planets in the twelfth house, therefore, can actually be vehicles for connecting you with your Higher Being. In that sense, those planets can suggest exalted gifts and talents, even genius potential. It's notable that in horoscopes of people who are well known in the arts, sometimes considered visionaries who take their field to a new level, a high percentage have a cluster of planets in their twelfth house.

When an infant arrives in a body and on the planet, there is a lot going on. Just getting used to a body is a major concern. Trying to figure out where you are, what is going on around you and what is expected from others can occupy most of your time and energy. If you have energy in your twelfth house, that task is easier. You at least have the opportunity to immediately recognize a part of yourself. You know a major part of who you are, what you are here to do and some primary gifts that you have to do it with. Why, then, does the twelfth house traditionally have such a negative connotation?

Most people are not raised by conscious parents. Our civilization has not evolved in a way that recognizes and supports the uniqueness and primacy of the individual entity. We are parented in a way that coerces us to fit in. Conditional patterns of love manipulate the individual into becoming who our parents want us to be as a child, and who society wants as a new member. For people with twelfth house energy, a very early childhood trauma is experienced as they realize they must make a decision. Do they maintain contact with who they really are and act out that truth, thereby running the risk of being rejected by their parents and sent back to the void? Or do they conform to their parents' expectations, ensuring their survival, but at the price of their gifts? Most people make the latter choice. They don't just abandon their tools and talents, however, they put them away in a safe place, where no one else can use or destroy them, where they will remain until the entity can return and reclaim them. They lock them up in the vault of the subconscious mind. Unfortunately, because this decision, is made in a pre-conscious state of early infancy, the energy gets lost, or at least forgotten about. You lose touch with that part of yourself, as if it's not even there. Since you can't express or use what isn't there, it can't possibly affect anybody else. You may be unclear about the energy and your manifestation of it, but those around you are not so confused.

Other people do feel the impact of your words and actions, and will respond accordingly. That response may baffle you, because you are not in touch with your own actions. They are emanating from your subconscious mind and hidden from you, but obvious to others, nonetheless. Unconscious words or actions can alienate others without your being aware of your part in the dynamic. These are your secret enemies, people whom you have attacked unknowingly and who are merely fighting back or defending themselves. From your point of view, no initial attack may have even taken place.

As you begin to become aware of this pattern you can feel helpless, as if you can't control your energy or your relation-ships; thus the association of the twelfth as the house of situations over which you feel no control. If the unconscious acting out persists, especially to an extreme degree or if motivated by unclear intention, you cause great harm to others or yourself. In the former case, you may have to be punished and incarcerated, in the latter, hospitalized. Therefore the twelfth is called the house of self-undoing.

If these kinds of experiences continue, your feelings of helplessness and hopelessness can impel you to want to escape from the syndrome. You may self-medicate, using drugs or alcohol to numb the pain, to eliminate the confusion, to tell yourself that everything is okay. Street drugs or by prescription, bar hopping or drinking alone, you are merely prolonging the pattern and sustaining the agony. This pattern also explains the tendency for twelfth house experience to generate lack of self-confidence. What's the way out? Go back to the vault, rediscover the hidden energies, and liberate them through consciousness to be used in clear and positive contexts. Unless or until that is done, the karma or action of unawareness continues and the karmic debts mount. To pay off the debts means to get in clear and conscious contact with each and every planetary energy in your twelfth house and manifest it consciously. To return to the vault means to work on yourself, to learn your way around the inner planes, to implement the tools of the twelfth house, to activate those parts of yourself that have been hidden from you.

If you were able to incarnate in a family of conscious, self-aware beings, or if you have been working to actualize yourself and are functioning as a conscious parent for your children the pattern is quite different. Awareness of the gifts was never lost in the first place. You, or your children, remain in contact with attributes that others must spend years recovering. Recovery can take place through psychotherapy or hypnotherapy or other techniques of bypassing your rational, critical mind and going to the source of awareness. Tapping into your creative imagination and manifesting the resulting inspiration can also help retrieve your misplaced tools. It's as if the techniques of reconnection and that to which you are re-bonding are one and the same.

Perhaps the best way of actualizing your twelfth house energy is by activating and liberating your higher spiritual being. The twelfth is the house of the subconscious mind until you mine its contents. It then becomes the house of the superconscious mind, the doorway through which we can have access to limitless wisdom and understanding. To take fullest advantage of that potential, allow yourself quality time alone on a daily basis. Writing down your dreams helps to clarify your psyche. Doing something creative each day helps to liberate your own gifts of inspiration, but meditation can help you to become intimately familiar with the Creative Source of Life itself and help you to know yourself as a being of limitless creative potential.

You can use that realization to discover your calling, or higher purpose. With significant energy in the twelfth house, it can take the form of the arts, healing or spiritual service. Healing in a twelfth house context can take the form of being oriented toward the psyche or the emotional body. You could work in prisons, hospitals or other facilities in which others who have no or limited control over themselves are kept. This is the same idea as before, but experienced from an entirely different perspective. Spiritual service can also take the form of volunteer work. Hospice work can be such a path.

As you become more consciously aware of and consistently use your twelfth house energy, the karmic debts are paid off. The only real debt was the need to develop the awareness of the energy and consciously choose how to manifest it in a new way. With the Sun in the twelfth house, the debt is to your own sense of self-awareness and self-love. The Moon in the twelfth suggests working through patterns of victimization or persecution by becoming more conscious in the eternal present about the subtle, emotional or psychic interaction between yourself and others. There could also have been childhood conditioning from your relationship to your mother that needs to be addressed. These could be having been literally left by her, having had to deal with some illness or disability she suffered, or having felt criticized and undermined by her when you were a child. Mercury in the twelfth requires that you be more conscious of your thoughts and to be more responsible in communicating them, being careful to avoid excessive criticism or analysis of yourself and others. Venus in the twelfth house helps to burn off relationship karma by becoming clearer about what you want and need in relationship. If used consciously it can enable you to learn how to go about getting what you want. In an unconscious expression it can serve to undermine you from getting it, starting with making a wrong choice of partner and possibly leading to or including hidden affairs or secret relationships.

Mars implies the need to get in touch with anger, learning what it feels like and how to discharge it in safe, appropriate ways. Try to become more aware of how your actions affect others. Mars in the twelfth can tend to express misplaced aggression in which you vent your anger at the wrong person or for the wrong reason or in an unacceptable way.

Mars in the twelfth also suggests the need to become more consciously in touch with your sexuality. Who and what turns you on? How to realistically pursue that relationship to a point of becoming sexual? Unconsciously, Mars in the twelfth can keep you stuck in sexual isolation or sexual fantasy.

Jupiter in the twelfth brings many opportunities to expand your mind in new directions and through new dimensions. Travel or being part of a spiritual community could be particularly beneficial. Saturn counsels the need for a greater sense of your own power to overcome vague fears and feelings of being out of control. Learn to be focused on establishing and enforcing limits and boundaries. Saturn in the twelfth enables you to profit from spiritual discipline by providing the dedication to do it and the concentration to benefit from it.

The trans-Saturnian planets in the twelfth house all bring specific tools to open your higher mind and develop your relationship to the superconscious. With Uranus in the twelfth you would enjoy meeting with like-minded friends to discuss or experience various kinds of esoterica that you all find inspiring. Neptune is at home here. It would help you to take advantage of an active dream life and your creative inspiration. Meditation (which helps develop a highly active and accurate intuitive mind) or service work will also serve to stimulate the higher octaves of consciousness. Pluto in the twelfth needs to learn how to take advantage of its keen depth of insight. It is often able to understand someone's motivations. To liberate yourself from Pluto karma here, however, means to learn about and accept your own motivations. You can always release and let go of what you don't like. You are an emotionally intense person, so learn how to express what you feel. Pluto in the twelfth house can lead to periodic emotional explosions when unreleased feelings finally boil over. You may have a fear of that, which is what impels you to keep the lid on emotional expression in the first place. In the long run it is that lid, the unwillingness to express your deepest feelings and passions that causes the explosion.

As the eleventh house deals with collective consciousness, the twelfth house deals with the collective subconscious; the ability to tap into the archetypal experiences or images that relate to the universal psyche. Planets in the twelfth house are gifts that can enable you to identify with Oneness and to learn from the highest levels and the highest teachers accessible.

PISCES AND THE BODY

Anatomically, Pisces rules the lymphatic system, the body's first line of defense against bacteria and viruses. If there is high toxicity in the body or if fighting an infection, the lymph glands swell. With a lot of Pisces energy, or if Pisces is your ascending sign or on the cusp of the sixth house (health), your lymph glands tend to be more sensitive to physical invasion, just as the Pisces nat . . . . o be sensitive to psychic or emotional invasion.

Pisces a' . . .ules the duodenum, which connects the stomach to the small intestine. This is a part of the body where ulcers tend to form. Ulcers can be caused by different factors. One is excessive and persistent worry especially if stimulated by a diet that is improper and unhealthy.

Pisces rules the feet. This could suggest anything from deformed feet to ones that give you trouble. However, it could also indicate a tendency to take good care of your feet. You might be particular about the type of shoe that you wear, being more concerned with fit than style. Rubbing your feet or getting reflexology treatments may be ways of providing care for your feet. The feet also ground you. Pisces can be ungrounded, so by paying attention to your feet you can counteract that tendency. Walking as an exercise, wearing soft soled shoes or being barefooted can also provide greater opportunity for grounding.

Neptune rules the pineal gland. The pineal gland is found in the frontal area of the brain, above and between the eyes. It is part of the endocrine system and as such it is the physical manifestation of the sixth *chakra* or the third eye. This is the *chakra* that becomes activated as you dedicate more time and energy to developing your spiritual awareness. The French philosopher Rene Descartes called the pineal gland "the seat of the soul." It is the doorway to universal consciousness. To become more focused on the sixth level through meditation, is to expand your intuition and be more tuned to higher inspiration. The pineal gland becomes more activated in adolescence, an indication that this is a time when you have a natural flow of energy that can help you develop spiritually and intuitively.

Neptune can also indicate psychogenic disorders; physical problems that are mental or emotional in origin. To treat the body only, without dealing with the underlying internal roots, is to affect only half a cure or none at all. Psychogenic illness can also manifest as alcoholism, drug addiction, hallucinations or diseases that are obscure or hard to diagnose. These syndromes can often be resolved through psychotherapy, hypnotherapy or psychic or shamanic healing.

CONCLUSIONS

Pisces is the final sign of the zodiac. It offers an experience of completion, but also one of reintegration. When Pisces is significant in your natal chart it facilitates the development of the most extensive perspective on the nature of life. Each year as Pisces fades into Aries, the sign of new beginnings, your life can recommence in a new way with fresh awareness and renewed inspiration.

Pisces is the third of the water signs. The first, Cancer, promotes emotional and intuitive experience from the most internal and personal point of view. As a cardinal sign, its experience is immediate and in flux. The second, Scorpio, is more oriented toward depth of personal feeling within the context of relationship. This could be a relationship to life as a whole or within an intimate partnership. As a fixed sign, Scorpio has great depth of passion, but can also get stuck in certain internal states or patterns. Pisces, the mutable member of this triad, is the most amorphous and tends to be less restricted in scope than either Cancer or Scorpio. Although its emotional experience may be less focused than Cancer, less intense than Scorpio and less self-aware than either, it has the greatest range of response. It is able to resonate with and understand the inner world of others. If Cancer represents personal emotional experience and Scorpio is the transformation of that experience, Pisces offers the results of that transformation.

Pisces is the fourth of the mutable signs, each of which contributes a type of service to the world. The first is Gemini, which serves through networking, gathering information and communicating in spontaneous ways. Its opposite sign, Sagittarius, combines the bits of data into concepts, thought-forms and systems that can be learned and exchanged in more formal ways by larger numbers of people. Opposite Pisces is Virgo. The Virgo-Pisces axis makes its contribution by facilitating integration and transition. Virgo facilitates the process of moving from the inner world and the personal life out into the realm of relationship to others and into experience in the larger world. Virgo uses a detail-oriented, organized, logical approach to assimilation of information and integration of that material into the practical. Pisces reverses that process, relying more on intuitive understanding to guide the direction of life. It is the experience of surrendering to the flow of energy in the most expansive context possible. From its own internal life and process, Pisces discovers how to take what it has learned into open interaction with the world. What Pisces can learn from Virgo is how to discern fact from fantasy, reality from idealism and perception from projection. Through this discriminative process, Pisces can learn when it is appropriate to remain within and when and how it is more important to integrate itself back into the social and physical world. Through this process of selection, the Piscean experience can help you to realize all the ways that your experience and your sense of self is similar to that of all other people. This realization helps to validate the premise that we all have a lot more in common than we have differences. It helps us to relate to others with compassion and empathy. Pisces stimulates the opportunity to serve your Higher Being, to grow beyond identification with the physical and to reunite in Oneness with Spirit.

The first eleven signs of the zodiac have a clear sense of themselves. Part of their journey is to look beyond self and learn that there is another Self which is greater than any individual self and which permeates and unites all things. From a spiritual point of view the first eleven signs need to learn to identify that force and learn how to identify with it. Pisces, the twelfth and final sign, has the opposite task. Pisces begins with the realization of the Oneness but must learn how to define and identify itself as a separate entity. As a Pisces you must learn where you stop and everyone else begins. Otherwise you could have a tendency to dissolve the ego-self and merge with whatever is around you. There is no attachment to who you have been previously. However, this could also enable you to be more in the eternal present and more aware of the ever-present creative force. That's certainly where the action of life is taking place. That which was already created lacks the same sense of presence and life. The potential difficulty with this perspective is that you can be so open as to be unnecessarily idealistic and vulnerable. If this is a problem for you, create frequent periods of isolation within which to wring out your psychic sponge. Take the time to purify your water, your internal environment.

As suggested by your totem—the two fish swimming in opposite directions, or around in circles—this can be a difficult task. The fish symbolize the double bodied nature of Pisces. Each of the fish represents a different mode of action and can be defined as the "upstream Pisces" and the "downstream Pisces." The downstream Pisces seeks to flow with the current of the river of life and eventually merge with the cosmic sea in consciousness of Self. In this mode you are centered and self-loving, maintaining an actively growing inner life through self-analysis. This type of Pisces is independent, a world traveler, someone who seeks a cross cultural perspective on life. This is Pisces the compassionate humanitarian and the empathetic healer. The downstream Pisces can identify with the Boddhisatva, who refuses the reward of personal liberation until all beings have been liberated.

The downstream Pisces can also manifest as the sign of the creative imagination which serves the world by bringing more beauty into it. The artist and the spiritual seeker can combine in forms of creative meditation such as dance, movement or *Tai Chi*, a soft and flowing martial art.

When, as a Pisces, you are swimming upstream you are fighting the current of the river of life, and are in an uncentered, unself-loving pattern. Here you can get caught in whirlpools of self-pity, self-criticism and self-destruction. Lacking self-confidence, feeling inadequate, overwhelmed, lost, or confused by life you can become easily influenced by external factors. Sometimes this dependency can be on other people, sometimes on self-destructive patterns such as alcoholism, drug abuse, or excesses of sleeping, eating or isolation. The upstream Pisces tend to wrap themselves in fantasy, illusion and to be plagued by self-deception and delusion.

Pisces is the mystic and the monk of the zodiac. As a Pisces you both need and feel comfortable in isolation. Being alone affords you the freedom to protect yourself from the harshness of the outer world, even as it can allow you to take maximum advantage of your inner world. For the past two thousand years, humanity has been experiencing the Piscean Age. During this period an exaggerated importance has been placed on aloneness. We have honored aloneness and created social institutions that insist on it. We separate God from humanity and humanity from Nature. We separate the nuclear family from the tribe and the individual from the family. We separate religion in the form of the Church from daily life and monastics from the community. Isolation has come to mean alienation. What was once a valuable way to grow has become a way of being limited, a way of establishing authoritarian hierarchies of haves and have-nots supported by a global value system that prioritizes profit over people, and consumerism over conservation.

The Piscean Age is ending. The dawn of the Aquarian Age, the Age of Humanity, is at hand. It's time for the mystics and the monks among us to descend from their mountains and ivory towers and join in the marketplace of humanity. The time has come to share mystical attunement, the joy of being, and insightful wisdom with the world through everyday, spontaneous interaction. It is also time for our collective humanity to evolve in such a way as to value individual experience and to provide reassurance and reinforcement that will allow us all to feel accepted and to function in day to day society.

The experience of mutable water is amorphous and can clearly manifest in limitless ways. Expressions of the Piscean archetype can be as different as the self-less saint is from the self-destructive drug addict, and as the self-inspired artist is to the self-deceiving psychopath. These are all members of the same family, all possible manifestations of this gentle sign. What they all share is a drive to transcend the self, to grow beyond the limits of self-imposed ego identification. In a healthy being, this manifests through dissolving attachments to the material world of form and change. You learn to look beyond identifying with your body, your class, your race or your gender. The key to this process is faith. Not wishing or hoping that there is something greater than we are. Faith means having absolute confidence in the connection between all things, knowing that that which is inside you is mirrored by what is outside. You see and feel that all of life is various facets of the same thing reflecting itself. What Pisces contributes to the human experience is the desire and ability to evolve, subtly and slowly, by merging with Spirit and feeling and knowing the Oneness of all Life.

THE MAKER'S DOZEN

The twelve signs of the zodiac are archetypes of human experience. They help us to be objectively aware of our attitudes and behaviors, our drives and motivations. Each individual natal horoscope is a picture that comprises many of those archetypes. All ten planets and some combination of signs and houses forge the road map that represents the fundamental patterns of options and potentials, possibilities and probabilities available to each person. To understand this system, to speak its language and to work with its variables is to become clearer about who you are. It's also possible, however, to get lost in the map. You can be limited by your present level of awareness and fail to penetrate the essential truth of your chart to the point that it helps you to expand your perspective and to become more self-actualized. You can become limited by the distinctions between yourself and others and fail to notice the similarities. You can even become so tantalized by the chart itself that you become trapped in the world of polarity and relativity. The Vedic scriptures claim that Truth and Ultimate Reality is unindividuated Spirit. When Spirit becomes form, it creates a material manifestation through the illusion of duality called *Maya*. You become totally focused on the day/night, male/female, birth/death combinations and fail to transcend your awareness by perceiving the Unity behind these apparent differences. When awareness is limited to only that which is perceivable through the senses you have become tricked into thinking that the illusion is real. You identify with many and forsake the One. You are limited to the field of opposites and fail to notice the stadium within which the game is being played.

Life is a clear, radiant endless mirror. From our perspective on the earth, that mirror is shattered into uncountable shards. To discover your true nature implies seeing the self reflected in as many of the pieces as possible. Through that process you can

376	The Maker's Dozen

learn how to reintegrate yourself into the human family, seeing yourself reproduced in varying combinations in all your brothers and sisters. Similarly, you can see how you are expressed through each of the zodiacal archetypes. Some will be more obvious, others barely noticeable at all based on their presence in your natal horoscope. As you become more familiar with all the options you can begin the process of identifying with the Whole of Life, the Oneness that is contained within and represented by all things. This is literally the process of learning who you are. Whether we are in an adolescent phase, in a mid-life transition or just beginning the process of self-discovery, the first question is, "Who am I?" Each sign provides a different answer. Each is a part of the total answer. By learning how to identify with each one, noticing how each is manifesting in your life, where or at what time period, you can use astrology as a method of expanding your consciousness to a point of self-realization.

Instead of asking, "Who am I," make the investigation a series of declarative statements and include keywords from each of the signs. Use all the archetypes in your life in ways that are appropriate and balanced. The statements are affirmations.

I know who I am by:

What I do and how I act (Aries).
What I value and what I have (Taurus).
What I think about and how I communicate (Gemini)
How I feel and how I relate to my home and family
(Cancer).
What I love and how I creatively express myself (Leo).
What I am devoted to and how I serve (Virgo).
How I relate to others and create harmony (Libra).
What I seek to transform and how I do it (Scorpio).
What I understand and my vision for the future
(Sagittarius).
What goals I establish and what I achieve (Capricorn).
The company I keep and the expression of my uniqueness
(Aquarius).
How I relate to all things and the feelings of love, joy and
bliss that flow through me (Pisces).

Seeing yourself in each of these ways prevents the projection of those that you don't like or that you feel uncomfortable with on to other people. You will no longer have the desire to be critical or judgmental of those signs that don't conform to what you think life is. The earth plane is a very special school. We are given endless opportunities to learn about who we really are so that we can eventually graduate and evolve to more exalted states of being. As you are working to integrate the twelve basic archetypes, strive to perceive them as different aspects of the same thing. In order to do so, it may be helpful to meditate on the five divine qualities, love, joy, light, peace and wisdom. As you embrace and embody these states it becomes easier to see yourself manifesting in each of the signs and to see yourself reflected by each person you see.

If you have few planets in fire signs, or if you are called upon to do something that requires courage and self-confidence, focus on the quality of light. Observe sunsets, stare deeply into a fire or notice the light mirrored and waving to you by every leaf of every tree. Light is less dependent upon material form than any other natural manifestation. It is the energy that pervades all substance and is the essence of Life itself. It is the spark that generates and sustains creative manifestation.

If you have little energy in earth signs, or if you are confronted by a situation that requires equanimity and patience, meditate on peace. This is the first divine quality through which your connection to and relationship with Spirit becomes obvious. You can experience peace when you let go of your burdens of worry and fear. It's as if you literally relax into an ocean of constancy and stability. Peace enables you to identify with that which is eternal and unchangeable.

If you have few planets in air signs, or if you are required to look beyond yourself and your previous understanding of things, strive to develop the quality of joy. This is a subtle state that is often overlooked and undervalued in a culture based on Puritan values of hard work and solemnity. Joy is a feeling that quickens the pulse, that enables you to feel full from the inside out, bringing a radiant smile to the face for no apparent reason. Mark Twain said that joy must be shared. When you experience that feeling the most obvious course of action is to be open and interactive with life.

If you have few planets in water signs, or if you are confronted by emotional pain and psychological confusion, meditate on the sublime state of wisdom. This quality unfolds within you as you consistently and actively participate in two experiences. One of these is meditation. By meditating daily you tune into the vibration of Higher Being. You discover an inner directive that impels you to do that which is right and proper for you at all times. Through meditation your intuition about life and your place in it becomes clear. Meditation also helps improve your ability to concentrate. This enables you to develop wisdom through another modality of being: paying attention. Notice everything about where you are and what is going on around you and how you feel about those experiences. To be part of the eternal present, feeling the flow of creative energy manifesting within and through you is to function as a centered person in the ever-changing play of life. From that perspective you acquire subtle understanding about the nature of life and a deep compassion about other people.

To combine, feel and identify with all four of these qualities is to also feel Divine Love flowing around and through you. You transcend the habit of seeing life from the various perspectives of each of the twelve signs and hence you break free from the constraints of illusion producing Maya. No longer bound by duality, you can achieve the highest goal of human experience: to perceive the Unity of Creation from the point of view of the Creator. You grow beyond identifying as a self and realize that the truth of your true Self is as a limitless being of radiant light, peace, joy and wisdom. This is your birthright and the result of striving and response to all challenges. It is the purpose and lesson of life.

BIBLIOGRAPHY

Bolen, Jean Shinoda, *Goddesses in Everywoman,* New York, Harper and Row, 1984.

Bolen, Jean Shinoda, *Gods in Everyman,* New York, Harper and Row, 1989.

Campbell, Joseph, *The Hero With a Thousand Faces,* Princeton, NJ: Princeton University Press, 1949.

Campbell, Joseph, *The Power of Myth,* New York: Doubleday, 1988

Clow, Barbara Hand, *Chiron,* St. Paul, MN: Llewellyn, 1990.

Collin, Rodney, *The Theory of Celestial Influence,* New York: Samuel Weiser, 1973.

Crowley, Aleister, *Astrology,* New York: Samuel Weiser, 1974.

DeVore, Nicholas, *Encyclopedia of Astrology,* New York: Philosophical Library, 1947.

Dobin, Joel C., *The Astrological Secrets of the Hebrew Sages,* New York: Inner Traditions International, Ltd., 1983.

Durant, Will, *Our Oriental Heritage,* New York: Simon & Schuster, 1954.

Durant, Will, *The Life of Greece,* New York: Simon & Schuster, 1939.

Eisler, Riane, *The Chalice and Blade,* San Francisco: Harper & Row, 1987.

George, Demetra, *Asteroid Goddesses,* San Diego, CA: ACS Publications, 1986.

Gleadow, Rubert, *The Origin of the Zodiac,* New York: Castle Books, 1968.

Grant, Michael, *Myths of the Greeks and Romans,* New York: Mentor, 1962.

Greene, Liz, *Saturn,* New York: Samuel Weiser, 1976.

Hackin, J., *Asiatic Mythology,* New York: Crescent Books

Hall, Manley Palmer, *An Encyclopedic Outline of Masonic, Hermetic, Qabbalistic and Rosicrucian Philosophy,* Los Angeles: The Philosophical Research Society, Inc., 1971.

Hand, Robert, *Horoscope Symbols,* Rockport, MA: Para Research, 1981.

Jocelyn, John, *Meditations on the Signs of the Zodiac,* San Francisco: Harper & Row, 1970.

Nauman, Eileen, *The American Book of Nutrition and Medical Astrology,* San Diego, CA: ACS Publishing, 1982.

Oken, Alan, *As Above, So Below,* New York: Bantam Books, 1973.

Rudhyar, Dane, *An Astrological Study of Psychological Complexes and Emotional Problems,* the Netherlands: Servire, 1966.

Smith, William, *Smaller Classical Dictionary,* New York: Dutton, 1958.

Wilhelm, Richard (translator), *The I Ching,,* Princeton, NJ: Princeton University Press, 1950.

Yogananda, Paramahansa, *Autobiography of a Yogi,* Los Angeles: Self-Realization Fellowship, 1946.

ABOUT THE AUTHOR

Rio Olesky earned a BA degree from the University of California at Berkeley in 1969 and an MA degree from San Francisco State University in 1972. He began his study of astrology in 1967 and started a private practice giving astrological readings in 1976. He has an extensive and loyal following in Northern California and has developed an international reputation, with clients throughout the United States, Canada, South America, Europe and Australia.

Since 1977 Rio has taught beginning astrology at Santa Rosa Junior college and an on-going weekly class to intermediate and advanced students. He has lectured at conferences and retreats in California, Oregon and Hawaii.

He has written articles for national magazines as well as a monthly column for local publications. He has been on numerous television and radio talk shows.

The main focus of Rio's life is spiritual, and he has maintained a daily practice of yogic meditation for twenty-five years. He uses astrology in both his personal life and to help his clients expand their potential to the greatest possible degree. His readings are constructed to empower his clients to get in touch with their inherent resources and to apply them to the process of learning their lessons, overcoming their challenges, and creating self-directed behavioral change.

Rio is married, has four children, one grandchild, and lives in Northern California.

READINGS BY RIO OLESKY

Natal Charts

An in-depth analysis of the primary energy patterns and traits available to you throughout your lifetime. Discusses your tools and resources plus the tensions and challenges to be resolved in all areas of life and on many levels of consciousness.

Update Charts

A delineation of energy patterns available to you now and in the future that offer new opportunities for personal growth and development. Specific issues that require choices or decisions in the present are highlighted.

Combination

A reading that combines the most significant features of your natal horoscope with highlights of the patterns of present time.

Compatibility

A method of assessing the strengths and weaknesses of a relationship using two different forms of chart comparison. The first, synastry, involves analyzing the two natal charts to discover what you offer and what you need. The second method, the composite chart, defines how the two of you function as a unit.

Children

This will help you to be more conscious as a parent of your child. It will help you to see in what areas to direct your child and in what areas to be more patient. It helps you and the child to be more well-adjusted and comfortable with his/her own path.

Astrocartography

Put your natal chart on a map. Locate places in the world most beneficial to achieving your desired goals. Also useful in seeing how influences have shifted from your place of birth to your place of residence. To move or not to move, and if so, where?

Readings can be done in person, over the phone or through the mail. For more information contact Rio Olesky, Box 807, Forestville, CA 95436.

CASSETTE TAPES BY RIO OLESKY

The Language of Astrology

A comprehensive basic course for beginners. Six cassette tapes containing information about all the signs, planets and houses. A handy way to learn the material while in the car or at home.

How to Interpret a Natal Horoscope

An introduction to chart analysis. A simple, yet comprehensive methodology for understanding the complexities of a natal chart.

The Horoscope As a Guide to Empowerment

How to work with specific planets in your natal chart to over-come obstacles in your life, become the person you want to be and create the life you want to live.

The Conjunction in Capricorn

In 1988-1993 the planets aligned in a pattern repeated only four times in the past 2500 years. These tapes show the potential for individual and collective change as a result of this alignment.

Uranus-Neptune Conjunction in Capricorn

This major planetary configuration occurred in 1993 and will influence consciousness change in both individual and collective experience. Learn how to take full advantage of this opportunity in this decade and beyond.

Venus: Relationship Communication Skills

This tape defines Venus in a comprehensive and detailed way to help you understand the dynamics of relationship in the contemporary world. Integrating the concepts can help you create harmonious and mutually fulfilling relationships.

Saturn: Actualizing Your Goals

A complete description of the nature of Saturn and the various ways to use its potential in facilitating achievement, personal liberation and empowerment. A useful tool to break old patterns of fear, isolation and blockage.

Moon and Pluto: Understanding Your Emotions

The energy of these planets helps you to become aware of your inner self. They connect you to your intuitive and mystical side. This tape discusses how to understand what these energies offer and how to work with them so that you can deepen your process of becoming whole.

Neptune: Intuition and Consciousness

This tape helps you to navigate the world of inner space. By developing your intuition you become more aware spiritually and more clear psychologically. Ultimately Neptune enables you to grow beyond the confines of the material world and identify more with spirit.

Levels of Love Through the Horoscope

There are different kinds and qualities of love. Love of self, love for partner, love for humanity. This tape explores how each of these expressions is found in the natal chart. It explains how to maximize you potential to feel and share each form of this special energy and create more joy and happiness for you and those around you.

For more information about these tapes contact: Pegasus Tapes, Box 419, Santa Ysabel, CA 92070.